Indianola

The Mother of
Western Texas

Indianola
The Mother of Western Texas

by Brownson Malsch

JACKET BY VIC BLACKBURN

SHOAL CREEK PUBLISHERS, INC.
P.O. BOX 9737   AUSTIN, TEXAS 78766

FIRST EDITION — NOVEMBER 1977
SECOND EDITION — JANUARY 1978

LITHOGRAPHED AND BOUND IN THE UNITED STATES OF AMERICA

Library of Congress Cataloging in Publication Data
Malsch, Brownson, 1910-
Indianola : the mother of western Texas.

Bibliography: p.
Includes index.
1. Indianola, Tex.--History.   I. Title.
F394.I5M35   *976.4'121*   *77-18119*

ISBN 0-88319-033-8

PREFACE

"An o'er true tale of flood and tide!"

"Such is the aspect of this shore;
'Tis Greece, but living Greece no more!"

Byron

There were two possible avenues of approach to relating the story of Indianola. One was to cover each major facet of her life (religion, education, etc.) as a unit, presenting it as a single basic subject complete unto itself from the beginning to the end in each case.

The other possibility was to put down events as they occurred in chronological order, month by month, year by year. The latter was chosen because it is the order of life, the manner in which history itself unfolds. Like those of Indianola, our own personal experiences come a day at a time as we move inexorably toward the climax. For Indianola, that climax was hurricane destruction and abandonment. In some chapters, this historical order requires delving into a number of diverse subjects and events in short periods of time in the development of the city. Nevertheless, the chronological method enables the reader to become immersed in the *evolving* life of the port and see those events through the eyes of residents there, who knew not what the outcome would be.

Neglected, even overlooked, by historians in this century, Indianola must be restored to her rightful place in the annals of Texas. The eyes of Texas must be refocused on the vastly important role she played in its development as Republic and State. This is the purpose of "Indianola, The Mother of Western Texas." It is a debt that those of us who know the saga of Indianola owe to her memory.

"So, Indianola, has it been with thee,

Thou once fair city by the moonlit sea!

Thy fame is ended and thy beauty fled —

Bleak memory calls thee from the silent dead.

Thy streets are nameless, and the sea-weeds grow

Along thy walks where life was wont to flow.

Forever dead! fore'er thy dream is o'er! —

Thou livst alone on Memory's barren shore.

The sun that sets, yet sets to rise again,

Will smile the same, yet smile on thee in vain;

While moonbeams dancing as the billows roar,

Will seem as bright, yet dance on thee no more."

FROM "INDIANOLA"
BY JEFF MCLEMORE, SEPTEMBER 1889.
PUBLISHED BY MAVERICK-CLARKE CO., 1904.

ACKNOWLEDGMENTS

This book is the result of the efforts of many people. First, there were men and women who, as former residents, shared their personal experiences in and knowledge of Indianola with an eager young listener a half century ago. There is deep gratitude to the late Mesdames Robert (Pauline Shirkey) Clark and Isaac A. (Alice McCoppin) Reed, and to Francis E. Huck, of Victoria, Texas. All brought Indianola back to life for me!

The kindnesses of the late Mr. and Mrs. S. G. Reed of Houston were innumerable. The son of Isaac A. and stepson of Alice McCoppin Reed, S. G. Reed was away at college when his father perished at his post in the Indianola weather station tower during the hurricane of 1886. Fully aware of my early interest in the history of the port city, he happily shared his memories with me. Later, his widow graciously gave me his collection of documents and files, after family members had set aside certain personal papers they wished to keep.

From the beginning years of research, there was encouragement from Bronte Club Librarian Mrs. Hal Ashworth, from Mrs. Ben Jordan and Mrs. J. M. Brownson, all of Victoria. George F. Simons of Edna willingly contributed his personal knowledge of people and events in the bay area. Delving into the Texas State Library and Archives began when they were housed in the capitol building in Austin. There, Miss Harriet Smither delightedly brought out material that had reposed, untouched, in the files for decades, and gave wholehearted support to the long-term endeavor.

As my opportunities for research expanded in recent years, the utmost cooperation was received from staff members of the University of Texas Library, Barker Texas History Center, Austin; Rosenberg Library, Galveston; Texas State Library and Archives, and General Land Office, Austin; Victoria Public Library and Victoria College Library; San Antonio Public Library; Texas Room of the Houston Public Library; New Orleans Public Library; National Archives and Library of Congress, Washington; Postal Service; Departments of Agriculture, Commerce, Defense, Interior and Health, Education and Welfare, and other public and private repositories.

The most sincere thanks go to Mrs. James Ardel Moore of Waco and to the Leibold sisters of Victoria for making available family memorabilia vital to recording details of Indianola's life and death. I am indebted to Monsignor William H. Oberste of Corpus Christi and His Excellency, Thos. J. Drury, Bishop of Corpus Christi, for their interest and assistance in pinpointing facts regarding the Catholic history of Indianola.

To Mrs. Walter Ray Cook and other staff members in the office of Mrs. Mary Lois McMahon, Calhoun County Clerk, Port Lavaca, there is gratitude for patience and willing assistance in ferreting out corroborative records.

Lt. E. K. Mullan, United States Coast Guard Public Affairs Officer, Eighth Coast Guard District, New Orleans, took a lively interest in guiding me to pertinent records and photographs. To him, I am indebted, as I am to John L. Lochhead, Librarian, The Mariners Museum, Newport News, Va.; Collin B. Hamer, Jr., New Orleans Public Library; Elizabeth W. McElroy, National Oceanic and Atmospheric Administration, Washington; Donald E. Cooke, President, Edraydo, Inc., Wayne, Pa. and Mrs. L. T. Barrow of Houston.

A word of special appreciation goes to Mrs. Bobbe Kornegay, Librarian, Jackson County Library, Edna, Texas, for her untiring efforts to aid in following leads and obtaining records available on inter-library loan.

This work could not have been completed without access to the archives of the Victoria *Advocate* (originally the *Texian Advocate*, founded in 1846). Sincere thanks go to those *Advocate* staff members who so generously and enthusiastically helped.

And, how very fortunate I was to have the counsel and encouragement of my dear wife, Louise. Her great grandmother, Mrs. Karl (Anna Charlotte Stubbeman) Kaapke, was a resident of the ill-fated city almost from the beginning and was, with children, rescued on September 16, 1875 from her flooded and disintegrating home across the street from the courthouse. To Louise, I say "thank you" for thoughtful, constructive criticism, for reading and rereading, for typing and for unwavering support of the project of compiling the history of Indianola.

A monumental difficulty was presented by hurricane destruction of family and corporate records at Indianola, by the loss of privately owned photographs of the city and her inhabitants, and by the annihilation of the treasure of priceless glass plates in the photographic studios there. The search to fill gaps led to the distant and widely separated places named. It was because of the efforts of all the individuals who became involved that success was achieved.

INTRODUCTION

Indianola, The Mother of Western Texas, is the saga of a city that was born, flourished, and died on the Texas coast between 1844 and 1887. It was located in Calhoun County on the west shore of Matagorda Bay, about halfway between Port O'Connor and Port Lavaca.

The author is Brownson Malsch, a native of nearby Victoria, Texas, who became interested in Indianola more than half a century ago. The Malsch home was in a "nest" of former Indianolans, men and women who had been adult residents of the ill-fated little city when it was destroyed by hurricanes. Naturally they were pleased to have a young listener sit on their front porch steps and take full notes on the stories they had to tell. "It was a thrilling opportunity to learn at first hand," he told us, "and I made the most of it while those people were physically and mentally active. Through the years that followed, Indianola was never far from the surface of my thoughts. In every likely spot I searched for records of the city and her inhabitants. Because of the two hurricanes, such records were few and far between, but bit by bit they added up to a substantial collection."

He sought out the pieces and fitted them together with loving care. The result is an absorbing account told in the exact language of the eyewitnesses themselves. But there is much more here than the story of a storm — much more. He puts the events into perspective, giving us a whole new page for Texas history. The text glows with the names of specific individuals and places.

Champions of ethnic minorities will be delighted to find here a vivid description of what the Germans contributed to our culture. Civil War buffs will be surprised to learn that the Indianolans, many of whom had just arrived from Europe and owned no slaves, got along very well with the Yankee troops of occupation.

The main thrust of the story, of course, is the part Indianola played in opening up a supply route from Indianola through Victoria to San Antonio and on to California, with the economic interplay of steamships, oxcarts, highways, and railroads. Not only was Indianola the first Texas port at which U. S. Government supplies were unloaded for Western Texas, as well as the New Mexico and Arizona Territories; there were also shipments of silver, lead, copper and other exports flowing into Indianola from Chihuahua.

This book will become a Texas city, county, Confederate, and railroad collector's classic. There is much to be learned here by the medical profession about the history of disease in Texas, and for the meteorologist it should be required reading for the freshman course. Where else can you find the complete story of a hurricane that originated southwest of the Cape Verde Islands off the coast of Africa, crossed the Atlantic to the Lesser Antilles, to Cuba, the eastern Gulf of Mexico, and on to Indianola, then moved ashore, carrying a large schooner five miles inland, then veering northeast through Indianola, on to Delaware, and back across the Atlantic north of the British Isles?

Despite the powerful descriptions of the violent forces of nature that are to be found in this volume, however, the scenes that will linger in our memory for years to come will be such delightful little episodes as the German artists who presented a performance of "Stereomonoscopic Dissolving Views and Polaroscopic Fire Works," and especially the last Christmas on the eve of the Civil War, when, following the German custom, Santa Claus paid his visit after supper on Christmas Eve, accompanied by Black Peter who carried bundles of switches and bags of ashes to leave for bad boys and girls. Of course, no child ever found just switches and ashes under the tree, but the thought of the possibility kept them on their good behavior in the days before Christmas.

Read this volume now for pleasure, and then keep it for reference. The Texas State Historical Association will have to draw on it heavily in preparing Volume IV of *The Handbook of Texas*.

MALCOLM D. McLEAN
PROFESSOR OF HISTORY AND SPANISH
THE UNIVERSITY OF TEXAS AT ARLINGTON

October 1, 1977

CONTENTS

ILLUSTRATIONS

I.

The Seed Is Planted

It is not unusual for a city to be put to death by warfare, by natural disaster, or even by pestilence. Consider the fate of Carthage, of St. Pierre on Martinique, of Port Royal on Jamaica, of Pompeii and Herculaneum . . . the mysterious abandonment of Chichen Itza. What is unusual is to find a city which not only died engulfed in agony, but which was born of human suffering!

Such a city was Indianola. Her birth was the direct result of calamitous difficulties encountered by early immigrants from Germany who were brought to the shores of the Republic of Texas by the Adelsverein, beginning in 1844. Her death was due to her near sea level location on Matagorda Bay and the visitation of two "once-in-a-century" hurricanes within a span of only 11 years.

During the period between 1844 and 1886, Indianola grew from a plague-infested immigrant camp to a cosmopolitan port city. At her zenith before the storm of 1875, she was second only to Galveston in the state and was regarded by that place as an annoying threat to its commercial and maritime supremacy. Wielding vast influence on the development of Western Texas, as the land west of the Colorado River was then called, Indianola left her imprint on that great region. She became the port for the Chihuahua trade, was the eastern terminus of the shortest overland route to California, was the funnel through which tens of thousands of immigrants from Germany, Switzerland and France came to Texas . . . to say nothing of the influx of settlers who migrated from the southern and eastern United States to the new lands of the west. Over her wharves moved the necessities and luxuries of life for the inhabitants of Western Texas, as well as the ordnance and other supplies for the chain of forts that shielded "civilized" Texas from the untamed Indian tribes. Scores of towns in Western Texas were born from her womb and nourished at her breast.

Prior to the sprouting of the crude, makeshift settlement that was destined to become "The Mother of Western Texas," the prairies bordering Matagorda Bay were thinly populated. At the eastern end of the bay there was the town of Matagorda, situated on the left bank of the Colorado River near its mouth. With a population of about 1,200, Matagorda boasted the distinction of having a newspaper, the *Bulletin*, from 1837 to 1839, one of the few in the Republic.[1] She struggled to become a seaport of significance, but failed. A silt bar deposited by the river in the long, narrow eastern arm of the bay prevented ocean-going ships from reaching the town. Vessels entering the bay through Pass Cavallo could approach Matagorda no nearer than four miles.[2] There, cargoes were transferred to lighters, whose shallow draught enabled them to cross the bar.

Linnville, a village of approximately 200 in 1839, had been founded about 1831 by John (Juan) J. Linn on the west bank of upper Lavaca Bay. But, Linnville was to die before Indianola was born. Looted and burned by Comanche Indians on August 8, 1840, following their raid through Victoria, the settlement was abandoned.[3] A few survivors moved south and established a new, smaller community which was to receive the name Lavaca, later Port Lavaca.[4]

The City of Calhoun was projected in 1839 on the northeastern end of Matagorda Island opposite Pelican Island, and overlooking the Gulf of Mexico at Pass Cavallo. Calhoun came into brief existence as a result of action by the Congress of the Republic of Texas on January 21, 1839, requiring Secretary of the Treasury Asa Brigham to have a section of land there surveyed as a seaport.[5]

Members of the Congress saw the need for a deep-water port on Western Matagorda Bay. Such a port would be expected to aid in opening the empty stretches of Western Texas to immigration. An increase in population would lead to expanded trade opportunities. That, in turn, would mean more revenues for the near penniless Republic. It was also intended that Calhoun would be a port through which embryonic Austin might be more conveniently supplied with manufactured goods.

There was an even more compelling reason. Although the seat of government was still at the town of Houston in early 1839, it was a foregone conclusion that the new capital of the Republic of Texas was to be on the Colorado River at the very edge of the frontier. President Lamar had personally selected the site. He used his influence to secure Congressional approval, which was given despite the dangerously exposed location of the planned capital, coupled with the opposition of Sam Houston. Development of the virgin land to the west would create a buffer zone and give protection to the inhabitants of the new town, including the lawmakers, many of whom viewed the anticipated move from Houston with feelings of uneasiness for their personal safety.

The basic reasoning for projecting Calhoun was sound, but the critical error was made in pinpointing Matagorda Island as the designated site. The members of Congress handed Brigham an assignment for which failure was inevitable. It was a political, not a commercial, decision.

Had the Congress of the Republic designated the western shore of Matagorda Bay from Alligator Head to Indian Point, the projected town would have succeeded. There, wagons from the interior could reach the beach, just off which there was water of sufficient depth to accommodate any vessel that could enter Pass Cavallo. Matagorda Island was inaccessible except by boat, and there was no protected harbor. The anchorage at the east end of the island at Pass Cavallo was subjected to a swift current of tidal water rushing into and out of the bay. Congress obviously lacked chorographical knowledge of the area. It would remain for a German prince to inspect that western shore of Matagorda Bay in 1844 and understand its potential value. Karl, Prinz zu Solms-Braunfels was, unwittingly, responsible for the birth of Indianola.

The plat of the City of Calhoun was prepared by Edward Linn, brother of Juan Linn and surveyor for Victoria County which, at that time, extended to the Gulf of Mexico and embraced Matagorda Island. It was an ambitious plan, encompassing 173 city blocks divided into lots for sale. In addition, there were blocks set aside for public purposes. One was to be the site for a Methodist church, one for a Catholic, one for a Presbyterian and one for a "Protestant" church, two for public squares, one for a market, one for a "fish market," and one each for male and female academies. Provision was also made for a block at the corner of the town facing the Gulf, on which a fort was to be constructed for the protection of the pass.[6] In 1842, Alexander Somervell, hero of San Jacinto and Secretary of War in the cabinet of President David G. Burnet, was appointed collector of customs at Calhoun.

The continued fear of Mexican invasion of Texas by sea was the probable reason for decreeing that a fortification be at Calhoun. On January 14, 1843, the Congress appropriated $1,000 to be used in "defense of the pass into Matagorda bay." How the funds were to be expended was not stipulated.[7]

The location chosen for the City of Calhoun quickly proved to be unsuitable for a commercial port. Purchasers of lots were almost non-existent. Calhoun remained the headquarters of the collector of customs until 1844. The Congress of the Republic, in joint resolution on February 2, recognized the failure of its plan and ordered the removal of the custom house "from Port Calhoun to Port Caballo." The Secretary of the Treasury was "authorized and required to have moved the Custom house, and such other public building or buildings of the Port of

Calhoun, the present location, to Port Caballo, provided the proprietors of Port Caballo donate to the government a suitable lot or lots in said town for the erection of the public buildings." The day before the death of Calhoun was ordered, the Congress had authorized Sylvanus Dunham of Matagorda County to establish a ferry from Port Caballo on Decrow's Point to the opposite shore at Port Calhoun. Dunham's project was doomed to failure with the demise of the Republic-sponsored town.[8]

A short-lived settlement named Palacios had been laid out by 1839 on the point of land on the east side of Trespalacios Bay between Matagorda Bay and Oyster Lake. From a maritime view, it was a satisfactory choice of site, inasmuch as deep water was close to shore. However, a conflict developed over the title to the land on which Palacios lay, so the port failed to develop.[9] Sixty-three years later, another Palacios was founded near the northeastern end of Trespalacios Bay.

Texana was the only other community in the vicinity of Matagorda and Lavaca Bays of sufficient size during the Republic to merit being called a town. At the head of navigation on the Navidad River, a tributary of the Lavaca which flows into Lavaca Bay, Texana was, in 1839, slowly recovering from the ravages of being put to the torch during the Revolution.

There had been a flurry of activity in the bay area during and immediately following the Texas Revolution. Sailing vessels loaded with volunteers and military supplies came in through Pass Cavallo and discharged at army supply depots at Cox's Point, at Linnville, at Dimitt's Landing on the right bank of the Lavaca River, or at LaBaca, a small settlement on the left bank of that stream. Men heading for Colonel James W. Fannin's command drilled at Texana before moving on.[10] During that period, Clara Lisle, fiancée of James Bowie, resided in Texana.[11]

Continuing to November 1837, the Army of the Republic of Texas maintained a total of seven consecutively occupied camps above Lavaca Bay. The first was Camp LaBaca (sometimes referred to as LaBacca or as Lavaca). Under command of General Thomas J. Rusk, Camp LaBaca was in sight of the bay. General Felix Huston succeeded Rusk in October 1836, when the latter departed to assume his post of Secretary of War in President Houston's cabinet. Huston was himself succeeded by General Albert Sidney Johnston as commanding officer of the military installations, all of which were in the vicinity of Texana.[12]

On the abandonment, in early November 1837, of the seventh and last camp, named Chambers in honor of Thomas Jefferson Chambers, Captain James Jevon's company of regulars was transferred to Cox's Point. Later in the month, the company was again transferred, that time to Indian Point at the junction of Matagorda and Lavaca Bays. There it remained for a short time before being withdrawn from the area.[13]

After the removal of the military forces at the end of 1837, the bay region had lapsed into a state of somnolence, out of which it was jolted by that August 1840 Indian attack on Victoria and Linnville. A faint stirring of commercial enterprise was manifested the following month. On September 21, 1840, the firm of Ferguson and Harrell began weekly passenger and freight service with the little paddle-wheel steamer *Swan*. It was inaugurated between Texana and Port Caballo. At the Decrow's Point port, passengers and freight were transferred to and from the few ships that plied the waters of the western Gulf of Mexico.

Except for the weekly plume of smoke from the wood burning *Swan* and the occasional sighting of a transient sailing vessel, the languor of the bay was undisturbed. A few solitary residence structures could be seen at widely separated locations. Had he been able to return, Rene Robert Cavelier, Sieur de la Salle would have found the shores of Matagorda Bay and its tributaries to have been only slightly different in appearance from the time he and his ill-fated colonists came through Pass Cavallo on February 20, 1685.[14] It was still an empty, lonely region.

But, unknown to the isolated pioneers of Matagorda Bay, change was in the making. The formation of the Adelsverein (society of nobility) at Biebrich am Rhein in Germany on April 20, 1842, was for the stated purpose of providing assistance for the emigration of several thousand Germans to the Republic of Texas. Basic purposes for this interest in sponsoring those willing to emigrate were to ease tensions resulting from widespread political turmoil, and to relieve dangerous pressures caused by economic depression and its accompanying high rate of unemployment. Encouragement to emigrate was to be given to the known radical political activists. Emigrant groups were, in theory at least, to be carefully chosen in order to provide a balance of artisans, mechanics, physicians, farmers and representatives of all other crafts necessary for the success of communities established in a part of the world remote from the Fatherland.

Land was to be purchased by the Adelsverein or, hopefully, secured as grants from the Republic of Texas for settlement by German colonists.[15] Each head of an average household was required to deposit 600 gulden (about $240), and each single person 300 gulden. Half of this sum was to be used by the Adelsverein to furnish transportation from Germany to the projected colony, as well as housing, once there. The other half was to provide a credit upon which the emigrants could draw for tools and farming equipment, also food rations to sustain them until the first harvest.[16]

Counts Joseph Boos-Waldeck and Victor von Leiningen were dispatched to Texas with instructions to secure land by purchase or grant. Of the two, Boos-Waldeck was the more astute. On his return to Germany in 1844, after buying the 4,428 acre plantation in Fayette County which he named "Nassau," he counseled against large scale emigration to Texas, citing the almost prohibitive cost involved. That cost was seen by Boos-Waldeck to far exceed the deposit required of the emigrants to cover transportation and housing. The lack of business acumen on the part of the managing officials of the Adelsverein, plus the fact that they did not want to receive advice contrary to the course they had already set, resulted in their brushing aside the recommendations of Boos-Waldeck. Incensed by the rebuff, and realizing that his knowledge of Texas and experience there were of no consequence in the minds of the directors of the society, Boos-Waldeck promptly resigned his membership.[17]

Even more unfortunate for the welfare of the hapless Germans who, beginning in 1844, were to become victims of careless planning and worse administration by the officers of the society, von Leiningen was made president of a restructured Verein on March 24, 1844. The meeting at Mainz on that date created a new organization, its stated aim being the "protection" of the Germans emigrating to Texas. Its abysmal failure has been recorded in writings on the subject.

Blissfully ignorant of the almost total lack of facilities for the reception, accommodation and transportation of immigrants from the coast of Texas to the interior, the society began planning the gathering and dispatching of shiploads of families. Prince Karl zu Solms-Braunfels was appointed commissioner general for the projected colony and sailed for Texas in May 1844.[18] Although he did not know it, hard on his heels was the first contingent of immigrants.

He was thunderstruck and wholly unprepared when the brig *Weser* arrived at Galveston in July 1844, with the first group of colonists. There was no land on which he could place them. A permanent port for disembarkation had not even been considered. Prince Karl left his bewildered countrymen to fend for themselves at Galveston and hurriedly began the task of finding a more desirable place for the reception of future shiploads.

He narrowed his choice to the west bank of Matagorda and Lavaca Bays. From the shore line, a direct route could be laid out to the lands of Western Texas where it was anticipated that sites might be secured for the colony. The village of Port Lavaca was considered, Prince Karl describing it as "a town of four houses."[19] However, the hazards of navigation through and over the sand and mud bars in Lavaca Bay dimmed its promise as a haven. Had deep water been available, Port Lavaca would have been ideal. Its situation on a high bluff, and its consequent freedom from swampy terrain and flooding by storms were definite advantages. But, too often were vessels grounded on Lavaca Bay bars.

The prince then looked over the point of land where Lavaca and Matagorda Bays join. Perhaps it would be better described as a bulge in the shore. Being below Gallinipper Bar, which was the most troublesome of those en route to Lavaca, this spot called "Indian Point" had water of sufficient depth to permit sailing vessels to anchor near the beach and have their cargoes and passengers lightered. Vessels that could enter Matagorda Bay through Pass Cavallo could come to Indian Point without difficulty.[20]

Actually situated on an island, Indian Point was separated from the flat mainland by a string of small, brackish lakes, all connected by shallow bayous. The long, narrow island was composed of a low ridge of fine, white, crushed shell which had been formed by wave action through the ages. It was clean. Even heavy and prolonged rains were not troublesome, as the firmly packed shell provided a natural all-weather surface. There was little wood, and no safe drinking water, other than that collected from rainfall. Nevertheless, those two drawbacks did not deter Prince Karl from deciding that the Indian Point area would be the most suitable beginning for the long road into Western Texas. Its lying west of the Trinity, Brazos and Colorado meant that there were no great streams to cross on the way inland. The Guadalupe, a crystal clear, spring fed river, had numerous fords upstream that made an easy passage possible.

Samuel Addison White held title to the land at Indian Point by virtue of Headright Certificate number 37, issued by the board of land commissioners for Jackson County. Survey had been made in 1842, after which White built a small house there.[21] Sensing opportunity for development of the property, and personal profit, White was receptive to overtures from the prince. He agreed to permit the landing and encampment of German immigrants a few hundred yards southeast of his residence, as proposed by Solms-Braunfels. Details would be worked out at a later date. There would be plenty of time for the principles of agreement to be drafted . . . they thought. Prince Karl would notify the Verein in Germany to suspend emigration until land was obtained in the interior of Texas and transportation was lined up.

White had come to Texas in 1830 and had settled in present-day Jackson County.[22] One of the surveyors of the Power and Hewetson Colony, he had also surveyed the Texana townsite for Dr. F. F. Wells and Mrs. Pamelia Porter. White was a participant in the drafting of the revolutionary resolution against the Mexican government, which was adopted at the nearby Lavaca-Navidad Meeting of July 17, 1835. His first military action had been in the Battle of Velasco. He was a captain in the Army of the Republic of Texas. White had previously read law with the Wharton brothers, John Austin and William Harris. (On its organization in 1846, Wharton County was named in their honor.)[23]

Neither Prince Karl nor Samuel Addison White was ready for the reception of colonists when the brig *Johann Dethardt* (Captain Th. Lüdering) arrived in Galveston on November 23, 1844.[24] After a short layover, the *Johann Dethardt* sailed for Pass Cavallo and Matagorda Bay. That vessel was followed by the *Herrschel* (Captain J. Lamke) on December 8 and the *Ferdinand* (Captain A. Hagedorn) on December 14. The brig *Apollo* arrived at Galveston on December 20, 1844. Like the *Johann Dethardt*, *Herrschel* and *Ferdinand*, she too sailed on to Matagorda Bay. To White's credit, he did everything within his limited means to ease the problems facing the Germans.

That first Christmas in Texas, thousands of miles from home, was a frightening experience for them. They had been grievously misled by the Verein. There was no place to go. There were no buildings on the bay to house and protect them from the cold wind and rain of Texas "northers." Theirs was a desperate plight, and they quickly realized it.

However, being possessed of great moral strength, confident that "der liebe Gott" would see them through their tribulations, they set to work to erect temporary shelters to protect body and possessions.

Providentially, Prince Karl was able to interest the Rev. Louis Ervendberg, Texas' first German Protestant minister, in coming to Indian Point in the service of the Verein and extending a Christian welcome to the people who, like the ancient Israelites, were in a foreign and inhospitable land.[25] For the German children, a brave attempt was made at a traditional observance of their beloved Weihnachtsfest, with a Christmas tree. Some accounts give it as a small oak, others as a cedar. Whatever it was, the little tree was decorated with loving care, carols were sung and gifts were presented to the delighted children. On the following morning, the 25th, the first Holy Communion service on the soil of what was to become Indianola was led by Evangelical Lutheran minister Ervendberg, who endeared himself to adult and child alike by his kindness and his solicitude for their welfare.

Those families were the vanguard of the great migration that was to bring many thousands of Germans to Texas during the next three decades. They would likely have questioned the statement, yet it can be said that the first immigrants who landed at Indian Point were fortunate. Their stay on the coast was short. Transportation was secured to aid in moving them from the vicinity of Indian Point soon after the New Year. Their first stop was Agua Dulce on Chocolate Creek, 12 miles from the bay. Where they were headed was uncertain, even to their leaders. The Fisher-Miller grant, in which the Verein had become involved, was between the Colorado and Llano Rivers, some 300 miles distant, unmapped and inhabited by hostile Indians. A halfway station was needed, but there was none. To fill that urgent need, Prince Karl left the immigrant train at Spring Creek, just above Victoria, and set out to find and purchase a tract of land to be used for the initial settlement.

Not all of the newly arrived immigrants left the bay in January, 1845. Johann Schwartz (Swartz) and his family lacked enthusiasm to blindly follow the prince. Both the Verein and Prince Karl were discredited in their minds by the bungling that was clearly evident . . . the lack of facilities to receive, house, feed and transport the Germans, and no suitable land on which to place them. Schwartz bought from Samuel Addison White a small acreage three miles down the bay shore, near Powder Horn Bayou, purchased the necessary lumber which was brought by schooner from Galveston, and erected the first house on the site of what was to become the port of (Lower) Indianola. When Johann Schwartz died in that house on Wednesday night, October 31, 1860, the Indianola *Courier* referred to him in its edition of November 3 as "an old and highly esteemed citizen . . . the oldest inhabitant of Indianola, being the first settler on the present site of the city, where he built the first house, which he occupied up to the hour of his death . . . ."

By March 5, the immigrant train had crept to McCoy Creek, 78 miles from Indian Point. Through sheer good fortune, Prince Karl had learned about Las Fontanas and, on March 14, 1845, had been successful in negotiating for the purchase of what became known as the Comal Tract. Las Fontanas (the fountains), as the Spanish knew them, were to prove to be by far the largest springs in all of Texas. The short river which they fed became a source of water power unequalled in the state.

When word of the land purchase reached the immigrants at McCoy Creek, they struck camp and made their weary way to the garden spot, coming to their journey's end on March 21, 1845, one week to the day after the prince had signed the purchase agreement. Their spirits revived by the sight of the snow-sprinkled hills, they set to work laying out a town, to be known as Neu Braunfels in honor of Prince Karl's home, and dividing the surrounding land into small farm plots.[26] Neu (New) Braunfels became the Mecca toward which subsequent legions of immigrants were to try to make their way from Indian Point.

Though the difficulties of the first shiploads were many, a truly awful situation faced those who came in late 1845 and in 1846. The already confused state of immigration affairs in Texas had reached crisis proportions in 1845. Inadequate financing in Germany had led to exhaustion of local credit of the Adelsverein. Prince Karl's good intentions were exceeded by his lack of managerial ability. Quarrels with Henry Fisher (Heinrich Fischer) had helped bring about a chaotic condition in company affairs in the Republic.

The prince's sudden departure from New Braunfels less than a month after its establishment indicated his awareness of what lay ahead, and his desire to wash his hands of the whole project. He left the settlement prior to the arrival of his successor, Johann Ottfried Freiherr (Baron) von Meusebach, who had been appointed commissioner general by the Verein in Germany on February 24, 1845. Von Meusebach reached Galveston in April, went on to Indian Point to survey the landing area, and soon ended up in New Braunfels, where he was apprised of Solms-Braunfels' sudden leave-taking. Quickly discovering that the local financial and administrative affairs of the society bordered on disaster, and lacking an accounting by his predecessor, von Meusebach resolved to follow Prince Karl to Galveston. There, he hoped to locate and confront him before he sailed. He did, indeed, find the prince at the port. Solms-Braunfels had been unable to depart because of an attachment that had been filed by a creditor suspicious of his motives in abruptly attempting to leave the jurisdiction of the Republic of Texas.[27]

Von Meusebach paid off the $10,000 attachment, after having received from the prince a commitment that he would urge the directorate in Germany to send at once, without waiting for a report, twice as much additional credit as the Baron then had at his disposal. That, the directorate did not do. The failure of the officials to extend the necessary credit was a basic factor in the development of the dreadful condition that enveloped the thousands of immigrants who were stranded at Indian Point later in the year.

After having purchased (on credit) land for the establishment of Friedrichsburg (now Fredericksburg), von Meusebach learned by letter received in October 1845 that 4,000 more immigrants were being embarked, destined for Indian Point, and that a credit of only $24,000 had been opened with a New Orleans banker. During the fall, winter and spring of 1845-1846, 5,247 men, women and children arrived in 36 ships, 24 from Bremen and 12 from Antwerp.[28]

In 1845, Dr. Joseph Martin Reuss reached Texas from his native Münnerstadt, Bavaria. He settled at Indian Point, where he began the practice of medicine among the immigrants and opened an apothecary shop. There were no single women there, a lack keenly felt. While in Galveston in late November, Dr. Reuss met and was charmed by a German fräulein, Anna Gesine Stubbeman, who had just arrived alone. The immigrant vessel on which she journeyed from Europe had encountered a storm in the Gulf near the Texas coast. Passengers were obliged to cast overboard all of their possessions in order to lighten the ship and endeavor to prevent its foundering. Fräulein Stubbeman reached Galveston with only the clothes on her back, her large chest of clothing and other personal effects having been lost in the frantic effort by crew and passengers to save themselves. She went to work as a maid in the Tremont Hotel, and it was there that Dr. Reuss saw her.

Following their marriage on December 2, after a whirlwind courtship, they sailed to the point where, for the next 30 years, they were leaders in the business and social life of the community. Anna Gesine had her counterparts many times over during the period of emigration from Germany. She and those counterparts are numberd among the pioneers of the women's liberation movement. Independent in spirit and endowed with a sense of destiny, they joihed the exodus to the new land of Texas in order to get away from repressive customs at home. Once established at Indian Point as the wife of a prosperous physician, Frau Anna Gesine Reuss sent for other members of her family, one by one. They came, married and began new lives in the promised land.[29]

Another young German who had a leading role in the development of the budding port on Matagorda Bay was Henry Runge. At the age of 29, he had come to the United States, entering at Baltimore. Attracted to New Orleans, he remained there for a short time. Moving on to Indian Point late in 1845, he opened a bank in a tent, the first in the area and one of the early institutions of its kind in Texas.[30]

The winter season of 1845-1846 was one of extreme cold and unusually heavy rainfall in Texas. The coastal flatlands were turned into quagmires and the streams into unfordable torrents. With more initiative and foresight than Prince Karl, new Commissioner General Meusebach had arranged for the erection of barracks, and had acquired tents to be used at Indian Point as housing for the inpouring families. Despite his endeavors, the shelter was insufficient to protect all against the harmful effects of inclement weather. Respiratory diseases spread like wildfire throughout the camp along the beach, and great numbers of the immigrants perished.

It was during that time, and in part because of the grim difficulties, that the beginnings of commerce became firmly rooted at Indian Point. Another young German by the name of Henry (Heinrich) Huck had come to New York via London and then made his way to New Orleans. In 1844, he had visited Texas but returned to the Crescent City. He was part of the small German colony there which was made up of immigrants, most of whom had come to the northern United States and then been drawn to New Orleans by its prosperity and attendant opportunities for business investment. When news of the plight of the Germans on Matagorda Bay reached New Orleans late in 1845, Henry Huck lost no time in acting. Having financial resources to enable him to do so, he purchased sufficient lumber to load to capacity the schooner *Native*. With that cargo, and a large supply of medicines, he sailed for Indian Point.

Huck opened the first lumberyard and found customers among Germans who, despairing of ever reaching the lands of the Verein, bought small parcels of ground from White. Using material from Huck's lumberyard, they began to erect houses. Samuel Addison White's hope for a town on the bay showed signs of realization. Prince Karl had satisfied his own ego by designating the landing place as Karlshafen or Carlshafen (Karl's Harbor), though that name was used only by the Germans. To the other Texans, the settlement would continue to be known as Indian Point until 1849.

Feeling deeply the privations being endured by the immigrants, Henry Huck, acting in concert with Dr. Reuss, freely supplied them with medicines at no cost. Huck also gave, without charge, lumber with which coffins for the innumerable dead were constructed.[31]

Von Meusebach was to eventually provide the answer to the immigrants' prayers through his business ability, his dedication to their interests and his wisdom in seeking and making treaties of peace with the Comanche Indians. As a result of the treaties, those Germans who finally made their way from Indian Point to the Hill Country lived in harmony with the tribes. The only Indian difficulties they encountered were instances of depredations by renegades. However, before the sun broke through their clouds of despair, the families moving through Indian Point were to face more troubles.

The Congress of the United States acted on December 29, 1845, to admit Texas into the Union. The end of the Republic actually came on February 19, 1846, when its flag was lowered and that of the United States was raised in its place at Austin. At that ceremony, the officials of the new State of Texas were inaugurated. Notable as those events were, they received scant attention from the stranded German colonists.

By March 1846, von Meusebach had made arrangements with the Torrey brothers (John F. and David K.), then of Houston, for the movement of immigrants from Indian Point. About 100 teams arrived that month to the joy of the people. However, the transfer of the Germans to New Braunfels proved to be a difficult task. The wagons would sink to the axles in the mud of the water-soaked prairie and could only be pulled along with exhausting effort on the part of the animals, even as the families would strive to assist by lifting and shoving the vehicles. Progress was yard by yard. Some of the people left the wagon trains at

Victoria and remained there. Others gave up at various points further along the route. The thought most shared was the wish that they had never heard of or seen Texas. Who could blame them for their disillusionment? Few families had been spared loss by death, either on the bay or en route to the Hill Country.

As weather conditions began to improve in late March, the hopes of the great multitude remaining at Indian Point rose. The drying of the prairie and the return of streams to their normal rate of flow meant that Torrey Brothers would be able to shorten the time required for the round trips between Indian Point and the colony at New Braunfels. But, on April 3 heavy rains began to fall again, and the next journey from the bay to the Comal required almost four weeks one way.

Then the ultimate calamity befell them. War broke out between the United States and Mexico in May. Almost overnight, the American government scooped up every available team and wagon in Texas. The Army paid far more for draft animals and vehicles, as well as higher wages to the teamsters, than could individuals, including von Meusebach. As a result of the temptation of generous payment in gold, the contract between the society and the Torreys was repudiated by the latter and their equipment turned to military use.[32]

It is not difficult to visualize the feeling of gloom that engulfed the colonists at Indian Point. Perhaps their volunteering was a reaction to frustrations faced in their desire to reach New Braunfels and Fredericksburg, or it may have been a genuine wish to serve the United States, to which Texas had just been annexed. Whatever the reason, a company of youthful volunteers was organized at Indian Point by Augustus Buchel, who had arrived from Antwerp late in 1845. Captain Buchel had received his military training in Mainz am Rhein in Hesse, and at the Ecole Militaire in Paris. He had been an instructor in the Turkish Army and had served as a mercenary in the forces of regent Queen Maria Christina during the Carlist War in Spain. The company he formed on the bay was a part of the First Texas Rifle Volunteers under Albert Sidney Johnston.[33] Additional German youths stranded at Indian Point enlisted in other companies. There is no precise record of the total number of such volunteers, though some 500 are believed to have gone into the service.

Buchel advanced to the rank of major during the Mexican War and was cited for meritorious service in the Battle of Buena Vista. The first sergeant in Buchel's company was Emil Krieswitz (Krieswicz) who later became the German Indian Agent and, with von Meusebach, was largely responsible for the amicable relations between the Hill Country colonists and the Comanches. Clemens Hartman, a private in the company, was the surveyor of the later division of the town of Indian Point between White and Theodore Miller, acting for the German Emigration Company, in 1848.[34]

The state of affairs caused by the Mexican War and resultant lack of transportation sealed the doom of hundreds of immigrants. As the heat of summer came on, a combination of things caused their plight to become hopeless. The crowded housing conditions in the camp swelled by a steady inflow of arrivals, polluted drinking water and lack of adequate sanitation were bad enough. To that situation there was added an agonizing plague of mosquitoes from which there was little protection, an invasion of green stinging flies and hordes of disease-carrying house flies! Epidemics of typhoid, cholera and cerebro-spinal meningitis took the lives of adults and children. Frau Reuss, Frau Huck, Mrs. White and the few other women who had become permanent residents of Indian Point worked valiantly to aid the stricken. From their kitchens came kettles of broth to nourish the sick. They fed and helped care for small children whose mothers were prostrated by fever and nausea. At first, they aided in laying out the dead, but the enormity of the epidemic that swept over the Verein's camp was soon overwhelming. It quickly reached the stage that mass graves were filled with bodies wrapped in blankets. There was no time to construct wooden coffins. The dead had to be interred at once. Whole families were wiped out in some cases. In others, children were orphaned. Estimates of the number who died at Indian Point during that summer of 1846 have ranged from a minimum of 400 to more than 1,200. One source makes the assertion that 2,000 perished!

Wild fear overwhelmed the people. Many abandoned their belongings and started out on foot, determined to walk to the colonies on the Comal and Pedernales Rivers. Over 200 died along the way. Those who did manage to struggle on to New Braunfels and Fredericksburg carried with them germs of disease, which infected those previously healthful communities. The scene all the way from Indian Point to distant Fredericksburg became one of indescribable misery. Only slowly did the survivors of the overland trek regain strength and become able to resume the effort of endeavoring to establish homes in the new country to which they had been led, unwitting victims of stupidity on the part of officials of the Verein, which by that time was approaching bankruptcy.[35]

For those survivors, the excitement and enthusiasm, which they had displayed in Germany upon hearing tales of the wonders and opportunities of Texas, had evaporated. Their dreams of a new life of freedom and abundance were wiped out by the reality of death on every hand, and privation for the living remainder. Yet, even in that summer of tribulation, there were some immigrants who did not panic. Facing up to the hard facts, they carefully appraised their options in order to salvage what they could. Their decision was to abandon the Adelsverein, settle at Indian Point and, like Johann Schwartz, Dr. J. M. Reuss, Henry Huck and Henry Runge, find ways to earn a livelihood and establish themselves in this new home. That decision was their salvation. They only hoped to exist. What came their way was the prosperity and the political freedom they had sought through the empty promises of the Verein.

II.

A Twin Birth —
Town and County

The year 1846 saw three parallel currents of events flowing at Indian Point. There was the continuing scramble of most of the German immigrants to find the means to move on to the colonies. At the same time that feverish activity was in progress, the legislative mill in Austin was grinding out the bill that created Calhoun County on April 4.[1]

Named in honor of American statesman John C. Calhoun, the new county received the greater part of its territory from Victoria. Jackson County was obliged by the law to cede most of its sea coast, which lay on Lavaca, Cox, Keller, Carancahua and Matagorda Bays. The county of Matagorda to the east contributed a minute portion. The hamlet of Lavaca was designated as the seat of government and elections were ordered for choosing officials. One of the immigrants, Theodore Miller, was elected Chief Justice. He had settled on Indian Point, was the agent of the German Emigration Company and held power of attorney from von Meusebach. Henry J. Huck was elected probate judge.[2] He had not sought the office and was only persuaded to allow his name to be placed on the ballot by the insistence of immigrants to whom he had given unbounded aid.

German surveyor George Thielepape became justice of the peace for Precinct 2, which included the Indian Point area. Rudolph Binderwald, first lieutenant in Augustus Buchel's company of volunteers, was elected a justice of the peace but failed to qualify because he went off to the Mexican War. The following year, Dr. Reuss was elected county coroner to replace Henry Ducher, who resigned, and Augustus Fromme was selected to be a justice of the peace.[3]

The organization of Calhoun County, and the participation of a large number of the Germans in the election of officials, caused increased public attention to be focused on Indian Point. The swelling movement of immigrants to the bay shore at the point, and the need for warehouses, stores and other commercial facilities, prompted the third noteworthy event of 1846 . . . Samuel A. White and William M. Cook acting in concert for the formal establishment of a town. Cook had acquired a half interest in the land there by deed dated August 11, 1845.[4] Although small tracts had previously been sold to individuals, the growing demand for land made imperative a semblance of order in the transfer of ownership and in the description of each parcel.

Thielepape had already been employed by White to survey lots, blocks and streets and had begun his work. The article of agreement between White and Cook was dated August 28, 1846, and signed in the presence of County Clerk Isaac Brugh at his office in Lavaca.[5] But, lurking in the background was a possible cloud on the title. Two weeks after the agreement was executed, White sold to A. W. G. Davis for $800 lots 1 and 2, Block 14 "in the town of Indian Point . . . upon which the said White now resides, and also a garden, which has been cultivated for four years and is enclosed by a ditch and hedge, containing about 1/2 acre . . . White and his heirs and assigns agree to forever defend the title to said premises against the claim or claims, either in law or equity (by) Fernando Deleon and against the claim or claims of all persons whatsoever claiming through said Deleon."

Don Fernando De Leon was commissioner and head of one of the original 41 families in Don Martin De Leon's colony of Guadalupe Victoria, established in 1824. That colony extended to Matagorda Bay and land there was included in several of the Mexican grants. Post-revolution conflicts of interest and claims of forfeiture of title were the basis of this and other "clouds" in the Indian Point region.

Thielepape's plat of the town of Indian Point embraced 733 building lots on 82 blocks. Four streets paralleled the bay, and 22 short streets were at right angles to the shore. Twenty-three blocks along the bay contained 140 water lots, which fronted on the beach with no street intervening. Having direct access to the bay, those lots were intended as sites for warehouses and stores to be located adjacent to wharves yet to be constructed. The center of two blocks between Main and Third Streets, numbers 35 and 36, was set aside ostensibly as a public square. It would later develop that the unstated purpose of the square was to serve as a proposed site for a courthouse. The promoters of Indian Point were looking ahead to the time when there would be agitation for the removal of the county seat of government from Lavaca. A large block, number 11, was designated as a market square. It was situated in the exact center of the town.[6]

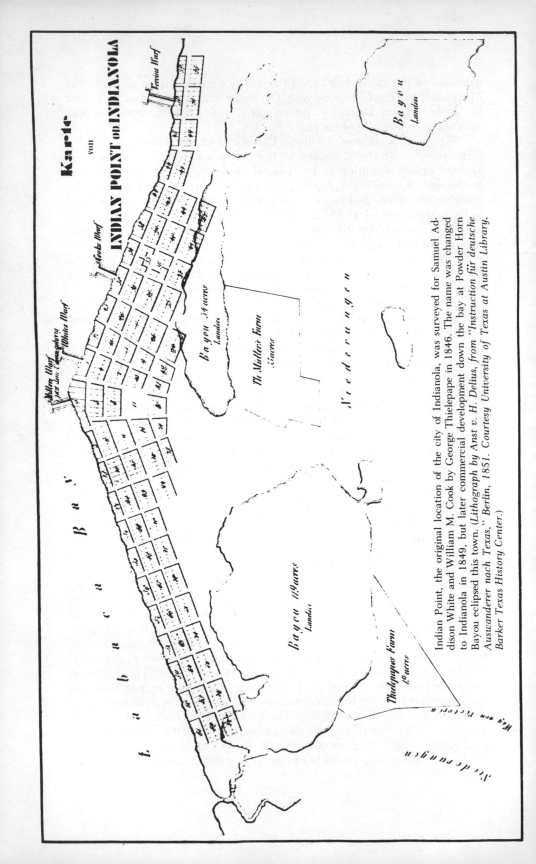

Karte

VIII

INDIAN POINT od INDIANOLA

Indian Point, the original location of the city of Indianola, was surveyed for Samuel Addison White and William M. Cook by George Thielepape in 1846. The name was changed to Indianola in 1849, but later commercial development down the bay at Powder Horn Bayou eclipsed this town. (Lithograph by Arnst v. H. Delius, from "Instruction für deutsche Auswanderer nach Texas," Berlin, 1851. Courtesy University of Texas at Austin Library, Barker Texas History Center.)

The first street paralleling the bay was officially listed as "Main Street," though it was frequently referred to as "First." The next in order were Second, Third and Fourth. The short streets running to the bay had widely different names (showing more imagination on the part of the owners) such as Austin, Bay and Front.

With the formal establishment of Indian Point in 1846, the promise of growth and prosperity that was seen for it began to interest "Americans," who came to inspect the site. Some remained to purchase property and open commercial enterprises. Port Lavacans, noting the events 12 miles down the bay, cast worried glances at Indian Point.

The meager early maritime traffic had moved through Lavaca after the destruction of Linnville. There was no other mainland port on the western shore of the bay to handle it. However, the repeated difficulties encountered with the bars of Lavaca Bay made it imperative for ship owners to seek an alternate spot for discharging the cargoes of vessels whose draught prevented their passing over the formidable Gallinipper Bar. Gallinipper completely obstructed passage of even the smaller boats when the effect of normal low tide was intensified by the strong north winds that prevail in Texas during much of the fall, winter and spring. Those north winds, by forcing bay water out through Pass Cavallo and lowering the level to the danger point in the shallow channel through the bar, played havoc with the ambitions of Port Lavaca and handed a golden opportunity to Indian Point. The deeper water at the latter place made its eventual selection as the alternate site a foregone conclusion.

Aside from the German immigration movement, traffic in the bay, though still very small by Galveston standards, began to expand. As the annexation of Texas had become apparent in 1845, the inevitability of war with Mexico had been recognized in the War Department of the American government. When annexation was effected and the conflict did begin, the United States was prepared to send shipments of men and arms direct to Matagorda Bay for movement inland to the frontier. Because it was the nearest point on the coast to the outposts projected on the frontier of Western Texas after statehood was achieved, that fact played a decisive role in the development of the new port of Indian Point.

During the Mexican War, government-chartered steam propelled ships entered through Pass Cavallo with men and materiel. Those of shallow draught made their way to Lavaca, the larger being obliged to cast anchor off Indian Point and lighter to shore. The heavy military traffic continued until the spring of 1847 and firmly established Indian Point as a commercial port of call in the western Gulf of Mexico. The lack of wharves at which ships could dock was soon corrected.

Prior to the surge of shipping activity connected with the war effort, no packet had operated between New Orleans or Galveston and Matagorda Bay. Other than the boats that came to Indian Point loaded with German immigrants, only occasional small sailing vessels called at irregular intervals. The latter were almost all second-rate tramps. Packets plied the Gulf between New Orleans and Galveston, but difficult problems had been posed for travelers wishing to go further west to

Matagorda Bay. A wait of from one to three weeks often proved necessary at New Orleans, if a person insisted on direct service. With favorable wind conditions, the voyage could be made from New Orleans to Pass Cavallo in four days. On the other hand, a schooner could be becalmed and 20 days would elapse before she arrived at the pass. The cost to a traveler for such a trip was $25. Usually, passengers would go to Galveston on a packet and then transfer to a small coastal ship for completion of the voyage.[7]

Even after arrival in the bay, captains of tramp sailing vessels displayed their independence by dawdling on delivery of freight to the towns of Matagorda, Lavaca and (after 1845) Indian Point. Being nearest the pass, the point usually received the quickest service, another mark in its favor.

There were two notable exceptions to the generally unsatisfactory state of shipping and traveling. They were the schooners *European*, commanded by Captain J. D. Brower, and *America*, Maloney-master. Those boats, under the direction of their able captains, became noted for their cleanliness, superior cabin accommodations, and courtesy of crew. Despite the fact that they operated without regular schedules, the *European* and *America* were eagerly sought as the preferred means of transportation between New Orleans, Galveston and the Bay. The *European*, with accommodations for 12 cabin passengers, and the *America*, which could carry 30 in "fine cabin style," were finally placed in service as packets from New Orleans to Indian Point, Lavaca and Matagorda in August 1847. Another schooner that was above average was the *Adeline* but she was slower, often requiring six weeks for a round trip.[8]

Despite the obvious handicap posed by inadequate maritime transportation facilities, Matagorda Bay continued to attract the attention of both men and women who came in person to review the situation and assess business prospects. One such notable Texan was Mrs. Angelina Belle Eberly, the heroine of the "Archive War" at Austin in 1842. At that time, she was operating the Eberly House in the capital city, to which place she had moved in 1839.[9] Mrs. Eberly was a practical business woman, aware of the promise of a booming future for the towns on the west side of Matagorda Bay. It was obvious that money could be made there. She prudently leased "a tavern house and lots" in Port Lavaca on April 16, 1847, so she could weigh prospects before making a financial investment in the purchase of property.

The lease was executed between Mrs. Eberly and Edward Clegg for the term of 12 months.[10] Excepted in the property covered by the lease were the bar and a room adjoining, and the stables. Mrs. Eberly was a successful hotel keeper and had no interest in operating a bar or a livery stable. Included in the lease were the household and kitchen furniture and fixtures. A bill of particulars was supplied, stating the quality and condition of the furniture, it being agreed that the furniture would be returned at the expiration of the lease "in as good order and condition as when received, with allowance for normal wear and tear." $180 was payable on July 15, 1847, and a like amount on October 15, on January 15, 1848, and on April 15, 1848, at which time the building and contents were to be turned back to Clegg.

In addition, Mrs. Eberly agreed to board Edward Clegg, his wife, child and servant, for the sum of $30 per month. A room in the tavern was to be made available to the Cleggs, but they were to supply their own bedding. Furthermore, Clegg agreed "to keep and maintain the said Mrs. Eberly in the quiet and peaceable possession of said premises for and during the lease aforesaid." She wanted no meddling on his part in her running of the establishment.

The reason that lay behind Edward Clegg's willingness to lease his Port Lavaca tavern to Mrs. Eberly was not long in becoming evident. Clegg opened the Planter's House at Indian Point to serve the expanding flow of travel through the port. His act was not lost on Mrs. Eberly, who deemed it confirmation of the wisdom of her leasing, not purchasing, Clegg's property in Lavaca. At the expiration of the lease, she moved to Indian Point.

The increasing commercial and passenger traffic into and out of Matagorda Bay was duly noted by the United States government. On September 7, 1847, a post office was established at Indian Point with John W. Pope postmaster in charge. The pressing need for navigational aids to shipping through Pass Cavallo brought about the purchase on November 22, 1847, of the south half of five acres of land on Matagorda Island, with 50 varas frontage on the pass, from Thomas Jefferson Chambers for $250. On December 9, 1848, the government purchased five additional acres for $500. The land was to be used as the site for a lighthouse and keeper's residence.[11]

The Congress of the Republic of Texas had taken steps on February 3, 1845, looking toward the placement of a lighthouse at the pass. The sum of $1,500 had been set aside for building the tower and equipping it with "the necessary apparatus for lights." It was to be constructed "on the west side of Passo Caballo, near the spot on which the flag staff now stands within or near the site of Port Calhoun . . ." However, the adoption of the joint resolution by the United States Congress on February 28, 1845, offering Texas statehood, and the sequence of events that followed during the year, squelched the planned building of the lighthouse. Why, it was asked in Austin, should the Republic expend this sum when, in a matter of months, the construction and maintenance of such a navigational aid would be the responsibility of the American government?

Evidence of the growth of Indian Point was C. Chipman's 1847 announcement as architect and builder, offering his services in the drawing of plans and specifications for buildings, as well as in contracting for their erection. H. Runge & Co. now operated as commission and forwarding merchants, in addition to banking, Henry Runge having been joined in business by his brother Herman. At Indian Point they had "a large and commodious warehouse with cool cellar for wet barrels." By the end of the year, other commission and forwarding agents were

Charles Eckhardt and Murphree & Brown, a partnership between David Murphree and John Henry Brown. A native of Tennessee, Murphree was a veteran of San Jacinto and had taken part in the campaign against Rafael Vasquez following the Mexican general's occupation of San Antonio in 1842. Murphree also commanded a battalion during the Somervell Expedition.[12]

On January 20, 1848, a formal agreement was signed by Samuel Addison White and Theodore Miller, the latter acting as agent of the German Emigration Company. The company was the successor of the bankrupt Adelsverein, and was also identified as the "Lavaca, Guadalupe and San Saba Rail Road Company."[13] The agreement covered the division of White's property at Indian Point, the company receiving title to one third of the lots and blocks undonated and undisposed of by White as of that date. On its part, the company agreed to continue to make Indian Point the landing place for the German immigrants into Texas who were brought by the company by virtue of its charter.[14] It was stipulated that Miller, in his capacity as agent for the German Emigration Company, would only have the power to sell or lease lots to actual settlers, the object being "to improve the town and prevent the land from falling into the hands of speculators." It was further provided that, in the event of dissolution of the company and absence of a successor, undisposed of lands in its name would revert to White.

Within less than five months after the execution of the agreement, the company, through Gustavus Dresel as trustee and agent, gave a trustee's deed on the property as collateral security to the Commercial and Agricultural Bank of Galveston in consideration of that firm's discounting $10,000 worth of drafts on headquarters in Biebrich, Germany. Dresel signed a similar deed to M. A. Dooley of Comal County in consideration of the receipt of $3,000.[15]

In January 1848, John B. Brown of Victoria established a regular weekly stagecoach service to Indian Point. Providing a relay of horses on the route, he was able to make the 40-mile run in one day, an impressive rate of speed for a horse-drawn vehicle on Texas roads.[16] Brown's immediate success generated competition on the Indian Point run from Harrison & McCulloch. In November 1847, that firm had inaugurated the United States Line of stages between Port Lavaca and Victoria. The increasing commercial importance of Indian Point, and Brown's success, led them to extend their route from Lavaca. Theirs was a four-horse stage weekly service to New Braunfels via Cuero, Gonzales and Seguin.[17] It connected with the Houston stage at Gonzales and the San Antonio to Austin line at New Braunfels. Edward Clegg was named the first agent at Lavaca, the depot being at the livery stable next door to his hotel which Mrs. Eberly then had under lease.

J. B. Brown's decision to establish the stagecoach run between Victoria and Indian Point had been sparked by the recent placing, by the New Orleans shipping firm of Harris & Morgan, of the steamship *Yacht* on a weekly schedule between Galveston and the Bay. She was the first commercial steam packet to be operated to the Matagorda Bay ports, and opened a new era in marine transportation. The stage line was designed to connect with the *Yacht* at Indian Point. She, in turn, was scheduled to make connection at Galveston with Harris & Morgan's larger steamers to and from New Orleans.[18] Management of the steamship firm was vested in Israel C. Harris and Henry R. Morgan, though actual ownership was in the hands of Charles Morgan of New York. Charles Morgan was to put the match to the future Indianola's explosive development into the principal port for Western Texas. Harris was Charles Morgan's son-in-law, having married his daughter Emily Ann. Henry R. was the second son of the senior Morgan.

Announcing a definite schedule and maintaining it were two entirely different matters, as concerned the *Yacht* and Matagorda Bay. Her initial terminus was to be Port Lavaca, with call at Indian Point, but trouble dogged her wake. On the very first trip, the *Yacht* experienced the difficulties that were to hound Lavaca and keep that town from developing into the great port it could have been, had natural deep water extended to its wharves. The *Yacht* went aground on the bars of Lavaca Bay on that first voyage, as well as on each of the following six that it undertook.

The Harris & Morgan office in New Orleans, not in possession of the facts and being pressured by Port Lavacans, discharged the captain for the repeated groundings. The citizens of Lavaca insisted that there was a sufficient depth of water over the bar, alleging that the problem was caused by inefficiency. That unfortunate captain's successor fared no better, for on his own first trip into Lavaca Bay past Indian Point, the *Yacht* again went aground on Gallinipper Bar. A quarrel ensued between the captain (Wilson) and the irate merchants of Port Lavaca. The former declared that it was both impracticable and unprofitable to run steamers to that port. For their part, Lavacans continued to publicly blame the repeated groundings on incompetence, but privately were filled with foreboding of disaster, realizing that the incidents and publicity were deeply hurtful to their interests.[19] It was hardly an auspicious manner in which to inaugurate a service!

Damage to the vessel was incurred, one such stranding necessitating repairs to the *Yacht* in the amount of $900, a substantial sum for that period. Another headache for Harris & Morgan was that the delays resulted in the *Yacht*'s failing to return to Galveston in time to get her passengers and freight aboard the New Orleans bound ships.

In order to overcome the problem, Harris & Morgan placed a small schooner in service in the bay to lighter the steamer from its anchorage to the short wharves at Port Lavaca. Use of the lighter necessitated several trips between the ship and the town. During the transfer of merchandise and passengers, the vessel lay at anchor, all hands idle. The time and the cost of lightering was expensive to the firm. Consideration had to be given to improvement of the situation. The decision reached in the office of Harris & Morgan on New Orleans' Tchoupitoulas Street was to cooperate in the construction of a long wharf at Indian Point where the *Yacht* could dock. It would be completed in the late fall.[20]

Indian Point received another welcome boost, this one from the widely read book by the explorer-merchant-author Viktor Bracht, who had come to Texas in 1845. In "Texas im Jahre 1848," he said, " . . . Matagorda Bay is just as extensive as Galveston Bay, and much better suited for navigation. It is true that in the northeast part, near the town of Matagorda, navigation is checked by sand bars so that even small coasting vessels have to unload four to six miles from town . . . In the northeastern outlet of the bay, called Lavaca Inlet, is found a quite difficult channel with less water than the one at Indian Point. Not all coasting vessels laden with freight that reach the latter can get to Port Lavaca . . . "

The development and burgeoning prosperity of Indian Point was more than her near neighbor could bear. During January 1848, Port Lavaca's petulant attitude toward her new rival came into the open with a scathing editorial in the Lavaca *Journal*. The article was especially critical of that dean of Indian Point leaders, the beloved Henry Huck, together with Captain Horace Baldwin. The newspaper accused them of bias, of being blinded by the desire for personal financial gain and of misrepresenting the facts of the commercial advantages of one town against the other.[21] The charges were emotional and exaggerated. That editorial in the *Journal* was the opening volley in a more or less one-sided feud that lasted as long as Indian Point (Indianola) existed. It was Port Lavaca that was usually on the offensive. Response from the people down the bay was patronizing in tone, which annoyed Port Lavacans all the more.

Soon after the steamship *Yacht* was placed in service, announcement was made through the *Texian Advocate* that the "A-1 copper and copper fastened Brig *Matagorda*, E. Purchase, Master," would sail from the bay on January 21, 1848, bound for New York. She was to be the first of a line of sailing vessels to operate between that city and the Bay. Launched on December 6, 1847, the *Matagorda* was built expressly for this route in the Gulf trade. A swift ship, she possessed fine stateroom accommodations with the most modern improvements and innovations for the comfort and convenience of her passengers. The *Matagorda* arrived at Indian Point on her maiden voyage on January 15 and unloaded a cargo of 90,000 feet of white pine lumber for Henry Huck's yard.[22]

The use of a thin copper sheathing on the wooden ships was of importance for two reasons. One was to foil the shipworm, *teredo navalis*, whose troublesome practice was to bore into the submerged timbers of vessels, as well as into the piling of wharves. *Teredo navalis* was the scourge of ship and wharf owners in the warm waters of the Atlantic Ocean and the Gulf of Mexico. The copper sheathing had a life of approximately ten years, eventually being destroyed by electrolytic reaction of the salt water, the copper and the iron nails used in construction. Without its protection, the underwater wood soon fell prey to the shipworms and became tunneled, seepage of water into the hold resulting. As the unrestricted borings increased, the point would be reached when the ship's pumps would be unable to keep the water level under control and the cargo would be damaged. Unless drydocked and repaired, the wooden vessel would be consigned to a watery grave.

The other reason for the use of the copper sheathing was to discourage the barnacles, which so eagerly affixed themselves to unprotected timber. A thick, rough incrustation of barnacles would impede the movement of a boat, lengthening the time required for a scheduled run by both sailing and steamships. Insofar as the steamers were concerned, the dragging effect of barnacle incrustation resulted in increased consumption of costly fuel.

Indian Point developed into a wholesale center from which merchants of inland towns could be supplied. Extensive stocks of groceries, hardware, lumber, clothing, furniture and other items were maintained there as early as 1848. Their ready availability meant that the merchants of the interior of Western Texas were no longer required to make substantial capital outlays for large inventories, as they had been obliged to do in the past when their shipments came at long intervals from New Orleans and New York. Barter was an accepted manner of doing business, whether wholesale or retail. At the Point, cotton, dry hides, tallow and pecans were taken in exchange for manufactured goods, coffee, sugar, etc. The agricultural items commanded fancy prices on the distant metropolitan markets, thus affording Indian Point businessmen an opportunity for additional profit.

The town's co-founder, Wm. M. Cook, moved into a large warehouse on the bay front that had been vacated by Clegg and Neal in January 1848. There he set up a commission business, specifying that he made no charge for wharfage or lighterage. Cook had immediately constructed his own short wharf which, with those of Theodore Miller, of Samuel A. White and of the Verein (or German Emigration Company) gave the port a total of four. It was a remarkable achievement in view of the fact that only 37 months had passed since its beginnings, with the landing of the first immigrants.

There was a continuing steady movement of European immigrants through Indian Point destined for Western Texas. The bankruptcy of the Adelsverein in 1847, and its subsequent disappearance from the scene, did not halt the flow of scholars and other intellectuals, of mechanics, professional men, farmers and merchants who brought their families to the new land, establishing towns, settling the countryside. Among these were the members of a large group of communists who landed at Indian Point in the summer of 1847.[23] There they purchased the supplies necessary for their planned commune of Bettina on the Llano River. In less than two months, they were on the site working on the construction of housing. However, their spirit of dedication and industry soon waned. Lack of discipline, and wholesale shirking of responsibilities, resulted in the failure of the project by mid-1848. Members drifted away and were soon absorbed into the thriving towns nearby whose prosperity was based on the capitalistic free enterprise system that had become so dear to the hearts of the thrifty, hardworking men and women in their new life in Texas.

Then the flood gates of emigration from Europe were opened by the political upheavals on the continent in 1848. Western Texas was the goal of the thousands of refugees who fled from the turmoil, economic stagnation and severely repressive policies of European governments seeking to halt the trend toward free-thinking and republicanism.

III.

Religion Comes to Town

An adequate supply of potable water was to remain a constant problem at Indian Point. There was no fresh stream nearby from which good water could be secured for household purposes and for placement in the boilers of steam powered ships. Green Lake, which could have provided a limitless quantity, was almost 20 miles distant. It might as well have been on the moon. The collection of rain water in cypress above-ground cisterns and in gigantic concrete reservoirs underground was necessarily resorted to. Rainfall was usually sufficient to maintain the cisterns, but in occasional prolonged dry spells, the shortage of water could become acute.

The summer of 1848 saw spotty drought conditions. Though Indian Point did receive a few showers that prevented the development of a critical water scarcity, residents across the bay on Matagorda Island were not so fortunate. A letter written at Saluria on August 8 and addressed to "Dear Sister Maverick," Mrs. Samuel A. Maverick of San Antonio, by her brother-in-law R. J. Clow mentions the difficulties encountered. " . . . There is only one cistern that has water in it, at the warehouse, the doctors being entirely out. Lizzie and myself have to wash in about a pint each of fresh water and then put it in a tub and preserve it to wash our feet, which luxury we indulge in twice a week. I mean in fresh water. And, after washing our feet, it is carefully preserved to wash baby clothes, I mean Mrs. McCreary's, and then it is . . . put into a barrel kept for the purpose and issued out carefully to the chickens and calves three times a week. I think from the economy we have learned by necessity to practice in regard to fresh water, we both would be good subjects to pass the great desert of Sahara . . . ''

In March 1848, there had been a buzz of interest in the new Bullard windmill, which offered hope of providing a dependable flow of water from shallow sands that underlay the coast country. Unfortunately, experimental digging proved that intrusion of salt water in the sands near the surface of the bay shore spoiled them for use. There was neither the equipment nor the know-how to drill into the deep strata where later exploration found abundant resources of pure artesian water. That would come in a future generation. As a result, the cisterns continued to be the source of the town's water during the remainder of its existence. Salt water from the bay was utilized extensively in the kitchens. When water closets were introduced, bay water was pumped to the overhead tanks, but caused constant difficulty because of its corrosive effect on metal parts.

Rainfall caused problems at Indian Point whether it was in abundance or in short supply. When there was a dearth of rain, cistern water was rationed, but heavy and prolonged downpours that caused the cisterns to overflow resulted in monumental problems for the wagon trains. They bogged on the earthen roads, there to remain until the surface dried. An all-weather route to the interior was a great need for uninterrupted movement of traffic into and out of the port. Railroads were still out of reach for Texans in April 1848. The next best thing was the laying out of new roads to utilize high, firm ground and, where possible, to by-pass sections which became mires in rainy weather. Where there was no alternative route around the latter, a plank road was sometimes laid.

Charles Eckhardt and Theodore Miller, acting for the merchants of Indian Point and the German Emigration Company, commissioned John A. King of DeWitt County to survey a new and shorter route from New Braunfels to Victoria, where it would connect with the roads then traveled from that town to the port. The purpose was to save time and effort on the part of wagoners, stages, immigrants, and the general public. King's work resulted in reducing the distance from Indian Point to New Braunfels by slightly more than 25 miles, and was especially noteworthy in that it avoided much bad ground and several stream crossings which had been a source of trouble. The old road ran from Victoria to Gonzales and Seguin to New Braunfels.

In that early time in Texas, before there were county road districts or a State Highway Department, little or no grading was done. A route would be surveyed and marked. The next step was for wagons, carriages, horsemen and stages to follow the marked trail and make their own road. In King's report, he said, "According to agreement, I have made the survey for the road leading from New Braunfels to this place and take great pleasure in making a report of the same. I commenced at the southeastern margin of the town [New Braunfels] and continued down the Guadalupe River, making as few angles as practicable so as to keep on good ground, shunning the sand on my right hand and avoiding the bottom, or stiff, land on my left until I arrived at the springs not far distant from Maj. Erskin's and near the pass of the Caporta Hills, making 25 miles. Thence making a rather serpentine survey for two miles which brought me to the top of the hill, making a good route, easy of ascent, but little sand. Thence in a true course for Yorktown and found the ground all the way admirably adapted to the making of a good road. Thence in a direction best suiting the object for Victoria. The route well watered and the greatest distance between watering places 10 miles. And, on the way, there are 16 places of never failing water . . . "[1]

The interest in trade routes from the bay went far beyond New Braunfels, Fredericksburg, Austin and San Antonio. The large amount of United States government traffic moving to Matagorda Bay in consequence of the war with Mexico was soon followed by shipments of commercial and military goods to Western Texas. In February 1848, the establishment of the Post of El Paso, later known as Fort Bliss, was authorized. This first of a series of Army outposts on the frontier was to profoundly affect the fortunes of Indian Point. Visions of trade with Northern Mexico, the New Mexico Territory and newly acquired California began to dance in the heads of the enterprising merchants of the bay. The excitement spread to other communities that might be benefited by such movement. The *Texian Advocate* of May 4 wrote, "The Passage to the Pacific . . . We had hoped that the General Government would, ere this, have ordered a survey of this route, which begins at Pass Cavallo on the Gulf of Mexico, passes up the Guadalupe River to Paso del Norte, thence to the Gila River and the Gulf of California.

"Besides this channel being the nearest and most favorable route to the navigable waters of the Pacific, it is unquestionably the route through which all Northern Mexico and Santa Fe are to be supplied with merchandise. Already, indeed, there is an extensive trade carried on between Western Texas and Chihuahua, which needs only to become a little better known to supplant the immense trade heretofore carried on from Independence [Missouri].

"The slightest knowledge of our Gulf Coast taken in connection with the fact that only two passes are to be found in the great chain of mountains extending from Oregon through Mexico will be entirely sufficient to make what we have said apparent to everyone. Galveston, Pass Cavallo and Aransas are the only places where shipping can reach a landing on the west side of the Gulf of Mexico. The Great South Pass and Paso del Norte are the only places where roads can be had across the mountains. These being the case, will not a glance at the map be sufficient to dispel every doubt as to the advantages of the route from Pass Cavallo?"

Another boost for a southern transcontinental route came from Dr. Levi Jones, who had recently moved to the Indian Point area from

Galveston. He had been the physician in attendance on Stephen F. Austin during the *empresario's* illness with pneumonia, and death at Columbia on December 27, 1836. One of the organizers of the Galveston City Company, and agent in its early years, Dr. Jones's attention had been caught by the opportunities for financial gain through commercial activities at Matagorda Bay. He became a leader in advancing its interests.

Jones published a promotional pamphlet in 1848 and in it he, too, referred to the advantages of a road from the bay to the Pacific. He said, "It is a curious fact, well worth recording, that about 40 years ago the late John J. Astor of New York, then extensively engaged in the fur trade on the Pacific, made application to the Spanish government for permission to construct a road and line of military posts from a point on the Pacific near San Diego, by way of Paso del Norte and San Antonio, to Matagorda Bay in Texas. For some cause not known, this application was refused. Thus did this sagacious man, at that early date, suggest what scientific discoveries have recently confirmed, that the true route for communication between the Atlantic and Pacific Oceans is the very one we advocate . . . "[2]

From this small acorn would grow the mighty oak of the Chihuahua and California trade through Indian Point, soon to be known as Indianola.

Dr. Jones reflected upon the role he played in the Galveston City Company, and the subsequent expansion of the island port. In his considered opinion, the possibilities for profit in the Matagorda Bay region were fully as great as those at Galveston, so he moved to take advantage of them. On July 9, 1848, there was filed in the office of the county clerk at Port Lavaca an indenture signed by Jones, Hiram G. Runnels, Hugh McLeod and James Love, all of Galveston. Included was the expressed intention to establish a commercial port town to be named LaSalle. It was to be located on a 5,000 acre tract on the west shore of Matagorda Bay below Powder Horn Bayou, and approximately six miles from Indian Point. By this agreement, the LaSalle City Company was formed.[3]

Dr. Jones had not cut out for himself an easy task, though he was a capable organizer and promoter. The obstacles he faced were enormous as he endeavored to buck the magnetic pull on routing of commercial traffic being exerted by Indian Point. Had he been able to take advantage of a golden opportunity presented by Morgan interests the following year, his ultimate success could have exceeded his wildest dreams. Why he did not remains a mystery.

After being placed in dry dock in New Orleans for repairs and reduction of draught, Harris & Morgan's *Yacht* had returned to the Matagorda Bay run in April 1848. Thus enabled to better navigate the shallow channel through Gallinipper Bar, the *Yacht* reached Port Lavaca in three days from New Orleans, one from Galveston.[4] In the face of pleasure at her reappearance, grumblings were beginning to be heard about what merchants and travelers considered her exorbitant rates. Suggestions were freely offered by the public that a reduction of 25% to 50% would be beneficial.[5] The New Orleans and Texas Mail Line Steamship Company turned a deaf ear to the proposals. There was to be no lowering of rates until other steam propelled vessels were placed in the lucrative Matagorda Bay service by rival owners in competition with Harris & Morgan.

Sailing ships from Boston, New York, Philadelphia, Baltimore, Pensacola, Mobile, New Orleans and lesser Gulf and Atlantic ports crowded the four wharves at Indian Point to discharge their assorted cargoes for the interior of Western Texas, and to take on raw materials consigned to the industrial north. Those sailing ships were to remain the backbone of Western Gulf maritime traffic for several years. The *Patriot* from Mobile was on a frequent schedule carrying from the Point a new Texas agricultural export, gama grass hay.[6] The native grass hay from the Guadalupe River valley was being shipped by Charles Eckhardt of Indian Point to New Orleans and Mobile. His first shipment of 1,400 bales commanded a premium price in the markets of those cities. The profitable venture led to Eckhardt's expansion as an exporter of Texas hay, and provided a certain market for the excess produced by farmers and ranchers in the coast country.

Eckhardt became the prime exporter of wool from Saxon sheep that had been brought to Fredericksburg from the Rhineland via Indian Point. He had studied the region around Fredericksburg and had concluded that it was the most suitable in Western Texas for the raising of sheep. Soon after he made that assessment for the wool-producing industry, a shipment of Merino sheep was brought into Indian Point from Spain. Destined for the Blair Ranch on the upper Guadalupe, the flock was attended by a Spanish shepherd and a "genuine shepherd dog." A demonstration of the canine's skillful control of the flock delighted the people of the port who gathered to witness the show. It was Blair's intention to cross the Merinos with the hardy Mexican sheep.[7]

The *Ocean Wave, Harrison, Pennsylvania, Tom Paine, Montana, Sears, Mary, Adeline, Matagorda, European, America* and *Victoria* were among the vessels whose officers and crew had become well known in Indian Point because of their frequent trips to the port. On each arrival, the eyes of the crews would be greeted by the sight of new buildings along the low shore. All stood out sharply against the horizon, as the point was deficient in trees. Only diminutive scrub oaks, the Texas umbrella tree, the pink-flowering tamarisk and the laurel grew satisfactorily in the poor soil. Through most of the year, the gaillardia spread its blanket of color over the land, sharing it in spring with white and yellow daisies, bluebonnets and the Indian paintbrush.

Oleanders had been introduced from Galveston, to which town they had, in turn, been imported from the islands of the West Indies. Hedges of the sweet-scented flowering shrub were to become as typical of the Indian Point scene as they have been of Galveston. They, and the tamarisk, were widely used as windbreaks against the strong prevailing southeast breeze.

Despite its infancy, Indian Point presented a neat and well-ordered appearance. In those beginning years, the residences were cottages, a few having an upper half-story or attic with dormer windows. The fine two-story, large private homes were to begin appearing in the middle 1850s, but in 1848 Indian Point was still a frontier town. However, the amenities of civilization were already beginning to ease the stark realities of life there and in Western Texas. Wallpaper, much in vogue east of the Mississippi, began reaching the Point's wholesale and retail market at that time, though it was slow to be accepted locally as being practical in the humid climate. The interior walls of homes on the bay were of smooth-fitted tongue-and-groove boards coated with a glossy paint, usually white.[8]

The influence of the large German population was apparent in the cleanliness of the town, which was a bilingual community from the start. Many of the older immigrants who settled at Indian Point lived out their life span without learning English. The same was true in other communities in the interior where thousands of the Germans took up residence. Schools of Indian Point were bilingual until June 1860, after which time English became the required language for instruction.[9]

Even in the first years most of the buildings were painted for protection against the elements. White was most frequently used, especially for business houses, but individualism did show up with some being painted gray, light blue, green, yellow and even red. Warehouses built of cypress lumber, which were between Main Street and the shore line, were the largest structures in town at that time. In them, merchandise discharged from or to be loaded onto the ships was stored temporarily. The unpainted cypress warehouses and the small sheds and other outbuildings, as well as fences, weathered beautifully in the atmosphere of Indian Point, taking on a delicate coloring of silvery gray that was aesthetically pleasing. The use of shutters on residences and commercial buildings was uniform. Those window coverings with movable slats were popular because they provided interior coolness and reduced the glare produced by strong sunlight reflected off the white shell on which the town was built.

For over three years, lots at Indian Point had been sold in response to local demand, but now Samuel A. White decided to promote their sale through a public offering. In the late spring, he placed an advertisement in New Orleans and Texas newspapers giving notice of the availability of building sites. "The proprietor will offer at public sale on the 6th day of July, 1848, a number of the most valuable and eligible lots in the town of Indian Point on the west side of Lavaca and Matagorda Bays at their junction, and at the head of nine feet of water in said bays. The proprietor does not desire to promote the sale of his town property by means of unmerited puffs, but contents himself with pointing to the eligible and healthful location of the place with its easy accessibility by both land and water, its rapid and permanent improvement within the last two years, and its present and increasing amount of commerce and shipping. Relying upon the manifest advantages and rapidly developing importance of Indian Point, he submits its claims to those who may be seeking a safe and profitable investment in town property without further comment. Terms of sale, 1/5 cash, the other 4/5 in two equal installments at 6 and 18 months."

German residents of the town were less than enthusiastic about White's plans to entice more "Americans" to invest in and settle at Indian Point. Their views on the institution of African slavery were at sharp variance with those of many Southern Americans. While not abolitionists in an active sense, the Germans, with very few exceptions, were opposed to slavery. It was against their nature, and abhorrent, to hold another human in bondage. Therefore, slave ownership at Indian Point was almost wholly confined to the "American element."[10]

Sam White's public sale of town lots at Indian Point was a success, more than 100 having been sold "to actual American settlers." A female school was established, as was a Presbyterian Sunday School with an enrollment of 52, a fine shell road had been built by July one mile straight out of town over the salt flat on the route to Victoria, and plans for a public wharf to ten feet of water were being pushed. That depth of water, with soft mud bottom, was reached within 400 varas of the beach.

Both the Presbyterians and Methodists had congregations in Indian Point by the summer of 1848.[11] There were many German Lutherans in the town, but it would be 1854 before a Lutheran church was formally organized there. The report of the 8th Session of the Texas Conference, Methodist Episcopal Church, held at Cedar Creek from December 29, 1847, to January 3, 1848, had stated, "The German work in the Southwest is included in a Victoria and Indian Point German Mission, with Henry Bauer in charge."

The Rev. Daniel Baker, D.D., pioneer Presbyterian missionary minister, visited Indian Point, Lavaca, Victoria and Texana in 1848. In a letter dated at Port Lavaca on July 18 and addressed to his son William, Dr. Baker said, "I still think Texas is the very place for me, and perhaps for you, also. It presents a new, wide and promising field for missionary enterprise. Yesterday I finished a meeting at Indian Point, some 8 or 9 miles distant from this on the bay. It is a flourishing village that has come into notice chiefly within the last 12 months; formerly being a place for German immigrants who were here in a state of transportation to the interior. Six months ago there were not, I suppose, 20 Americans in the place, now 100 or more. Recently lots have been sold in the amount of $4,000 and within 6 or 8 weeks past persons have come in to settle there whose property is valued at $250,000. Well, in this place, I have lately preached some 15 sermons and I am happy to say my efforts to do good have been greatly blessed. Six or 8 persons hopefully converted, the first who ever confessed conversion in the place; one of whom I baptised, the first adult ever baptised in the place. Moreover, I administered the Sacrament of the Lord's Supper, the first time this Sacrament also was ever administered in the place. About 20 persons of different communions sat down at the table. On Monday, took the requisite steps for organizing a Presbyterian Church of 11 members, the first church organized of any denomination.

"I ought to have mentioned that I succeeded in forming a Sabbath School here, embracing 8 teachers and 44 scholars. Astonishing. No one ever dreamed of half that number. Two of the converts, so called, were brought in at the right time, one to be Vice Superintendent and the other Librarian.'"[12] Dr. Baker was mistaken in his belief that his administration of the Sacrament of the Lord's Supper was the first such at Indian Point. That had been administered by the Lutheran pastor Louis Ervendberg on Christmas Day, 1844.

In his diary entry of Thursday, August 13, 1848, Dr. Baker observed, "Went again to Indian Point to preach a few days and administer the Sacrament next Sabbath. When we went last week, at the pressing invitation of Mr. W-, the proprietor of the village [Note: obviously Samuel Addison White], we were left to bear our own expense and, although he had provided a room for our accommodation, when we retired after preaching found there was no chair, table or bed in the room. At that late hour had to seek accommodations elsewhere. Hope a bed will be provided this time. Stayed with Mr. B-'s family, who lived in the attic story, and slept on a mattress in the ware room amid hogsheads of sugar, etc. . . ." It is possible that the "Mr. B-" to whom Dr. Baker referred was John Henry Brown, who had recently moved to Indian Point from Victoria. The Browns were Presbyterians and became leaders in the new church at Indian Point.

Dr. Baker's success was indicated by the fact that on August 17 he was satisfied to return to Port Lavaca, after preaching eight sermons at Indian Point, which he believed "is likely to be an important place before long." His achievements at Indian Point were not immediately matched at Port Lavaca, as the proposed organization of a Presbyterian church there was postponed, "for a few weeks," he having concluded that the citizens of that town were not quite ready for the step.

IV.

The Wave of the Future

By the Treaty of Guadalupe Hidalgo, which had been signed on February 2, 1848, and marked the end of the war between the United States and Mexico, the latter relinquished its claim to that part of Texas between the Nueces and Rio Grande Rivers, as well as to the great Southwest. The United States government paid Mexico $15,000,000 and assumed American claims against that nation. The transfer of that vast territory favorably affected the fortunes of Indian Point, as did the Gadsden Purchase of 1854.

The exodus of American troops from Mexico was not long in starting after the signing of the treaty. Colonel Hays's regiment of Texas Volunteers arrived in Matagorda Bay on May 12 from Vera Cruz on the steamship *Maria Birt* and was disbanded, the term of enlistment having expired. They had left the City of Mexico on April 30 and Vera Cruz on May 4.[1] Throughout the summer, there was an uninterrupted flow of homeward bound troops. The dead were also returned. The remains of the ill-fated Mier Expedition prisoners who died in 1843 were obtained as a result of the victory over Mexico and were brought back for interment on Monument Hill above LaGrange.

Commercial implications of Guadalupe Hidalgo were enormous. In editorial comment on June 22, 1848, the *Texian Advocate* at Victoria expressed views regarding the possibility of diversion of the Chihuahua trade from Santa Fe and Independence through Victoria and Matagorda Bay. The editors urged the formation of a company for the purpose of opening the trade route between the bay and Chihuahua. "The distance is very little more than 500 miles and, from information in our possession, we believe a road may be had which will vary little from a direct route." The paper pointed out that, in 1835, Captain D. B. Friar of Green Lake, "in company with Col. Milam," went from San Antonio to the Rio Grande, crossing that stream "just above the mouth of the Rio Puerco on the eighth day from San Antonio." After traveling up the Rio Grande for two days, "they met a party of Mexicans only three days from the City of Chihuahua, thus making the travel from San Antonio to the City of Chihuahua only 13 days."

The editors observed that, "An experienced mercantile friend suggests, however, that there is no occasion for American merchants going *into* the country at all, that it would be better to establish at some convenient point near the Mexican line, which is here the Rio Grande, a large depot and fort to which the Mexican traders and population might come and make their purchases. By this arrangement, the duties might be almost entirely avoided and the Mexicans would doubtless undertake the smuggling at a very low premium. . . ." It is curious that the respectable editors of the *Texian Advocate* would have encouraged the flouting of Mexican and American laws by tacit approval of smuggling activities!

Only five months later, on November 2, the newspaper reported on the prospect of actual experimentation with the trade route, though the commercial opening of the road would come in early 1850. Some of the Santa Fe and Chihuahua traders who had been operating from Independence were, at the time, examining the new routes through Western Texas to Northern Mexico. "We conversed a few days ago," said the *Advocate*, "with a Mr. Shaw (son of Chief Justice Shaw of Boston, a man of great wealth), who informed us that himself and a Mr. Glasgow of St. Louis were both on their way to San Antonio, where they would await the return of Col. Hays, upon whose favorable report of the route to Chihuahua it is their purpose to make an adventure the coming spring. The company to which they belong wields a capital of $12,000 and use in their trade 800 wagons. We hail this as a favorable omen for Western Texas, which must inevitably be enriched by the transit of the immense trade of all of the northern States of Mexico, and perhaps of California."

Of much concern to the people of Indian Point during that eventful summer of 1848 was the projection of a "railroad" from an, as yet, undetermined point on the Colorado River in Wharton County to the town of Columbia on the Brazos. The plan for its construction was similar to that suggested by Prince Karl in his sixth report to the directors of the Adelsverein for a "railroad" from Matagorda Bay to the German colonies. In both instances, it was intended that the "rails" would be of live oak and that mule power would be used to pull the cars until such time as iron rails and a steam locomotive could be secured.

According to the 1848 proposal, cargoes unloaded from boats in the Brazos River at Columbia would be transported overland to the banks of the Colorado above the log jam and there loaded on vessels that would carry them upstream as far as Austin.[2] Although several thousand dollars had been pledged, the project got no further from the drawing board than did the prince's Lavaca, Guadalupe and San Saba Rail Road Company. The failure of the Colorado-Brazos plan was welcomed by the merchants of Indian Point and Port Lavaca in one of their rare cooperative moods.

The Colorado River competitive threat had existed for several years during experiments with navigation. On March 8, 1846, the first steamboat had arrived at Austin, an event that caused newspaper editors to indulge in flights of fancy about the new capital becoming a great inland port. As a matter of fact, that little steamer, the *Kate Ward*, which was owned by the Colorado Navigation Company, was locked into the river by the log jam near its mouth. She had been built above the jam and her machinery installed on the spot. A flat bottom vessel, she had extremely shallow draught, which enabled her to maneuver through the constantly shifting channels of Colorado sand bars. She was equipped to remove snags that interfered with her passage. Great efforts were put forth by the navigation company to clear out the downstream log jam, but that feat proved to be beyond the financial ability of the towns along the river. Had the plan for the live oak railroad been carried to completion, the diversion of traffic from Matagorda Bay to the new route would have been a severe loss.

Then, Mother Nature took a hand in the matter. Although near-drought conditions prevailed along the middle coast, heavy and prolonged rains in the upper reaches of the Colorado resulted in excessively high water in the summer of 1848 that cut a temporary channel around the log jam, enabling the *Kate Ward* to make her way into East Matagorda Bay. She was then used in another exhaustive attempt to remove the jam, but it also failed. In a few years, the ever-growing mass of debris closed the new channel.[3] The *Kate Ward* ended up plying the Guadalupe River and the bays between Victoria and Indianola.

In August, the *Yacht* was again taken out of service for repairs in New Orleans, but this time her place on the run between Matagorda Bay and Galveston was filled by the *Globe* and the *Portland*, other Harris & Morgan vessels. It was observed that, "Judging from the number of troops that have been landed at New Orleans, it cannot be long before the *Galveston* and other Texas steamers will resume their places in the Mail Line from New Orleans to Texas."[4] That prediction was soon proved correct by the return to their owners of steamships that had been under lease to the United States government during the war with Mexico.

At the beginning of October 1848, a contingent of troops under Major Jefferson Van Horne reached the bay en route to San Antonio. By the following September, that force garrisoned the new outpost of El Paso del Norte.[5] Less than ten days after Van Horne's passage, news reached Indian Point of the discovery of gold in Northern California. Though the populace was electrified by the exaggerated reports, there is no record of anyone leaving the town and heading for the gold fields. Serious minded citizens reflected on the significance of the news and thoughtfully considered it to reinforce the recent pressure for a safe southern route to the Pacific . . . one that would, of course, begin on the western shore of Matagorda Bay.

Not all shared enthusiasm for Texas and the Southwest. The New York *Tribune* had just published a blast that was eagerly copied in state newspapers. It became a source of merriment to readers because of the patently snobbish and provincial attitude it evidenced. The *Tribune* said, in part, "Rhetoric aside . . . Texas is a miserable country, and its inhabitants a miserable population. She and the newly acquired territory west are destined to be an interminable source of turmoil and expense to the nation. They will cost the Government in current expenses far more than all the rest of our frontier, without taking into calculation the prime cost of annexation. . . the hundred millions expended in the late war. Their resources (superlatively over-rated and exaggerated) will never, in all time, contribute to the Union a tithe of the benefits which the false statements of interested parties and their continued cost to the General Government would give the nation to expect. Grain, Texas cannot grow to any extent. Her cotton trade must be next to nothing and her sugar trade literally nothing. Her grazing facilities are incomparably inferior to those of the whole Western region north of latitude 36½ from the Alleghany [sic] to the Rocky Mountains.

"Except a small patch of Eastern Texas, she has no productive soil because she has no seasons. Like most of Mexico, the rains of heaven are scarcely vouchsafed to her at all, and never in seasonable regularity. He who sows has no confidence that he will ever be permitted to reap. Not one season in five is productive to the laborer. Irrigation can only make the soil yield a sure return, and so small a proportion of the whole is susceptible of this artificial and expensive adjunct that it is merely trifling to consider it. The same is true of New Mexico and California. Texas is hopelessly bad, New Mexico, if possible, worse, and California worst!"

At the expiration of her lease on Edward Clegg's tavern in Port Lavaca on April 15, 1848, Mrs. Angelina Belle Eberly moved to Indian Point, where she began operating the American Hotel on Main Street. She advertised "private rooms for families." Not until the following year did she make her first purchase of property.

There had been increasing discussion of the need to change the name of Indian Point to one that better conveyed the impression of a community of importance. It had become the general belief that "Indian Point," though quaint, and appropriate to the site, failed nevertheless to project the proper image of the town. After debate on the matter, suggestions for a new name were solicited. That which was chosen, "Indianola," was proposed by Mrs. John Henry Brown. Her reasoning was that the first part of the current name (Indian) should be retained.

To that, there would be added the Spanish word for wave, *ola*. Surely, it must be admitted that the wave of the future was beginning to sweep over Western Texas from this very spot on Matagorda Bay. There was beauty in the name. It had a musical sound. "Indianola" was approved without dissent and a document dated February 1, 1849, was prepared for signature by the principal property owners, signifying their agreement to the change.[6]

Many months were to elapse before the name Indian Point passed out of popular usage. To avoid confusion in the public mind, advertisements that were circulated in distant places used both Indianola and Indian Point, until it was assumed that the fact of the change had become sufficiéntly well-known.

A sharp increase in the number of vessels operating into Matagorda Bay had occurred beginning late in 1848. Messrs. Harris and Morgan took due note of the more competitive situation their company faced. To expedite the handling of cargoes to Port Lavaca, which was still the terminus for their company, now known as the United States Mail Steamship Line, they replaced the sail lighter with the steam propeller *Jerry Smith*. Soon after its placement in lightering service, the company began running the sidewheel steamers *Portland* and *Galveston*, the largest of the fleet, through to the bay from New Orleans, only touching at Galveston. No longer was it necessary for passengers and cargoes to be transferred at Galveston to the *Yacht* for movement to Indianola and Port Lavaca. Most significantly, both cabin and deck passenger fares were reduced by 20%.[7]

Harris & Morgan also made a revision of freight tariffs, though the new rates were partially unsatisfactory to shippers and receivers alike. There was little complaint about the charge of 80 cents per barrel from New Orleans on such items as flour, coffee, sugar, salt and other measurable goods. The rates for certain other listed articles created a bone of contention with patrons. On boxes of soap, claret, candles, starch, etc., the charge was "3 bitts per box." On that basis, the specially named articles greatly over-averaged 80 cents per barrel.

Despite the criticism, shipping and travel on vessels of the United States Mail Steamship Line had obvious advantages. The boats were clean and prompt, almost to the hour. Passengers from Austin, Gonzales, San Antonio, New Braunfels and the other inland towns could arrive at Indianola in the morning and be assured of departure on steamers leaving in the evening. Immigrants from the states east of the Mississippi could arrange their affairs so they would not remain in New Orleans more than a few hours. That regularity was a key to the successful development of the stage lines operating into and out of Indianola on fixed schedules tied in with those of the ships. Safety was another factor in Harris & Morgan's favor. Since the firm had begun operations to Matagorda Bay, no boat or cargo had been lost, a feat that could not be matched by the sailing vessels.

The cargo capacity of the steamers, and that strict adherence to timetables, meant that they soon took over most of the livestock shipments from Indianola. The sailing vessels had done yeoman service in creating a profitable market for Texas coast country range cattle by transporting them on the hoof from the bay to New Orleans. Although cattle represented the bulk of the shipments, other animals were also carried at times. On September 24, 1848, the schooner *Louise Antoinette* had sailed with a cargo of 120 beef cattle, six mules and an unstated number of frightened deer.

In December 1848, James D. Cochran, H. H. Rogers and S. A. White had opened a beef canning plant on the outskirts of Indian Point. It met with only moderate success. The transportation of live cattle on foot remained the preferred method of sending range beef to the distant metropolitan markets. Twenty years would pass before mechanically refrigerated beef began to move out of Indianola.

V.

Morgan Lights the Fuse!

Port Lavaca committed near hara-kiri in 1849 for inexplicable reasons. Few things she could have done would have harmed her more. Nothing she could have done would have given rival Indianola a greater boost. After considerable wrangling, authorities at Lavaca increased the fees charged shipping firms for the privilege of docking at that port. As Galveston was to learn to her sorrow later, Charles Morgan was a man who could not be pushed around. When Port Lavaca refused to reconsider the cost increase, Morgan washed his hands of that place and designated a landing below Indianola (old Indian Point) as the terminus for the Harris & Morgan line in Matagorda Bay.[1]

Too late did Port Lavacans realize the folly of their action. Despite aggressive efforts to surmount the staggering blow of the loss of Morgan Line traffic, from 1849 on Port Lavaca was destined to play second fiddle to Indianola until the latter was shattered by the hurricanes of 1875 and 1886, and then abandoned. However, the death of Indianola meant little to Port Lavaca in a commercial sense. So widespread and devastating were the effects on Matagorda Bay of the two hurricanes that the entire region sank into a paralyzed economic state, from which it did not begin to emerge for more than half a century.

The place chosen by Charles Morgan was where Powder Horn Bayou connects Powder Horn Lake, or Bay as some refer to it, with

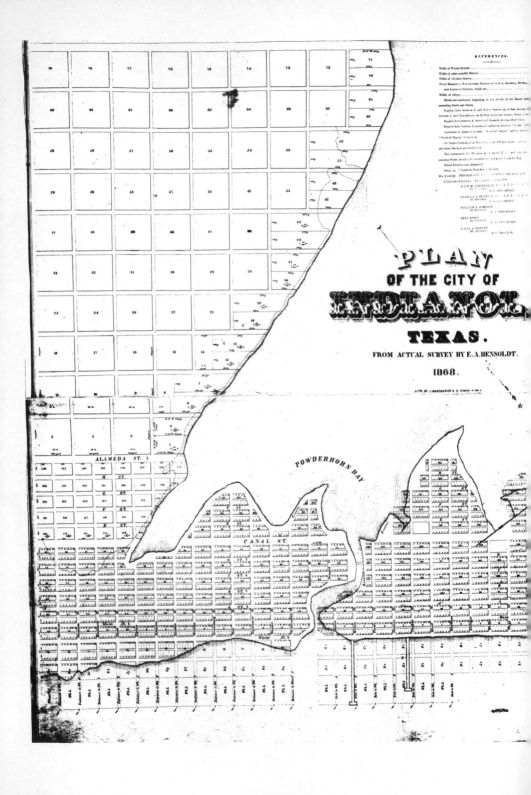

PLAN
OF THE CITY OF
INDIANOLA
TEXAS.
FROM ACTUAL SURVEY BY E. A. HENSOLDT.
1868.

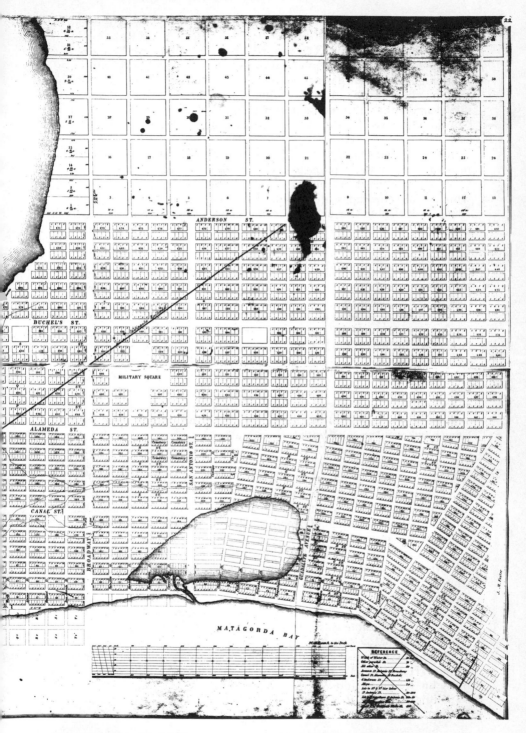

Map of the City of Indianola, as resurveyed by E. A. Hensoldt in 1868. (*Lithograph by J. Manouvrier, New Orleans. Courtesy University of Texas at Austin Library, Barker Texas History Center.*)

Matagorda Bay. Three miles below old Indian Point, it was there that Johann Schwartz had built his residence in 1845. Port Lavaca had not caught Morgan napping. The shrewd Connecticut Yankee had already taken steps to have the western shore of the bay examined with care, soundings made and charts prepared. When Port Lavaca acted, he knew exactly where he would go. His chosen new terminus offered water of sufficient depth to accommodate any ship that would be able to enter the bay through Pass Cavallo, which lay only about 15 miles to the southeast.[2]

The business community of Indianola was delighted with Morgan's move and began to lay plans to take full advantage of the new situation. One step was the development of an addition to the established town which would encompass the Powder Horn area. Included in the addition was part of the old German immigrant camp site, Karlshafen, stretched along the bay front below the point. The dynamic John Henry Brown was a prime mover in the expansion. It was not surprising that the project became known as "Brown's Addition to Indianola." He was joined in the development by Samuel Addison White, Wm. M. Cook and Baldridge, Sparks & Co. as proprietors. W. C. A. Thielepape was employed to survey the property and lay out streets and blocks.[3]

It was envisioned that the Main Street of Indianola would continue down the beach and be designated by the same name in the addition. However, instead of using Second, Third and Fourth Streets, those paralleling the bay there would be called A, B, C and on up to S, as they progressed inland from the shore. The waterfront street of the addition was given the appropriate name of "Water." There were to be five grand avenues in the grid of streets, each of these being 150 feet in width. Water Street was laid out 80 feet wide. Other streets were 70 and 80 feet. Each block was surveyed with a 20-foot alley.

Included in the plan were a cemetery of four blocks area, a church, a school and a market square, plus four public squares, one of which was named "Austin." A military square of five blocks arranged in the form of a Greek cross, and a courthouse square completed the list of property dedicated to public purposes.[4] There was dire portent for Lavaca in the fact that both Indianola and Brown's Addition to Indianola had set aside space for a county courthouse.

As was true of other Texas communities that came into being following the establishment of the Republic and annexation to the United States, the pervading sense of patriotism was evidenced in the naming of streets. The first street west from Powder Horn Bayou was Bowie, and then there were Milam, Travis, Fannin and Crockett. Others were Lamar, Houston, Rusk, Alamo, Goliad and San Jacinto.[5] There was Hays, in honor of Texas Ranger Captain John Coffee "Jack" Hays. Walker and Gillespie were tributes to Hays's associates in the persons of Samuel Hamilton Walker and Richard Addison Gillespie. Ward, Burleson, Kaufman and Worth recognized the services rendered to Texas by William Ward, Edward Burleson, David Spangler Kaufman and William Jenkins Worth.

Places and events connected with the recent Mexican War were memorialized in the streets named Palo Alto, Cerro Gordo, Buena Vista, Monterrey, Contreras, Puebla, Orizaba and Chapultepec. Other names with various connotations were Trinidad, Sophora, Brazos, Chocolate, Calliope, Clio, Hermoso, Cherokee, Lipan, Calhoun, Lavaca and Matagorda.

East of Powder Horn Bayou were Opelousas, Navasota, Manahula, Llano, Karnes, Johnston, Juanita, Hidalgo, Grandbury, Frio, Esperanza, Dimmit (sic), Carancahua, Benevides and Anaqua.

The grand avenues were Broadway, San Antonio, Guadalupe, Canal and Alameda. Carried through to its ultimate limits in 1868, the plan of the City of Indianola, as Brown's Addition later came to be known, covered 834 building blocks, 64 wharf lots and, on the outskirts, 142 farm lots, most of which were ten acres in size. As the plan was expanded to the west, two more grand avenues, Buchel and Anderson, were added.[6] When lithographer J. Manouvrier of New Orleans prepared a map of Indianola according to a re-survey by E. A. Hensoldt in 1868, errors were made in the spelling of names of some streets. Calliope was shown as Calliopa, and one "r" was dropped from Monterrey. Most embarrassing was that Crockett was minus a "t," an oversight by Manouvrier that caused an outcry from Davy Crockett *apasionados*.

For the time being, in the early 1850s, old Indian Point was recognized as Indianola and Brown's Addition was generally referred to as Powder Horn. After the passage of a few years and the growth of the Powder Horn portion of the community, the former Indian Point would come to be known as "Old Town" and the Powder Horn area would be Indianola proper. By some they would be called "Upper" and "Lower" Indianola. That gradual transition occurred during the decade before the war.

The United States Army's early selection of Indianola as a depot for the Quartermaster and Subsistence Departments, through which supplies would be brought in for the military outposts on the frontier, gave impetus to the development of the port. The steamer *Fashion* had been placed in regular service for the government to bring in horses, mules, wagons and teamsters. These, and other supplies from various Gulf and Atlantic ports, were landed at what was known as the "Government Wharf" at the Point. It had a length of 250 feet, reaching to six and a half feet of water. On the wharf there was laid a narrow gauge railroad which extended to the warehouses on shore. The small flat-cars were pulled by teams of docile mules. Depot facilities were on lots leased by the government. Supplies were stored in five buildings. There were also a blacksmith shop and a stable with 2,240 square feet for stalls, tack and feed.[7]

The census of 1850 disclosed that Mrs. Eberly had become the principal property holder in the town of Indianola, her assets being valued at $50,000. Although there were several hotels with dining rooms, Mrs. Eberly's principal competitor was the Alhambra. Its bar and oyster saloon attracted a large segment of the traveling public. Mrs.

Eberly catered to families, her rooms being in constant demand. The Alhambra was operated by Casimir and Matilda Villeneuve, he a 35-year-old native of France, and she a 22-year-old Kentuckian. At the time, Mrs. Eberly was 46.

Villeneuve was a firm believer in the power of newspaper advertising. His ads were to be found in papers of New Orleans and Texas, as well as in the *State Gazette*. They were enticing to many travelers. His insertion for January 1850, in the *Texian Advocate* said, "This establishment has been fitted up in the best manner for the accommodation of visitors and the traveling community. The Bar is always furnished with genuine wines, ale, Porter, cider, brandies and other liquors, imported expressly for this establishment . . . and the Oyster Saloon is constantly supplied with the largest kinds of Peninsular Oysters served up with every variety of style. The Billiard Room . . . is retired and exceedingly comfortable, and the tables, maces, cues &c are new and of the latest and most approved workmanship. In fact, the proprietor invites all who are fond of good eating and drinking to give him a call and judge for themselves."

Calhoun County records contain an 1850 inventory of the personal property of Matilda Villeneuve. It indicates that her money was underwriting the business. She made a good investment, as it prospered throughout its existence.

The *Texian Advocate* of Victoria, which remained the news organ for Indianola until the founding of the first newspaper there in January 1852, was attuned to the interests of the bay. The prosperity of Victoria was directly linked to that of the port. In its issue of February 1, 1850, the *Advocate*, in a spirit of jubilation hailed the reality of trade with the far western country. The likelihood had been recognized in 1848 when there first appeared the possibility of diversion of traffic from the long-used route to Northern Mexico via Santa Fe and Independence.

The *Advocate* editors were justified in their enthusiasm. They set out reasons for it in an editorial which was headed "The Santa Fe, Paso del Norte and Chihuahua Trade." Asserting that Matagorda Bay, rather than Independence, was the natural channel for the movement of that commerce, the paper quoted economic facts of life to back its claims. ". . . Cost of freight to Matagorda Bay from New York is half that from New York to St. Louis . . . The distance from Independence to Santa Fe is 900 miles, and Paso del Norte 1160, and to Chihuahua over 1300 miles. From Matagorda Bay on a direct route to Paso del Norte 750 miles, to Chihuahua 750 miles."

Although it is doubtful that the editors had personally traveled either, they commented that the road from Indianola was the better of the two. "It passes through country [adequately] supplied with wood and water. Most [of the region] is capable of settlement. The road from Independence to Santa Fe passes, for the most part, through a sandy waste, scarcely producing grass for the sustenance of mules or oxen . . . This road can be traveled at all seasons of the year . . . that from Independence at only one period of the year. The road [from Indianola] is not at present greatly infested with Indians, and will soon be completely free from them. The Independence route can never be made safe from their depredations so long as the Indians are permitted to roam over the great western deserts."

The editors concluded by remarking, "Our attention was again directed to the subject of the Santa Fe and Chihuahua trade with the arrival in our town a few days since of Mr. Aubrey with a train of 18 wagons [from Indianola] direct for Santa Fe by way of Paso del Norte . . . This may be regarded as the opening of the Santa Fe and Chihuahua trade . . . As such, we hail it as the most important commercial event which has transpired since our residence in the west."

Aubrey had noted that "Victoria has advantages over any other place on or near the bay as the terminus of the land carriage for this trade," to which the paper added, "That is, provided our river is susceptible of constant and regular navigation." However, transportation on the Guadalupe River from Victoria to the bay left much to be desired. The *Kate Ward* would continue to operate between that town and Indianola and other vessels would come and go on the river scene, but their schedules were slow and, because of shallow draught, cargoes were light.

A series of disasters had plagued shipping in the bay during the winter of 1849-1850. The first concerned the brig *Matagorda*. She had departed New York on December 21. On the night after sailing, she had encountered such bitterly cold weather that most of her crew members received severe frostbite injury. After a passage of 21 days, the *Matagorda* arrived at Indianola, some of her crew in such piteous condition that several had to undergo amputation of frostbitten limbs.[8]

On February 10, the steamer *Telegraph*, first of a new line inaugurating direct service between New Orleans and Matagorda Bay, met with the same fate as the *Yacht*, when her own run to Port Lavaca was begun in January 1848. The *Telegraph* went aground on Gallinipper Bar, where she remained for 24 days. Just after the last of the cargo had been removed from the stranded ship by the *Mary Somers*, a strong norther blew in, lowering the water level in the bar channel and so buffeting the *Mary Somers* that she was forced onto the reef. She was held fast until the turn of the wind and normal tide three days later.[9]

The fine bark *Monterey* [sic] commanded by Captain Mitchell, out of New York bound for Indianola, Lavaca and Matagorda, was cast ashore on Matagorda Island by the same norther that grounded the *Mary Somers*. The beached vessel, with her damaged cargo, was sold on February 18 for the account of the underwriters. The *Monterey* was intended to run as a packet between the bay and New York.[10]

As though the troubles besetting the shipping interests were not enough, much of Western Texas was suffering from an epidemic of cholera, more severe at inland points than on the coast. At Victoria, several newly arrived German immigrants had succumbed, and the town was greatly alarmed. The resident Quartermaster, U. S. Army Major John P. J. O'Brien, died at his residence in Indianola from the disease.

His sudden death occurred while his family members were visiting in New Orleans. They learned of his demise on their arrival at the port following his burial in the Indianola Cemetery with religious ceremonies held by the Rev. John A. Jacobs, pastor of the Indianola Catholic Church.

Major O'Brien had served in the Florida Campaign and so distinguished himself at Buena Vista during the Mexican War that he received the personal approbation of Major General Zachary Taylor in the field. At a public meeting held in the Indianola schoolhouse on March 31, testimonials of respect for Major O'Brien were adopted. A committee was appointed to select and purchase "an appropriate piece of silver to be engraved and presented to the widow and children as a token of the sentiments of the citizens of Indianola."[11] One week after officiating at the funeral of Major O'Brien, 80-year-old Father Jacobs died from cholera.

In a more cheerful vein, the *Texian Advocate* reported that "The 2nd of March, 1850, the anniversary of the independence of Texas, was handsomely celebrated by the citizens of Indianola. All the vessels in the harbour honored the day by unfurling all their banners.

"At nine o'clock, a procession consisting of the Sons of Temperance, ladies, gentlemen and military officers of the city was formed at the Planter's House by Messrs. C. Etter and John F. Segui as marshals, and moved under the martial strains of music to Mrs. Eberly's hotel, where the Rev. Mr. Orr offered a most feeling prayer. The Declaration of Texan Independence, prefaced by appropriate introductory remarks, was read by John Henry Brown, after which an oration was pronounced by Wm. J. Howerton, Esq. The assemblage then separated, the utmost harmony and good feeling having been manifested. In the afternoon, appropriate salutes were fired, and in the evening a pleasant party was entertained at the Planter's House. The whole scene closed beautifully, but old Boreas followed immediately in the shape of a 'ranting, snorting norther.' "[12]

On April 12, the steamer *Envoy* was brought to Indianola by her owner and captain (Moore). His plan was to move on to the Guadalupe, steam upriver to Victoria and there offer his vessel for sale. Of the ship, the *Advocate* said, "The *Envoy* is a sternwheel boat of 113 tons burthen, 122 feet long, 15 feet beam and 5½ feet hold. She draws 2 feet of water light and will carry 600 bales of cotton on 3 feet water. She is a strong boat and well adapted to carry both freight and passengers.

"Capt. Moore brought the *Envoy* into our river for the purpose of selling her. Whether he will succeed in so doing, we are unable at present to say . . . Within the next 12 months, a great increase in trade and travel of Western Texas will certainly take place. The Santa Fe trade has already commenced, and ultimately nearly all that vast and important trade will pass through Pass Cavallo. What portion of it will stop at Victoria will depend very much upon the action of our people . . . "

At the end of March, a new and more direct road had been opened from Victoria, through Yorktown, to San Antonio. Troops from the Eighth Infantry had been actively employed under the direction of

Lieutenant LeRoy in making the survey, opening and finishing the route. A government-sponsored project, its primary purpose was for the movement of military traffic from Indianola to San Antonio. The distance from Victoria to San Antonio had been measured at exactly 95 miles.

The road had scarcely been opened when Messrs. Lewis and Groesbeck of San Antonio began the hauling of government freight being unloaded from six schooners at Indianola. Some of the military goods were destined for San Antonio, but the bulk would be hauled direct to El Paso. In March, the *Palmetto* had arrived at Port Lavaca with a cargo consigned to a Mr. Wiggins for the Chihuahua trade. George Wentworth, one of the leading Chihuahua traders, had made arrangements with Brown and Cochran at Indianola to act as his consignees for merchandise arriving on the *Ben Milam.* Both Wiggins and Wentworth had previously been Missouri traders, moving goods through Independence. In the fall of 1849, they made a trial run from Matagorda Bay to Chihuahua via Victoria, San Antonio and Fredericksburg. The partnership of Coons and Aubrey was increasingly turning a large volume of Chihuahua trade from Independence to the bay.[13] It was this lucrative traffic that Logan and Sterne, *Advocate* editors, hoped would begin at Victoria instead of Matagorda Bay. In their efforts, they were joined by Captain Jesse O. Wheeler who, at the moment, was seeking 140 yoke of oxen for use on what came to be known as "The Chihuahua Trail."

The emphasis on commerce did not cause neglect of spiritual matters. George W. Freeman, Provisional Bishop, Protestant Episcopal Church in the Diocese of Texas, arrived at Indianola on a missionary journey in April 1850. In his report, the bishop said, "I reached Indianola the same day at evening. The next day, I baptized Robert William, the infant son of James H. Hughes, Esq. and Julia Cornelia, his wife; the parents and the grandfather, Robert Hughes, Esq. of Galveston, being sponsors. After dinner, started in the sail boat of Captain Brower for Port Lavaca where, although the wind was blowing a gale from the north, I arrived in safety in little more than an hour."

Bishop Freeman spent the fifth Sunday in Lent at Lavaca, held service and preached twice. There he found "quite a number of church families . . . who would much rejoice to be favored with the stated ministrations of a Clergyman of the Church." The following day, he proceeded to Victoria, where he remained until the next Wednesday. On Tuesday night, " . . . due notice having been given," he wrote, "I preached in the Court House. The congregation was quite large and attentive, and the responses were audibly made. On this occasion, I baptized Martha Edwards and John Samuel, children of Dr. John Ragland and Rachel, his wife; the mother and Mrs. Margaret E. Harrison being sponsors. There were several families of Church people, including 2 communicants, at that place. A minister should officiate at Victoria, Port Lavaca and Indianola in rotation [and] would accomplish much good by furnishing spiritual nourishment to many members of the fold of Christ who are now as sheep without a shepherd. In a few years [he would] build up a church in a region which is obviously destined at no distant day to sustain a large population."[14]

In April of 1850, Indianola was a veritable beehive of activity. All of the wharves were at capacity, with sailing vessels and steamers tied up bow to stern, while others rode at anchor in the bay waiting their turn to come in. The streets were crowded with wagons and Mexican *carretas.* Others, unable to approach the warehouses and wharves, remained in camps nearby.

The vehicular traffic was a bonanza for dealers in hay and feed, for blacksmiths and public sellers of precious water. The merchandise movement was compared to an outpouring of the Horn of Plenty to commission and forwarding agents. Hotels, restaurants and stage lines were overwhelmed by the heavy passenger traffic. Stage operators strove to acquire more coaches to satisfy demand. Whereas one loaded stagecoach had been arriving in Victoria in the evening, now three or more came rattling into town, often having left at Indianola passengers who could not be elbowed into the seats.

Taking notice of the bustle, John Henry Brown, in a letter written at Indianola on April 15, 1850, said, in part, "The schooner *P. B. Savery* arrived at our wharves two or three days since loaded entirely with wagons for the great trade of Lewis, Groesbeck and Coons. The schooner *Native* . . . is also discharging a full cargo [of] 1,154 packages consigned to one of our houses for the same gentlemen. [A] schooner arrived this morning with a full cargo for the government. Several other vessels have been in for the government during the last two weeks. Now numerous arrivals, together with the busy preparations for the great El Paso train, create much stir here. Only think of some 550 to 600 wagons fitting out at a single town at one time! You may well imagine our streets are crowded continually. Everybody is employed, and everything wears a most cheering aspect . . . ."

Government facilities at Indianola were frequently swamped by the expanding movement of freight into the warehouses and, as quickly as transportation could be secured, on out to the frontier. The ingenuity of the Commissary Department's Captain J. L. Calvin was taxed to arrange with teamsters the handling of government stores to the far distant forts that had been established for protection against marauding Indians.[15]

A procession of the wagon trains of Lewis, Groesbeck, Coons and Aubrey got under way the last week of April. It consisted of approximately 400 vehicles, of which almost half were heavy wagons, each drawn by six mules or six to eight oxen. The balance of the units in the El Paso train were the picturesque two-wheel Mexican carts, which were pulled by at least four oxen.[16] It was a colorful sight, and still a source of excitement along the route, although long wagon trains moving between Indianola and Western Texas, Northern Mexico and the New Mexico Territory were becoming commonplace.

The massive flow of goods through Matagorda Bay was noted by the merchants of the upper Colorado River Valley. The distance from Austin to Houston was about the same as that to Indianola. Soil conditions on the road to the Bayou City were such that, below Columbus, wagons would encounter paralyzing mud and flooding streams after the frequent heavy rains that were characteristic of that section of the state. From Austin to Indianola and Lavaca, road conditions were better. The primary advantage to merchants of the route to Matagorda Bay from Austin and other towns of the upper Colorado was that, because the average transit time of wagons was less than on the road to Houston, that speed of movement lowered the unit cost of transportation. The lowered unit cost increased the financial return of the merchant fraternity.[17]

Dr. Levi Jones began active promotion of his projected port. As agent for the LaSalle City Company, he placed advertisements in the newspapers of Texas, New Orleans and New York acclaiming the advantages and prospects of the planned town. In them, he announced a sale of lots on Friday, May 31, 1850. Samuel Addison White's success in public sale of lots at Indian Point two years earlier encouraged Jones.

He certainly counted on the bulk of the trade with Chihuahua and the American Southwest moving through Matagorda Bay and wanted a piece of the action for LaSalle. Due to his lobbying efforts, a railroad charter had been granted by the Third Legislature on February 11, 1850, for a rail line to extend from LaSalle to El Paso. It was expected that the great flow of trade and travel to California would soon follow the new route directly down the right bank of the Gila River. Jones planned that the completed railroad would funnel the movement through the port of LaSalle.

Results of the public sale of lots were disappointing but the company continued to hammer away at promotion of the town. By July, construction had begun on the long wharf. It was being built by William Hawley of Galveston, one of the leading wharf contractors on the Texas coast. An aspect favorable to the town was announcement by the LaSalle City Company of settlement of the disputes relative to land title there. The compromise resulted in Dr. Jones being named agent for Albert T. Burnley, et al.[18] That title problem also involved the land at Powder Horn and Indianola, but the compromise did not clarify the matter at those sites. Dr. Jones tried to use that for the benefit of LaSalle later on. The ensuing legal battles were carried to the Supreme Court of the United States.

As befitted a man of Dr. Jones's experience and background, the most brilliant social affair thus far held on the bay was hosted by him at Casimir and Matilda Villeneuve's Alhambra House in Indianola on July 12. The event was, ostensibly, to celebrate the launching of LaSalle. The guest list was carefully drawn. In addition to those Indianolans who were invited, other distinguished individuals came from Austin, San Antonio, New Orleans, Lavaca, Victoria, Saluria, Matagorda and Galveston, "to partake of a collation and other enjoyments and entertainments at the hospitable hands [of Dr. Jones] . . . At 3 o'clock p.m., the gentlemen assembled in the saloon of the Alhambra House, where the festive board was laden with the choicest viands of the land. Turtle soup was served up brown. Gen. Joseph Bates of Galveston presided during the opening services but, with a few friends, was compelled to leave early in the 'action' in consequence of the steamer's departure." After toasts, the party adjourned for the purpose of allowing time for preparation for a "ball after tea." That evening, the elegantly attired ladies and gentlemen turned out in force for the grand ball which "went off in fine style and much to the delight of all."[19]

Dr. Jones was a clever salesman, so much so that he was successsful in persuading several Indianolans to transfer their business houses to LaSalle. One was Charles Mason, whose thriving forwarding and commission firm was one of the largest in the port. Mason, then 38, a native of Augusta, Georgia, was followed by James D. Cochran, whose partnership with John Henry Brown was dissolved so he could take his assets to LaSalle.

Indianola merchant Chambers Etter, who had succeeded Brown as local agent for the *Texian Advocate*, solicited advertising for that newspaper. One of his regular patrons was Charles Mason. Etter, being aware that LaSalle was virtually unknown, always put an Indianola dateline under Mason's ads for his LaSalle business. Etter did the same for Mrs. Eberly when she finally succumbed to Jones's wiles and, late in the year, began the operation of a hotel at LaSalle on a lease basis. She did not remain at LaSalle long, but made her final move to the Powder Horn area in Brown's Addition, where she remained in business until her death from heart failure.

Mrs. Eberly, Mason, Cochran and others were intrigued by Dr. Jones's promotion of the LaSalle and El Paso Railway Company. He was able to convince numerous people that he would succeed in financing the road. Approval was given for the LS&EP to begin at LaSalle, "or any other point on Matagorda Bay to any point near El Paso," with a view of being continued to the Pacific Coast. The charter required that construction begin within three years from June 1, 1850, and that 200 miles be completed within five years thereafter. The Fourth Legislature, in extra session, revised the charter to authorize a period of five years from February 5, 1853, for construction to commence, and six years for the building of 200 miles. Eight sections of land to the mile were granted, if work on the road were started prior to February 5, 1855, and ten miles completed by February 5, 1857.[20]

As was true of so many other visionary Texas railroad projects that lacked adequate backing, Jones was unable to start the line, and the charter was finally forfeited. Had Charles Morgan not transferred his terminus from Port Lavaca to the Powder Horn area just three miles above LaSalle, the latter might have prospered because it offered deeper water than did Old Indian Point. It did not have that advantage over Powder Horn. Whether Jones tried to influence Charles Morgan to bring his ships to LaSalle is not of record. As it was, LaSalle remained largely a "paper town" and, when the Federal forces came into Matagorda Bay during the War Between the States, the inhabitants there fled the scene and took up residence in Indianola. LaSalle was never reoccupied!

VI.

The Boundary Commission Arrives

The constantly crowded condition of the wharves at Indianola resulted in the *Kate Ward* changing her bay terminus from that port to Saluria on Matagorda Island. The delays encountered while waiting to dock had proved too costly for the practice to continue. After additional wharf facilities were constructed near Powder Horn Bayou in Brown's Addition, the *Kate Ward* again changed her bay destination, that time from Saluria to the Powder Horn long wharf.

The Houston *Telegraph* took note of the movement of upper Colorado River valley traffic to and from Matagorda Bay. The *Telegraph* observed that the editor of the *Advocate* had been boasting, "and with very good reason," that a steadily increasing amount of that trade was moving through the bay. The *Telegraph* urged citizens of Houston to take steps that would make it advantageous to the Colorado River planters and merchants to procure their supplies at Houston "instead of the new towns at the West. We admire the noble spirit of enterprise that has been displayed by our Western friends during the last 3 or 4 years," said that paper.

Speaking in a frank manner, the *Texian Advocate* retorted, "We venture the assertion that the day has passed by when the merchants of Houston can make such improvements that it will be for the interest of the Colorado River planters and merchants to procure their supplies at

Houston instead of the 'new towns at the West.' " The *Advocate* pointed to the difference in freight rates. "They find that, instead of paying $2.25 per 100 lbs. of freight from Houston to Austin, they can get it from Lavaca or Indianola at $1.50, and sometimes at a less price, and from Victoria at $1.25 per 100 lbs. . . . Pass Cavallo is the natural outlet for the trade of the Colorado Valley above Columbus, whether the Colorado River is navigable or not. Until the navigation of that noble stream is completed, the towns of Victoria, Lavaca, Indianola or Texana afford much greater facilities, all things considered . . . "[1]

It was precisely because of the recognized threat posed by Matagorda Bay ports that business men of Houston and Harrisburg had already moved to attempt to secure control over the routing of the enlarging trade of Central Texas. For that purpose, they obtained a state charter on February 10, 1850, for the Buffalo Bayou, Brazos and Colorado Railway Company, one day prior to the granting of the charter for the LaSalle and El Paso Railway Company. The chartering of the BBB&C, which was to begin at Harrisburg and whose avowed terminus was Austin, made clear to Indianola leaders the reason for John Grant Tod's visits to their port and to Victoria. One of the incorporators of the BBB&C, Tod had made a covert study of the possible extent of traffic diversion that Indianola posed for Houston and Harrisburg. However, construction on the BBB&C did not begin until 1852, and in the meantime Central Texas freight moved in great volume through Matagorda Bay.

The bay's advantages were again highlighted on June 28 when Captain Parker H. French passed through Victoria with a wagon train of 200 emigrants bound from New York to San Francisco. From that city, they were headed for the gold country of Northern California. French's fee for transporting the emigrants to the Golden Gate was $250 each.[2] He was the harbinger of a new California movement of people who wished to avoid the long, hazardous voyage around Cape Horn, or that across the disease-infested jungles of Central America.

A few days after French's passage, sailing and steamships were buffeted when a severe squall came across the bay at Indianola and caused damage there. The lighter *Jerry Smith* and the Guadalupe River steamer *Envoy* were lashed to the *Palmetto* which was, at the time, moored near the wharves. The force of the gale tore the *Palmetto* from her anchored position and drove her aground near the beach. The *Jerry Smith* suffered extensive damage to her upper works, whereas the *Envoy*, being on the leeward side of the *Palmetto*, came through the blow virtually unscathed. The schooner *Ann*, which was lying at LaSalle where she had just discharged a cargo of 78,000 feet of lumber, was uninjured. The *Ann* was the first vessel to dock at the new LaSalle wharf, which was nearing completion. When the final nail was driven on August 1, that pier extended into ten feet of water. The second ship to use the LaSalle wharf was the schooner *Aurora Borealis* (Captain Hudson) which arrived from Mobile on July 17, with 76,000 feet of lumber consigned to D. H. McDonald. Drawing nine feet, three inches, the *Aurora Borealis* was able to tie up and unload at the wharf instead of having to use a lighter, a fact that was duly noted by the merchants of Indianola.[3]

During the last week of July 1850, the schooner *Ann Elizabeth* from Baltimore, and the steamer *Fashion* from Tampa Bay arrived at the government wharf at Indianola with cargoes consigned to the Quartermaster of the United States Boundary Commission. In consequence of the 1848 Treaty of Guadalupe Hidalgo, both Mexico and the United States had set up commissions charged with the joint responsibility of surveying and marking the boundary between the two nations. During succeeding weeks, other vessels carrying equipment for the Commission reached Indianola. Some material remained at the port, the balance being moved on to Victoria. Commission Quartermaster James Myer had established his office at Victoria and immediately advertised for "100 good, serviceable mules to work in harness and 40 gentle saddle horses, for which a liberal price in cash will be paid." He also advertised for "a few good teamsters . . . who can come well recommended . . . "[4]

Dr. Levi Jones had sailed from Indianola on July 20 aboard the steamer *Portland*. He was headed for New York, his intention being to secure eastern capital for his town of LaSalle, and for the LaSalle and El Paso Railway Company. Before his return to Texas, he was to visit Washington. Among his fellow passengers on the *Portland* were Judge John H. Rollins, one of the United States Indian Agents in Texas, who was on his way to Mississippi, and Colonel George T. Howard. Upon the latter's arrival in Texas in 1836, he had joined the Army of the Republic. Acquiring fame for his activities designed to control Indian depredations, Howard also participated in the Santa Fe Expedition, joined Alexander Somervell's Expedition, had served Bexar County as sheriff, assisted Henri Castro in his colonization work, and was in the Texas Volunteer Cavalry in the Mexican War. In 1848, Howard gave financial assistance to and was a part of the Chihuahua–El Paso Pioneer Expedition, which had been aimed at exploring the feasibility of trade and the laying out of a road from San Antonio through the little known and largely unmapped portion of Western Texas. His experience and ability were recognized by the United States government in his appointment in 1850 as an Indian Agent in Texas. Two months later, he was named superintendent of the Agents in the state.[5]

By August, vessels bound to and from Indianola and Lavaca began making LaSalle a regular port of call. On the 20th, the steamship *Galveston*, drawing 9½ feet water, arrived from New York to tie up at LaSalle. She had aboard Lieutenant Colonel John McClellan and 105 members of the Boundary Commission force. A few civilians disembarked at LaSalle, but the Commission members, together with their baggage, provisions and wagons, remained aboard to go on to Indianola, where they were lightered to the Government wharf. Also at the LaSalle wharf was the schooner *Jane Elizabeth* from Baltimore discharging 1,000 barrels of stone coal, as well at the steamer *Envoy* from Victoria, the *Mary Somers*, the schooners *Ward*, *Dayton* and *Tom Paine* from Matagorda, and the *Colonel Brown* from Texana.[6] It was obvious to

Indianolans that the deep water wharf at LaSalle posed a threat and a challenge that had to be met, and quickly!

Arriving aboard the steamer *Portland* on August 29 was Commissioner John Russell Bartlett of Rhode Island, and the balance of the men assigned to his command. Bartlett had been appointed by President Zachary Taylor as the United States Commissioner charged with the responsibility of surveying and marking the boundary between this nation and Mexico. He was to meet his Mexican counterpart, General Pedro Garcia Conde, at El Paso del Norte and, in concert with him, run the boundary line from that point to the Pacific Ocean.

The first task of Bartlett and Garcia Conde was to be the reaching of agreement on the exact place on the Rio Grande where the westward survey would begin. The result was the Bartlett-Conde Compromise, which was brought about by an error that was discovered in the Disturnell Map of 1847, which was specified by the two governments as the guide to be used in the survey. Observations there revealed that there was a mistake in the map of about two degrees (over 130 miles) in the location of the Rio Grande. The settlement of El Paso del Norte (present-day Juarez, Chihuahua, Mexico) was shown to be about eight minutes south of the 32nd parallel. Its site was actually 30 minutes south.

In addition to Commissioner Bartlett and Lieutenant Colonel McClellan, who was chief astronomer and head of the Topographical Scientific Corps, there were at Indianola Lieutenant Isaac G. Strain, United States Navy, Lieutenant A. W. Whipple, and about 50 others whose duties were those of staff officers, astronomers, mineralogists, naturalists, artists, surveyors and related assignments. The balance of the 120 man Commission was composed of mechanics and laborers.[7]

Fully aware of the significance of this event in the history of the United States, of Texas and of Indianola, the citizens of the town rose to the occasion by giving a supper in honor of Commission members. In true Texas style, they did not call it a dinner or a banquet. The problem of a hall of sufficient size to accommodate the participants in the affair, seated at table, was solved by selecting the large warehouse of John Henry Brown, which was emptied of its merchandise contents for the occasion. Mrs. Eberly was in charge of the committee of ladies responsible for food arrangements. A press report carried in the *Texian Advocate* of September 6, 1850, gave some details of the event.

"Mr. Charles Mason presided," said the *Advocate*, "assisted by Capt. Julius A. Pratt as vice president. Among the invited guests, not attached to the Commission, were Lieut. Lear, U. S. Army, and Judge Rollins, Indian Agent. We pass over the ceremonies and briefly give the toasts and leading features of the entertainment.

"Upon a call from the President for an opening sentiment from John Henry Brown, that gentleman gave Hon. John R. Bartlett, his officers and men: 'Our brethren from the north, south, east and west we welcome to the shores of Texas and in the long, arduous and important mission on which they have embarked, we wish them triumphant success and a speedy and safe return to their families and friends.'

"Mr. Bartlett responded and gave a succinct account of the nature and design of the Commission, its preparation for scientific observations, the survey of a railroad route to the Pacific &c, and in conclusion gave: 'Indianola and Matagorda Bay: Their paramount importance are felt and acknowledged as the probable future termination of a great route from the Atlantic to the Pacific.'

"Upon a call, Lieut. Strain, U. S. Navy, gave: 'The Ladies of Indianola. The prosperity of Indianola. Indianola, the beauty of its name is only equalled by its hospitality.' Also toasted were the heroes of San Jacinto.

" 'The Union, the whole union and nothing but the union,' by Capt. Edward Barry of D. C. 'Our worthy hostess, Mrs. Angelina B. Eberly. We revere her as one of the early mothers of Texas, and thank her for her kindness to ourselves while here.' Three cheers.

"Music and songs by Mr. Bull of New York and Robert C. Murphy of Ohio. With great applause.

" 'To the health of the celebrated Texan Ranger Jack Hays, and to the health of Mrs. Hays, considered one of the most estimable ladies in Texas.' Three cheers.

"Toast to our fellow townsman, John Walker, the man of 1812.

"Toasts to the captain of the U. S. steamer *Mary Somers.*

"Another toast to 'The Ladies of Indianola, Angels of Heaven inhabiting Earth.' "

The newspaper account indicates that the number and frequency of toasts increased the enthusiasm of the citizens and guests. There followed a recitation of innumerable toasts, speeches and declarations, far too detailed to list. The report ended, "The affair continued until midnight, the arrival of the Sabbath."

After leaving Indianola, the Boundary Commission encamped on the Coleto Creek northwest of Victoria. There, Quartermaster Myer completed the purchasing of draft animals, both mules and oxen, and saddle horses. The Commission broke camp the last week in September, moving on to San Antonio. Remaining in that town for only a few days, the march was resumed toward the meeting place with Mexican Commissioner Garcia Conde and his company. The caravan arrived at the Post of El Paso on the Texas side of the Rio Grande opposite El Paso del Norte. There Bartlett awaited the arrival of Garcia Conde.[8] As Bartlett had pointed out at the Indianola supper, one of the duties of his mission was to make observations for a contemplated railroad route from the Gulf of Mexico to the Pacific. It was partly due to his report, and to the Bartlett-Conde Compromise, that the United States initiated the move to purchase from Mexico in 1854 for $10,000,000 the 45,535 square mile tract south of the Gila River as a feasible route for a transcontinental rail line.

In September, the postmaster general announced the establishment of new mail routes in Western Texas to supplement those already in operation. Directly affecting Matagorda Bay towns and Victoria were: "From Indianola, via McGrew's to Victoria. From Victoria, via Mission

Valley, King's and Sulphur Springs to San Antonio. From San Antonio, via Eagle Pass and Presidio del Norte, to El Paso and Dona Ana. From Goliad to Cibolo Springs, Bexar County. From Lavaca, Calhoun County, to Texana, Jackson County. From Texana, via Wharton and R. J. Calder's, to Columbia."

Other news from the national capital disclosed that Dr. Levi Jones's pilgrimage to Washington had paid dividends to him. His appointment as collector of customs for the District of Saluria was made public in September.

The large portion of the California movement of travelers and of commercial traffic, newly diverted through Indianola from the Cape Horn and Central America routes, made the admission of that state to the Union on September 9, 1850, of more than passing interest. Although Indianolans had taken an active part in public discussions more than a year before the Compromise of 1850, and had forcefully expressed themselves to the Congress regarding the political time bomb of the Texas claim to the New Mexico territory east of the Rio Grande, passions had subsided. There remained some opposition in Indianola to the proposed land cession, and to the so-called Ten Million Bill, by which the United States was to acquire undisputed title to the land north of the 32nd parallel and west of the 103rd meridian. Under provisions of the bill, Texas was to receive $10,000,000 from the Federal government. However, in the October 28 referendum, the balloting at Indianola was three to one in favor of the measure. In the special election of that date, Clark L. Owen of Jackson County was elected representative over Benjamin J. White, from that same county. Indianolans supported Owen five to one. He had campaigned in favor of, and White against, the cession and payment. Governor Bell affixed his signature to the bill on November 25, 1850, and Texas thus relinquished her claim to that region which extended into present-day Colorado and Wyoming.[9]

Little local concern was expressed over the fact that the Compromise provided for the admission of California as a free state, nor were Indianolans agog over the passage of the Fugitive Slave Bill. Anxiety had become apparent regarding the growing friction that was beginning to suggest national division over slavery. To the people of Indianola, the real question was that of state rights. They believed that slavery was a side issue that could be settled without harm to the national fabric. The locally expressed sentiment was that the Ten Million Bill had "saved the Union." It was wishful thinking that in ten years would be proved wrong.[10]

Although there was talk of secession in the South in 1850, at Indianola the most important matter was that of business profits. Several lines of commercial activity were vital to the prosperity of the port. One of these was the movement of cattle. The largest early shipper of beef cattle on the hoof was Solomon G. Cunningham. In 1850, Cunningham purchased J. M. Foster's livestock holding pens on the bay. Though he was not the first, Foster had begun shipment of live cattle to New Orleans in 1849.

As his business grew, Cunningham was obliged to reach out into Western Texas in the purchase of stock, which was driven to the bay and held there for outbound shipment. His expansion required the construction of additional pens, which he placed on land bought along the bank of Powder Horn Bayou. Because of that acquisition, he became embroiled in the legal snarl concerning clear title to land around Powder Horn Bayou and Lake. Cunningham was one of the defendants in a lawsuit brought by Dr. Levi Jones, *et al*, alleging unlawful occupation of the property.[11]

Another leading source of revenue in Indianola was the lumber trade. In October 1850, there were seven vessels running regularly from Mobile and Pensacola to Indianola solely engaged in the movement of lumber, and still the demand in Western Texas exceeded the supply. Cypress and juniper shingles averaged $4.50 to $5.00 per thousand in Indianola yards. Yellow pine lumber was priced at $20.00 per thousand, a substantial reduction from the going price of $30.00 per thousand in 1846 as the port was beginning to develop. The transportation of lumber from Indianola to the inland towns provided employment for a great number of teamsters, as well as for laborers handling the loading and the unloading at the port and upstate. Anyone who wanted to work could do so.[12] A persistent shortage in the labor force existed until after the outbreak of the War Between the States, and again became a fact of commercial life in Indianola following the conclusion of hostilities.

Also in 1850, mail boats were placed in service on a weekly schedule between Indianola, Saluria, Corpus Christi and Brownsville. Mail to Laredo was delivered by boat to Corpus Christi and then moved overland to destination. Three of Harris & Morgan's United States Mail Line steamers, the *Palmetto* (Captain Jerry Smith), the *Galveston* (Captain J. R. Crane) and the *Portland* (Captain H. E. Boehner) were running regularly with mail between New Orleans and Matagorda Bay. On their way into and out of the bay, the steamers touched at Decrow's Point and Saluria. Though Harris & Morgan, now located at No. 7 Canal Street in New Orleans, boasted about the luxury and superior stateroom accommodations of the vessels, bay opinion of the seaworthiness of the *Portland* differed from that of her owners. On October 2, the *Portland* narrowly escaped being wrecked in a storm off Galveston Bar. The passengers averred that their remaining alive and whole was due more to the "presence of mind and untiring efforts" of the captain than to the safe, sea-going quality of the ship.[13]

Editorial sentiment expressed in the *Texian Advocate* was that, "She is an old and unsafe vessel and Messrs. Harris & Morgan should . . . withdraw her from the trade and fill her place with a good boat. They have already made enough off our people," the paper continued, "and while they enjoy the monopoly they now do, they should at least give us good, safe, seagoing vessels. We pay them enough . . . for the privileges and benefits we receive from their steamers. The *Portland* should have been laid up long ago. She invariably makes long trips and is always behind time," though Harris & Morgan challenged that statement . . .

"We are told that the vessel is much injured and leaking so bad while coming from Galveston to the Pass that although the pumps were kept in active operation all the time, they failed to keep the water out of the hold. We trust this old rotten steamer has now made her last trip to the Bay. Capt. Boehner is worthy to command a good vessel."

Harris & Morgan, faced with the harsh realities of the situation and pressured by strong public opinion, caved in and announced that the arrival of the *Portland* at Indianola on October 20 was to be the last regularly scheduled trip of the venerable boat. On that farewell voyage, Captain Boehner at the helm, she brought in 30 passengers and a full cargo of miscellaneous merchandise, the run from New Orleans having been made in five days. Later, the old ship ended her life on the bottom of Matagorda Bay as a wreck and hazard to navigation a few hundred feet offshore from the foot of Esperanza Street, across Powder Horn Bayou from the main business district of Indianola.

To meet competition from the LaSalle wharf, Captain John A. Rogers purchased the entire interest in a new wharf at Indianola in early October and laid plans to extend it to a water depth of ten feet. It would then be the longest that had been built, to that time, on Matagorda Bay. Rogers' wharf helped turn the tide and hold for Indianola the traffic that was beginning to be diverted to LaSalle where the deep-draught ships could dock and eliminate the costly services of lighters.[14]

A new record was set for speed of transit between New York and Indianola with the arrival of the schooner *Catherine Hall*. She tied up at the wharf on October 19, only 14 days after sailing from New York. The *Emily Weaver* came in from New York at the same time, loaded with troops for the frontier. The comment was made that "our place is crowded with the body of soldiers arrived today from New York and, true to their reputation in general, they are 'considerably in the wind' tonight." The *Nebraska* and *Tallahassee*, both from New York, were docked alongside the *McNeal* from Galveston and the *Alida* from Mobile.[15] Two immigrant ships direct from Germany to Indianola arrived two days later. The *Emily Weaver* brought word that, at the time of her departure from New York, 47 vessels were loading at that port for the passage around Cape Horn to California. The news spurred local interest in taking steps to more actively advertise and promote the movement of that traffic through Matagorda Bay.

In November 1850, the *William Penn* arrived at Indianola on her way to provide additional freight and passenger service on the Guadalupe River between Victoria and the bay. Commanded by her owner, Captain Jesse Obadiah Wheeler of Victoria, the *William Penn* was intended to supplement the *Kate Ward*, which had been purchased by Captain Wheeler after her original use on the Colorado. More than any other person, Captain Wheeler was responsible for the development of water transportation to that town.

Another maritime-connected event, this one a personal triumph for Dr. Levi Jones that followed his visit to Washington in July, came to public attention. News reached the bay that the 31st Congress had provided, in Section 15 of Public Act No. 44, that the United States custom house be removed from Saluria to LaSalle. Dr. Jones, as the recently appointed collector of customs for the Saluria District, took office in LaSalle at the time of the transfer in December.

During November 1850, Messrs. Harris and Morgan of New Orleans spent more than a week in Indianola, interrogating businessmen and studying the shipping facilities of the port. Thomas Decrow had completed a strong and substantial wharf at his place on Decrow's Point at the tip of Matagorda Peninsula. Inasmuch as the H&M steamers touched at the Point and Saluria, both inbound and outbound, Decrow was making a valiant effort to secure a portion of the freight to be trans-shipped. He repaired and enlarged his warehouse at the foot of the wharf. As a lure to shippers and receivers, Decrow made no charge for wharfage in any case for vessels, and none for merchandise unless such items remained on the wharf more than 24 hours. Over 24 hours, the fee was three cents per barrel per day. He also offered storage in his large warehouse at rates competitive with Indianola, Port Lavaca and Saluria.[16] Nevertheless, the venture was not significantly successful. Victoria-bound goods that ships discharged at the Pass were usually left at Hawes's warehouse at Saluria. To reach that place, the river steamers *Kate Ward*, *William Penn* and *Envoy* could remain out of the clutches of the powerful tide surging through Pass Cavallo.

The United States Congress finally approved, in Public Act No. 47, $15,000 for the long-planned lighthouse on Matagorda Island at the pass. Though impatiently awaited, the lighthouse was not soon erected, two years passing before that event. But, lighthouse or not, maritime traffic through Pass Cavallo continued to swell.

As a result of their lengthy stay at Indianola, Messrs. Harris and Morgan announced that two new steamers were to be added to those of the line running between New Orleans and Matagorda Bay. Their action produced exultation in Indianola. The first to go into service was the *Louisiana*, which was followed before the end of December by the *Mexico*. Both were new vessels of 1,200 tons burthen each, incorporating the most modern methods of construction. Luxurious in staterooms and public saloons, the *Louisiana* and *Mexico* joined the *Palmetto* and *Galveston*, enabling the steamship company to operate on a schedule of arrivals and departures every five days out of New Orleans to and from Indianola, via Galveston.[17]

VII.

The First Newspaper

The decade of the 1850s witnessed enlargement of the Indianola trade territory in Western Texas, and far-reaching changes in the town itself. There was the mushrooming growth of Brown's Addition at Powder Horn Bayou, and the simultaneous decline of Indianola proper, former Indian Point. The first newspaper was established, the lighthouse was erected at the pass, legislative authority was secured to incorporate the community, the county seat was moved, the camels landed, and railroad construction was started.

There was no let-up in immigration through Indianola. Articles in newspapers of Western Texas pointed to the influx of settlers, the expressed attitude being pleasure at the fact. Typical of these were three separate comments in the *Texian Advocate*. On January 25, 1850, the *Advocate* had spoken of the "constant stream of emigration [sic] moving along the Valley of the Guadalupe of late . . . coming principally from Germany." The editors observed that "a large proportion of these emigrants are families of wealth and distinction, characterized by refinement and education. We give them a hearty welcome to our fertile plains: and what will be to them a desideratum far outweighing all considerations of affluence and power, we tender them all the privileges and immunities of our free institutions."

Six weeks later, on March 8, the paper said, "We rejoice to see the vast number of emigrants [sic] now flocking into our rich and beautiful country. At no time in the last four years has the increase of our population been so rapid and so valuable as at present. Every steamer is literally crowded with emigrants . . . from the Southern States, nearly all of whom bring with them one to 60 negroes. As the real worth and advantages of Texas become known abroad will this immigration continue to flock to our state. Our country is large, our lands are good and cheap, and our climate delightful. Our soil will produce sugar, cotton, corn, small grain and every description of vegetable. What more can be desired?"

Again, on October 3, the *Advocate* remarked, "We are informed a heavy German emigration is expected at Indianola. Some vessels are . . . direct from Bremen and Antwerp. Capt. Augustus Buchel has been appointed agent of the company at Indianola . . . "

At the beginning of 1851, Harris & Morgan's United States Mail Line of steamships sustained its first loss on the New Orleans to Indianola run. The great danger of Pass Cavallo had always been the incessant shifting of the channels and bars, occasioned by the tremendous flow of water in and out of the bay with each tide. Boat passage had to be undertaken with caution, and at certain times, to take full advantage of the high tides, as well as favorable wind direction. The shipping line had its own pilots stationed at the pass, men qualified to keep abreast of the changing relation of bars and channels, and thus competent to guide the vessels through the deepest water.

At 4:00 p.m. on January 9, 1851, the steamship *Palmetto* fell victim to the treachery of Pass Cavallo. Under the expert handling of her captain, Jeremiah Smith, and one of the several Morgan line pilots, the *Palmetto* had negotiated the pass without incident ever since she was placed in service to the bay. However, on this attempted entrance from the Gulf of Mexico, she ran hard aground on a new and unsuspected bar. Despite the jolt of the grounding, at first no alarm was felt by the passengers or crew. It was believed that it would be possible to work her loose without harm. That circumstance was not to prevail. In the late evening, the wind velocity increased, the sea became very rough and the *Palmetto* was caused to thump violently on the bar, the repeated blows causing the development of a dangerous leak.

Residents of both Saluria and Decrow's Point watched helplessly, and with fascination, as the *Palmetto* struggled to free herself, her great side wheels thrashing the water and the ship shuddering from bow to stern. The roughness of the sea precluded the launching of lifeboats. About 10 o'clock that night, the ship beat off the bar but proved to be so grievously injured that it was necessary to beach her on Matagorda Island immediately to save the now frantic passengers. No lives were lost, all persons escaping through the roaring surf in the darkness and onto the island, with aid from inhabitants on shore.

The mail was saved, but the cargo was a near total loss, as was the baggage belonging to the passengers. Charles Morgan's policy was to carry no insurance on his ships, a fact frequently used in advertising. It was thus employed to point up the safety of the vessels for the individuals using them for personal transportation, as well as for the movement of freight . . . implying that they were so safe that Morgan did not deem it necessary or prudent to pay out large sums for insurance coverage. In this accident, the *Palmetto's* owner, Charles Morgan, acting through his son-in-law I. C. Harris and son Henry Morgan, attached no blame to Captain Smith or Pilot Harrison for the unfortunate occurrence.[1]

Immediately following the loss of the *Palmetto*, Harris & Morgan discontinued the practice of their ships touching at Saluria. Although it was not so stated, it was surmised on the bay that they attributed the grounding of the *Palmetto* to the fact that the vessels, under the old routing, were obliged to leave the main channel in the pass and maneuver their way to both Saluria and Decrow's Point. The management announced that henceforth "passengers for *all* points in Matagorda Bay will be landed at Indianola, as well as freight for Matagorda and Saluria."[2] Though Saluria was eliminated, the ships did not cease calling at Decrow's Point at that time.

In January, a new packet service, the Philadelphia and Indianola Line, was inaugurated between those two cities by Levi Eldridge & Company. The first vessel to leave the Pennsylvania port was the brig *T. W. Smith* loaded with goods provided by the United States government for three Indian agencies in Texas. William A. McAdoo was transferred by the company from Philadelphia to Indianola as the agent for the line in Texas.[3]

As a consequence of the loss of the *Palmetto*, I. C. Harris, accompanied by Captain Jeremiah Smith, departed New Orleans on February 25 for New York for the purpose of contracting for the construction of two new steamships of 1,300 tons burthen each. Harris & Morgan put the *Globe* (Captain Place) in the line to fill the gap resulting from the destruction of the *Palmetto*. The announced schedule provided for departure from New Orleans on the 5th, 10th, 15th, 20th, 25th and 30th. From Indianola, there was a vessel departing the day following. Thus, the matched ships passed one another in the Gulf of Mexico between the Southwest Pass of the Mississippi River and Galveston on each trip. H. E. Boehner, former captain of the retired *Portland*, was appointed agent for Harris & Morgan at Indianola. Another change was the assignment of the *Yacht* to a run from Galveston to Aransas Pass and Brownsville via Indianola every two weeks, carrying mail on a new government contract.[4]

Efforts to improve travel between the bay and Victoria led to the announcement, on February 13, of a "New Road to Indianola." The article stated, "It may be of interest to the public to know that there is a new road opened to Indianola via Green Lake. The great difficulty in reaching Indianola from the interior has been the bad hog wallows at, above and below Chocolate Creek, embracing some 7 or 8 miles.

"Instead of going by Chocolate, the new route continues from McGrew's and White's neighborhood along the ridge to Green Lake, thence directly to Indianola. From Indianola to Green Lake by the road is not over 16 miles, thence to White's 5 miles . . . say 21 miles . . . making a saving in distance of one mile or more. But, the great advantage of the Green Lake road is that there is no bad hog wallow on it. About two-thirds of the distance is that peculiar kind of soil between the real stiff and sandy, a medium with an inclination to hog wallow but not enough to prevent carriages from trotting most of the time. The other one-third is an excellent sandy soil, the best on the coast. Having carefully gone over the route, I think there is a great difference in favor of the Green Lake road. Mr. Carlisle, Mr. Friar and other experienced wagoners so consider it and travel it altogether. From the Lake to White's the road is first rate.

"The only difficulty is that from the water basin near Indianola, there is no permanent fresh water till we reach the Lake, about 14 miles. But, on the other hand, Green Lake is one of the best camping places in the country; the finest water and grass in great abundance, good settlements all around, milk, butter, poultry, eggs, etc. always to be obtained, and these are important items . . . It may also be remarked that the Government trains are running by the Lake."[5]

In February 1851, members of the congregation of the Indianola Presbyterian Church awarded the contract for the erection of the first house of worship in the town. Completion date was targeted for May 1. It was an unusual arrangement. The Presbyterians, being the largest denomination there, had been able to raise a substantial sum of money toward erection of a building, but not enough. So, the Methodists, Catholics, Episcopalians and Lutherans, none of whom had yet built a permanent church edifice, made contributions to the Presbyterian building fund which, in total, made the awarding of the contract possible. It was agreed that, when the time came that each of the other denominations was ready to proceed with the construction of a sanctuary, the Presbyterians would reciprocate by making an equal cash gift to their individual building drives. That was done, in every case, during the next several years.

The Presbyterians made their new church available to other denominational groups for use in worship on schedules that were mutually satisfactory.[6] It was a joint effort that was characteristic of the spirit of cooperation and helpfulness that pervaded Indianola. The arrangement was an improved situation for all, as they had been meeting in various places, such as the schoolhouse, in bay front warehouses, even in residences.

The Saltmarsh Stage Line, which had the contract for transporting United States mail from Indianola via Lavaca, McGrew's, Victoria and Sulphur Springs to San Antonio, increased the number of trips each week, beginning in March 1851. Its contract route out of Indianola via Lavaca precluded use of the improved road by Green Lake. Originally on a fixed semi-weekly schedule, Saltmarsh began running his coaches through, tied in with the arrival and departure of the H&M steamers. The new system was favored by inland towns because there would no longer be delay at Indianola through holding mail and passengers until the next semi-weekly scheduled stage departure from the bay. Hotel operators, saloon keepers and merchants at Indianola did not share that enthusiasm. Under the revised plan of operation, as soon as mail, passengers and baggage came ashore and could be loaded in the stagecoach, it started for San Antonio.

The *Texian Advocate*, on March 20, 1851, spoke with understandable pride of the advancement in means of travel from Indianola to Victoria in recent years. "It looks a little odd to us to see the fine new Troy coaches running through our town. What a contrast! A few years ago we had no stages and people were contented to travel by individual Spanish ponies. These were succeeded by common Jersey wagons, which were looked upon as a great convenience. Now, only think of riding in regular stages, brand new Troy coaches at that! Another improvement will be railroad cars driven by steam, which will nearly annihilate time and space. But, there is no telling what a few more years will bring."

Lieutenant Colonel James D. Graham, chief astronomer and head of the Scientific Corps, succeeding Lieutenant Colonel John McClellan, arrived at Indianola in late April 1851 enroute to the Post of El Paso where he was to assume his duties in the United States Boundary Commission. Colonel Graham had run the boundary between the U. S. and Texas in 1840, between Maine and New Brunswick in 1842-43 and had, in 1850, resurveyed the Mason and Dixon Line. As a youth, he had been a member of Major Stephen H. Long's expedition to the Rocky Mountains in 1819-20.[7]

On his arrival at Indianola, Colonel Graham carried with him a copy of the ratified treaty of Guadalupe Hildalgo for guidance of the Boundary Commission. While in town, Graham made observations at the request of John Henry Brown to determine the latitude of the port. In a letter to Brown, datelined Indianola, April 28, Graham said, " . . . From a hasty reduction of a portion of the observations I made on the night of the 25th instant, it appears that the latitude of this place is 28 degrees, 33 minutes and 19 seconds north. The point of observation was in your garden about 30 feet south of your dwelling house. When all the observations made that night come to be reduced, the mean result may vary a few seconds from the above statement, but the difference will not be appreciable, I think, for ordinary, practical purposes."

At the time Colonel Graham reached Indianola, large lots of supplies for the Boundary Commission were being landed at the government wharf. They were then hauled by wagon train to the Post of El Paso and to stations on the Gila River. Another government shipment arriving consisted of a total of 2,000 horses to be used as mounts for troops on the frontier.

The steamship *Delta* (Captain Gibson) returned to Indianola from Caney in Matagorda County, where she had been operating on Caney Creek for two years. The *Delta* made her first run up the Guadalupe River to Victoria in June. She had on board General Alexander

Somervell and a large party of citizens from Indianola and Saluria. The *Delta* carried a miscellaneous cargo consigned to Victoria merchants. Always ready to sponsor or participate in social events at the drop of a hat, the people of Victoria made quick arrangements for a ball in honor of the visitors, and to suitably celebrate the placement of still another vessel in freight and passenger service from the bay to their town.[8] The absence of the *Envoy* from the river had played a part in the decision of Captain Gibson to try his hand at negotiating the shallow, narrow and tortuous Guadalupe. Off for needed repairs in dry dock in Indianola, the *Envoy* returned before the end of the summer of 1851.

June 25 saw the passage of another short, though severe, storm through Matagorda Bay. Pronounced the most disastrous experienced there to date, the blow caused widespread wind and water damage to buildings at Saluria. Of more serious nature to the people of that Matagorda Island town was that the tides, highest in memory, permitted waves to inject sufficient salt water in the cisterns to render their contents unfit for use. After the storm abated, Salurians were obliged to clean out the cisterns so rain water could again be collected.

Every wharf at Port Lavaca was destroyed. Ross's warehouse was swept away and others on the bayfront sustained damage in varying degrees. The schooner *William and Mary*, which was anchored at the wharf of R. M. Forbes & Co. was cast onto the beach where she remained, high and dry, after the subsiding of the storm tide. Wind damage to buildings in Port Lavaca was widespread.

The main force of the storm struck Indianola at 2:00 p.m., increasing in severity through the night, after which the wind diminished. The *William Penn*, which was secured to White & Co.'s wharf at Old Town, was torn from her mooring, driven toward shore and was sunk in five feet of water. Though upright, her hull was submerged. Later it was proved that she suffered no serious structural damage. The upper works were the most extensively affected. Numerous small boats ended up on the beach where they were knocked to pieces, among them the sloop *Commercial*. The government wharf, White & Co.'s wharf and that of August Fromme were all badly battered by the pounding of the waves. The back portion of several buildings on the water front received damage, including those of C. A. Ogsbury, H. Runge, Jacob Maas and Casimir Villeneuve. The *Mexico* was torn from her anchors and grounded on a bar in the bay. The *Mexico* was to remain so hard aground that, in order to float her, it became necessary to remove her machinery. After refloating, the machinery was reinstalled.

At Powder Horn (Brown's Addition), the vessels anchored in the bayou and lake escaped injury, as they were partially protected by the spit of land between the lake and the bay. The storm tide did not go over it, and that gave a false sense of security insofar as the Powder Horn region was concerned. A portion of the railroad track on the LaSalle wharf was torn loose and dumped into the bay. In the Gulf, the steamship *Maria Birt* was lost, but all on board at the time succeeded in making their escape and reaching land.[9]

Of great annoyance to Victorians was the receipt of news that mail for their town, San Antonio and Western Texas was lost in the bay. It had just arrived at Indianola on the *Mexico*. For some unknown reason, the mail had been transferred to a sloop for movement to Port Lavaca, but the boat capsized and its cargo was strewn in the bay.[10] The *Texian Advocate* fulminated against Indianola Postmaster David Lewis. "Why," the paper asked, "was our mail placed on board the boat to be sent to Lavaca when Saltmarsh's stage was at Indianola ready to start for Victoria?" As a result of subsequent harsh criticism and numerous protests regarding the incident, all mail destined to inland points through Victoria was thenceforth carried from Indianola only by stage, as had been the contract arrangement. None would be sent to Lavaca by boat except that addressed to the town itself, and to Texana and other settlements served by mail route out of Lavaca.

That was not the only "storm" on Matagorda Bay. Dr. Levi Jones created consternation by legal action he took in Federal Court in Galveston. In it, he sought to have Solomon G. Cunningham fined and imprisoned "for building a beef pen, wharf, etc. and shipping beeves from Powder Horn at the lower end of the town of Indianola." The several parcels of land whose title was in dispute had been mainly in the possession of Samuel A. White since 1838, 1839 and 1840 "by virtue of location, cultivation and residence." Dr. Jones, as proprietor for the town of LaSalle, and as agent for others claiming ownership of the land through inheritance or purchase from the original Mexican grantees, sought to enjoin all improvements within several hundred yards of Powder Horn Bayou. Included in his suit as defendants were John Henry Brown, who held under White, C. A. Ogsbury, Charles Mason, John F. Segui, James D. Cochran, Chambers Etter, D. H. McDonald and other holders of real property in Brown's Addition.

On a final hearing at Galveston in June 1851, Federal District Judge J. C. Watrous dismissed the motion against Cunningham and others. As one Indianolan expressed his feelings in the *Advocate* of July 3, "This leaves Powder Horn, one of the best harbors on the Gulf, open to the public to whom it rightfully belongs. It is a noble stream, navigable for 10 or 12 miles, has a depth for some distance of 15 feet and a width at the mouth of 200 to 300 feet, and afterwards becomes a bay of one to two miles in width. The monopoly as private property of such a stream and body of water, including a large harbor of unsurpassed safety, is too absurd to need comment." Nevertheless, the matter did not end with Judge Watrous' dismissal.

Beginning in the summer of 1851, and continuing without break, except for the war years, Indianola was supplied with ice harvested on New England ponds in mid-winter and transported south by refrigerator ships. At Indianola, it was placed in an icehouse whose thick wooden walls were insulated with packed sawdust. At first a thrilling novelty, natural ice became a commonplace item for home use, for hotels, restaurants, bars, drug stores and confectionaries where ice cream and chilled drinks were offered to the trade.

Upon the introduction of New England ice to the Indianola market in 1851, Casimir Villeneuve, inveterate showman that he was, packed a big block of it in sawdust in a heavy wooden crate and sent it by special wagon to the office of the *Texian Advocate* at Victoria. An obvious advertising gesture, Villeneuve received his reward, though his name was misspelled. In the edition of August 7, the editors exclaimed, "Ice. We are indebted to the kindness of friend Cassimer [sic] of the Alhambra House, Indianola, for a large lump of ice. We divided it out equally among our neighbors and the boys, who had a glorification over it. They did not forget to remember the kind and thoughtful donor. We return our thanks for the favor and hope our friend may never lack for customers. Cassimer keeps the best hotel in Western Texas and has his table always loaded with the best the market affords, done up in the best French style!"

Not only was the Matagorda Bay area providing opportunities for substantial financial returns on commercial investments, but it was also being recognized for the pleasures of recreation enjoyed by Western Texans. Rumors were rife in Indianola that plans were in the making for the erection of a large resort hotel in Brown's Addition. Other public houses were being constructed on the bay. One was that of John Huff at Decrow's Point on Matagorda Peninsula overlooking Pass Cavallo. Laying groundwork for patronage in the summer of 1852, Huff began to advertise his new establishment in November 1851. He took "pleasure in informing his friends, the Planters of the country, and the traveling public, that he has opened the above Hotel [Huff's Hotel, Decrow's Point] for their accommodation, and hopes by a close application to business to meet with a liberal share of public patronage. Decrow's Point is the healthiest place on the Bay and an excellent place for fishing and bathing. Persons wishing to spend a few months during the summer season on the coast could not select a better place. The steamships running between New Orleans and Matagorda and Lavaca Bays touch at Decrow's Point."[11]

The sea coast of Texas attracted the "moneyed class" from up-state. Inland residents found the fresh sea breezes to be invigorating, and the boundless variety of seafood was a gourmet's delight. There was crabbing and fishing off the beaches and short piers constructed by hotels for the exclusive use of their patrons. The collection of empty seashells, coral fragments, live conchs, bits of floating pumice, and the investigation of driftwood scoured to off-white by the salt water was a source of joy to children. For the ladies who sat in the shade of the hotel galleries, there were bits of gossip to exchange. The Indianola hotel rumors soon proved to have a foundation of fact with the acknowledgment that Casimir and Matilda Villeneuve were making plans to erect the Casimir House in Brown's Addition. It would accommodate 150 overnight guests.

Indianola's prosperity was not being matched by its would-be competitor, LaSalle, which was beginning to experience difficulties. A change in the structure of the LaSalle City Company left Dr. Jones as president, but resulted in some new faces on the board of directors. Subsequent to the shuffle, it consisted of Fielding Jones, Charles Mason, William P. Ballinger and Henry B. Martin, in addition to Levi Jones. The town they were endeavoring to get on its feet was so overshadowed by nearby Indianola that its ultimate success began to be questioned. Few individuals were willing to invest in LaSalle lots. It remained for the War Between the States to cut its commercial throat and allow it to die.

January 1852 brought the establishment of the Indianola *Bulletin*, a weekly newspaper with John Henry Brown as editor and Robert C. Brady as foreman of the print shop. For almost six years since its formal establishment in 1846, Indian Point-Indianola had looked upon the *Texian Advocate* as its mouthpiece. Now the *Advocate* carried in its January 3, 1852, edition a statement and advertisement headed, "The Indianola Bulletin. The subscriber proposes to commence, in the month of January 1852, the publication of a weekly newpaper in Indianola, Texas bearing the above title. The size of the sheet will be the same as the principal papers of Western Texas. It will be more strictly commercial, agricultural and miscellaneous than political, and on all subjects will be independent.

"We deem it unnecessary to indulge in many promises, or publish a lengthy prospectus, relying upon the tone and character of the paper itself for a liberal support from an intelligent public. Suffice it to say that both of the undersigned have been more or less connected with the press from early life; both are practical printers and shall spare no chance to render the Indianola Bulletin an early and truthful herald of the news of the day and a useful paper to all classes of the community in which we live.

"The Editorial Department will be under the control of John Henry Brown, the Mechanical Department under the control of Robert C. Brady.

"All postmasters in Western Texas, and such friends as this prospectus may be sent to, are respectfully requested to receive and forward subscriptions. They will please send in such names as they may have, to reach here by the 20th January.

"Terms: If paid in advance or within 3 months $3.00
    If not paid in advance but within 6 months $3.50
    If not in 6 but within 12 months $4.00
Indianola, December, 1851.
       BROWN & BRADY"

The Indianola *Bulletin* became a highly respected paper in Western Texas with above average news coverage and editorial content. Its editions were examples of correct composition and clear printing, attesting the skill and high standards of Robert Brady.

Editor Brown was a restless man who possessed a keen, analytical mind. Combined with a flair for writing that gave his work easy readability, his quick perception enabled him to provide his readers with a journal that commanded a large and rapidly growing clientele. By December of its first year, circulation exceeded 700. Brown had been born in Pike County, Missouri, in 1820. He worked on a country newspaper before coming to Texas to live, for a while, with his uncle Major James Kerr, in Jackson County. Employed by the *Texas Sentinel* in Austin in 1840, he became acquainted with Mrs. Eberly. Brown was in Captain Jack Hays's company of Texas Rangers, was wounded in the Battle of Salado on September 18, 1842, and participated in the expedition to Mexico led by General Alexander Somervell later in the year. While in Missouri on a visit, he married Mary Mitchel of Groton, Connecticut, on July 9, 1843.

On returning to Texas with his bride, Brown was employed by Logan and Sterne on the *Texian Advocate*. Moving to Galveston from Indianola in 1854, he bought into the Galveston *Civilian*, and represented that county in the Texas Legislature from 1855 to 1857. Brown and his family moved to Belton in 1858 where he edited the Belton *Democrat*. He represented Bell and Lampasas Counties in the Secession Convention of 1861, and then served in the Confederate Army.

To Mexico in 1864, Brown became commissioner of immigration under Emperor Maximilian. In New Orleans in 1870 and back to Indianola the following year as co-editor of the *Bulletin*, he next moved to Dallas and was elected to represent it in the 13th Legislature. He was the representative of Dallas, Tarrant and Ellis Counties in the Constitutional Convention of 1875. Among the several public offices he held after moving to Dallas was that of mayor of the city from 1885 to 1887. In his later years, John Henry Brown became the author of several notable historical works, his most famous being "History of Texas from 1685 to 1892" and "Indian Wars and Pioneers of Texas."[12]

Under Brown and Brady, the motto of the Indianola *Bulletin* was "Devoted to Commerce, Agriculture and the Dissemination of General Information." When Andrew Marschalk succeeded Brown as editor and publisher, he placed under the masthead, "Independent in Everything, Neutral in Nothing." After W. H. Woodward purchased an interest in the *Bulletin* in 1855 and, with Andrew Marschalk, Jr., operated the newspaper, they displayed the motto, " 'Tis a Base Abandonment of Reason to Resign our Right of Thought."

The *Indianolian*, which began publication in July 1857 as the town's second newspaper, Alfred P. Bennett, editor, proclaimed its mission to be "A Weekly Journal Devoted to News, Politics, Literature, Education and the Interests, General and Local, of the City of Indianola." Then came the third newspaper, the Indianola *Courier*, whose editor was William T. Yancey. Editor Yancey carried under his masthead, "A General News, Business and Family Journal — Independent on All Subjects," but by October of 1859 that was changed to "Pledg'd to no Party's Arbitrary Sway. We Follow Truth Where'er She Leads the Way." The *Courier* merged with the *Bulletin* and, for a while, operated under the name of the Indianola *Courier and Commercial Bulletin*.

During the War Between the States, Indianola papers, like others in the South, were caught in the newsprint shortage. If they published at all, they did so in abbreviated form and at long, irregular intervals. After hostilities ceased and newsprint was again available, S. A. Benton edited and published the Indianola *Times* beginning in 1866, using as his motto, "Courtesy without Servility, Truth without Fear," facing as he did the stern control of military rule in the aftermath of war. The *Bulletin* resumed publication under its original name in 1866 with C. A. Ogsbury as editor. He continued the paper without interruption until the great hurricane of September 1875 destroyed his plant.

Newspaper advertising was relied upon heavily by businessmen of Indianola, and through it they reached far beyond the regional market. They used the papers in New Orleans, Galveston, Victoria, San Antonio and Austin to spread their message before regular and prospective patrons. A consistent distant medium was the *Texas State Gazette*, because of its wide circulation. Published in Austin, the *Gazette* was a powerful voice in Texas affairs throughout the years up to the war. It finally ceased operation and died about the time that Indianola met her end.

Casimir Villeneuve utilized the *State Gazette* to draw patronage to his Alhambra House, and then to the Casimir House in Indianola. As a commission and forwarding merchant, August Fromme advertised in the *Gazette*, as did Harris & Morgan, proclaiming the safety of their low pressure steamers plying between Indianola and New Orleans. Constantly expanding their service to the bay, H&M advertised in February the addition of the steamship *Meteor* to the run.[13] These and other Matagorda Bay businessmen successfully turned toward the port much of the commerce of Central Texas.

Also in February 1852, the "San Antonio, Seguin, Gonzales, Victoria and Indianola Semi-Weekly Stage Line" began operation, its lengthy name clearly defining to the traveling public its route. The owner was J. L. Allen of Indianola. Advertising "superior coaches, fine horses, polite and skillful drivers," the line ran in connection with the boats to and from New Orleans, as might be expected. Allen's headquarters were at Indianola. His stage line agents at Victoria and San Antonio were, respectively, J. L. Nickelson and C. R. Jamison.

Fares were:

From Indianola to	Victoria	$4.00
. . . .	Gonzales	8.00
. . . .	Seguin	10.50
. . . .	San Antonio	12.50
From San Antonio to	Seguin	$3.50
. . . .	Gonzales	6.50
. . . .	Victoria	10.00
. . . .	Indianola	12.50

The several stage lines running to the bay would hold sway for a few more years. When the efforts toward construction of a railroad finally succeeded, the improved mode of travel so severely cut into their revenues that all but one ceased service.

VIII.

A Heartrending Calamity

The Indianola *Bulletin*, less than three months old, scooped its contemporaries in the reporting of the wreck of the steamship *Independence* at Pass Cavallo on March 26, 1852. Had the circumstances not been so tragic, the story would have been the beat of which eager reporters dream. The factual report by the *Bulletin* began, "We have to announce the most heartrending and melancholy calamity that has occurred on this coast within our knowledge. The new steamship *Independence*, Capt. Charles Stoddard, on her first trip from New Orleans to this Bay, is a total wreck, the cargo almost entirely lost, and six lives lost."[1]

Typically Texan are the winds of the vernal equinox. In the coastal regions along the Gulf of Mexico, spring winds are erratic, quickly shifting direction in the vicinity of squalls, and changing from a zephyr to a gale in a matter of minutes. Exceeded in ferocity only by the hurricanes associated with the autumnal equinox, the treacherous winds of spring have exacted a heavy toll in human life and wrecked vessels on the Texas coast each year since the beginning of recorded history. In the case of the *Independence*, the trap was set by nature and was sprung by man failure.

The ship had attempted to cross the bar at 10 a.m. on March 26 without a pilot familiar with the pass. There were aboard about 120 passengers, officers and crew, and a large miscellaneous cargo. The *Louisiana*, drawing one foot more than the *Independence*, had come through the pass without incident three hours earlier. The *Independence* was not so fortunate.

Captain Stoddard erroneously endeavored to cross the bar about one mile north of the main channel. In a matter of minutes the *Independence* struck violently on the bar. It was almost instantly apparent that the ship was in a perilous situation. Her engine was crowded in an effort to force her over, but "she worked ahead so little as to cause great alarm and convince those on board that she must become a wreck," said the *Bulletin*. "Messrs. John Ayr and Laughlin M'Kay, part owners, were on board. It is enough for us to say that the attempt to come in without a pilot, to say the least, was censurable, but it is not our wish to harrow the feelings of those already in distress . . . "

The *Independence* had left New Orleans on Saturday, March 20, stopping at Galveston for discharge of passengers and freight. While there, the owners hosted a dinner on board to which leading citizens of Galveston were invited. Mrs. John Henry Brown's mother and sister, and the latter's husband were on the *Independence*. Charles W. Eldridge of Mt. Carmel, Illinois, the brother-in-law, wrote on March 30 from Indianola detailing experiences of those on the ship.

"There was a very heavy swell upon the sea [after departure from Galveston on Thursday morning] causing the ship, lightened as she was, to roll very much. So much as to keep mother close to her berth, as well as myself, most of the time, whilst Hannah was scarcely affected by seasickness at all." Eldridge continued, "Thursday night came on before we could reach the Bay and, as the Pass could not be made in the night, we lay off until the morning of Friday, when I was aroused by Mr. Cochran, Mr. Brown's former partner who was on board, knocking on our stateroom door asking if we did not wish to see the ship go through the pass.

"I threw open my window blind and looked out upon a sea of breakers into which, to my astonishment, we seemed to be directly going. I hastened on my clothes and scarce had time to get outside when we struck. Around us was the sea white with foam, as we were stranded in the midst of fearful breakers. I then learned that we had attempted the crossing without a coast pilot, that the captain had been influenced by one of the part owners, Capt. Ayres [sic] to go in, mistaking the waving of a flag on shore as a signal for the channel . . .

"There was still hope we could get off," said Eldridge. "The power of the engine was exerted to its utmost capacity, but it only served to increase the force of the thumps upon the sand bar. I then witnessed a scene that looked like a last extremity. Orders were given to 'lighten ship,' and goods of all descriptions were, without ceremony, cast into the waters, and they continued casting overboard . . . from between decks until the sea was covered with a floating mass of boxes, barrels, casks, furniture, etc., etc. drifting with the waves and tide as far as the eye could see."

The Indianola *Bulletin* report continued, "Soon after the vessel struck, Capt. Wm. Nichols, one of the pilots, boarded her, and Mr. Morgan attempted to do so but was swamped in the breakers and narrowly escaped with his life. About noon, the ladies declining the hazard of the frail boats alongside, Judge Webb of Austin, Mr. James D. Cochran of Lockhart, and three Germans were brought off.[2] Directly after, one of the vessel's yawls, manned by Mr. Hubble Hovey, the chief mate, and two men took on the young bride of Lt. W. E. Jones, U. S. Rifles, the wife and three children of Mr. Stephen Minot (late of Kingston, Jamaica and moving to Gonzales), and young Mr. Horrell of St. Louis, Mo., nephew to Gen. Somervell, and instantly followed a scene of agony and horror, the recital of which chills the blood.

"The boat filled in leaving the ship and capsized in the furious breakers. The mate, in a noble effort to sustain Mrs. Jones, sank with her to rise no more and, before aid could be had, the greatest consternation and shrieks prevailing on board, Mrs. Minot and three children perished together, the helpless innocents clinging to her to the last. Both husbands were witnesses to the horrid scene. Mr. Horrell was rescued in a lifeless condition, but restored by prompt attention. No further effort was made during that day to carry off the passengers, all the boats being dashed to pieces."

The view from aboard ship was given by Eldridge. "I can scarcely relate to you the succeeding incidents in the relation that they occurred . . . the weather was more threatening, the sea increasing . . . one of our boats was lowered, she immediately filled and swamped, broke her fastenings and was lost . . . another was got down successfully and, astern the wheelhouse by the ship's side, was ready . . .

"We were advised that this boat was now ready. Mother was willing, but I could not persuade Hannah. The sight of the breakers was too terrifying. Mr. Nichols came down the ship's side. I told him they would not go this time. He returned to the deck, the wheel was put in motion and the boat filled with water . . . We were then notified that the second boat had been cleared of water and would try to land some passengers. I again put forth my entreaties for Hannah and Mother to go."

Eldridge continued, "Mrs. Lieut. Jones and Mr. Minot's family had consented to go. I told Lieut. Jones we would go down and see who was to command her, and then decide. We all went down to the second deck and found our first mate, in whom we had the utmost confidence of any in our crew, going with her. They at last concluded to go. I assisted Mrs. Jones on board. Mr. Hovey, the mate, received her and told her he would save her. I also assisted the three beautiful children of Mr. and Mrs. Minot on board. I had urged my dear wife as first on board. She stood on the ship's brink, her foot had its last hold . . . At this moment, there was a revolution of the wheel that covered them all with water, another wave that made into the boat. I said no more.

"A Mr. Horrell of St. Louis took their place and the boat cast loose. I hastened up on deck and, ah, fearful to relate, the boat . . . was swamped and before our eyes, beyond our reach, all were struggling in the water. The young and beautiful bride of Lieut. Jones, the excellent Mrs. Minot and her three most lovely children, Mr. Horrell and crew. And oh, the cries of anguish, the groans, the lamentations, shrieks and prayers of those on board. No tongue can describe them, no imagination can picture the terrible scene. On the bottom and clinging to the capsized boat we could see some. The two little girls were noticed, embraced in each other's arms before they sank forever. Mrs. Jones caught Mr. Hovey around the neck, from which he could not disengage himself. They drowned together. . . . She was seen after he had disappeared, supposedly supported by him . . . They succeeded in picking up the crew, except Mr. Hovey, Mr. Horrell in a drowning state. They were hoisted on board with ropes and, with prompt efforts, Mr. Horrell was restored . . .

"The sadness . . . the awful gloom that this tragedy cast over us all, you may faintly imagine. It made us realize the brink over which we were all hanging and deeply were our sympathies enlisted toward the suffering relics of those departed ones. Mr. Minot . . . had endeared himself to all by his kindliness and urbanity. He was almost distracted. At one fell swoop he had been robbed of all. The calmness of Lieut. Jones was almost fearful."

The steam propeller *J. W. Rabun* (Captain R. Holton Kerr) having been advised of the wreck went down and anchored inside the breakers on Saturday morning, the 27th, about 400 yards in front of the *Independence*. In conjunction with Captains Nichols, Cummings, Decrow, Morgan and others, valiant efforts were made with the *Rabun's* yawls to rescue the passengers. About noon, they were successful in removing Mrs. Lucy Mitchel of Groton, Connecticut, and Mrs. Eldridge (the mother and sister of Mrs. Brown), with four other women and an infant. However, the increased violence of the breakers and the loss of boats forced suspension of the rescue operation.

"In the meantime," said the *Bulletin*, Messrs. Webb and Cochran reached the U. S. Mail steamer *Louisiana*, Capt. James Lawless, at the Indianola anchorage at 3½ p.m. same day with the sad news. She had on a full head of steam in waiting for the New Orleans passengers who were nearby on a sloop, and in 30 minutes they were on board and this noble steamship under heavy press of steam for the wreck. Our senior (Mr. Brown), happening to be at the anchorage and learning that his relatives before named were on the wreck, went down on the *Louisiana* and from that time witnessed all that passed.

"In the stream at Decrow's, Capt. Kerr met us, he being in a yawl, came on board and . . . he, Capt. Lawless and the other gentlemen . . . already named acted in concert. The *Louisiana* came to two miles above the wreck under Pelican Island and manned her two life boats and one of the quarter boats, Capts. Lawless, Kerr and four men in No. 1, Mr. H. Potter Dimond, chief mate, commanding No. 2, and Peter Foster, 2nd mate, the quarter boat. Arriving in front of the wreck about 300 yards distant (now one-half hour to sunset) and the breakers rolling like hills, Mr. Dimond was ordered if possible to reach the vessel, and never did any man make a more noble and daring effort. Whilst in the midst of the breakers, his boat swamped and rolled over and over, the crew clinging to her and by almost superhuman effort got through one-half a mile above the *Independence*. It was now dark and the sea becoming more dangerous, but the dauntless Dimond bailed his boat and made a second attempt to save the lives of others at the hazard of his own, in which his boat again swamped, floated inside the breakers and was again bailed. Yet undaunted, he made a third struggle and for the third time was swamped when, finding his men failing, with a reluctant heart he gave up the effort and floated inside, two of the crew being in almost lifeless condition.

"It was now 10 o'clock," said the *Bulletin*, "the wind rising rapidly and all hope for the night gone. Fires were built on shore, signals set and dispositions made for a daylight effort on the morrow. During the later part of the night, distress guns were fired by the *Independence* which, with the roar of the surf, added to the horrors around.

"At daybreak [Sunday, the 28th] the work was resumed. Additional help came in the persons of Capt. James Duke and others from the Bay, and about 8:00 o'clock the first life boat was taken off and transferred to the *Rabun*. At 3 p.m. all were safely on the same vessel, the last gun was fired and, amid loud huzzas, the distress signal was hauled down and the ill-fated ship, already broken in two, abandoned to the mercy of the sea . . .

"Up to our latest arrival from the Pass, but one of the dead bodies had been reclaimed — the eldest child of Mr. Stephen Minot, a lovely girl of 12 years. This most intelligent and estimable gentleman has been bereft of his entire family and a valuable property by the late calamity."

IX.

The County Seat Is Moved

Indianola was only six years old when the editor of the *Texian Advocate* traveled to Matagorda Bay in May 1852 to visit the town and its rival Port Lavaca. His observations pointed up the spirit of competition that existed between them, but clearly recognized Indianola's ascendancy. Of his trip, he wrote, in part, "We visited these flourishing towns on our Bay last week and were astonished at the growth of the former and its progressive spirit, whilst we noticed that the latter [Lavaca] still enjoys a very heavy forwarding business and an extensive trade with the up-country. Harris & Morgan's line of steamers runs to Indianola, and the *United States*, the *Rabun*, and other transient steamers run up to Lavaca.

"We were pleased to note," said the *Advocate*, "that all evidence of petty bickerings, if that ever existed, had passed away and that harmony prevails between the citizens of the two places, the residents making frequent and cordial visits from one point to the other . . . The 'Lavaca Navigation Company' seem determined in [the] prosecution of their enterprise to deepen the channel up to their wharves . . . so that steamers that come into the Pass may easily reach that place . . . The requisite dredging machinery, we were informed, was about being ordered from Troy, N. Y. , being somewhat similar to that being used by Mr. Bradbury in digging out the Galveston channel . . . ."

The *United States* (Captain Young) had as her agent at Lavaca, T. Jenkins & Co. A regular packet between New Orleans and Lavaca, the *United States'* schedule provided for departure from the wharf at Port Lavaca every two weeks, touching at Indianola and Galveston. Another low pressure steamer, the *James L. Day* (Captain W. H. Talbot) was placed in service between Lavaca and New Orleans on Wednesday, June 16, to operate on a semi-monthly schedule. Being of light draught, the *James L. Day* could dock at the Lavaca wharf, thus avoiding the necessity for lighterage. Of 700 tons burthen, she had an inducement for passengers that the *United States* did not offer. The *Day* did not carry cattle. Travelers who were fastidious booked passage on her instead of the *United States*.[1]

For their new bridge over Chocolate Bayou between Indianola and Lavaca, Ogden and Milby, with permission from the county court, set tolls for crossing, agreeably promising to reduce them when travel increased to the extent that lowered rates would be economically feasible. A fee of 50¢ was charged for wagons pulled by two or more horses, or by two or more yoke of oxen. Pleasure carriages and two-horse buggies paid 30¢. Mexican two-wheel carts paid 25¢ and horsemen were charged 20¢. Pedestrians paid five cents, the same fee that was charged per head for sheep, hogs, horses and cattle.[2]

June 30 saw the organization in Indianola of Western Texas Lodge, Independent Order of Odd Fellows under the administration of Anson Jones, Grand Master in Texas. Elected as officers by the charter members were A. K. Peiser, Noble Grand; H. E. Boehner, Vice Grand; D. S. Woodward, Secretary; F. E. Hughes, Treasurer; George Heald, Warden and J. T. Winnemore, Special Deputy.[3]

During the summer of 1852, a gnawing fear plagued Port Lavacans, and now rumor became fact. A petition, which met all requirements of the law, was presented to the Commissioners Court by Indianolans proposing that the Calhoun County seat of government be moved from Lavaca to their town down the bay, and that an election be called to give the voters an opportunity to express their wishes in the matter. The question was presented to the people of the county and an overwhelming majority gave approval to the transfer.

John Henry Brown, Dr. F. E. Hughes, Chambers Etter, Henry J. Huck, John H. Dale, Henry Beaumont, H. E. Boehner, R. D. Martin, J. M. Camp, Duncan Beaumont, S. M. Peiser, Wm. M. Cook, C. A. Harper, George M. Beecher and Wm. M. Varnell, all of Indianola, gave satisfactory bond to the court to furnish buildings there suitable for county purposes free for six months. S. A. White and Wm. M. Cook presented to the court deeds of donation to the county of the public square embraced in Blocks 35 and 36, as well as all of Block 162 and Farm Lot 7 in Block 226.

The commissioners decreed that all public offices and the archives of the county, which by law were to be kept at the county seat, be removed to Indianola on or before August 21, 1852. The court further ordered that James Ashworth be authorized to accept the buildings offered for county use there. The sum of $25 was set aside to cover the cost of transporting the archives of the district and county clerks from Port Lavaca to Indianola. Wesley Ogden was appointed a committee of one to examine the ground donated for location of the county building, and also to receive plans and estimates for building a courthouse and jail. He was to report to the court in September.[4]

Thus, the "public square" that had been set aside in the plan of Indian Point in 1846 was now recognized for its true purpose, that of accommodating a courthouse. Block 162 was intended to be the site of the county jail and workhouse. The two and three-fourths acre farm lot was turned over to Calhoun County with no strings attached, the deed simply stating that it would be used for such purposes as Chief Justice Jefferson Beaumont and the court might decide.[5]

Early in August, the people of Indianola held a "railroad meeting," with Samuel Addison White as chairman and Duncan Beaumont, secretary. Pointing to the lack of progress on plans for a railroad to be called the San Antonio & Mexican Gulf and their belief that doubt had been cast on the eventual construction of the road out of San Antonio, ten resolutions were offered and adopted. Participants in the meeting stated their understandable conviction that the most suitable route for either a railroad or a plank road from Matagorda Bay would be one beginning at Powder Horn Bayou, running up the beach to Indianola (Old Town), thence to Gonzales via Victoria. Harry Beaumont, C. A. Harper, H. E. Boehner, Jacob Maas, H. J. Huck, W. H. Woodward and Wm. M. Cook were appointed temporary trustees. The consensus was that the trustees should receive subscriptions, collect funds and put under contract the building of such a railroad. It was also agreed that subscriptions previously made to the San Antonio & Mexican Gulf along its proposed route be withdrawn and turned to this new project, all to be done as soon as a charter could be secured from the State. Suggested name for the line was the Indianola and Guadalupe Valley Railroad Company.[6]

The *Texian Advocate* enthusiastically reported the action taken by Indianolans and commented editorially on August 21, "We commend the spirit of our neighboring town and so far as we have heard expression given to public feeling here, we may state that their project meets with hearty favor . . . The trouble lies in getting the charter. If that could be had by early winter, we feel sanguine that enough stock could be secured forthwith to build a railroad from the Bay to this place, with an eye on its extension to Gonzales, Lockhart and Austin."

A "railroad meeting" was called for Victoria, to be held in the courthouse on Saturday, August 28. The advance news story said, " . . . Victoria and Calhoun County, with our towns, can build a road, and it is their aim to do it. We have witnessed with unmingled admiration and interest the action of our fellow citizens of Indianola in reference to their own and the interests of Victoria upon this very question, and we wish by a public demonstration to prove to them how heartily we will cooperate with them in their views. Whilst we would thus aid ourselves, we would show to the San Antonio Company how completely independent we are able to render ourselves with chaffering and juggling, which alone have distinguished their proceedings as regards the people of both Victoria and Calhoun . . . "[7]

Chairman of the Victoria meeting was Sylvester Sutton, with John H. Stewart acting as secretary. Reporting on the August 28 session, the *Advocate* said, "Never did we see a more spirited meeting than we had in this place on Saturday evening, last, the object being to concert some arrangements whereby our efforts might be brought to unite with the movement recently made by the people of Indianola for a Rail Road from Powder Horn to Victoria . . . "

Two firsts at Indianola were noted as August slid into September. One was that the Presbyterians there were hosts for the meeting of the Presbytery of Western Texas in their town. The three-day conference was conducted in the Presbyterian sanctuary which had been completed with the help of other local denominations. The significance of the other happening was to be discovered in the future. At the time no one in the town knew the role that Indianola would play in a most unusual set of experiments, though officials in Washington did in fact map plans that involved Indianola. Newspaper attention was given to the recommendation of Secretary of War Charles M. Conrad that Congress appropriate $20,000 for a test of the practicability of using camels for the transportation of government freight, including ammunition, in Western Texas, through the New Mexico Territory and on to the Pacific Ocean.[8]

Also in September, the Villeneuves purchased from Baldridge, Sparks & Co. and Wm. M. Cook lots in Block 7 of Brown's Addition to Indianola for the purpose of erecting the Casimir House. Seven blocks from Powder Horn Bayou, it would have frontage on Main, Ward and Water Streets. Only one city block would separate it from the entrance to the long wharf where Harris & Morgan's New Orleans steamers arrived and departed.[9] Casimir and Matilda Villeneuve were to make it into one of the most popular hotels in Western Texas, widely known for its luxurious accommodations, elegant bar and completely outfitted game rooms.

Reaching out to garner an ever larger share of the commerce of Western and Central Texas, 13 Indianola business firms devised a plan of offering costly premiums as agricultural awards. In order to participate in the program, the producers would, of course, be obliged to route their goods to and through Indianola. In its issue of October 16, 1852, the *Texas State Gazette* said, "The following 'Circular to the People of Western Texas' has been sent to us by the editors of the Indianola *Bulletin* with a request that we publish it. We do so most cheerfully, as it is a laudable effort not only to advance the interests of Indianola as a commercial town, but it is well calculated to stimulate and encourage the leading pursuit of Texas, that of agriculture. The example is worthy of imitation by all the commercial towns on our coast:

" 'Indianola, Texas, October 1, 1852.

" 'The subscribers, Merchants of Indianola, desirous of encouraging the Traders and Producers of Western Texas in their respective avocations, have determined to offer a set of beautifully wrought *silver premiums* to them, upon the following basis:

" 'To the Country Merchant who brings in the largest number of Bales of Cotton for sale or shipment, a Silver Cup, Pitcher or Goblet, worth Forty Dollars.

" 'To the Planter bringing in the largest number of Bales of Cotton, the produce of his own plantation, (or if the same is shipped through any merchant) a Silver Cup, Pitcher or Goblet worth Forty Dollars.

" 'For the best packed lot of Cotton (if five bales or over), a similar premium of Twenty Dollars.

" 'For the largest amount of Hides and Peltries, a similar premium of Twenty Dollars.

" 'For the largest lot of Pecans shipped or sold by a Country Merchant, a similar premium of Twenty Dollars.

" 'For the largest lot of Pecans shipped or sold by any one Farmer or Planter, a similar premium of Twenty Dollars.

" 'For the largest amount of Pecans shipped or sold by any person, the picking of himself alone, a similar premium of Ten Dollars.

" 'For the best Hogshead of Texas-grown Sugar brought in for sale, a similar Premium of Twenty Dollars.

" 'The period of receipts to extend from the first day of September, 1852, to the 31st day of March, 1853. On the day last named, a Committee of Awards, consisting of Henry Runge, John H. Dale, Jacob Maas, A. K. Peiser, Duncan Beaumont and W. B. Fulkerson will proceed to compare the receipts of Produce and award the Premiums.

" 'Persons desirous of contending for the Premiums will, from time to time, report their receipts to Mr. Chambers Etter, by whom a full and fair statement will be kept for their guidance, and at all times subject to the inspection of the Committee of Awards, or other parties.

" 'The Merchants of Indianola have adopted this course as the first step towards the formation of a Permanent Association in the place for the encouragement of Agriculture, Mechanical Arts, and every branch of Home Production within our State.

" 'Signed by the following wholesale and retail firms in Indianola:

H. S. Fulkerson & Co.	*Jacob Maas*
Baldridge, Sparks & Co.	*H. Runge & Co.*
George S. Menefee & Co.	*S. A. White*
Chambers Etter & Co.	*John H. Dale*
Peiser & Brother	*Thomas D. Woodward*
Huck & Ogsbury	*John A Settle'* "
Lewis & Hughes	

Progress at Indianola in 1852 was not confined to landbased operations. The brig *Russell* (Captain E. K. Cooper) had arrived in May, her cargo being the prefabricated parts for the cast iron lighthouse to be placed on Matagorda Island at Pass Cavallo. The *Russell* had already discharged at Galveston the material for the lighthouse on Bolivar Point. Murray & Hazelhurst of Baltimore had the contract for their erection and proceeded first to complete the one at Bolivar. The crew then came to Matagorda Bay and began assembling the Pass Cavallo lighthouse. On completion, it was a 79 foot tower painted red, white and black with horizontal stripes, stationing a Third Order lens 96 feet above sea level.

The lamps, fueled by colza oil, had concentric wicks. The flame was magnified and concentrated by special built-up echelon lens. The revolving light, operated by clockwork and weights, showed a flash every 90 seconds. It was visible for 16 miles.[10] Indianolans crowded the waterfront on the first evening of the new light's operation. At dusk, the lamp was lighted, its first flash being greeted by loud cheers from the assembled citizens, the sounding of whistles by steamers in the harbor and the firing of guns.

Baldridge, Sparks & Co. had begun their new wharf near Powder Horn Bayou in August. Sixteen feet wide and 1,500 feet long, the wharf rested on four parallel rows of palmetto log piles, which were joined at the top by large beams of cypress timber fastened with iron bolts. It was floored with heavy cypress lumber. The palmetto piles were driven into the soft floor of the bay by a floating pile driver. At the outer end of the wharf, the T-head (on which a warehouse was built) was large enough for five vessels to dock at the same time.[11] Palmetto logs were used in the wharf construction to thwart the shipworm, *teredo navalis*, so destructive to wooden piles submerged in warm salt water.

On shore, the firm erected another warehouse and a double store building, each 52 x 104 feet in size. The editor of the *Texian Advocate* commented, on October 23, 1852, "We paid a flying visit to our neighboring town of Indianola in the early part of this week and were pleased to note the evidences of progress which presented themselves on every hand. We have never seen a town grow faster than that has during the last nine months. We visited the magnificent improvements of Baldridge, Sparks & Co. at Powder Horn. Their new wharf is . . . certainly one of the most substantial structures we have ever seen . . . " As the wharf was being completed, lumber was unloaded on the ground for erection of the Casimir House.

With the transfer of the county government from Lavaca to Indianola, political affairs began to attract the attention of citizens of the new capital. At the November 15 meeting of the Commissioners Court, matters pertaining to the move were taken up. The owner of the sloop *Fashion*, Captain White, had submitted a bill in amount of five dollars for transporting a prisoner from Port Lavaca to the new jail which had just been completed at a cost of $598.25. The tight-fisted court allowed four dollars for the prisoner removal. J. A. Settle was paid one dollar for a padlock for the jail, Julius A. Pratt $2.25 for handcuffs, John G. Kerchey $8.50 for construction of a table and benches for the courtroom, R. Pompset six dollars for three additional benches and J. H. Davis $6.25 for moving the archives from Lavaca to Indianola. For stationery to be used in the county clerk's office, the court authorized

Built in 1852, the Pass Cavallo lighthouse on Matagorda Island was relocated in 1873 two miles from its first site. The light is now automated and uses the original lens. The weights which formerly operated the clockwork to turn the lens are still in place. (*Courtesy U. S. Department of Transportation, U. S. Coast Guard.*)

$5.98. Two stoves were purchased for $23.50, one for the district and the other for the county clerks' offices. Firewood was bought for $13.50.[12] Jackson County was the chief source of wood fuel, it being brought to Indianola by boat from the loading dock at Texana.

Hugh W. Hawes appeared before the court at the November meeting, petitioning for the right to operate ferries, and to charge toll, over Pearce and McHenry Bayous between the mainland at Alligator Head and Saluria on Matagorda Island. Hawes's petition was conditioned on court approval of a request from Dr. Levi Jones for the construction and maintenance of a road between the two towns. Approval was given to Hawes's proposal and ferry toll rates were set: "Wagons with 6 oxen or horses, $1.00; wagons with 4 oxen or horses, 75¢; pleasure carriages, 75¢; carts or drays, 50¢; horse and rider, 50¢; pedestrians, 25¢; horses and cattle, 10¢ each."

Jones was joined in his request for the road by Thomas Rooke, Henry Jones and Sam Harding. The route they contemplated was from the end of Main Street in Indianola to Brown's Addition, where it crossed Powder Horn Bayou. It then paralleled the shoreline to the wharf at LaSalle, and on to the point on the bay at Alligator Head. The court authorized the new road, the first of several it would be called upon to approve out of Indianola.

As early as 1846, Masons moving to Indian Point felt the need for a local lodge home. The following year, the Grand Lodge of Texas was petitioned to grant a charter for a lodge there. It was granted in 1850 to Indianola Lodge #65, later changed to #84. On December 4, 1852, the lodge purchased from the estate of Horace Baldwin Lot 3, Block 18 in Brown's Addition. The property faced the bay front on Water Street between Goliad and San Jacinto. There the members erected their two story building.[13]

The Legislature approved an act to incorporate the City of Indianola on February 7, 1853, and to set boundaries. They were specified to "begin on the north at the mouth of White's Bayou; thence down Matagorda Bay so as to include the harbor in front of Powder Horn Bayou; thence with said Bayou and Lake to a point one mile in a straight line southwest from the said Bay of Matagorda; thence in a straight line to a point one mile due southwest from the mouth of White's Bayou; thence to the said place of beginning."

Included was the stipulation that, "Whenever the proper courts of law shall decide that the titles of Benito Morales and Juan Cano are valid ones, all the lands within their original grants which by this act are placed or described within the limits of said corporation, shall be considered as stricken out therefrom and altogether exempted from all the provisions of this charter."[14] Once more, the cloud on land titles was seen.

The act further provided for the election of a mayor, recorder and eight aldermen. As soon as the city council was qualified under the law, its first assigned duty was to appoint a city treasurer, a tax assessor-collector and a city marshal. Such other appointive offices as would prove necessary to the orderly conduct of municipal affairs were authorized by the Legislature.

Despite initial optimism, the railroad from Powder Horn Bayou to Victoria moved no nearer realization than the talk stage. At the first meeting in Indianola, an alternate plan had been suggested. It was for a plank road, which would be an all-weather turnpike and less costly to construct. Railroad funding problems resulted in the alternate plan being adopted, though reluctantly, and charter applied for. It was granted by the State on February 7, 1853, to the Indianola and Victoria Plank and Turnpike Road Company. Again, the promoters were unable to get the project off the ground. Three years would pass before there was a revival of interest in railroad construction. For that, Port Lavaca would be responsible, as it continued to struggle desperately to secure a position of commercial dominance over Indianola.

The six month period during which Indianola citizens furnished quarters to Calhoun County free of charge ended March 1, 1853. The court executed a lease agreement with August Fromme on February 21 to continue occupancy of the building, known as "the Eckhardt property," then serving as the courthouse. For the use of the entire structure and lot, including cistern privileges, the county paid Fromme $25 per month.[15]

Actual construction of a courthouse at Indianola was to be delayed for several years. A primary reason for procrastination was indecision about where the building should be located. Evident at the time was the surging growth of Brown's Addition to Indianola at Powder Horn Bayou. There was a gradual realization that that portion of the town was destined to be the center of commercial activity for the community. Officials were reluctant to authorize the expenditure of funds for a courthouse at Indianola (old Indian Point) as, one by one, the business firms were moving down the bay. Having received from the state a grant to aid in construction, commissioners discussed the proper procedure for handling the money in order to avoid more criticism than would normally be theirs. Members of the court instructed that the state funds, then in the hands of the county treasurer, be loaned at interest for periods not exceeding six months, with adequate collateral in the form of real estate. Rate of interest was set at 10% annually.[16]

Another mishap occurred in connection with the mail in September. This was bound from Western Texas to Victoria, Indianola, Port Lavaca, Galveston, New Orleans and beyond, and was lost in Peach Creek near Gonzales. The northbound coach had made a safe crossing of the stream at the ford only two hours earlier, but a hard rain upstream caused the water level to rise past the danger point. The driver of the southbound stage, not exercising caution, plunged the heavy vehicle into the stream. Force of the water quickly overturned the coach, scattering passengers, baggage, mail and horses. Two of the animals were drowned. The mail and baggage were swept away. The driver and all passengers managed to save themselves, however one man lost a large sum of money which he was carrying on his person.[17]

The specter of yellow fever reared its head for the first time in epidemic form in 1853. It spread through the eastern and southern states and finally reached the Texas coast. As was true of all towns through which travelers moved, Indianola was not spared. Because this was the first severe occurrence of the disease since the beginning of the town, quarantine procedures had not been developed there. The city would not be caught unawares the next time!

When it became evident that yellow fever was spreading rapidly and posing a serious threat to the community, the new city administration appointed a Board of Health to take charge. Members were H. E. Boehner, Henry Runge, A. K. Peiser, Dr. William H. Dallam, Dr. J. C. Lawrence and Dr. F. E. Hughes. Along with the formation of the Board of Health, the Indianola City Hospital was established, with Dr. Hughes as physician.[18]

The cause of yellow fever, and the means by which the infecting organism was transmitted, was still a complete mystery. For generations, fear of the killer disease had spread terror. Various theories had been propounded as to the cause, and how it might be controlled. One obvious benefit of the theories was based on the suspicion expressed by some that the mosquito was possibly involved, but to what extent and how no one had the remotest idea. Because of the thought that the mosquito played an unknown role, concerted efforts were made to eliminate standing water as breeding places. At its first meeting on August 30, the Board of Health reported that, ". . . . Much has been done to improve the sanitary conditions of the city by the removal of vegetable and animal deposits, and the filling up of unhealthy pools and ponds in the suburbs."[19]

September brought a dramatic upsurge in the number of cases of the fever. In the week ending September 20 alone, 14 deaths were recorded in Indianola. Galveston was hard hit, deaths from the disease there averaging ten to 12 per day. Houston, Port Lavaca and Victoria all listed fatalities. At New Orleans, 7,537 yellow fever deaths had been recorded in the four months from May 20 to September 16. It was enough to strike fear into the hearts of the bravest.[20]

On September 24, 1853, the *Texian Advocate* editorialized on the disease under the heading, "Yellow Fever — Who Shall Decide When Doctors Disagree?" The newspaper summarized opinions as to whether the disease was infectious, asking whether it might be communicated to a city by persons who contracted it elsewhere, as had long been argued pro and con by the medical profession. "Quarantine regulations, almost universally resorted to by large cities upon the advice of eminent physicians well instructed by long experience, together with those fears which are so natural upon hearing of the ravages of a fatal epidemic in a neighboring city, have heretofore inclined a large majority of mankind to believe that yellow fever is infectious.

"This position was greatly strengthened by the current reporting that the present epidemic was brought to New Orleans by the bark *Mary H. Kemball* from Rio de Janeiro, via Jamaica. But, upon a careful investigation of facts, it turns out that previous to the arrival of the *Mary H. Kemball*, there had been 21 deaths from yellow fever at New Orleans. The first death from that disease was a laborer, a native of Ireland, who died on the 27th of May, direct from Liverpool. The second case was a German from Bremen, the third was from Ireland dead June 7 just from Liverpool. The fourth was from Bremen, died June 7. The fifth was an Englishman from Liverpool, died June 10. The sixth was 15 days from Boston, died 11th June. From this time onward, the cases rapidly increased . . . until 21 deaths had occurred. The cases above enumerated nearly all died with black vomit," said the *Advocate*.

"These facts destroy a strong argument in favor of the theory of infection . . . and when we consider the fact that the most rigid quarantine regulations have in every instance failed to arrest or ward off the disease, the probabilities amount almost to certainty that the cause of yellow fever must exist in a town independent of imported infection before it can prevail as an epidemic.

"If such be the case, the removal of all local causes of disease . . . cleanliness, temperance, a careful attention to all morbid symptoms would be much cheaper, more efficient and less detrimental to private and public interests than oppressive and ruinous quarantines." So much for newspaper opinion on a matter about which the editor knew no more than did learned physicians of the period!

There was "time out" from worry about yellow fever as the newspapers delved into a bit of history. In October 1853, the Indianola *Bulletin* commented, "We have on our table the second number of the Texan Mercury, published at Seguin by Bucanan [sic] and Burke, a handsome sheet. The first number was lost with the mail in Peach Creek. Every old Texian we ever heard speak on the subject prefers being styled a 'Tex-i-an,' instead of Texan.

"When the Advocate started in Victoria in 1846, 'Texan' was its preface to 'Advocate,' but the editors received so many letters and verbal messages protesting against the omission of the 'i' they at once yielded and, by doing so, gained fully a hundred subscribers. A band of 20 or more old citizens in Jackson County mutually agreed they would never support the paper unless the change was made. There is, perhaps, no fixed rule to govern the case, but to our ears there is more euphony in Texian than in Texan. At any rate, since the discussion of the subject by the New Orleans Bulletin at the commencement of the revolution in 1835, it has been the custom of the people in writing and speaking to refer to themselves as 'Texians.' Very few but do not otherwise . . . among the latter we have the Western Texan at San Antonio and now the Texan Mercury."

The yellow fever epidemic continued to rage unabated, though each town affected attempted to play down the seriousness of the situation and made claims as to the healthfulness of their respective communities. In the edition of October 15, the *Advocate* yielded to the urge to again editorialize on the subject. "Several cases of yellow fever have been brought into Victoria, all but one of which proved fatal. The first two cases occurred six weeks ago, yet no citizen of this place has taken it. Our citizens nursed the sick and buried the dead. Will the Galveston News inform us why, upon the theory of infection or contagion, our town has thus escaped?" That statement had reference to a difference of opinion between the two newspapers.

Although no yellow fever cases had been reported there, the October term of district court scheduled at Texana was canceled as a result of the pressure of public sentiment. The people of Texana were opposed to an influx of "outsiders," being afraid they might serve as carriers of the scourge.[21]

In that issue of the 15th, the *Texian Advocate* printed additional reports on yellow fever in the coastal plains. ". . . . At Galveston, the deaths averaged 7 per day for the last 3 days ending on the 6th October. The News hopes that the epidemic will terminate there in a week or two more. At Houston, the News says there is no abatement of the disease.

"From Indianola, we have no late news. The Bulletin of last week was received here by the last mail. It is reported, however, that the disease has been rather worse there for a few days past. At Lavaca, we are informed, the disease continues to be fatal. Mr. Keen, a merchant of Lavaca, writing to a citizen of this place October 11 says, 'The epidemic is still raging with unabated vigor, [and] 126 cases have occurred, out of which there have been 26 deaths . . . .'

"At Victoria, the health is pretty good. No case of yellow fever has originated here, nor is there at this time a case in town. Dr. Hayne, whose letter of the 27th ult. we published giving information of the appearance of the fatal epidemic at Lavaca, and also his partner, Dr. Johnson, are both dead."

A half century would pass before all of the pieces of the yellow fever jigsaw puzzle would fit in place.

X.

The Government Depot

In line with instructions of the War Department, Brevet Lieutenant Colonel W. G. Freeman, who was assistant adjutant general, made an inspection of the Eighth Military Department in Texas. His report, dated at San Antonio on October 1, 1853, began with Indianola, which city he had reached by sea on May 26 from Washington. Inspection at Indianola was begun on the day of his arrival.

In referring to the Indianola Depot, Lieutenant Colonel Freeman said, in part, "This Depot, which is used by the Quartermaster's and Subsistence Departments of the Army, is situated in the town of Indianola, on Matagorda Bay, about 20 miles from the bar of Pass Cavallo . . . All supplies coming by sea for the principal depots at San Antonio and Austin are landed at this point and conveyed hence by wagons, the distances to the places being, respectively, 140 miles W. N. W. and 160 miles N. N. W.

"From eight to ten feet water can be carried over the Pass Cavallo bar at ordinary tides, and nine feet can be brought to the wharf at Powder Horn Bayou, 3½ miles S. E. of Indianola. At the Depot wharf itself there is only a depth of 6½ feet water. The buildings of the Depot consist of five structures (60 x 30) for supplies, a small blacksmith shop, and a stable (32 x 70 feet) all constructed of rough lumber, at a total expense, probably, of $2,500. They are, however, fully adequate to the purposes required of them. These houses are built on ground leased by the United States. A wharf, 250 feet long and on which is laid a railroad, is connected with this land, and for the exclusive use of the wharf and the lease of the ground, the Government pays a monthly rent of eighty dollars. The owner of the wharf binds himself to keep it in repair against dangers by sea or collisions of shipping, the United States defraying the expenses of ordinary wear and tear."

Colonel Freeman continued, "Quartermaster's Department. Bvt. Major E. B. Babbitt, Assistant Quartermaster, is usually in charge of this department of the Depot, but at the time of my visit he was at San Antonio acting as Chief Quartermaster of the 8th Department, and his duties at the Depot were performed, temporarily, by 2nd Lieut. George C. Barber [sic], 8th Infantry. The quantity of supplies on hand was very limited, most of those received being intended for transshipment to the interior and sent off as fast as landed. The articles in store were, however, in good preservation, and due scrutiny seemed to be exercised to prevent waste or misapplication.

"The persons employed in the Department are one clerk at $85 per month, one forage master at $40, one veterinary surgeon at $30, one blacksmith at $35, seven teamsters at $20 each and one watchman and four labourers at $20 (each). All these men, except the clerk, receive in addition to the pay specified one ration per day. The monthly expenditures for the pay of persons employed and rent ($80 for lease of grounds and $12 for Quartermaster's and Commissary's Office) amounts to $522. This is the ordinary expenditure, exclusive of the purchase of supplies. When additional labour is required, it can be obtained at $1 per day, the labourer furnishing his own subsistence.

"Subsistence Department. Second Lieut. George C. Barber, 8th Infantry, has been in charge of this Department since May 22, 1852. One clerk at $25, one labourer at $25 and one at $20 per month are employed, making the ordinary disbursements amount to $70. Only a small amount of provisions was in store, and it is desirable that this should always be the case, as from the dampness of the climate they are liable to spoil if kept too long near the coast. The issues are, usually, inconsiderable and confined mostly to teamsters and detachments of recruits en route to their regiments. Nearly all the provisions received are intended for consumption at the interior posts. I am of the opinion, therefore, that the Assistant Quartermaster of the station should be required to discharge the duties of the Subsistence in addition to those of his own Department. This is now done and, I believe, without inconvenience to the service of either Department, by the Assistant Quartermaster in charge of the San Antonio Depot, the operations of which are probably more extensive than those of all the other Depots in Texas combined. By this arrangement, Lieut. Barber could join his regiment, now suffering greatly from the want of officers, and from which he has been detached upwards of sixteen months. Having deemed it my duty to make this recommendation, I take pleasure in adding that all accounts concur in representing Lieut. Barber as an officer of much promise and great moral worth. The condition in which I found his books, papers and the property in his charge bears testimony to an intelligent and faithful performance of duty.

"Since the above remarks were written," reported Freeman, "I have heard of Lieut. Barber's death, but I shall, nevertheless, let them stand unaltered, as they are now as just to his memory as they were due to him when living." Lieutenant Barber (Barbour) was one of the many victims of the yellow fever epidemic at Indianola in the summer of 1853.

"Leaving Indianola at 4 p.m., May 26th, I proceeded via Lavaca, Victoria, Yorktown and the Sulphur Springs, to San Antonio, to fit out for my tour. The distance, as has been previously stated, is 140 miles, and the road with the exception of the portion [some 40 miles] to Victoria, which runs over a 'hog wallow' prairie almost impassible [sic] in wet weather, is very good ordinarily and sufficiently well watered. Occasionally trains are kept back, involving sometimes the loss of animals, by the swelling of the streams on the route, which in this country frequently rise twenty feet in a few hours, but the waters subside almost as rapidly, and such detentions rarely exceed two days."[1]

On the Indianola political scene, the initial experiment with lending the state's courthouse grant at interest proved satisfactory. The commissioners then ordered, on February 18, 1854, a six months extension of the plan. Provision was made that the minimum of each loan would be $500 and, further, that real estate taken as security should be "at the rate of one fourth value on improved and one half real value on unimproved property."

Major E. B. Babbitt had returned to Indianola from his temporary assignment at San Antonio early in 1854 and, as elder, was the lay representative of the Indianola Presbyterian Church at the meeting of the Presbytery of Western Texas held there from March 24 to 27. It was the second time in as many years that the Presbytery had convened at Indianola.

During deliberations, delegates to Presbytery resolved to apply to the Board of Domestic Missions for "pecuniary aid" for certain ministers, namely, "Rev. W. B. Tidbell at Corpus Christi, Twelvemile Motts, Lamar and St. Joseph's Island; Rev. James Wallis at Bethany Church, Texana; Rev. W. C. Blair at Green Lake and Hinds [sic] Bay, and Rev. J. M. Connelly at Cuero, Clinton, Coletto and Sandies." In the selection of Commissioners to General Assembly, J. M. Cochran of Indianola and Joel T. Case of Victoria were chosen as principal and alternate from the ministry. As laymen, Major Babbitt and W. N. B. Miller were approved by ballot as principal and alternate, respectively. At the meeting, Presbytery dissolved the pastoral relationship between Case and the Victoria church. Case had been named to an agency on behalf of Aranama College, the Presbyterian educational institution at Goliad, whose principal had fallen victim to yellow fever the previous autumn.[2]

By April 1854, James and A. C. Ashworth had joined the migration to the Powder Horn area and were doing business there as grocers and commission merchants. They had moved from Indianola proper, now being increasingly referred to as "Old Town" or "Upper Indianola" to distinguish it from the portion developing rapidly in Brown's Addition and which was being called Indianola. The *Bulletin* office had already moved down the bay. Fletcher S. Stockdale transferred his law office from Old Town to the Powder Horn section, where he rented quarters above J. A. Settle's store. Stockdale had come to Matagorda Bay in 1846 when Indian Point was born and had taken an active role in promotion of the commercial, cultural and religious interests of the community. Admitted to the bar in Kentucky, he was to represent the 26th District in the Texas Senate of the Seventh and Eighth Legislatures.

Attorney J. S. Jones had followed Stockdale's lead and relocated his office near the bayou. William M. Varnell, commission and forwarding merchant, simply floated his warehouse building down the bay, hauled it ashore and was ready for business at the new stand. Over the next several years, Old Town was transformed into a chiefly residential area.

The move was unfortunate. Elevation of land at Old Town was several feet above that near Powder Horn Bayou. Although Old Town was separated from inland higher ground by a string of small lakes connected by bayous, that higher ground was only a short distance away. At Powder Horn, the town was being built on land barely above sea level. Worst of all, for several miles to the rear there stretched Powder Horn Lake and a low, marshy area. The stage was thus being set for destruction in future hurricanes by the water of high storm tides building up in the lake and on the flats. Then with the veering of the wind as the eye of the hurricane passed, the pressure of a gigantic flood was released as the 15-foot high water rushed back to its normal level in the bay, carrying buildings with it and drowning hundreds of inhabitants. Old Town would not suffer as acutely from that situation. However, in 1854, the settlers at Indianola were not wise to the ways of hurricanes ("West Indian Cyclones" they were popularly called) and were simply unaware of the peril to which they were exposing lives and property.

At the May 1, 1854, meeting, the Commissioners Court acted to comply with the state law of January 31 ordering the establishment of a public school system. The county was divided into four districts. No. 1 encompassed Lavaca and environs, including the settlements on each side of Chocolate Bay and Bayou. District No. 2 covered Green Lake, Long Mott, "and settlements on Espiritu Santo Bay." Indianola and suburbs comprised No. 3. District No. 4 was Matagorda Island.[3]

Two weeks later, the court instructed that an announcement be placed in the *Bulletin* that proposals for plans and specifications for a courthouse would be received, stipulating that the structure be of either brick or concrete. Payment of $25 was authorized for the plan submitted to, and adopted by, the court. However, action on construction of the building was still a long way off. Chief Justice Jefferson Beaumont read a letter from Wm. M. Varnell on August 21 in which he offered to donate to the county two acres of land in the rear of the town, further stating he would pay $100 in labor or cash for building a road across the pond which lay between town and the proffered site. Varnell requested the court to meet him on the ground at a time to be set by the members. That afternoon was designated to view the location.[4] Varnell's offer was rejected . . . another mistake.

On Monday, September 18, 1854, a storm struck the upper Texas coast. Every vessel in Matagorda Bay was wrecked, the wharves at Old Town were destroyed and much damage was again done at Port Lavaca. The Powder Horn area and LaSalle escaped with only moderately harmful effects. However, further to the east where the wind velocity was higher, the town of Matagorda was dealt a savage blow. Many of the buildings were shattered, among them the Methodist and Episcopal churches. Accompanying news of the storm's effect on the bay, was a statement that several cases of yellow fever had been confirmed at Indianola. During the following weeks, the disease was to spread and, once more, take a heavy toll among the residents there, at Lavaca and other coastal communities.[5]

At the fifth annual convention of the Protestant Episcopal Church in the Diocese of Texas, held in Houston in 1854, the Rev. C. S. Hedges was present representing St. John's Church, Indianola, and Grace Church, Port Lavaca. In his address to the convention, Provisional Bishop George W. Freeman said, in part, "On Friday, April the 21st, I proceeded by sail boat down the Bay to Indianola, where I was met by the Rev. Mr. Hedges. Service was held at night. Mr. Hedges being unwell, I read prayers and preached. In the morning of the next day, Mr. Hedges read prayers and I preached again. In the evening, I proceeded, accompanied by Mr. Hedges, to Port Lavaca. On Sunday, April the 23rd, the Rev. Mr. Hedges reading prayers, I preached twice and confirmed three persons.

"The two churches of Indianola and Lavaca have suffered much from the epidemic [yellow fever] of last summer and fall [1853], and many valuable members have been swept away. At the latter place, of seven vestrymen, five were carried off by the epidemic and one by consumption, so that but one of the original vestrymen was living at the time of my visit. Thus, the worthy missionary has virtually to begin his work again. There is, still, much to encourage him. Having, by his faithful adherence to his post during the ravages of the pestilence, acquired the respect and confidence of the people, he may well look forward to a measure of success that will amply reward him for his labors of love . . . "

The Rev. Mr. Hedges, in reporting on the two infant Episcopal churches, stated, " . . . The ladies of Lavaca have raised about $150 for the purchase of a bell and other church purposes. The ladies of Indianola have raised about $300 towards the building of a church . . . The congregations at Indianola and Lavaca both suffered severely from the epidemic. At Indianola, we lost our Senior Warden, the pious and amiable Lieut. Barbour, U. S. Army, together with many friends of the Church. At Lavaca, almost the entire congregation were carried off by the sickness. Thus, we were compelled to begin almost anew . . . " Both congregations continued to be critically weakened by recurring ravages of yellow fever.

In the September 1854 meeting, the Commissioners Court adopted the architectural plan for the courthouse submitted by Edward Beaumont. He was paid the $25 previously authorized. Public notice was given for the reception of bids covering construction, opening date to be the fourth Monday in December. However, that turned out to be Christmas Day, necessitating a one-day postponement. When the court met on December 26, no bids for construction of the courthouse were received, whereupon a new submission date was set for February 1855. And, on December 26, no decision was made on the location of the planned building. That, too, was postponed once more.[6]

The spring of 1855 was rain-short along the Texas coast. The southern end of Stevens Bayou, immediately behind Lower Indianola, had become dry by late April. The same was true for many of the cisterns, a situation that led to great inconvenience and discomfort for the people of the town.[7] There was little cheer in the news brought by the *Perseverance* that citizens of Galveston were paying $2.50 per barrel for drinking water. As if that were not enough, the ice house had not yet received its first shipment from New England.[8] Water was strictly rationed in households. Hotels and restaurants ceased serving it free with meals. Before the emergency ended, a glass of rain water cost more than a stein of beer, the going price for which was five cents. The critical nature of the water famine resulted in a boom for cistern builders. In an effort to prevent a recurrence, auxiliary cisterns were constructed and tied in with the downspouts from gutters on residences and business houses.

Lovers of music, the German residents of Indianola had, from the beginning, joined informally in the presentation of choral programs to local audiences. Following the organization of the Indianola Saengerbund, members went to San Antonio where they participated in the Second Annual Saengerfest in 1854. Some became involved in political actions there which included the approval of controversial resolutions on freedom and human rights. Some "Americans" considered the actions to be subversive and a direct slap at the institution of slavery. Indianola was represented at the Saengerfest in New Braunfels in 1855, as well as at subsequent meetings. At Indianola, the Saengerbund presented complete musical programs on special occasions. Members regularly participated in patriotic and religious affairs in which music played a part.

In a lengthy address made to Mayor H. E. Boehner and the aldermen of Indianola on May 5, 1855, Dr. William D. Kelly expounded on the best method of protecting the city from recurrent sieges of yellow fever. His was a scholarly address, considering the limited understanding of the disease at that time.

Dr. Kelly urged the Council to take the necessary steps to acquire a permanent building for the City Hospital, and to plan adequate financing to provide medical care for all sufferers from the disease. He reminded council members that, in the previous year, yellow fever had decimated the population of the city by a total equal to the increase through birth and immigration.

Speaking of the accepted medical care of yellow fever patients exhibiting one of the four differing categories of symptoms, Dr. Kelly outlined what a well-equipped and staffed hospital could provide in the way of curative treatment, ranging from "bleeding and an ice cap" for one; "cathartics combined with mercurials" for the second; "cups, leeches, fomentations and ice swallowed in small quantities" for the third, and "gentle tonics and stimulants" for the fourth. He closed his presentation by saying, "I have omitted to mention that temperance, the use of wholesome food, protection from the sun, keeping within doors at night when its power is most active, mental tranquility, sea bathing at least once per day, avoidance of too great fatigue in the hot season, constitute the surest protection against this, as well as most epidemic diseases."[9]

Impressed by Dr. Kelly's persuasive eloquence, and prodded by other physicians of the city, the Council drafted and passed on May 31 an ordinance entitled, "Relating to City Hospital," which clarified and improved on previous decrees in the matter of protection of the health of the community. It provided for leasing a more suitable building for the City Hospital and supplying it with "necessary furniture, bedding, &c, for the comfort of the sick that may be at any time admitted into the same." The Council authorized the Hospital Committee to make permanent arrangements for supplying the institution with medicines and "such articles of food as may be needed."

Designation of a physician as City Health Officer at a fixed salary was approved. His specified duties were to include treating all patients placed in the hospital by city authorities, visiting "all steamers or other vessels arriving at this Port from sea, bearing immigrants," and reporting to the mayor or chairman of the Board of Health all cases of sickness coming to his attention. In particular, he was to report all persons "affected with a disease of a contagious or epidemic nature, and he shall, during the existence of any epidemic in the City, make a weekly report to the Mayor of the patients received and discharged, in all cases stating the disease . . . "

The Board of Health was empowered to employ a capable male nurse at a fixed salary per month, "who shall remain at the Hospital and give his attention, under the advice of the City Physician, to the sick in his charge [and] take care of all furniture or other property belonging to the Hospital." A further provision was that, "if at any time the number of patients should become too great for one person to attend to them properly, a sufficient number [of nurses] shall be employed, for the time being."

The Council members held a tight rein by stipulating that, "no patient shall be admitted into the Hospital without a permit from the Mayor or Chairman of the Board of Health, provided, however, that the City Physician may be instructed by the City Council to admit patients during the existence of an epidemic in the City." All money or property found in the possession of any person admitted to the hospital was required to be inventoried and cared for. It was also set forth that, "in all cases where a person has a sufficiency of means to pay for the same . . . [he] shall be required to pay three dollars per day" for every day he might receive treatment as a patient there.

Hotel, tavern and boardinghouse keepers were required to report to the mayor, chairman of the Board of Health or the city physician (city health officer), within 24 hours, all sick persons arriving at their places, and all persons taken ill after arrival. There was a penalty for failure to comply. "Any persons violating this section, on conviction thereof by any Court of proper jurisdiction, shall be fined for such offence not less than two nor more than fifty dollars."

At the following meeting, the Council, yielding to complaints from some citizens concerned about an influx of ladies of the night who were cashing in on the free-spending habits of the sailors, approved another ordinance. That one was entitled, "To Suppress Houses of Ill-fame in the City of Indianola." It was short and to the point.

The ordinance provided that it would be unlawful for any person to not only keep a house of ill-fame within the city limits, but also to permit a structure to be used as a bawdy house. In an effort to close all possible loopholes, Council ordered that, " . . . any lodger who keeps only a single room for the use of a Bawdry in this City shall be held to be within the purview and meaning of the first Section of this ordinance."

The penalty for violation was more severe than that set for hotel, tavern or boardinghouse keepers found guilty of disregarding the provisions of the health ordinance. " [A] person found guilty of violating any of the provisions of this ordinance shall be fined in any sum not to exceed one hundred dollars, or to be imprisoned in the city prison not to exceed 30 days . . . " This edict was not strictly enforced, so the "problem" remained.

The struggle for commercial supremacy that raged between Port Lavaca and Indianola periodically was again brought into the open. Lavacans had been agitating for removal to their town of the United States Government Depot located at Old Town. The on-site investigation by Lieutenant Michler, and his subsequent report, was no consolation to the citizens of Port Lavaca, but it was prophetic in its reference to the Powder Horn portion of Indianola. Michler's report, in part, was printed with pleasure by the editor of the Indianola *Bulletin* on June 15, 1855. In it, he expressed the conviction that there would be no advantage gained by removal of the Depot from Old Town to Lavaca. "If, however," Michler said, "it is the determination of the Government to build its own houses and its own wharves, then [Upper] Indianola, as well as Lavaca, should be thrown out of all consideration and a third place selected, one which, as long as communication with the interior is by land, possesses all the other advantages . . . together with storage . . .

"The place I refer to is the point of land to the south and at the mouth of Powder Horn Bayou. The entrance of this Bayou is from 100 to

200 feet in width, then gradually widening it spreads out into a large lake. The depth of water in this Bayou varies from 12 to 18 feet. You enter it over a narrow bar which must be crossed. The least depth of water over it is five feet. The Bay [Note: Powder Horn Lake] is an excellent harbor for small vessels able to cross this bar."

Michler then proceeded to enumerate advantages possessed by Lower Indianola and also said, "By throwing out a wharf from the point mentioned above from three to four hundred feet, you come into 12 feet of water. At this place . . . all vessels and steamers come to anchor which are able to enter Pass Cavallo, and all would be enabled to run alongside the wharf and lie to, in safety. The fact that the Steamers select this place for anchorage is the best evidence of its safety. As to the latter, which is the main point in the choice of a harbor, examine its position and you find it protected by an opposite point of the main land, and by the middle grounds, from the heavy seas occasioned by the severe weathers, and by the main land from the heavy southeast gales. In addition to this, it affords the best anchorage because we find here better holding ground than at any other point.

"If trade should ever justify the expense of deepening the bar composed of soft mud, which easily could be done, then the Bayou could be used and would afford an excellent harbor. In every respect, as far as wood, water, the nature of the country &c are concerned, it has the same advantages as [Upper] Indianola. The trouble and expense, wear and tear, of lighterage is done away. The selection of this place would only increase the length of the road . . . by three miles . . . If the Government intend to build their own warehouses, then I would recommend the selection of Powder Horn Bayou as being the best harbor . . . ."

In the May 21 meeting, the Commissioners Court had granted permission to James McCoppin to establish, for the use of the public, a ferry across Powder Horn Bayou. McCoppin presented a performance bond of $1,000, whereupon the court granted him a license without charge and set tolls to be charged. Also at that meeting, a sealed bid had been submitted by R. E. Sutton for the building of a courthouse of either brick or concrete for the sum of $9,000. After studying the bid for the period of a week, the court met again on the 28th and instructed the chief justice to accept Sutton's bid, stipulating that he execute a $22,000 performance bond. The court further required that the building be constructed to "slant perfect" for 12 months after completion, that it be of concrete, the latter to be "composed of sand, shell or pebbles, lime and cement," and that in making the concrete, "there shall be one-third as much cement used as lime, and that Thomaston lime and the best quality cement alone shall be used." When constructed, the aggregate was composed of shell. The durability of the resultant concrete was exceptional.

Indianolans believed that the long delay in designation of a site and in construction of a courthouse somewhere in the three-mile-long Indianola townsite now had to be resolved. The court was under intense pressure to erect the structure in Old Town, whose remaining residents were striving to stem its decline. Michler's report worked against that location. Caution continued to be the watchword of the court.

To further complicate matters, J. H. Baldridge and Fletcher S. Stockdale offered to donate to the county a choice block of land in Lower Indianola as the site of the courthouse and jail. Nevertheless, on May 28, the vacillating court ordered the chief justice to purchase lots 1, 2, 3, 4 and 5 in block 38, according to Chambers Etter's map of Indianola, provided the cost would not exceed $75 per lot. The action perplexed many citizens. There was suspicion that the new proposal was merely a delaying tactic. The *Bulletin* published the news that "The Courthouse Committee have selected the vacant ground on the beach immediately in front of the residences of Dr. Kelly and Dr. Baldwin. This is a beautiful location, and now that the question has been settled, we hope the work will be commenced immediately." Although on the surface the matter appeared to be resolved, there would be more delay.

The inter-town rivalry popped out again with an article in the Port Lavaca *Herald* leveling accusations against Indianola for what it asserted were exaggerated claims as to her port facilities. In a lengthy editorial reply on July 20, 1855, *Bulletin* editor A. Marschalk said, in part, "Your business men are already aware that there is not enough water to your place to accommodate the vessels demanded by the trade of this Bay. It is no 'fanfarronade' friend Herald for any man to say that a ship drawing 10 feet cannot sail in 6 feet 6 inches of water. We have made statements as to the capacity of this harbor and position for a town that are incontrovertible. You know it, and the Sea Captains and Bay Pilots know it. Any man who doubts it or wants proof can go out into the Bay and sound for himself. But the large steamers do come to our wharf and have tried in vain to get to yours. Fact. You know it! Why did they not go there?

"For three years, your especial friends Harris & Morgan tried to get their vessels to you and could not, but lightered their freight to you for nothing, and so, throwing the whole force of their tremendous capital, experience and influence FOR your place and AGAINST this, till taught by sand bars, reefs, wrecks and delays that they COULD NOT go above here. Depend upon it, that it is not H&M's love for this place or hatred for yours that induced this step. They are not omnipotent, any more than you are. They cannot make large steamers swim in a mud hole . . . We are older than you are, friend Herald, and venture you this advice. Take a boat and sound the Bay, or take a seat and watch the lighters and vessels sticking in the mud near your place, and you can find DATA to base an article on . . . "

Editor Marschalk failed to include in his reasons the increase by Lavaca of wharfage fees in 1849. It was commonly supposed that increase was the sole reason that caused Charles Morgan, acting through Harris & Morgan to designate Powder Horn as the future landing for his steamers. However, evidence suggests that the company was ready for the move and perhaps seized on the wharfage fee boost as an excuse to do what was already being planned.

XI.

The Camels Are Coming

Nearing the end of his short tenure as editor of the Indianola *Bulletin*, A. Marschalk was inclined to be more outspoken in his views on matters concerning his adopted city of residence. He was fiercely loyal to Indianola. As one of those who had vigorously opposed the Ten Million Bill, he complained that some of the Texas creditors were asserting that the ten million dollars received by the state were supposed to be used simply to pay them. He commented, "The act which vested the money in Texas recites the consideration. It was for boundaries, for cession of land, *and* to enable us to settle with our creditors. The land was the most important consideration. We transferred sixty seven millions of acres to the federal government for the pitiful [sum] of ten millions of dollars."

On the locally important matter of the coast survey by the United States government, editor Marschalk extolled the advantages offered to maritime commerce by Matagorda Bay, and pressed for swift action in proper marking of the channels in that body of water.

Then he exploded on July 27 at claims made by Galveston regarding the depth of water at the entrances to the several ports of Texas. He said, "The following we clip from the Victoria *Advocate*:[1]

" 'Depth of Water at the Entrance of the Harbors of Texas

Sabine	From 8 to 10 feet
Galveston	" 12 to 13 "
Brazos River	" 5 to 7 "
Pass Cavallo	" 10 to 11 "
Aransas	" 7 to 10 "
Corpus Christi	" 5 to 7 "
Brazos Santiago	" 6 to 7 "

Galveston Civilian

" 'According to the above statement, the pass leading into Galveston Bay is two feet deeper than that leading into Matagorda Bay. Such, however, is not the fact, nor has it been since the occurrence of the great storm [Note: 1854] that cleared out the accidental obstructions from the latter channel. As this is a subject upon which the public should be informed, we have taken considerable pains to obtain reliable information and, if necessary, we intend to publish such proof upon the subject as will be entirely satisfactory. We have no doubt that the editors of the Civilian, as well as the citizens of Galveston, generally, are sincere in believing that theirs is the deepest channel, and that the above statement is literally true, for such was the case until the fortunate and unexpected improvement of Pass Cavallo by the recent storm.' "

In no mood to be so mild in expression, Marschalk bitingly commented, "We would be glad to harbor the charitable feelings of the Advocate if we did not know better, that is, as far as the Editors of the Civilian are concerned. One of the editors of that paper well knows that the statement is not correct from personal observation.[2] No man can pass over the route and both bars so often, possessing any ordinary observation, without knowing by repeatedly hearing the soundings of the lead cried, the statement to be erroneous. It is a well ascertained fact that Pass Cavallo has from one foot to 18 inches of water more than Galveston bar. The citizens of Galveston, who have no other information on the subject, do no doubt believe the statement true . . . Pass Cavallo has ten per cent more water than the entrance to any other harbor on the coast of Texas. More than that, [it] is straight and wide, and that is more than can be said of any other."

Had Marschalk been in Indianola in later years, he would have taken umbrage at some editions of the *Texas Almanac*, which began publication in Galveston in January 1857. Touted as an organ of general information on Texas, the *Almanac* was regarded by rivals of the port of Galveston as a not so subtle means of boosting that city and slighting others which were considered to pose threats to her commercial supremacy. That was especially true of the Matagorda Bay ports.

While making arrangements to move to San Antonio, editor Marschalk expressed his love of the sea in two comments that summer of '55. "We visited the other day Capt. Boehner's schooner the *J. P. Ross* and were much pleased to see the improvements he has made on her. She is now ready to receive the new masts, which have been ordered from

Pensacola, and which are looked for by the schooner *Emma DeRussey* . . . She will then be in first rate order to take her place in the line between here and New Orleans as a regular packet under command of Capt. B. We only regret that we are so situated that we cannot enjoy the first trip with him."

Referring to another vessel, the *Emma of Indianola*, Marschalk commented, "This handsome little schooner belonging to our enterprising neighbor Harry Wilson, recently built in Indianola by Mr. Samuel McBride, being just finished a few days since, Mr. Wilson invited some of his friends on board to test her sailing qualities. We have not heard how she performed, but from what we saw of her from the window of our sanctum, we think she must have fully realized the expectations of her owner and builder."[3] The *Emma of Indianola* was to serve as a lighter in the bay.

In his final comment in the *Bulletin* on August 24, Marschalk expressed sadness in leaving Indianola for San Antonio and said, " . . . In what I have done in connection with the Bulletin, I have but prepared the way, and my mantle descends upon, a 'greater than I:' I lay down the sword, he will take up the battle axe. W. H. Woodward, Esq. will hereafter undertake the editorial department of the Bulletin. You all do know him, and in abler hands I cannot leave it . . . "

Woodward had his statement prepared for publication in the same issue of the newspaper. In it, he set out the philosophy that would guide it under his leadership. He pulled no punches. Woodward stated, "In assuming the post of Editor of the Bulletin, I hope and feel that I know the duties and responsibilities that will devolve on me as such, and in obedience to a time-honored custom, I herewith submit to the public a synopsis of the line of policy by which I intend to be governed as a public journalist.

"As Editor of the Bulletin, in all cases I intend to be governed by the dictates of what I may conceive to be sound principle, regardless of the policy or impolicy of this or that measure, this or that man, clique or party — and, believing that in times of great political excitement, when the country is rent by contending factions, it is the duty of every patriot, and more especially so of those who are conductors of the press, to speak out, I unhesitatingly fling my banner to the breeze and proclaim to the world my principles."

In terms understandable to the residents of a maritime city, Woodward said, "I shall espouse the cause of the Democratic Republican party, with the Constitution for my polar star, and Washington, Jefferson, Madison, Webster, Clay and Jackson as my beacon lights — having ever in view the preservation and perpetuity of our glorious confederacy." The possibility of disunion was being recognized on every hand.

"I shall oppose the doctrines and dogmas of the [so-called] Know Nothing or American Order: first, because I believe it to be an organization created by disappointed ambition and broken down political hacks, conceived in iniquity and begotten in demagogism;

second, because I believe that its principles are inimical to the best interests of the country and contrary to the spirit and genius of our institutions, and, finally, because I believe that their doctrines afford the greatest elements of political discord ever witnessed in this, or any other country."

Taking note of the changing political order, "I have ever acted in my humble sphere with the Whig party; having been born under the genial sunlight of Kentucky with Henry Clay as my political god-father, I could not well have been otherwise than a Whig. But now that my party is disbanded, broken down, dissolved and lost in the chaos of disorganization, I see no refuge but in the conservatism of the great Apostles of American Liberty, Jefferson, Madison, Webster and others. If I shall be able to dispel one speck from the cloud that hangs over the destinies of this Republic, my highest ambition will be gratified.

"It will be my purpose in the conduct of this Journal to deal with candor and courtesy towards those with whom I may differ in opinion, either politically or otherwise, holding myself responsible for any editorial matter that may appear in its columns, yet ever ready to repair any injury or wrong that I may unintentionally fall into . . . "

The *Bulletin* became an area newspaper, with agents in towns as far as 130 miles distant from Indianola. They were, K. M. Dowden - Port Lavaca, John Law - Gonzales, R. Jones - China Grove, B. J. Pridgen - Price's Creek, E. C. Anderson - Seguin, Major Perryman - Valley, S. Friou - Maysville, Dr. John Sutherland - Sutherland Springs, J. T. Ford and I. T. Brugh - Texana, G. W. Garnett - Victoria, Crockett Cardwell - Cuero, J. P. Kindred - Concrete, J. C. Stribling - Belmont, J. S. Johnston - Bastrop, Samuel Renick - Hamilton, B. W. Gillock - Ecleto and J. T. Kilgore - Yorktown. Henry M. Hyams was agent for the Indianola *Bulletin* in New Orleans.

As was true of the wreck of the *Independence* in 1852, the *Bulletin* scooped its contemporaries in reporting the arrival of the exotic cargo of the *Supply*. The camels reached Indianola from the Near East and Northern Africa on May 14, 1856. The expedition for their purchase was under the direction of Brevet Major Henry C. Wayne and the animals were brought into the Gulf of Mexico on the U. S. Navy store ship *Supply*, commanded by Lieutenant D. D. Porter.

The *Supply* sailed from Smyrna on February 15. Advance arrangements had been made by the War Department for the erection of a huge corral at Indianola in which the camels were to be placed, after unloading and prior to movement to Western Texas. The construction of the corral, and its purpose, was reported in the *Bulletin* of April 12, thus giving the first real publicity to an event that would capture the fancy of the nation in that generation, and all which have followed.

Coming through Pass Cavallo on April 29, 1856, the *Supply* anchored inside the bay to await the arrival from Indianola of the steamship *Fashion*, to which it was intended to transfer the camels for lightering. Because of her draught, the *Supply* was unable to tie up at a wharf. For several days, continuing heavy swells in the bay thwarted all

The USS *Supply*, which brought to Indianola the shipments of camels imported by the War Department in 1856 and 1857 for military experimentation in Western Texas. At left is the warship USS *Vermont*. (Courtesy *U. S. Department of the Navy and Smithsonian Institution. From Skerritt Collection, Bethlehem Steel Corporation Archives.*)

efforts to place the animals aboard the *Fashion*. The pitching and rolling of the ships made the unloading from the *Supply* extremely hazardous, insofar as the camels were concerned. Attempts were made to move them from one vessel to the other. Lifted singly from the *Supply* and then swung over the side, the danger of injury was so great that decision was finally made to go to the Southwest Pass of the Mississippi River and there effect the transfer in smooth water. The *Supply* arrived at Southwest Pass on May 8, the *Fashion* coming alongside the following day. On the glassy surface of the Mississippi, the 34 camels were successfully moved to the *Fashion*, which then brought them to Indianola where they were put ashore on Wednesday, May 14, to the relief of Major Wayne and the inordinate pleasure of the beasts.[4]

In his letter report to Secretary of War Jefferson Davis, Major Wayne, writing from Indianola on the 14th said, "I have the honor to report my arrival here with the camels. The animals were safely landed, all, by 11½ a.m. at Powder Horn. They are in good condition, considering their long confinement on shipboard and the tossing upon the sea that they have been subjected to and, with the exception of a few boils and swollen legs, are apparently in good health. On being landed and feeling once again the solid earth beneath them, they became excited to an almost uncontrollable degree, rearing, kicking, crying out, breaking halters and, by other fantastic tricks, demonstrating their enjoyment of the liberty of the soil. Some of the males, becoming even pugnacious in their excitement, were with difficulty restrained from attacking each other."

Business activity at Indianola came to a halt on the morning of arrival. Almost the entire population congregated on the bay shore and in second story windows of buildings facing Water Street, to watch the proceedings. It was the opportunity of a lifetime.

Major Wayne continued in his letter to the Secretary, "Saddling them as soon as it could be done, they were gently led to this place [Note: . Old Town], arranged in the stable put up for them by Captain Van Bokkelen, and secured. This occupied us until about 8 p.m. My attention for two or three days must be given exclusively to the animals, which will prevent me for that time from writing to you fully, either in regard to them or to the suggestion conveyed to me by General Jesup of again visiting the east."[5]

The choice of Indianola as the landing point for the camels gave her a place in history of unique importance. On her soil there began one of the most extraordinary experiments in the history of the War Department, the long-planned trial of camels in the transportation of military supplies on the frontier of Texas. Eventually, the testing extended through the New Mexico Territory to California. The basis for the novel trial was the natural ability of camels to survive, even thrive, in arid regions of Western Asia and Northern Africa, to parts of which the climate and terrain of the American Southwest were similar. It was to be carried out in a vast region in which springs, running streams, even water holes, were widely separated. Camels would eat the spiny vegetation characteristic of both parts of the world, and could travel without drinking water over distances that would cost the lives of horses, mules and oxen used as draft or pack animals. The success of the plan seemed assured.

As soon as word of their arrival at Indianola reached inland towns, great numbers of people hastened to the port to view the grotesque creatures. Both species of camel were represented: the Bactrian with two humps, and the Arabian with one. In addition, there was a male which was a cross between the two, and which Major Wayne called a "Booghdee."[6]

The Arabian camel stands about seven feet to the top of the single hump. Although it is usually referred to as a dromedary, to distinguish it from its two-hump kin, the true dromedary is a special breed of the Arabian camel developed for riding as well as for racing. When used for riding in the desert regions of Asia and Africa, the true dromedary has the ability to maintain a pace of ten miles an hour all day. However, Major Wayne's chief interest lay in purchasing pack animals, both Arabian and Bactrian, on his mission for the War Department. Both are considered docile animals, not from gentle disposition or the development of affection for their masters, but rather because of their basic stupidity. Camels are incapable of reciprocating affection, as are horses and dogs. They are ill-tempered and sullen, much given to quarreling with their companions. The very small brain, which weighs only about one pound, equips them for instinctive survival in their natural harsh environment, and enables them to learn to kneel for loading and unloading. They act much as robots of flesh and blood.

The sight of the plodding camels being led through the streets of Indianola, bells tinkling, was an experience to be remembered by the spectators for the balance of their years. Also of great interest to the people were three natives who had accompanied Major Wayne on the trip from the Mediterranean in order to tend the camels, and who remained with him in Texas to help manage them during the experiment.

Major Wayne later reported to Secretary of War Davis, "The camels, so far, have done well, seem to enjoy good health and to be rapidly recovering from the effects of their sea trip. The males are rather fierce and troublesome, but as soon as I can get their packs fitted to them sometime next week, perhaps I shall see what effect a little gentle work between this place and Powder Horn will have upon their tempers . . . "[7]

He further commented, "I have treated the camels with perhaps more care than their naturally hardy constitutions really required. We have camels that, for short distances, will easily transport twelve and fifteen hundred pounds." Then, referring to an incident in which the strength of the animals was demonstrated to the townspeople of Indianola, he said, "Needing hay at the camel yard, I directed one of the men to take a camel to the Quartermaster's forage house and bring up four bales. Desirous of seeing what effect it would produce upon the public mind, I mingled in the crowd that gathered around the camel as it came into town. When made to kneel down to receive its load, and two bales weighing in all 613 pounds were packed on, I heard doubts expressed around me as to the animal's ability to rise under them. When two more bales were put on, making the gross weight of the load 1,256 pounds, incredulity as to his ability to rise, much less carry it, found vent in positive assertion, and as I then became recognized, I observed that I was regarded by some compassionate individuals as about to make a splendid failure. To convey to you the surprise and sudden change of sentiment when the camel, at the signal, rose and walked off with his four bales of hay would be impossible . . . "[8]

In his book *Texas Camel Tales*, the late Chris Emmett quoted Joe Fimble of Victoria, who was a youth residing in Indianola in 1856. According to Emmett, Fimble said, "When the keepers of the animals would move them around from place to place, a rider on a horse would be sent ahead of the camels [and] shout to the teamsters on the road, 'Get out of the road, the camels are coming!' This was done for the reason that . . . the teams, both horses and mules, were frightened at the scent and sight of the camels. The ox teams were not scared of them. One day I was at Chocolate Bayou, having a horse tied behind a wagon leading him, when I met the camels. That horse enacted a terrible scene. He snorted, pitched and kicked, trying to get away. My team was one of oxen, which accounts for me not having a runaway team. The camels finally passed me and moved on inland, and I never saw them again after that."

For three weeks, the camels were a familiar sight in Indianola as they were led about in exercise to prepare them for the coming trek to Western Texas. On June 4, the procession left the corral near the bay, slowly and majestically making its way across the prairie toward Victoria, Indianolans watching as long as it could be seen.

The late Mrs. Robert Clark of Victoria was a child of ten when the caravan halted a short distance from the Shirkey plantation home south of that town. The house was near the Indianola-Victoria road. There, Major Wayne pitched camp to give the animals a rest. Two events occurred that indelibly impressed the occasion on her mind. One was that Major Wayne allowed the little girl to ride on one of the animals for a distance of about two miles. The other was that her mother knit a pair of socks from camel hair and sent them, through Wayne, to President Franklin Pierce,[9] thus displaying a keen "sense of history." In a letter to Davis, dated at San Antonio on August 12, 1856, the major said, "My dear sir: I have the honor to enclose herewith a pair of socks knit for the President by Mrs. Mary A. Shirkey of Victoria, Texas (lately of Virginia) from the pile of one of our camels.

"In her letter to me accompanying the socks, Mrs. Shirkey says, 'I have been much longer preparing the socks than I thought I should be when you left my house. I knit one and found it too coarse. I then spun some finer and knit the pair I have sent you. If I had the machinery, I could have made a much better specimen of what the camel's wool could do in Texas. I have spun the first thread and made the first article of clothing out of the wool in this country. I think if it was carded in the factory, it would do much better; all the long hair would drop out from the fine wool.' "

Major Wayne continued, "The fleece from which these socks were knit consisted of the loose dead hair of the past year that I had clipped off on the 9th of June to relieve the animal from its weight and heat. The fact of its being dead, not living hair may have, perhaps, some influence upon the softness of the fabric woven from it. The socks, at any rate, demonstrate the practical utility of the camel's pile and convey an idea of its probable value should the animal live and thrive among us."[10] President Pierce acknowledged with thanks, in a letter to Mrs. Shirkey, his receipt of the camel's hair socks. At the same time, he sent, as a token of his appreciation, an engraved silver cup bearing an inscription and his name.

A second shipment of camels, 41 in number, was landed in Indianola on February 10, 1857, from the steamer *Suwanee*. They had been transferred to that vessel from the *Supply* in the Southwest Pass of the Mississippi River, as the first had been in the preceding year. Though halted by the outbreak of the War Between the States in 1861, the test use of the camels was basically successful in Western Texas. Some of the animals were used by Confederate forces in the movement of supplies, when they took control of the frontier forts from the Federals. Others were caught and used by individuals as draft and pack animals. Those which escaped to the wild bred and produced offspring. For half a century, descendants of the two shipments of camels were to be found loose in widely separated parts of the Southwest and Northern Mexico, until they were captured or exterminated by man.

The wavering of the county court in the matter of selection of a site for the permanent courthouse of Calhoun County had come to an end early in 1856. At the February 18 meeting of the court, the effect of the cross-pressures of public opinion became evident. Commissioner Martin, who had made the motion the previous May that the county buy the land in Block 38 on the bay front, now moved that the order to the chief justice be revoked. A unanimous vote of approval was cast. Then, the court acted to accept the proposition made by residents of Lower Indianola to donate a square of land on the bay as the site for the building.

That block, number 14, was bounded by Main, Houston, Rusk and Water Streets. In front of the square. the bay shore bulged half a block beyond Water, providing a handsome setting. The designated location for the new courthouse was slightly less than a mile from Powder Horn Bayou. On January 2, 1857, all money on loan from the courthouse state grant was called in. It was needed to pay for work on the building then under construction. The commissioners authorized C. A. Ogsbury to move the frame structure still being used to house county offices from Old Town to Lower Indianola.[11]

Now it was Port Lavaca's turn to fray the nerves of Indianolans. Turnabout seemed fair play! The actual beginning of construction of the San Antonio and Mexican Gulf Railroad in 1856 at Lavaca shocked the business community of Indianola and caused renewed effort to be exerted toward development of rail service beginning at Powder Horn Bayou. It was too much for Indianolans that the SA&MG had been started and that it was intended to be built through Victoria and on to San Antonio. The threat to Indianola's prosperity was too ominous to be ignored.

Efforts of Indianolans resulted in the passage by the Legislature, on September 1, 1856, of still another railroad act, this one to incorporate the Powder Horn, Victoria and Gonzales Rail Road Company. Commissioners designated in the act to open books and receive subscriptions to the authorized capital stock of $5,000,000 were Andrew Dove, Joseph H. Baldridge, Jesse O. Wheeler, David Murphree, Preston Rose, F. S. Stockdale, D. M. Stapp, H. Runge, John J. Linn, Edward Bellinger, Augustus H. Jones, Benjamin B. Peck, William Monroe, Thomas H. Hardiman, John B. McMahan, W. S. Oldham, John M. Swisher, Thomas B. Johnston, Joseph F. Johnston and Wm. Venable.[12]

The act provided that the corporation be invested with the right of locating, owning and maintaining a railway, ". . .commencing on La Vaca [sic] Bay as near the mouth of Powder Horn Bayou as practicable and thence running on the most practicable direct route to Victoria, thence as near a direct line to Gonzales." Lack of geographical knowledge in Austin resulted in reference to the La Vaca Bay, though as a matter of fact, Powder Horn Bayou empties into Matagorda Bay some three miles below that body's junction with Lavaca. Section 6 of the act permitted not only the purchase, but also condemnation, of land necessary for constructing the railroad and providing space for depots, shops, etc. Provision was made for appeal by land owners, and the determination by the appropriate county court, of compensation to be paid for land condemned for railroad purposes.

Authorization was given to the company to extend the line from Gonzales to Austin, provided certain stipulations were met as to the rate of construction. Title for 16 sections of public land was to be given by the state for each mile of the first 25, "and also for each subsequent twenty miles of road." It was required that construction must begin within 12 months and that 25 miles be completed within three years. That requirement proved impossible to meet, as sufficient capital could not be raised to permit the start of the building program, much to the chagrin of Indianolans who were nervously watching the railroad-building activity at Lavaca.

By 1858, the SA&MG had constructed and was operating a five mile stretch of track from Port Lavaca. It terminated in the open prairie. That stub end was the scene of lively action. S. G. Reed points out in his book, *A History of the Texas Railroads*, that, "It was put to use right away, as indicated by the following extract from the report of the State Engineer for the year 1858: 'The road bed, ties, iron, etc. are first class. The completed portion of the road is in constant use. The remarkable fact may be stated that this five miles of road — terminating in the open prairie at a point remote from any settlement or public highway — has not only been of vast service to the people of Western Texas, but has actually over paid running expenses. I witnessed the immense business it was doing; the noise and bustle, the hundreds of wagons and teams and teamsters drawn to the present terminus or station in the open prairie. I have never seen or heard of an instance like it.' " Reed further comments, "The business handled was that which had formerly been carted to and from Port Lavaca. This indicates the condition of the roads in that section at that time." The situation would have sealed Indianola's fate in 1858 had she not possessed the natural deep water that Port Lavaca lacked.

Organization of the Western Texas Wharf Company at Indianola had been made a matter of public record on October 8, 1856. The purpose of the company was to erect a new long wharf near Powder Horn Bayou for the better accommodation of vessels of the Southern Steamship Company, as the Harris and Morgan line was then known. With a total value of $25,000, 250 shares of stock were authorized. Henry Runge was elected chairman of the board. Other directors were John E. Garey, Henry J. Huck, William H. Woodward and Herman Iken. The largest shareholder was Southern Steamship Company with 50, valued at $5,000. H. Runge & Co. bought 20 shares. William Hogan, H. N. Caldwell, E. F. Brown and Casimir Villeneuve each owned ten shares. Those holding five shares each were W. H. Woodward, Fletcher S. Stockdale, C. A. Ogsbury, A. Fromme & Co., John E. Garey, Jacob Maas, Isaac A. Reed and Henry J. Huck. R. Dossat and Charles H. Hughes each purchased three, Charles C. Howerton two and George S. Menefee, J. H. Duncan, G. W. Volk and Edw. Wood one each, for a total of 162. The remaining 88 shares were then made available to the general public for purchase as an investment.[13]

Right after the New Year of 1857, the steamship *Daniel Webster* arrived in the bay on her maiden voyage. She was the first vessel in Commodore Cornelius Vanderbilt's new line which had been established in spite competition with Harris and Morgan's Southern Steamship Company.[14] Vanderbilt was a bitter rival of Charles Morgan and made repeated efforts to undermine the latter's dominant position in the maritime commerce of the Gulf of Mexico. The two men's "no-holds-barred" fight extended to the route to California via Nicaragua.

Hugh W. Hawes sold to the United States for the token sum of one dollar a 50-foot-square block of land on the north bank of McHenry Bayou, opposite the town of Saluria and fronting the store of Captain Baker. On it was erected a short wooden tower called "Saluria Light," which was visible for six miles. Eighty years later, the government took over from Hawes's heirs their Matagorda Island property for use as a World War II bombing range, and then thwarted their efforts to secure its return after it had served its wartime purpose.

The prosperity of Indianola and Lavaca in 1856 was evidenced in a comparison of the value of town lots between Calhoun and other counties. The assessed value of Calhoun County town lots in that year was $259,680. This compared with a value of $117,560 for Victoria County, $17,280 for DeWitt, $73,680 for Goliad, $37,800 for Jackson and $119,300 for Comal. In money loaned at interest, Calhoun held high rank in the state. First place was claimed by Galveston County with $120,625 out. Bexar was second with $40,000 and Calhoun was next with $24,460. In fourth place was Harris County with $23,900. In value of merchandise on hand, Calhoun County was fourth in Texas. Harris County held first rank with $477,850, Galveston County was second with $375,000, Bexar was third with $374,080 and Calhoun followed with $161,020.

The Galveston *News* reported on a maritime disaster that involved Harris & Morgan's *Louisiana*, en route from Indianola to Galveston and New Orleans. "A few minutes after one o'clock on the morning of May 31, 1857, the steamship *Louisiana*, Capt. Henry Shepherd [sic] from Indianola to Galveston with a large number of passengers, was discovered to be on fire when about five miles from this city.[15]

"As soon as Captain Shepherd ascertained it would be impossible to quench the flames, he ordered the steamer's prow turned shoreward and attempted to beach her. Before this could be accomplished, the engineers had been driven from their posts, and everyone attempted to save himself as best he could. In the confusion generally incident to such calamities, one of the lifeboats was burned before it could be launched, and another was staved to pieces against the side of the steamer. The third boat . . . was safely launched and landed its freight on the beach outside the city. The remainder of the passengers, being driven from the steamer by the flames, precipitated themselves into the Gulf and clung to such pieces of timber and furniture as had been thrown overboard.

"As soon as the fire was discovered in Galveston, boats were dispatched to the scene of the calamity and succeeded in saving many lives. The scene in the city on the return of the boats which had been sent to the rescue was a saddening one, and as the burned and blackened corpses were placed on the Central Wharf, crowds gazed upon them, expecting to recognize friends or relatives who were on the vessel. The number of lives lost by this disaster was thirty-five. The steamer burnt to the water's edge, when she sank in twelve fathoms of water."

At the May 1857 meeting of the Calhoun County Court, it was ordered that "henceforth there be two polling places in Precinct 2." One ballot box was specified for Old Town and the other for Lower Indianola. By that time, construction of the courthouse had progressed to the point that a contract was entered into between Chief Justice George S. Menefee, acting on behalf of the county, and James Ranahan for plastering the new building. Terms of the agreement provided that Ranahan would finish the interior walls with two coats of plaster. The agreed price for the interior walls, exclusive of the courtroom, halls and stairwells, was 25¢ per square yard for lathing and plaster, to be done in brown finish. Cost of lathing and two coats of plaster for the ceilings was 40¢ per square yard. On the exterior walls, 50¢ per square yard was agreed upon, with penciled-in blocks in imitation of stone.

The problem of safekeeping of prisoners continued to cause concern to the court. The jail at Indianola not being secure, prisoners sentenced to long confinement had to be transported to Victoria or Galveston, at considerable expense to Calhoun County. To correct the situation, the court began investigating the cost of construction of an iron cell to be fitted into the jail. At the August meeting, a bid was received from Close & Cushman of Galveston in amount of $600 for the building of a jail cell, but not including its installation. That bid was later accepted.[16]

The United States Post Office Department signed a contract with James E. Birch of Swansea, Massachusetts, in June 1857 for a mail route from San Antonio, Texas, to San Diego, California. Compensation was set at $149,000 annually, two trips monthly in each direction being provided for. The coaches were scheduled to leave both San Antonio and San Diego at 6 a.m. on the 9th and 24th of each month. The initial trial run was made from San Antonio, leaving on July 9, and the second departed that place on the 24th. The first regularly scheduled trip started on August 9. The mail was carried in "fine, new square-bodied coaches drawn by five mules, two at the wheels and three abreast in the lead. This arrangement of the team is found to work exceedingly well as, thus arranged, one driver can command the whole, whilst a six mule team would require two drivers. The average speed made over the fine natural roads of the West is six miles per hour." Price of through passage was $200. Accommodations were "as good as circumstances will admit, the stages being so arranged that passengers can recline in them comfortably, and take their sleep while traveling. The provisions are the best that the nature of so long a trip will allow."[17] Reading between the lines, it can be seen that the accommodations and provisions were Spartan.

Birch had employed Major J. C. Woods as agent and general superintendent before leaving New York en route to California by boat to complete arrangments at that end of the line. On his return to New York, Birch traveled on the steamer *Central America*. He, along with 421 other passengers, died when that ship sank off the Florida coast in a hurricane on September 11, 1857.

As administratrix of his estate, Mrs. Birch sold her interest in the new mail and stage route to O. H. Kelton of Charleston, South Carolina. Kelton then appointed Abner Barrows as his agent. Woods remained as superintendent.[18]

The people of Indianola were keenly interested in the San Antonio and San Diego Mail Route. The Southern Steamship Company was the principal channel through which passengers and mail from the East were routed from New Orleans to Indianola, thence by stage to San Antonio, where transfer was made to the SA&SD. Although mail had been carried on contract over this long western route previously, the new operation was the first to offer accommodations for travelers along with transportation of mail.

Sentiments of Indianolans were summed up in the expression by the *Texas Almanac:* "We, therefore, assume that the establishment of this line must lead to the speedy and rapid settlement of the country throughout the entire distance, giving us, within a very few years, a continuous succession of farms, ranches, hotels, military posts, stage offices, &c, from one ocean to the other. There can be no doubt that this is very soon destined to be the great overland inter-oceanic thoroughfare of the nation, affording not only a safer but a quicker and cheaper passage to and from California over our own territory than can now be had by the present circuitous routes through the sickly regions of foreign countries.[19] Indianolans envisioned the new enterprise as a source of increased business for their port, being tied into the mail route as its true terminus, by extension, on the Gulf coast.

XII.

Boom at Powder Horn

During 1857, an additional steamship service was provided between New Orleans, Galveston and Indianola via Cornelius Vanderbilt's so-called "new inland route." It offered a "saving of one day's time, as well as reduced rates for passage, freight and insurance." It was actually a combination rail-steamship route. Inaugurated on Sunday, May 10, the service utilized the tracks of the New Orleans, Opelousas and Great Western Railroad from Algiers to the town of Brashear on the left bank of the Atchafalaya River at Berwick's Bay, a distance of 80 miles. At Brashear, passengers and freight were transferred to the steamers *Opelousas* and *Galveston*, "new and splendid steamships . . . built expressly for this route . . ." Each was of 1200 tons burthen.

Passengers left New Orleans from the railroad depot at the Algiers ferry landing opposite Jackson Square at 10 a.m. each Sunday and Thursday. The *Opelousas* (Captain A. Van Horne Ellis) departed Brashear on Sunday afternoon, following arrival of the train from Algiers. The *Galveston* (Captain David Wilson) left Brashear every Thursday as soon as the passengers, mail and freight were transferred from the train to the vessel. Returning, the *Opelousas* departed Indianola each Wednesday morning and Galveston the following day at 1 p.m. The *Galveston*'s schedule called for leaving Indianola every Saturday, and Galveston on Sunday.[1]

Records of the movement of these and all other vessels operating into and out of the Port of Indianola were maintained by the collector of customs for the District of Saluria. Reporting from Indianola on September 5, 1857, D. M. Stapp, Dr. Levi Jones's successor for the district, outlined the territory it then encompassed. Stapp stated, "[it] includes all that part of the State of Texas south and west of Matagorda and Wharton, including said counties, and north and east of and including Nueces County." He listed the port of entry under his jurisdiction as LaSalle, with ports of delivery being Lavaca, Matagorda, Aransas, Copano, Corpus Christi, San Antonio and Eagle Pass. The annual salary of the collector was $1,250.[2]

The customs collection District of Texas had been established on December 31, 1845, two days after the formal annexation of the Republic by the United States. It included the entire new state. Galveston was the designated port of entry. Sabine, Velasco, Matagorda, Port Cavallo (or Caballo), Lavaca and Corpus Christi were named ports of delivery.

The collection District of Saluria was formed on March 3, 1847, to include all that part of Texas south and west of Matagorda and Wharton, including those counties. The town of Saluria on the northeastern tip of Matagorda Island was the first port of entry. Ports of delivery then were Matagorda, Aransas, Lavaca, Corpus Christi and Copano. The District of Brazos de Santiago was carved out of Saluria District on March 3, 1849, the District of Paso del Norte on August 2, 1854, and the District of Corpus Christi on July 28, 1866. The District of Saluria was closed to all types of commerce by the Union blockade during the war, from April 16, 1861, to June 24, 1865. Indianola was made its port of entry in 1866.[3]

By late 1857 the new courthouse at Indianola was finally nearing completion. James Ranahan presented his bill on November 17 for payment due under the plastering contract, and for extra work. The total was $785.19. The commissioners ordered payment of one half ($392.59) to be made on May 1, 1858, and the balance on November 1, 1858. Apparently satisfied with this arrangement, Ranahan then offered to plaster the upper story courtroom and the walls of the halls and stairwells for $150, payment to be in two installments on the same dates set by the court for his previous work. The members of the court approved his proposition and also contracted with him, for the sum of $5.50 each, to finish the eight fireplaces and hearths, "so fires could be built with safety."

Postponement of payment to Ranahan was because Calhoun County was operating in the red, having overspent revenues by $2,000. Observing that income was insufficient to meet necessary expenditures, and recognizing outspoken dissatisfaction on the part of warrant holders, the court acted through State Representative Fletcher S. Stockdale to request the Legislature to allow it the privilege of levying a county tax equal to that of the state. In its petition, the court pointed out that the county had used the state grant entirely for courthouse construction and had not placed any of it in the general revenue fund, ". . . as so many of her sister counties have done, but has strictly complied with the terms of the law concerning those donations." The court observed that Calhoun "now has a courthouse costing $15,000, of concrete, equal to if not superior to any in the State," and further that the county "is under lasting obligation to the power that contributed."[4]

The petition for tax aid received a sympathetic hearing under the skilled handling of Representative Stockdale. An act approved February 16, 1858, gave Calhoun County authority to levy and collect an ad valorem tax of 12½¢ per $100 valuation on property, both real and personal. Six weeks prior to that legislation, approval had been given a measure providing that, beginning February 1, "All force sales . . . made of Real Estate or negroes, and all sales made by executors and administrators of Real Estate or negroes in the County of Calhoun shall be made at the door of the Casimir House in the city of Indianola," the hotel operated by the affable Frenchman and his wife. It seems logical that the nearest thing Indianola ever had to a slave block would be at the Casimir House. The Villeneuves, who bought, owned and sold slaves, found that for their own purposes in the operation of their hotel's housekeeping department and its dining room, the profit from the use of well-trained, polite and obedient slaves was far greater than that realized by plantation owners who utilized them in the business of husbandry.

Yet another time Indianola knocked on the door of the Legislature. Still nettled and deeply apprehensive over Lavaca's success, and striving to secure the building of a railroad from their town, business leaders were able to get the cooperative state body to pass an act for the purpose. This was to incorporate the Indianola Railroad Company, the once-projected Powder Horn, Victoria and Gonzales road having proved to be another dud. The date was January 21, 1858. Commissioners named to manage the affairs of the new corporation were Henry Runge, Darwin M. Stapp, William P. Milby, D. E. Crosland, John E. Garey and William H. Woodward.[5] This latest road was destined to move forward but not reach completion before the outbreak of the war brought all such activities to a jolting halt.

H. M. Mayo, in his monographs on early Texas rail lines that eventually became part of the Southern Pacific system, said, ". . . The Indianola Railroad Company was chartered to build a railway from Indianola . . . to a connection with the line to Victoria. [Note: he referred to the San Antonio and Mexican Gulf from Port Lavaca]. After the grading had been partially completed, it was taken over by the S.A.&M.G. This road was completed to Lavaca Junction, now Clarke [sic], during 1859 and 1860 and apparently operated under its charter title until April 22, 1871, when it was consolidated with the San Antonio and Mexican Gulf." Unfortunately, he gave no source reference for the statement that the Indianola Railroad was taken over by the SA&MG and that it was completed to the junction prior to the war. No proof can be found that it was in operation at that time. As late as the fall of 1860, news reports related unsuccessful efforts to negotiate the purchase of iron rails to be laid. The road bed had been graded, and some ties had reached Indianola, yet all available evidence points to the fact that they were still on the ground near the bay shore when the conflict began. Mr. Francis Huck and Mrs. Robert Clark, both of whom were adult residents of Indianola at the time of the 1875 hurricane, stated that there was no railroad service to that port until the early part of the decade of the 1870s.[6]

As Western Texas increased in population, its commercial import and export traffic grew in proportion. Cotton handled through Indianola in 1859 increased in volume 250% over 1858. The number of barrels of measurement goods moving over Indianola's wharves rose 63% during the same period. Lumber imports showed an increase of 66%. Exports of cattle rose 65%, of wool 55% and hides 43%. Similar upward surges were reported in machinery, clothing, furniture, sugar, molasses, corn, wine, bacon, butter, pecans, peltries, sheep, horses, mules, copper, lead, silver and the myriad other items of commerce.[7]

The rush of immigrants to Western Texas, and the general passenger movement through Indianola to the Southwest, resulted in demands for hotel accommodations and restaurant facilities that could only be met by additional construction. Clothing, hardware and grocery dealers shared in the bonanza, as did local banking houses. Many of those bound for the interior made substantial purchases of supplies needed for homesteading. Merchants from eastern and southeastern United States who had pulled up stakes, joined the rush, and were resettling in Western Texas, remained in Indianola long enough to make financial arrangements for goods to be shipped for their stores as soon as quarters could be secured at their respective destinations.

Commercial activity boomed despite repeated epidemics of yellow fever which affected the town in varying degrees of severity, as they did the other communities on or near the Texas coast. In 1858, one of Indianola's many victims was William F. Hubert, pastor of the Methodist Episcopal Church. Hubert served the Methodist congregation at Lavaca as well as Indianola, and endeared himself to the members of both churches by visitation, prayers and solicitude for their welfare during the epidemic that eventually took his own life. Robert N. Drake was assigned to succeed Hubert at Indianola and Lavaca. He, in turn, was followed by Hiram G. Carden in 1859 and Orceneth Asbury Fisher in 1860.

The Rev. George W. Freeman, Missionary Bishop of Arkansas, had been given supervision of Episcopal churches in the Republic of Texas in 1844. He continued in this position after Texas joined the Union. In 1849, a separate diocese was created for the state. During the 15 years that he served as Missionary Bishop of Texas, Freeman visited Indianola frequently. In the 1859 convention of the Protestant Episcopal in Texas, which assembled in Trinity Church, Galveston, the election of Texas' first resident Episcopal bishop was conducted. On Friday, May 6, the Rev. Alexander Gregg of South Carolina was unanimously elected to that office.[8]

Following his confirmation in Richmond, Virginia, at the General Convention, Bishop Gregg journeyed to Texas, arriving with his family, furniture and slaves in January 1860. For the next 14 years he was the active leader of Episcopalians in Texas, the entire state being his diocese. Texas was divided by the General Convention in 1874 and Missionary Districts created for Western and Northern Texas. Bishop Gregg came to Indianola regularly until its Church of the Ascension was placed in the new Missionary District of Western Texas in 1874. It was then under the charge of the Rt. Rev. R. W. B. Elliott, Bishop of San Antonio.

In mundane matters, the avarice of some elements of the Galveston business community intermittently grated on the nerves of individuals in other Texas towns. Although she was unquestionably the state's principal port in the early years, Galveston viewed with displeasure, and some apprehension, other growing communities nearby, such as Indianola and Houston, upon which she looked as potentially dangerous rivals. Nevertheless, conceit over her role in the economy of Texas led to attitudes and decisions on the island that cost Galveston that position of commercial leadership. She failed to learn from Port Lavaca's experience of 1849 and was to so anger Charles Morgan that she drove him into the waiting open arms of Houston. Morgan, at his own expense, in exchange for stock in the Buffalo Bayou Ship Channel Company, widened and deepened the channel across Galveston Bay and up Buffalo Bayou past its confluence with the San Jacinto River.[9] Morgan's action led to the development of the Houston Ship Channel and contributed to Galveston's decline as a terminus for rail and steamship lines.

It was against Galveston's boasting and exaggerations that the Indianola *Courier and Commercial Bulletin* complained in its edition of May 21, 1859: "Will the Galveston Civilian, which seems disposed to conduct everything else fairly, inform us why it is that it claims for Galveston the exports of Indianola? In every issue of the Weekly (we are not accommodated with the Daily) Civilian, we notice among the exports from Galveston by the New Orleans steamers the items of cargo which were shipped at this place. Does the fact of a vessel entering Galveston, in transitu, from this port to New Orleans give that place a claim upon the shipments from this port? There is no reshipment. The vessel only receives there additions to her cargo, and proceeds on her voyage. By what right, then, can the Civilian claim that the whole cargo is exported from Galveston? Galveston is not 'Texas,' nor is it the only port in Texas.

"Suppose the steamers, after leaving Galveston, touch at Sabine to receive additional freight. According to the Civilian's rule, the whole cargo of each, including freights from Indianola, Galveston and Sabine, would belong to the exports of the latter place; and in the same way, Indianola would be entitled to the exports to New Orleans from the Rio Grande, because this is the way port of the steamers engaged in that trade. We claim nothing here but that which belongs to us, nothing that is not put on board vessels in our port, either from on shore or directly from lighters trading between this and other bay and river ports.

Believing it is right, we commend such a course to the Civilian. If not adopted, we at least hope it will give some sort of excuse for the unjust course it now pursues." The reporting practice about which the *Courier-Bulletin* protested casts doubt on the reliability of export figures publicized by Galveston during the period in question.

The boiling of the national political pot in 1859 was drawing increased attention by Indianolans. Local affairs were likewise exciting. On July 30, James Madison Brackenridge withdrew from the three-way race for state representative from Jackson and Calhoun counties. He was the brother of George W. Brackenridge, then Jackson County surveyor, later San Antonio banker and philanthropist. J. M. Brackenridge was a resident of Texana. His withdrawal left the field to Colonel James H. Duncan of Calhoun County and Judge John Sutherland Menefee, former chief justice of Jackson County, currently residing in Texana.[10] Brackenridge's bowing out of the competition was to no avail, insofar as aiding his fellow townsman, Menefee, was concerned. Duncan won the election, despite Menefee's distinguished record as a veteran of San Jacinto and his having held the offices of postmaster at Texana, of county clerk, of representative in the Fourth Congress of the Republic, and of chief justice.

A wide range of matters received the attention of the commissioners as the decade neared its end. Finishing up the courthouse, they acknowledged satisfactory completion of the painting of the building by R. B. Vandevoort and ordered that a warrant for $185 be issued to him, payable in six months. The delayed payment illustrated that the financial situation was still providing its share of headaches to officials and warrant holders alike. Sheriff C. C. Howerton was authorized to enter into a contract "with any person . . . for furnishing and setting in a proper manner in the courthouse yard China, Cottonwood and other trees, at a cost not to exceed $50." The chief justice was instructed to secure the necessary services for the completion of the district courtroom "by making the bar and other necessary conveniences for holding court, and to be done in a manner suitable to the building."

Close & Cushman of Galveston completed fabrication of the iron cell for the jail and delivered it on the bay shore at the foot of the wharf. Examination of the cell by the commissioners showed that its construction was in line with specifications, whereupon approval was given to the issuance of a warrant in payment. It bore interest at the rate of 12½% until maturity.[11] Because of loose stock, there being no strict regulations governing confinement of horses, mules and cattle within lots or corrals, home owners kept their property fenced to protect flower and vegetable gardens. On completion of the courthouse, a stout wooden fence was erected around the entire square, with stiles for ingress and egress. It was necessary for proper maintenance of the grounds and the safeguarding of the young trees from hungry stock roaming on the grass-short shell beach portion of the Indianola township.

George Heald, a resident of Saluria, petitioned the court for permission to operate ferries over the bayous between his town and

Alligator Head, succeeding H. W. Hawes. The requested authority was granted to Heald on February 21, 1859, and license fee set at $10 annually. Heald was required to enter into a $1,000 performance bond and rate of tolls was set in detail by the court. On the next day, the commissioners granted permission to State Representative James H. Duncan to operate a ferry over the Guadalupe River "at the place known as 'White's Ferry.' " This was near Green Lake on the road from Indianola to Refugio. The court set an annual license fee of $20, but entered nothing in the records as to performance bond requirement or tolls to be charged. Was this absence of restrictions a move on the part of the officials to ingratiate themselves with the recently elected legislator? In all other permits, bond was required and tolls set.

April 1 saw the purchase of a lightning rod for the courthouse cupola at a cost of $36.50 and payment of $12 to G. Cox for making a coffin and burying a pauper at Lavaca. In the next month, James McCoppin's license for operation of the ferry across Powder Horn Bayou expired and he applied for renewal. Approval was given, providing for the same license fee and performance bond (ten dollars and $1,000), on the condition "that the said James McCoppin will at all times keep good and sufficient boats for the use of such ferry, and will also keep the banks on each side of the ferry in good repair, and so graded and leveled that the rise shall not exceed two feet in every seven from the water's edge to the top of the bank. . . "

The commissioners examined the tabular statements and rates of the several teachers in the public schools of the county, and approved payment to Mrs. C. A. Ring for $220.90, Mrs. A. F. Threlkeld $15.20, Frederick Goepfert $229.80, J. M. Bickford $111.70, H. B. Cleveland $27.50 and Fred Dietzel $376.90.[12]

Ten months after Close & Cushman delivered the iron cell for the jail, it was still sitting on the ground where it was placed by the stevedores. The county clerk was instructed by the court on May 18, 1859, to advertise one time in the Indianola *Courier-Bulletin* for proposals on the removal of the cell "from its present situation near the wharf to the jail on the courthouse lot."

The county was still in the financial woods, despite the authorization by the Legislature in the previous year to assess a tax equal to that of the state. Like the fable of the old woman and the little fish, the commissioners wished for more. The clerk was ordered, in the name of the court, to petition the Legislature in its next session for a remission of the entire state ad valorem tax to Calhoun County "for the next ensuing four years."

Increasing political unrest was blamed for several instances of lawlessness in the county. Public demand that was made for protective measures resulted in an order by the court that patrols be established in each of the county districts. Initially, 20 men were appointed for a period of 90 days from May 18, 1859. They were: District No. 1, W. P. Vaughn (captain), Alex Hensley, G. W. Cox, William Longnecker and James W. Snodgrass. For District No. 2, there were William M. Blair (captain), D. Lipscomb, John Miller, D. Beaumont and Robert Snodgrass. Appointees in District No. 3 were W. H. Woodward (captain), R. D. Martin, James Ashworth, B. F. Yates and J. B. Burke. In District No. 4, J. B. Baker was named captain. Patrol members were C. Coen, George Parr, Hugh W. Hawes and Thomas Taylor. The court further specified that the list of patrol members be advertised in the Indianola *Courier-Bulletin* and Lavaca *Herald* in order that the "citizens might be informed."

Three months after advertising for proposals to move and install the jail cell, it was still sitting on the bay shore gathering rust in the salt air. The cell on the beach became an object of ridicule. Scornful public remarks finally motivated the court to go on record August 16, 1859, that, in its opinion, "a necessity exists for the removal of the iron cage from its present position near the wharf to the county jail. It is therefore ordered that the clerk of this court draw upon the county treasurer for the sum of $60 to be paid out of the school fund, warrant to be drawn in favor of C. C. Howerton, for the removal of said iron cage and its permanent fixture in the county jail." Why school funds were used to install the cell in the jail is an unanswered question.

Commissioners approved the expenditure of $137.20 for lumber and labor in the construction of a bridge over Stevens Bayou for more direct access to the cemetery, and to the road leading toward Green Lake. Henry Huck was paid $42.33 for lumber for construction of a water closet at the courthouse, the first in Indianola. Kempel and Kaapke received $30 for their labor in construction of the ultra modern unit. The discharge pipe led to the bay in front of the courthouse. H. Runge was paid $24 for a stove and coal for use by the county clerk during the previous winter of 1858-59, and W. E. Mitchell received $5 for making a coffin and burying an indigent man who died at the hospital.[13]

The opening of the 1859-60 school year was marked by R. W. Yates beginning the fourth term of his private "Indianola Male and Female School" on Monday, September 5. H. B. Cleveland started registering pupils for his newly established "School for Boys and Girls" in a building owned by B. F. Yates on Main Street. A bit of family rivalry can be seen. Cleveland advertised that, "All the branches of education usually taught in school will be taught by him, at prices from two to five dollars per month."

Another event in the cultural development of the city was the offering of instruction in the art of sketching. A notice in the *Courier-Bulletin* placed by Otto L. Schnaubert announced "to the ladies and gentlemen of Indianola that he is prepared to give lessons in Drawing, and solicits their patronage. He will call at the residence of pupils to give instruction, if desired. The charge will be Fifty Cents for each lesson, or Five Dollars for a course of ten lessons. Mr. S- can be found at the boarding house of Mrs. Meyers, where he will exhibit testimonials of his skill."[14] Schnaubert succeeded and remained in Indianola as a permanent resident. He became an established artist with a large clientele in the fashionable pastime of sketching.

B. F. Yates was an Indianola alderman. In those years, conflict of interest received little attention, so Yates was able to contract with the Council, of which he was a member, for work in the city's behalf. One such agreement was contained in the report of the Council meeting of July 28, at which Yates, R. D. Martin, T. Rooke and E. Wood were present in their official capacities. Wood presided in the absence of Mayor James Ashworth. Alderman Martin also received pay authorization at that meeting. Hospital Steward A. D. Perry's bill of $182 was approved for payment, as was one from Daniel Hoffman in the amount of $5.25 for the installation of lights in the hospital building. Martin presented a bill for $21 covering the making of an unreported number of coffins and "burying the dead." Martin's invoice was paid out of the hospital fund, indicating that the burials were of indigent patients who had died there. Yates was paid $106.50 for filling up streets. For the same purpose M. E. Davis received $106.25. City Marshal Sam Turner was reimbursed $2.50 for removing dead animals from the town, in accordance with orders from the Board of Health.[15]

As was true of Calhoun County, the city of Indianola was short of funds, a not unusual situation for expanding communities. Population, and the attendant demand for city services, was increasing at a rate more rapid than that of revenues. In an effort to remedy the problem, Council passed and implemented, in the summer of 1859, an ordinance "to provide for raising a revenue by taxation in the City of Indianola." It provided for nine specific categories to be tapped for funds. The first set a direct ad valorem tax of "one-fourth of one per cent upon each hundred dollars value of all property, real and personal, excepting horned cattle and merchandise, and such occupations and professions hereinafter named as pay a special license, or as may hereafter be excepted."

In the second category, an annual direct license tax of ten dollars was imposed for individuals or companies "doing a Receiving, Commission and Forwarding business; of each and every person or firm engaged in vending goods, wares or merchandise; of each and every person engaged in the business of auctioneering; pursuing the occupation of a Real Estate, money or Exchange Broker; keeping any tavern, restaurant, cook shop or eating house for pay or emolument . . ." (3) An annual license tax of $50 was set for retailers of vinous liquors and (4) $20 for beer retailers (saloons).

The ordinance called for (5) a $20 annual tax on each billiard table used for revenue; (6) $25 for livery stables (not including carts and drays); (7) five dollars for each hackney coach, omnibus, buggy, cart, dray or other vehicle for hire; (8) $20 for each nine or ten pin alley and (9) a $2.50 fee for every performance by theaters and/or traveling theatrical companies for which admission was charged.[16]

Mayor Ashworth also affixed his name to three other ordinances. One was of no material significance to the citizens of the town. It merely changed the date of Council meetings. Of importance to the health and appearance of Indianola was that which established a regular garbage and rubbish pickup. It stipulated that on each Saturday the householder would be required to deposit refuse material in a convenient place in the street or alley. Responsibility for hauling was assigned to the Hospital Committee, which was authorized "to cause a cart to be employed" for the purpose. That committee was also designated to select a dump area in a location "consistent with the health of the city." To ensure compliance on the part of citizens, the city marshal was assigned the duty of enforcement, the penalty to be five dollars "for each and every refusal so to comply, to be recovered, with costs, before the Mayor on the complaint and report of the Marshal." As an incentive to the marshal to fulfill his duty, he was entitled to ten per cent of all fines collected.[17]

Not part of the garbage pickup were the familiar "slop buckets" that were suspended on the outside of the alley fences, or on the back walls of residential privies. Into those pails were scraped leftover food from dining tables. Larger containers were to be found outside the rear doors of restaurant and hotel kitchens. The pails were emptied daily into barrels in wagons, and the contents used as swill for swine kept in pens beyond the city limits. It was a convenient way for the semi-liquid kitchen refuse to be disposed of. The use of the swill served as a means of livelihood for persons, usually negroes, engaged as swineherds.

Local anxiety over the possibility of an armed insurrection by slaves incited by abolitionists, such as that which had been exposed and nipped in the bud in Colorado County in 1856, was the basis for the third ordinance, "Concerning Slaves Within the Limits of the City of Indianola." It was principally a curfew that applied not only to slaves but also to free negroes as well. There were stringent regulations concerning freedom of movement and action. The heart of the ordinance stated that it would not be lawful for any negro or slave to be off the premises of his or her master, owner or employer after 9 p.m. without a written permit from that master, owner or employer.

The ordinance further stipulated that it was the duty of the city marshal to commit to jail any offending free negro or slave. It also authorized white persons to apprehend an offending free negro or slave and to deliver such violator into the custody of the marshal.

Punishment of violators was severe. A guilty free negro or slave was required to receive not less than ten nor more than 39 lashes, "and shall not be discharged from custody until the payment, by the master, owner or employer ... of a fee of two dollars ... together with all costs." However, it was possible to procure remission of the punishment upon the payment of five dollars and costs.

Even more restrictive was the provision, "That each and every negro or slave caught playing cards or any gambling game within the limits of the City of Indianola, shall be punished by the City Marshal by the infliction of thirty nine lashes, and the Marshal be entitled to a fee of one dollar for each negro or slave so punished under the provisions of this section, to be collected of the owner, master or employer of such negro or slave."

The new ordinance gave the aldermen authority to, at any time, appoint a patrol of five persons from among the citizens, "Who may be required by the City Marshal, under a penalty of one dollar for each and every refusal to turn out, not oftener than once a week, to assist him in patrolling said city and carrying out the provisions of this ordinance, which patrol shall be on duty one month, when the Board shall appoint another patrol for the second month, and so on . . .." The marshal was named as ex officio captain of the patrol. It was his duty to call out the patrol whenever he deemed it necessary to preserve peace.[18]

A fourth ordinance was enacted at about the same time, but it was signed by Thomas Rooke, mayor pro tem, acting in the absence of Mayor Ashworth. Its purpose was to regulate vessels and seamen coming into Powder Horn Bayou, and to provide for raising a special fund for the improvement of the bayou as a harbor for small boats.[19]

On its left bank, the confluence of Powder Horn Bayou with Matagorda Bay was at the corner of Bowie and Water Streets. On its right bank, the confluence was at the intersection of Carancahua and Water. Its situation in the heart of the commercial district of Indianola provided a convenient and protected harbor for the smaller vessels of the bay. They included fishing, shrimping and oystering boats, as well as the sailing ships in freight and passenger service between Indianola and Matagorda Bay ports, and shallow draught boats which used the inland passageways through Espiritu Santo, San Antonio, Aransas, Copano and Corpus Christi Bays, and the Laguna Madre. Those inland passageways, shielded from the Gulf of Mexico by the line of low, sandy islands, were to play a significant role in the movement of freight during the War Between the States when Federal gunboats patrolled the open sea.

The successful use of the inland passages was a factor in creating the dream that later developed into the reality of the Texas Intracoastal Canal. Had Indianola survived the two great hurricanes, Powder Horn Lake would doubtless have been dredged and opened as a harbor for deep sea vessels in much the same way that Corpus Christi developed her excellent port facilities in an area shielded from the buffeting of waves in her bay.

In a burst of pride, the *Courier-Bulletin* exulted in its edition of October 29, 1859, "The name of our city is spreading its popularity. We notice that a new steamboat, lately finished for the New Orleans and Red River trade, has received the name of *Indianola*. There is now a steamship, a steamboat, a brig and a schooner bearing the name. There are four post offices of the name in the United States — besides this place, one in Illinois, one in Iowa and another in Kansas. . . ."[20]

The same spirit of pride was evident in the statement that, "Our city has grown to such importance that newcomers have difficulty in finding localities, and draymen and others can no longer be directed as formerly: — 'next door to Mr. A,' or 'the old B- house,' or 'just this side of the Court House,' or 'the new house opposite the old F- storehouse brought down by C-.' It is time now that some better method should be adopted. We suggest to the city authorities that it would be a great convenience if they would cause the names of the streets to be put up at each corner."[21] The newspaper further observed, "The Gazette says that the walls of the State Capitol are defaced by unseemly hieroglyphics and cautions the ladies not to scrutinise [sic] them. Our Court House is in the same fix and our County Clerk don't [sic] like it, either, as we judge from an advertisement over his signature offering a reward for the dirty scribbler. We hope he will be caught and punished severely."[22]

In another comment on the capital city, Indianolans read with amused interest that, "The Austin Gazette says that a lively time is anticipated in that city this winter. Among other extensive preparations that are being made for the 'comfort and accommodation' of the throng of members, floor and lobby, of the Legislature and distinguished visitors expected, we notice that two fine saloons are shortly to be opened in that city. They are both located NEAR THE CAPITOL."[23]

Quarreling between Indianola and Lavaca reached white heat when the latter imposed a quarantine against their neighboring community. In its issue of October 22, 1859, the *Courier-Bulletin* had carried two items on suspected cases of yellow fever. The first referred to the city up the bay. "A man died on the wharf at Lavaca one day this week," said the paper, "and the report went out that his death was from yellow fever, but it was found on investigation to be from want and intemperance."

Of Indianola the paper said, "The sch'r *Mary H. Banks*, the arrival of which from Galveston has been previously reported, after discharging her cargo went off into the stream and lay at anchor. One of the crew died on Sunday morning last, it is said of yellow fever, which was probably true. The man was coffined and brought on shore and immediately buried. Another case of sickness was reported on the same vessel, but she sailed on Monday without delaying to prove its nature. There was but little communication with this vessel while in port, and it was not thought that her isolated position was dangerous."

The following week, the newspaper reported, under the heading "Yellow Fever," that, "Among the passengers by the steamship *Chas. Morgan*, which arrived here on Wednesday of last week [October 19], were Richard Monaghan and his wife, and J. L. Gray. The former had come from New York to New Orleans by sea, and remained there seven days before embarking for this place via Galveston. They arrived here sick, though a physician was not sent for until Sunday last, when their disease was pronounced yellow fever. Monaghan died on Tuesday, and his wife the following day. The husband was a son of Owen Monaghan of New York City, and the maiden name of his wife was Cecilia Hagan. They leave two small children, one an infant.

"Mr. Gray was returning from Washington City to his home in Refugio County. He was unwell when he arrived, but was not taken down for a day or two after. He died Thursday night last of yellow fever. These parties were attended by experienced and skillful physicians, but whose best efforts proved unsuccessful.

"The disease was confined to these parties and we can still say with truth that, with the exception of these imported cases, there has not been a case of yellow fever here this season. The advanced state of the season, and the really cold weather we have experienced, enables us to state with confidence that our city is now beyond danger. The runaways we think can now come back with feelings of perfect safety — if there is any virtue in frost. Our city is perfectly healthy, and the Doctors are enjoying an 'elegant leisure.' ''

Whether Port Lavaca's quarantine was based on hysteria or had commercial implications is unknown. Perhaps both were involved. It is apparent that Indianola regarded the second to be the motive. The *Courier-Bulletin's* scathing editorial, "The Lavaca Quarantine," said, "It was well known to us that a portion of the people of Lavaca were so infatuated as to be blindly desperate, and that others were so boldly unprincipled that they would do many things devoid of sense, and regardless of consequences, in their eagerness to gratify covetous passions and selfish designs. We knew that they had done many foolish things and were capable of doing others that would not square by the rule of honesty — but, we were not prepared to believe that a controlling number existed there to put in force so silly and disgusting, so disgraceful and contemptible a proceeding as is revealed by the operation of the halfway quarantine they have pretended to establish."

The newspaper complained that, "The unfair purpose is so clearly manifest, and the proceeding is so shamelessly flouted that we are balked for terms by which to characterize the low meanness and the high impudence exhibited. They pretend to have established a quarantine against all infected ports, and this is its operation. Eagerly catching up a rumor that there was yellow fever in Indianola, which they ought to have known was false because of the hourly means of establishing the truth, they declare it an infected port and the communication by land shall be stopped — but, they do not stop it. While the daily stage is required to disgorge its passengers at the Buzzard Roost outside of town, the driver is permitted to enter and mingle indiscriminately with the people. While persons living in or passing through Indianola were not allowed to enter the sacred precincts of Lavaca, lightermen were permitted to go on board and receive freight from steamers just arrived at our wharves fresh from infected ports, and then go to Lavaca and discharge their freights without molestation. But, although they might go on board the steamers direct from Galveston, they were instructed not to come up into town, or else they should not return."

Editor Yancey then acidly observed, "Besides this, after the ridiculous farce had been in operation several days, a committee was appointed to come down and ascertain whether there was yellow fever here or not — as though a Committee might not convey the disease as well as anybody else. That Committee was told by everybody of whom inquiry was made that there was no yellow fever here, but a citizen of Lavaca told the Committee that a man had died here the night before (Tuesday) — which was positively untrue — and went back to report on that evidence that there was yellow fever here. A day or two after, a hack driver was given a permit, signed by the Health Officer, to come here and return to Lavaca — the quarantine still in operation — as though the disease was not communicable through hack drivers . . .

"Not a case of yellow fever has occurred here this season, and these things go to prove that they did not believe we had the disease. The sole purpose was to create the impression in order that Lavaca might reap advantages by turning the downward bound produce into that place. This was accomplished in several instances . . . "

Then he called on the prudent residents of Lavaca to disassociate themselves from what he regarded as a sham and an outrage. "In rebuke of former trickery in the same quarter, we have always made a distinction between the good and bad, but as this last act was performed in a corporate capacity, the honest and fair-dealing will have to relieve themselves of the odium which now attaches to the whole.

"It is further known that at the fork of the roads a few miles out of Lavaca, a yellow flag is hoisted upon a pole and a man is stationed there to point and shrug ominously and equivocate concerning yellow fever at Indianola, and thus frighten the teamsters into Lavaca. A gentleman here tells us that he has reliable information of this fact, and it was confirmed in our presence by a teamster. We have also seen letters from interior towns enquiring into the truth of the various rumors that have been maliciously set afloat.

"Some of our people proposed to 'fight the devil with fire' and, by retaliation, cut them off from all communication with the shipping in our port. This could have been easily done, but we are glad such counsel did not prevail. One wrong never justifies, though it palliates, another."[24]

Followup comment in the next edition stated, "We understand that our exposure of the trickery resorted to by some of the people of Lavaca has excited their ire to a high pitch. Well, 'let the galled jades wince.' We have not charged the people there as a body with the responsibility of the partial quarantine though, until they repudiate it, they might be held so. But we said, and do know, that the operation of the quarantine was a very silly or a very mean piece of business. We stated facts for proof, without caring who was to blame for their existence, nor how much they might be angered by the exposure."

In a separate piece, Editor Yancey said, "We have been told that we were mistaken about the Lavaca quarantine being in operation against Indianola at the time the hack driver came down with the pass. It may be, but if the 'trick' was not then in operation, what was the use for a permit? It is said that the quarantine, which commenced on Sunday of last week was taken off, or 'lifted,' so far as Indianola was concerned on the Wednesday or Thursday following. If true

       'Since so soon the thing was done for,
       The wonder is what 'twas begun for,'

unless there was an OBJECT to be accomplished, and such object as we explained last week.

"P. S. We learn that the portcullis has again been dropped, in consequence of frightful reports about the imported cases we have elsewhere alluded to, but the thing still operates lamely. A party from here in search of a runaway sailor was allowed to enter without *interruption*. The 'yaller flag' still floats proudly to the breeze. *Vive la bagatelle!*"[25]

As further evidence of the "plot" by Port Lavaca, Editor Yancey published an "Extract from a letter written by a reliable gentleman in Mission Valley to a friend in this place, under date of October 24th: 'The Lavaca people have told all the teamsters that seven or eight have died of yellow fever at Indianola and that if they cross the bridge, they shall not return.[26] I met some who had, in this way, been forced to take freight at almost nothing.' "

And, in another piece, Yancey delightedly exclaimed, "RETURNED - Our friend Casimir Villeneuve, Consul of Napoleon at the port of Indianola, and proprietor of the best hotel in Texas, returned yesterday morning from his trip to 'La Belle France,' bringing evidence of having spent a 'glorious time'in his hearty and satisfied appearance and jolly good humor. Had we not retained as hostages *Madame et fils*, we fear we should not so soon have had the gratification of chronicling his safe return. Of course, he has brought some nice things for the patrons of his place of *grande chere et beau feu*; but we hope *non le chasse-cousin*. Now, *tuer le diable par la queue*."

Indian depredations, a recurring problem of settlers from the earliest days, continued to plague Western Texas, despite the military outposts supplied through Indianola. As far back as 1850, General David E. Twiggs, Commander of the Department of the West, had expressed fears of serious difficulties between Indians and the citizens of Texas. He was then reported to favor calling into service a regiment of volunteers to stop raids.

On February 14, 1852, the *Texian Advocate*, in an editorial, had asked, "What is to be done with the Indians of Texas? Six years have passed since the United States assumed control of the Indians in Texas . . . ,"and the paper complained that the whole policy of the government with respect to them was totally unsuited to the conditions and circumstances of the times. The *Advocate* proposed the establishment of reservations to which the Indians "would be transferred, and on which they would be taught agriculture and the mechanical arts . . . "

The Indians grew increasingly bold as they struggled to ward off encroachment by the white man on their traditional hunting grounds. Except for the Fredericksburg area, where settlers enjoyed better than average relations with the tribes, thefts and murders were commonplace. Ambush was frequent in much of the Hill Country and, in 1855, the San Antonio *Ledger* had mentioned cases of raids not more than 15 miles from the city. A mass meeting was held in San Antonio on October 5, 1859, to consider protection of the frontier from Indian attacks. The assembled citizens lodged a strong protest against the "General Government's" policy of issuing firearms and ammunition to tribes through the agents.[27]

Indianola had continuing interest in the enlargement of the military force guarding Western Texas from attacks by Indians, as well as from raids across the Rio Grande from Mexico. Her newspapers dutifully recorded all reported instances of Indian and border outrages. Along with citizens of the interior of Western Texas, who were directly exposed to the ever present threat of attack, Indianolans plied Texas' representatives and senators in the national government with letters urging a tough and positive stand on the dual problem.

During the period from 1855 to 1861, Robert E. Lee was assigned to frontier duty in Texas. Lee was well known in Indianola, having visited it on official business, as well as traveling through the port. He observed his 50th birthday on January 19, 1857, while at Fort Brown in Brownsville, "and from there he went to San Antonio on February 6, only to be ordered to a new [military] court at Indianola. Before the time arrived for that tribunal to start, he was ordered back to Fort Brown once more. Thence he went overland to Indianola, arriving by March 20 . . . The court at Indianola adjourned within 10 days, and Lee started back to Camp Cooper by way of San Antonio and Fort Mason."[28]

Returning to Washington in 1859 as administrator of the estate of his late father-in-law, Lee commanded the company that captured the abolitionist John Brown at Harper's Ferry. He returned to Texas in 1860 via New Orleans, from which city he departed by steamer for Indianola on February 15. Reaching Indianola four days later, he traveled on to San Antonio, where he assumed command of the 8th Military District.[29] It was Lee who brought to a halt the so-called "Cortinas War" on the lower Rio Grande.

After having endured nine years of raids, the pressure of influential men was finally brought to bear on Washington. Juan Cortinas' continued interference with commercial activities was financially painful to border merchants and to shipping interests, among them Harris & Morgan. The fact that Fort Brown had been abandoned by United States forces enabled Cortinas to indulge in his reign of terror without restraint. Demands were made by Texans that a military presence be returned to the fort and all necessary means taken to restore order.

On October 25, 1859, a telegram was sent from Washington to I. C. Harris, president of the Southern Steamship Company, at New Orleans. "Your dispatch to the Secretary of War is received. Commander of Department of Texas has been directed to regarrison Fort Brown immediately by two companies of artillery from Fort Clark."[30] The show of force was only partially successful. Control of the situation was finally achieved by Lieutenant Colonel Robert E. Lee, who departed San Antonio on March 15, 1860, en route to Ringgold Barracks and Fort Brown. His orders were to secure an agreement from the Mexican government that it would stop Cortinas' forays into Texas. If such agreement could not be obtained, he had instructions to cross the Rio Grande and pursue Cortinas until captured.

Lee's diplomacy prevailed and forestalled what could have developed into a full-blown international incident. No invasion of

Mexico was necessary, if, indeed, it was ever really seriously contemplated, and Cortinas was obliged to cease his nefarious activities on the American side of the Rio Bravo del Norte. Indianolans were jubilant, and supposed that the success of this show of force would persuade the War Department to recognize the advantages of substantially increasing the number of men assigned to the 8th Military District, whose posts would be supplied through the Government Depot at the port.

On the very day that Lee left San Antonio en route to the Rio Grande, a pall of sorrow spread over Indianola at the news of the death of Mrs. Angelina Belle Eberly. The reported cause of her death on March 15 was "oscillation of the heart, following an illness of 19 days." There was an outpouring of grief at the loss, in her 63rd year, of this, the most distinguished woman in the history of Indianola.

Mrs. Eberly's survivor and heir to her substantial estate was a 10-year-old grandson, Peyton Bell Lytle. Young Peyton had been born to Mrs. Eberly's daughter Margaret Eveline, who was married on October 28, 1848, to J. T. Lytle of Port Lavaca. The romance had blossomed during the time Mrs. Eberly had Edward Clegg's tavern there under lease. Margaret Eveline died at age 20, on October 12, 1850. The young father died three and a half years later, leaving Peyton in Mrs. Eberly's care.

The court appointed Fletcher S. Stockdale as the child's guardian and D. E. Crosland as administrator of Mrs. Eberly's estate.[31] Peyton Lytle died in Philadelphia, and was buried next to his grandmother at Indianola on February 15, 1873.

XIII.

War Clouds on the Horizon

The directors of the Indianola Railroad Company, meeting in that city on April 7, 1860, discussed the financing of construction of the line. The president, Henry Runge, was given authority by the board to borrow money and to issue and negotiate bonds, not to exceed $200,000. This was for the purpose of "raising money and procuring iron, cars, locomotives and all other materials and things necessary for the construction of said Indianola Railroad, and for its complete equipment after construction . . . "[1]

In addition to Runge, the directors were William H. Woodward, John E. Garey, H. J. Huck, John H. Dale and David C. Proctor, the last being secretary. The necessary capital would have to be raised in the East or, failing that, in Europe. Company officials recognized that the money problems of the San Antonio and Mexican Gulf, building out of Lavaca toward Victoria and, hopefully, to San Antonio, were based on the fact that its directors had depended on procuring financing in Texas. However, capital was in short supply in the state. Land was plentiful and held in great acreages by individuals who might have been called "land poor." Conversion of land to ready cash was difficult, except at disastrously low figures. True capitalists were almost non-existent in Texas.

View of Indianola from the *Texana*, September 1860. By 1860, Brown's Addition was generally referred to as Indianola; however, many people called the settlement Powder Horn. The original town of Indianola, three miles up the bay at Indian Point, was becoming known as Old Town. The building with cupola at the right is the new concrete courthouse. Powder Horn Lake stretches through the marsh land almost to the horizon. From it, Stevens Bayou snakes its way to the rear of the developing town. (*Lithograph by Helmuth Holtz. Courtesy Library of Congress.*)

Previously projected rail lines from Matagorda Bay failed to develop because most had tried to raise their funds in the state. The Buffalo Bayou, Brazos and Colorado Railway Company, which had already constructed 80 miles of track from Harrisburg to Alleyton near the east bank of the Colorado River opposite Columbus, had obtained financing through investors in Massachusetts.[2] The Indianolans intended to profit from the lessons learned.

While Runge and associates were deeply involved in planning for the building of the railroad, Episcopal Bishop Alexander Gregg, newly arrived in Texas from South Carolina, reached Indianola on April 16. There, and at Lavaca the following day, he preached and made a careful survey of the condition of the yellow fever-withered churches of the communities. Then he moved on to Victoria where he "preached at night . . . Rev. Mr. Quinby reading service." In his report to the annual convention at Austin in 1861, Bishop Gregg stated, in speaking of Victoria, "The time is not far distant when this growing town will have its parish to supply the want now painfully felt.

"Friday, 20th, at Goliad held service in the hall of the Methodist institute. Rev. Mr. Quinby read and I preached to a large congregation. This was the first Episcopal service ever held in the town.

"Sunday, 22nd, at Clinton . . . "

But, the Episcopal church was not the only entity in the area suffering from weakness. In February 1860, the continued emptiness of the Calhoun County purse was manifested by James Ranahan's vigorous protest that he had never received payment on the three warrants issued to him for plastering work on the courthouse. Backed into a corner, and unable to procrastinate further, the court ordered the treasurer to retain all funds received and pay them to Ranahan until the full amount of warrants 71, 72 and 82 was liquidated.[3]

The ever-readiness of that court to increase tax rates or add new levies was again displayed by action taken on May 21 when a special tax of 12½¢ on each $100 valuation was approved for the purpose of building a new jail in Indianola. The tax was to be in effect for one year and its revenue was deposited in a special fund to be used solely for jail construction.[4]

A contract was entered into between the court and J. Coutret of Indianola for construction of a concrete underground rainwater storage cistern for use of courthouse and jail personnel. It was to replace the cypress aboveground cistern which had served since the courthouse was completed, but whose size was inadequate. The contract provided that Coutret would build the cistern with a capacity of 6,000 to 7,000 gallons, that the walls would be 16 inches thick and that the builder would obligate himself to guarantee it to be sound and in good order to hold water for a period of 12 months from date of inspection and acceptance. Payment on delivery was set at three cents per gallon "for each and every gallon the same may contain by measurement." It was completed, inspected, measured and approved on August 20, with payment to Coutret authorized for 8,000 gallons, a total of $240.[5] The old wooden cistern was sold at public auction to James H. Duncan for $7.50.

The matter of bilingual education became a factor in the public schools of the county, requiring action by the commissioners. As a consequence of the large German population composed of families that had emigrated to Texas and, since 1845, had gone no further than Indianola to make their homes, instruction was given in both German and English. However, in order to comply with Legislative action, public school teachers were now required to certify on oath "that the English language is principally taught in their schools." Certification to that effect had become mandatory in order for teachers to receive their wages from the school fund. The question of bilingual education also had to be faced in that great part of the Hill Country where German settlements predominated. At Indianola, James A. Duggan, F. C. Goepfert, J. M. Bickford and Mrs. C. A. Ring all filed duly executed oaths in August.[6]

The county was in a growing state of unrest over national political problems. It was generally thought that the points of conflict could be settled amicably within a reasonable time, if cool heads were to prevail in national and state governments. One of the festering sores was the fact that among the throngs of passengers coming off ships docking at Indianola's wharves were scattered agitators from the North headed into the state. A large percentage of the populace considered them abolitionists come to create discord. In August, one of these was forcibly put on board an outbound vessel, the charge against him being suspicion of arson in the port.[7] The city's provision for a patrol to insure the safety of the town was called into operation, though some referred to it as a "vigilance committee."

As the national election, set for November 6, 1860, drew near, passions increased. The pronouncements of threats, and inflammatory statements made by over-zealous orators, fanned the flames of sectionalism. That distressed a minority whose vision enabled them to see that a breakup of the Union would inevitably be followed by fratricidal war, the consequences of which would be devastating to both sides. Despite calls for secession, it is doubtful that Indianolans actually supposed a division would come. They appeared to be confident that Southern sabre-rattling would cause the "other side" to back away from a no-return showdown. A similar line of "reasoning"seemed to be behind Northern belligerence. Soon it would be too late for anyone to back down.

At Indianola during the early fall of 1860, it was business as usual, with plans being made for the apparent bright future of the port. The *Courier-Bulletin* on November 3 said, "Business continues to improve from week to week as the season advances. Our streets are constantly thronged with wagons and teams, and all classes of business men, mechanics and laborers are constantly and actively employed. Many people seem to regard it as an extraordinary thing that we should go on prospering, notwithstanding the partial failure of the crops, forgetting that immigration has been steadily on the increase and new resources are being developed. The varied products of Western Texas make it independent of any particular crop, and in seasons when there is a full realization of the hopes in regard to each, the surplus, if properly husbanded, would provide for years of disaster. The development of the resources of Western Texas has not yet been fairly started and when our railroads, now commenced, are extended through the interior, its unbounded wealth of production will be poured into our laps!" Editor Yancey's rosy view seemed to be based on sound reasoning. Local shipbuilding continued at a brisk pace, and more steamers to serve the port were being added. McBride's shipyard on Powder Horn Bayou had just completed the steamer *A. B.* for the Texana trade and was currently overhauling the *Lizzie Lake*, which plied the Guadalupe River and the bay between Victoria and Indianola.

The newspaper carried a description of the *William G. Hewes*, which was launched at Wilmington, Delaware, on October 15. It had been built for Charles Morgan to be placed in the Gulf trade. "The new steamship is one of the largest iron ships ever built in the country," Yancey exulted, "her length being 250 feet, breadth of beam 36 and depth of hold 20. For strength and beauty of form, she cannot be surpassed. Her engine is to be a marine beam. She will also have a steel boiler, which is the only one of any size ever built in this country. Her saloons are to be of hardwood, finished and fitted up in the most gorgeous style." The vessel was named in honor of the president of the New Orleans, Opelousas and Great Western Railroad and would be commanded by James Lawless, former captain of the *Orizaba*.[8]

Good news for the port that overshadowed the political headaches was revealed by the November 3 edition in an article entitled "More Steamers for Indianola." It said, "We learn that it has been determined by the managers of the Southern Steamship Company to put an additional number of steamers in the line between New Orleans and Indianola direct, and the arrangement will be commenced by the middle of this month. This . . . is made to accommodate the increased trade and to relieve the three heavy outside steamers, the *Charles Morgan, Texas,* and *Mexico* . . ."[9]

"These five steamers [Note: the three named plus the *Matagorda* and the *Orizaba*] will be more punctual in their arrival and delivery of the mails. The steamers *Austin* and *Arizona* will continue to run . . . between New Orleans and Brazos Santiago, by way of Indianola going and returning . . . The additional steamers to be added are the *Atlantic* and *Suwanee* . . . This arrangement gives us nine steamers of the regular line, independent of the *Fashion*, not employed by the company, in our trade, and the schedules will give us at this port seven arrivals per week."

As reports of the national vote in the November 6 election trickled in to Indianola, it became evident that the Republican nominee, Abraham Lincoln, though receiving a majority of the electoral vote (180) was, nevertheless, to be a minority president, without control of the Congress. He had 40% of the popular vote, Douglas 29%, Breckenridge 18% and

Bell 13%. The worst fears had been realized. A surge of Old Texian patriotism swept the state and Lone Star flags were raised on every hand. There came widespread demands that Texas secede from the Union and resume her former status as an independent republic. The fever of excitement threw caution aside as the evils of "Black Republicanism" under Lincoln were discussed. As editor James Russell Lowell had written in the *Atlantic Monthly* prior to November 6, "We believe this election is a turning-point in our history," it was that, indeed. Talk of secession became rampant throughout the South and there was a swelling tide of resentment against the North that only a miracle could stem. No such miracle was forthcoming.

Commercial relations with New York gave Indianolans an insight on the views of business leaders there. Their own patron, Charles Morgan, privately deplored the possible aftermath of a Lincoln victory. In this concern, he was not alone. The attitude was not based on personal political affiliations, but resulted from conviction that the pre-election talk of Southern secession was not an idle threat. Morgan and his associates foresaw that, if secession did become a fact, there would be widespread and serious dislocation of business, with consequent financial loss to them.[10] As he feared, Morgan did suffer loss at the hands of Federals and Confederates alike.

After the fact of Lincoln's election was certain, Indianolans united in resolve to resist domination by "Black Republicanism." On November 21, a mass meeting was held. Typical of gatherings throughout Texas and the other Southern states, it whipped sentiment to white heat. The meeting was reported in the press under the headlines "GRAND MASS MEETING!!! — The Sovereigns in Council! — The Voice of Calhoun!! The Lone Star Flag again Unfurled!!! The People Rally Around it without Distinction of Party!"[11] Rated as the largest and most enthusiastic public meeting ever held in Calhoun County, its stated purpose was to afford a means of expression as to the course of action the citizens believed should be taken by the state "in view of the recent decisive expression of a determination on the part of the North to wield the powers of the Federal government for the subversion of Southern institutions by the overwhelming majority it has given in favor of the abolition candidate for the Presidency."

Just to gather at the courthouse for public discussion was not enough. There had to be a parade, and a night procession was much preferred because it provided the opportunity for display of "transparencies," whose slogans painted on glass were illuminated by candles or kerosene lamps. Carried high on poles, they were clearly visible and easily read by the sidewalk throng.

Leading the parade was a Lone Star flag which had been made by the ladies of Indianola and presented for the occasion. It was "saluted by enthusiastic greetings of applause." Next came the band, which rendered stirring martial music, and then the transparencies, "which imparted the feelings and sentiments which prevail in our community." The *Courier-Bulletin* listed the 28 transparencies, their wording giving a clue

to the emotions of Indianolans at that time. They were: "The Time has
Come! — State Rights — [a device of the] Lone Star — Room for 15 —
The Issue is Upon Us — Voice of the People — Calhoun County is Ready
— Union Only with Honor — Who is not for us is Against us — All
Welcome to our Ranks — The First 300 — The 2nd of March —
Revolutions Never Go Backwards — Millions in Number, One in Sen-
timent — Cotton is King — Crocketts and Bowies not all Dead — None
but Slaves Submit — No Room in Abe's Bosom for US — Texas is
Sovereign — The Alamo — The North has Broken the Symbols of Union
— Goliad and Gonzales, 1835 — Storming of Bexar — 21st of April,
1836 — No Submission — True to Ourselves — We are with South
Carolina — and the last, a device with the Lone Star in the center
surrounded by 14 other stars."

The seriousness of the demonstrators was shown by the amount of
diligent effort that went into the preparation of the transparencies. The
effect was spectacular and patriotically inspiring to participants and
onlookers alike. D. S. Woodward was parade marshal. He was assisted
in its management by A. H. Phillips, Jr., and W. H. Woodward. The
Lone Star flag at the head of the procession was borne by Sam McBride.

The crowd filled the courtroom and overflowed onto the grounds. So
popular was the cause that there was jockeying for positions of
leadership. Judge J. J. Holt was elected to chair the meeting and five
were named vice-presidents! They were Captain John R. Baker, J. R.
Fretwell, D. E. Crosland, Judge H. W. Hawes and A. H. Phillips, Jr. As a
compromise, three secretaries were selected — Colonel John B. Burke,
B. A. Whitney and *Courier-Bulletin* editor Wm. T. Yancey.

Upon taking the chair, President Holt made a "forcible speech," in
which he outlined the sequence of events that had prompted the
gathering, and emphasized the necessity for decisive action. His comments were greeted with prolonged applause, after which the band
played the "Marseillaise," the French national anthem which had
become a revolutionary symbol. Its rendition and the wild enthusiasm
that followed indicated the mood in Indianola on November 21, 1860.

A committee consisting of F. S. Stockdale, C. M. Coen, J. D.
Braman, J. S. Hubbard and H. W. Sessions was appointed by Holt to
draft and present resolutions that would express the sense of the meeting.
There can be little doubt but that the membership of the committee was
pre-arranged and that a tentative draft had been prepared prior to the
event. Nevertheless, the group dutifully retired to deliberate. When
George P. Finlay had finished further exciting the passions of the crowd
with a fiery speech, the committee returned to the courtroom and
presented their collective brainchild. The resolutions were so perfectly
expressive of the attitudes of the hour, that only their quotation ver-
batim can show the trend of thought typical of the state of Texas at the
time. Fletcher S. Stockdale, as committee chairman, made the presentation, to the rapt attention of the audience.

"Believing that the non-slaveholding States have, in casting their
votes for electors pledged to the election of Abraham Lincoln to the

Presidency, considerately and definitively declared their purpose to use the Federal Government for the destruction of the institution of African Slavery in the South, and the subversion of the rights and sovereignty of Texas, in the Confederacy; the Citizens of Calhoun County, without distinction of party in Mass Meeting assembled, declare:

"1st. That Texas, with a proper consideration for her honor, equality and sovereignty and the rights of her citizens, ought not to submit to the rule of a Black Republican administration; and that she cannot do so without sacrificing the glorious renown she has won in her past history.

"2nd. That the Chief Executive and all other State officers should facilitate the sovereignty of Texas in the expression, in regular form, of its judgment upon the grave question presented by the present state of affairs, through a convention of the people of the State: to which end his Excellency the Governor is hereby requested to convene the legislature at as early a day as practicable; and that our representatives in both branches of the legislature are instructed to support an early call for such convention.

"3d. That, until there is some action deemed authoritative upon the question, we request the Federal officials in the Revenue, Post Office and other departments to retain their offices; to be resigned, however, instantly when State action shall have been taken.

"4th. Asserting the right of Texas, upon her own sovereign judgment, to resume, peaceably, the powers she has delegated to the Federal Government when they have been or are about to be used to her injury, we look for no unconstitutional attempt at coercion by Federal power; but, being determined to resist force by force, if our State commands, we recommend the organization and equipment of one or more companies of Minute Men in each of the towns of this County.

"5th. That the President and Secretary forward a copy of these proceedings to the Governor and have the same published in the public journals.

F. S. STOCKDALE   J. D. BRAMAN

C. M. COEN   J. S. HUBBARD

H. W. SESSIONS."

Colonel Burke thought the wording of the second section was too mild and moved to amend it by inserting the words "and required" after the word "requested," so that it would read, "The Governor is hereby requested and required to convene the Legislature . . ." After debate between Colonel Burke and William Tate in favor, and F. S. Stockdale against the amendment, a vote was taken and the amendment lost.

On the motion of W. H. Woodward, the resolutions were adopted by acclamation. Stockdale, Tate and Phillips then responded to calls made upon them and "sustained their reputation as able and eloquent declaimers." All the speakers were emphatic in calling for resistance "at all hazards and to the last extremity to Black Republican domination, and were greeted by hearty, earnest and enthusiastic rounds of applause . . ." Approval was given to the printing of 500 copies of the proceedings, and the mailing of one copy to each county in Texas.

In closing, George Finlay read to the meeting "an article from Lincoln's Chicago organ, edited by John Wentworth, in which the purposes of the successful fanatics with regard to negro slavery were declared and the Southern people reviled, their courage sneered at, and dared to attempt resistance. The article excited no other feeling than contempt." Upon that note, the convocation adjourned.

Regarding the general election on November 6, it was stated in the news, "We are informed that not a single Mexican vote was offered at either poll in this precinct [Indianola and Old Town] at the late election, though there were quite a number of cartmen in the city."[12] A further comment was, "The Ranchero says that in seven precincts of Nueces County no polls were opened at the recent elections, and that owing to the late judicial election difficulties, not a single citizen of Mexican origin would even offer to vote."[13] These two incidents, among many, point to the general policy of intimidation, and consequent disfranchisement of native Texans of Mexican descent, that was conducted with little fanfare and no secrecy. The disregard of the rights of many loyal Texas-Mexicans who had, or whose fathers had, actively supported the cause of the Texas Revolution, was claimed to have been a factor in the inception of the so-called "Cortinas War."

The attention being paid to political bombast on both sides of the national controversy, and the talk of secession, influenced the money markets and the flow of commerce. The fears of Morgan and other business leaders in the North were beginning to be realized. There was growing uncertainty in the negotiating of foreign exchange, and the movement of cotton was thereby partially paralyzed.

The unsettled condition of the Northern money markets was having its harmful effects on the efforts of the officers of the Indianola Railroad Company to secure financing. Sufficient money had been acquired through the sale of stock to local investors to permit the grading of the roadbed and the purchase of some ties. Far more than Indianola was capable of supplying was needed for the purchase of rails for a connection with the SA&MG at Clark Station, as well as for rolling stock and buildings. As negotiations went forward slowly in New York in the late summer of 1860, it had appeared that there was good reason to believe that success would be achieved. Then, they were suddenly chilled by the prospect of election of Lincoln, and apprehension of financial embarrassment. Confirmation of Lincoln's election resulted in the New York commercial house withdrawing from the consultations. Secession had become so confidently expected that there was reluctance to invest in a state which might soon throw off the sovereignty of the United States government.[14]

Following this abrupt and disappointing turn of events, the railroad directors turned their attention to European financing, with the aim of obtaining sufficient funds to build the road to Austin. The goal of the BBB&C, which had reached Alleyton, was to continue on the east side of the Colorado River to Austin. That event would deprive Indianola of the freight and passenger traffic advantage the port enjoyed in the river valley. It was imperative that the Indianola railroad head off the BBB&C.

Henry Runge, president of the company, went from New York to Germany. His prospectus was received favorably, but time was required for a representative of the syndicate to make an on-scene appraisal of the plan and its likelihood of producing revenue sufficient to justify the investment. Upon the return of Runge and his family to Indianola, he expressed confidence that success would be achieved, if the political situation would calm. However, because it steadily deteriorated, and the secession of Texas became a fact by virtue of the vote of the people on February 23, 1861, the effort failed. The Indianola Railroad would not be completed for another decade.

The national turmoil had no effect on the success of the Gulf Coast Fair in Victoria on November 14, 15 and 16, 1860. Two Indianolans carried off premiums with their fine horses. Dan Sullivan's splendid mare "Kate Hayes" took first place for fast trotting, and Adam Murdock's native half-breed racer "Honest John" won first place as the best saddle gelding exhibited.[15] Indianola's two shipyards continued their booming business in construction of new and repair of older vessels. The steamer *Echo* was in McCoppin's yard for overhaul at the first of December. The new Indianola-built steamer *A.B.*, having passed trial runs, had been placed in regular passenger and freight service from Indianola to Texana, via Lavaca. The *Lizzie Lake*, after coming out of dry dock, was again in operation between Indianola, Kemper City and Victoria via the Guadalupe River. After repairs, the *Troy* had resumed her runs to Caney Creek.[16]

It is doubtful that, if they had been able to foresee the strangulation of their ports' commerce by blockade imposed and enforced by Federal gunboats, so many citizens of Indianola and Lavaca would have taken their strong pro-secession stand. The course of the future was hidden, as always, so they joined hundreds of thousands of other Southerners in applying insistent pressure on state government leaders who held back from the abyss. Following the November 21 mass meeting, 132 Calhoun County businessmen put their names to a petition "To his Excellency, Sam Houston, Governor of the State of Texas." It read, "The undersigned, citizens of Calhoun County, Texas, in view of the election of Abraham Lincoln to the Presidency of the United States, as the representative embodiment of the Black Republican principles, do earnestly request your Excellency to convene the Legislature of the State at as early a day as possible to consult and act upon the present condition of the country. (Signed)[17]

D. S. Woodward	Wm. A. Peirce	David Lewis
F. S. Stockdale	F. A. Knox	J. S. Coates
W. Longnecker	John Rogers	Jas. Ranahan
William Tate	Z. K. Fulton	J. S. Hubbard

C. Villeneuve
H. J. Knopp
L. Preisig
J. Johnson
John H. Dale
T. S. Miller
R. Judur
John Swartz
E. Baxter
Chas. Keller
Leon Rouff
D. Hoffman
G. D. Keys
J. Vanderveer
J. R. Hanna
J. M. Reuss
I. T. W. Mitchell
W. Riddle
T. D. Woodward
E. Kerr
D. E. Crosland
A. H. Phillips
Adam Murdock
W. Leonhardt
E. Muegge
Lud Sigmund
A. Buchel
C. C. Howerton
J. Hackenberg
Henry Sheppard
S. H. Sester
John Jerler
J. Maxwell
Jas. F. Madden
Charles Pop
R. Wouffie
A. Jordan
H. Sanders
C. H. Hazen
Chas. Kempel

J. G. Ohlendorff
J. R. Eason
M. Demonet
Thos. Rooke
J. A. Settle
C. Woodsworth
August Swartz
E. Huck
J. Robertson
Ed. Wood
C. M. Coen
G. W. Bethards
John Gray
R. Burke
W. A. Simon
D. W. Hatch
T. F. Chesley
T. J. Poole
L. Labe
J. J. Holt
D. C. Proctor
M. E. Davis
C. Lupp
C. Kleinecke
A. Nitsche
J. Nolan
W. H. Woodward
J. L. Allen
L. Bernard
S. Von Bramer
P. Knight
D. Roemer
A. Rahm
J. Dyron
M. Haller
R. W. Yates
W. Franke
J. Miller
H. Dahme
Henry Thiemann

S. McBride
B. Weinrich
F. B. Parker
J. H. Brown
W. M. Blair
James Ashworth
John Dooley
H. A. Runge
J. Lang
J. E. Garey
Alex. Cold
August Wagner
Sam Marx
Achilles Stapp
W. Sanderland
W. Bonefeldt
S. Strauss
Edward Clegg
J. M. Freny
G. Baer
W. P. Milby
G. P. Finlay
O. Gebler
H. J. Huck
D. M. Stapp
D. Schultz
W. T. Yancey
R. D. Martin
W. Taylor
J. Klaus
H. Newton
C. C. Mertz
P. Thurmond
W. Silbereisen
J. H. Haller
W. N. Bryant
S. D. Clark
Jac. Arto
J. D. Braman
G. Simon"

But Governor Houston was not in favor of convening the Legislature or calling a convention to consider secession. However, he said if the majority of the people of Texas favored it, he would not stand in the way. As the Galveston *Civilian* expressed it, "He will resign and let Lieut. Gov. Clark carry out the scheme, if a majority wish to go out of the Union." Clark was in sympathy with the movement.

Episcopal Bishop Alexander Gregg was back in Indianola on Sunday, November 25, for services in the Methodist church. While preaching in Indianola, the bishop baptized four children and confirmed five persons. At Saluria he baptized two children. His departure from Indianola being delayed by several days of bad weather which precluded travel, Gregg finally made his way to Lavaca and preached in the Methodist church on December 9, assisted by the Rev. Mr. Quinby who had come up from Brownsville. In Lavaca, Bishop Gregg baptized three children. "Large and attentive congregations were present at these services," the bishop reported. "In the course of another year, Lavaca and Indianola together should [again] have a settled clergyman." On the 12th, he was in Texana, where he held service at night in the Methodist church, assisted by Mr. Quinby. While in Texana, he baptized three children. "To the scattered sheep in this vicinity, it was a sincere pleasure to minister," commented the beloved clergyman.[18]

After an absence of several months in the North, where he went each summer, Professor Whitehead, "the accomplished musician and *maitre de danse*," returned to Indianola and reopened his school for the winter season. Local wags insinuated that Whitehead was one of the "fainthearted" whose affairs took them elsewhere every year during the months of the yellow fever period. Dancing was a favorite pastime of the people, "soirees and hops" being frequent at the Casimir House. In 1860, there was no discernible inclination to allow politics to dampen the pleasures of fashionable social events. In fact, the national turmoil seemed to add a spirit of zest to daily life.

Editor Yancey commented on December 1, "We understand that there was a live abolitionist in town the other day. He came in a hurry from the interior and took passage by the first steamer for a colder climate. It is rather tropical here for birds of the feather."

Even the maneuverings promoting secession took a back seat in Indianola when the Christmas season approached. The German-born residents had brought with them the tradition of the decorated and candle-lighted tree. A plentiful supply of cedars in counties not far from the coast made specimens of that tree readily available. A limited number of conifers came on ships from Boston. Tree ornaments were of two types, usually mixed on the branches. There were the homemade decorations: minute dolls, boats, birds, houses and the like, handcarved and painted during idle moments throughout the year; small, gaily painted sea shells, and festoons of the brilliant red, rock-hard seed of the laurel which abounded on Matagorda Bay shores. The seeds were drilled through and strung on heavy thread. Buttons of various kinds made fine festoons for the trees, though when the celebration was over they went back into the sewing basket. Highly valued were the exquisite and fragile glass ornaments from Germany, which were safeguarded and brought out each year as family heirlooms.

For lighting of the tree, there were the four-inch candles of bright colors, which were placed in metal holders that snapped, like a clothespin, on the branches. In the parlor, a full size bed sheet would be spread to catch the candle drippings and protect the carpet. The tree was placed in the center, almost touching the ceiling. At Indianola, Santa

Claus paid his visit after supper on Christmas Eve, accompanied by Black Peter who carried bundles of switches and bags of ashes to leave for bad boys and girls who did not deserve the gifts Santa had in his sack. Although no child ever found only switches and ashes under the tree, the thought of the possibility of that awful discovery was enough to make even the most incorrigible toe the line of good behavior in the days before Christmas.

Under the tree would be placed the toys and the once-in-a-year bags of assorted nuts. Piled around the base would be apples, oranges and bananas which were then luxury items. And, fireworks for the boys — as much a part of the Southern observance as was the tree itself.

Indianola's shops were loaded with holiday goods. The bakeries offered cakes, cookies, pies, spiced concoctions of all shapes and sizes, ornamented with tinted icing. The confectioneries stocked ball, stick and ribbon candies of every popular flavor, sugarcoated nuts, candied fruit and incomparable chocolates.

No Christmas celebration was complete without *lebkuchen*. As The Day neared, fragrant odors from household kitchens gave notice that the cookie jars would be filled to the brim, that mincemeat pies and fruit cakes were coming out of the wood range ovens. For the Christmas Day feast, there would be turtle soup, roast goose, raised pies of meat or game, broiled oysters, candied sweet potatoes, peas, asparagus and other delicacies. On the sideboard sat dishes of candied cherries, diced citron, raisins, currants, dried figs and other fruits, watermelon pickles and, when a ship from Central America or the Antilles arrived in time, ripe mangoes would be added.

Baked fresh on Christmas morning for the noonday banquet would be lemon pies with snow-white meringue toasted on top to a luscious deep tan, angel food, chocolate and rolled jelly cakes and pumpkin pies on whose slices mountains of whipped cream were heaped. Eggnog made with rich whipped cream and choice whiskey or brandy (in households of liberal outlook) was available in ample supply throughout the day, the children filching a spoonful whenever the backs of adults were turned.[19]

"Christmas is coming and soon will be here," said Editor Yancey. "We are reminded of this fact not only by the little boys with their fire-cracker nuisance and the bigger nuisance of pistol shooting by the bigger 'boys,' but [also] by the scarcity and increased price of the 'chicken fixins,' which are usually held back for that huckster's millenium. Eggs readily sell at 40 to 50 cents per dozen, and are scarce at that, while country butter and domestic fowls are about the hardest possible things to find in the market. Wild fowls are abundant in the air and on the fields and lakes, but their savory odor rarely rises from the tables of those who have no leisure for hunting them 'to the death.' " A note of yearning is detected in that sentence. Possibly Yancey included himself in the category of those who lacked leisure time for the hunt, though the wild fowl could be purchased from hunters or in the markets for little more than a pittance.

The Christmas Eve service in the several churches of Indianola always preceded the celebrations at home. Mention of the program at the Methodist Episcopal church provides a description of one such church-oriented event. "The Methodist Church was the scene of a very pleasant entertàinment on Christmas Eve. A Christmas tree had been erected and its branches were loaded with handsome ornaments and toys designed as presents for the children of the Sabbath School. A large crowd gathered to witness the display. The little ones were delighted with their share of the varied products of the beautiful illuminated tree, and their satisfaction gave pleasure to those who designed the agreeable project."[20]

Five years would pass before the next peacetime Christmas, and it would be a lean one in a port community striving to recover from the effects of Federal occupation and blockade that held it in a stranglehold until mid-year of 1865.

On the evening of December 27, 1860, members of Indianola Lodge No. 84, A. F. and A. M. , held a Christmas party and installation ceremony jointly with the Lavaca Lodge, to which family members were invited. Officers-elect of both Masonic lodges were installed in ceremonies at No. 84's hall. Following the installation, the throng moved to McCauley's Restaurant "where an abundant supply of edibles had been prepared for the occasion. The best of feeling prevailed, and the recovenant of friends was repeatedly toasted with hearty good will."[21] No. 84 officers installed were W. H. Woodward - Worshipful Master, B. F. Yates - Senior Warden, W. T. Yancey - Junior Warden, Adam Murdock - Treasurer, James Casey - Secretary, C. C. Howerton - Senior Deacon, James Morrison - Junior Deacon, J. J. Vanderveer and R. D. Martin - Stewards, and Samuel McBride - Tiler. Murdock, Casey, Vanderveer and McBride went into Confederate military service, as did several other members of the lodge.[22]

The officers of Lavaca Lodge No. 36 who were installed at that joint meeting were J. R. Fretwell - Worshipful Master, R. E. Sutton - Senior Warden, A. H. Phillips, Jr. - Junior Warden, Henry Earle - Treasurer and W. S. Laybrook - Secretary.[23]

On their return to their homes in San Antonio after a tour of the central and eastern United States, William Thielepape, Herman Lungkwitz and William DeRyee landed at Indianola. There they gave two performances, January 8 and 9, 1861, before packed houses at the courthouse of their "Stereomonoscopic Dissolving Views and Polaroscopic Fire Works." They were German artists and pioneers in photography who had joined forces to display their work. It was a startling innovation. DeRyee was among the first in the field of trans-parencies. His products provided a sensation for viewers. Their artistry and astonishing displays were described by the St. Louis *Daily Republican*, in which city DeRyee's transparencies were first shown to the public. In all, there were 23 performances in that city.

The newspaper comments had followed the premiere. "The lovers of the beautiful were treated to a surfeit well nigh last evening at the St.

Louis Opera House, as the magic exhibition unfolded the long and surpassingly brilliant display. There is a large curtain with a circle of black around it - the inside white - which is first wet, and then come from the stereoscope and polaroscope by some, to us, unknown science, a succession of pictures of Kings, Captains, Actors, Actresses, Candidates for President, Temples, Cities, Shipping, a Ship and Houses on Fire, the Seasons coming and going, Waterfalls, Snowstorms, and all the wonders of a modern dioramic display. When the fine, thoughtful form of Garibaldi came out, there was loud greeting of it by the audience - equalled by nothing that was exhibited but the wild greeting which was given Breckenridge and Douglas in turn.

"The drop curtain of the several parts was original, indeed, it being the unfolding of polaroscopic Miracles by a succession of unfoldings of wheels within wheels, such as Ezekiel's vision, spokes of which dart off into diamonds, stars &c — advances and recedes — folds in and rolls out and over, generally in Hogarth's line of beauty — the circle — often in other forms, but always in such a magic wonder that the effect on the house is a continuous expression of astonishment. The music behind the curtain was very pleasant and occasionally accompanied by a rich and practised voice." Such was the diversion provided Indianolans at the beginning of that momentous year of 1861. Leaving the performance, spectators marveled at the unbelievable wonders they had seen. It was a glimpse of scientific developments in the wings, waiting to come on stage.

They had no such glimpse into the events of the next three months. Had they been accorded an inkling of the consequences, what would have been their attitude toward the approaching Secession Convention? F. S. Stockdale of Indianola and John Henry Brown, now of Belton, participated in the convention. Brown was a member of the committee which drafted a "declaration of causes which impel the State of Texas to secede from the Federal Union."[24] Both men signed the declaration as members of the deliberating body.

As senator from the Twenty-Sixth District in the Seventh and Eighth Legislatures from 1857 to 1861, Stockdale was the author of the Senate majority report early in 1860 affirming the right of secession. Debate in the Senate had followed the submission, by Governor Houston, of a copy of the resolutions adopted in December 1859 by the legislature of South Carolina. When Houston forwarded the South Carolina resolutions to the Texas Legislature, it was accompanied by his own lengthy message in which he gave a powerful argument in opposition to the principle of secession. Leaders in that Senate debate were James W. Throckmorton supporting Houston's position, and Stockdale in favor of secession.[25] The latter was a delegate to the State Convention of the Democratic Party, which began in Galveston on April 2, 1860, and to the National Democratic Convention in Charleston, S.C., beginning on April 23, 1860.

Following the almost unanimous vote by the members of the Secession Convention on February 1, 1861, in favor of withdrawing

Star of the West, captured by Confederates off Indianola, April 17, 1861. What is regarded by historians as the first shot of the War Between the States was fired at her by a South Carolina battery on Morris Island in Charleston harbor on January 9, 1861. The name of the vessel is shown in reverse on the broad pennant under the whip. (*Courtesy The Mariners Museum, Newport News, Va. From the Elwin M. Eldredge Collection.*)

from the Union, the matter was submitted to the people of the state. Texans voted three to one approval on February 23. The Convention again met on March 2 to canvass the returns of the election and, on the 5th, took the final step to move Texas into the Confederacy.

As commander of United States forces in Texas, General David E. Twiggs was immediately faced with a dilemma — how to respond to demands for his surrender of Federal forces and equipment. Being a native of Georgia, it was obvious where his sympathy lay. The War Department sent him no instructions from Washington. Left to his own devices, Twiggs formally surrendered to the Texas militia. Two months later he was commissioned a major general in the Confederate Army.[26]

Upon Twiggs's surrender at San Antonio in March, permission was granted by Texas authorities for Federal troops in the state to march to Indianola, where they would embark for the United States. The United and Confederate States were not yet at war and hope remained that military conflict might still be averted. Some of the Federal soldiers did get to Indianola and were picked up by the *Daniel Webster* and other transports before news came of the beginning of hostilities at Fort Sumter. When word of the fall of the fort was received, Union troops en route to Indianola were placed in a precarious position. Now being considered the enemy, their permission to leave was rescinded. However, some were near Matagorda Bay and able to continue their march without difficulty. They expected to be taken aboard the transport *Star of the West*, which was lying at anchor off Pass Cavallo bar.[27]

Now a famous vessel, the *Star of the West* played a historic role by drawing the first shots that were fired in the conflict of interests between North and South, though a state of war did not then exist. Outgoing President James Buchanan had ordered the *Star of the West*, at that time a merchant steamship, to the relief of Fort Sumter in Charleston Harbor with troops and supplies. She departed New York on January 5, secrecy covering her purpose and destination. News leaks occurred, and military officials in Charleston were apprised of her mission during the day of January 8.

The *Star of the West* arrived off Charleston bar near midnight on the 8th. With daylight, she steamed over the bar and moved toward the fort. When she was still almost two miles from Fort Sumter, a South Carolina battery on Morris Island opened fire. The commander of the fort, Major Robert Anderson, being unaware of her identity and purpose, was not in a position to act in her defense. There was no direct hit on the ship by shells fired from the island battery. One shot ricocheted and struck her, but did little material damage. It became apparent to the ship's captain, John McGowan, that to proceed further would endanger the lives of those aboard and run the almost certain risk of being sunk, whereupon she was swung about and her course set for a return to New York.[28]

Those shots at the *Star of the West* on the early morning of January 9, 1861, are looked upon as the first which were fired in the War Between the States, and a prelude to the bombardment of Fort Sumter by South Carolina's guns on April 12. As Federal steamships with supplies for the fort were approaching Charleston harbor on that day, demand was made for Major Anderson to surrender. Upon his refusal to do so, shelling began and the war was under way in earnest. In that conflict, Indianola and Lavaca were to suffer more than any other cities in Texas.

XIV.

The Unwanted War Begins

Confederate plans for military preparedness on the Texas coast were under way prior to the beginning of open warfare, though communication problems led to some uncertainty. Earl Van Dorn, Colonel, Confederate States Army, wrote from Indianola on March 26, 1861, informing Secretary of War L. P. Walker at Montgomery of the fact that United States troops were camped at Green Lake, ". . . about twenty miles from the coast, awaiting transports to remove them. They are yet ignorant of their destination. I have seen but two of the officers, Maj. E. K. Smith and Lieut. Thornton Washington. The former has resigned and is on his way to Montgomery to offer his services to the Southern Confederacy . . . I think I shall have no difficulty in securing many of the troops and officers. I leave in a few minutes for the Green Lake Camp . . ."[1]

Hugh W. Hawes addressed a communication to John H. Reagan, a longtime personal friend, now postmaster general of the Confederacy on March 30. Writing from Saluria, Judge Hawes said, "I returned here yesterday evening from Powder Horn. Colonel Van Dorn has not succeeded in engaging many of the officers or soldiers to join the Army of the Confederate States.

"There are some 500 soldiers assembled here, and five sea-steamer transport vessels lying outside our bar [ready] to receive the troops . . . as they arrive, and the *Fashion* is chartered by Captain King to remain here and lighter the men to the sea vessels. I very much fear the plan of Lincoln is to delay delivering up Fort Sumter until the whole Texas Army can be concentrated for an attack on Pensacola and, by a brilliant stroke, arouse Northern enthusiasm in favor of coercion . . . Our towns are entirely undefended, and those now carrying the mails are at the mercy of an enemy having steamers that can cross our bars. Morgan and Harris are both at Powder Horn . . ."[2]

Van Dorn was called to Montgomery for strategy sessions in the War Department, looking toward development of a comprehensive plan for protection of Texas' ports in the event armed conflict became a reality. Pointing up coastal Texans' feeling of urgent need for positive and prompt action, Hawes dispatched another letter to Reagan, this one from Indianola on April 9. "In stirring times like these, I deem it proper to advise you of the state of things here. The *Mohawk*, the *Empire City* and the *Crusader* — I believe these to be the names of war vessels and sea transports — [are] lying at Saluria this morning. The *Fashion*, chartered by the United States Government, brought in about 12 o'clock today stores from the *Empire City*. There are 9 companies concentrated here and at Green Lake . . . for embarkation, mostly here. There is a strong wind blowing which will prevent, till it ceases, their embarkation and has already delayed it 4 days.

"The *Arizona* is at Brazos with 300 troops which were embarked three days since for this place to join the troops here, but she is yet detained outside the bar by heavy weather. There are 7 companies hastening to the coast from the upper posts for embarkation here. Our latest advices are warlike, and it may be important for President Davis to be informed of these facts, and I accordingly write this by steamer just leaving, it now being 1 p. m. . . . "[3]

Prior to receipt of Hawes's second letter by Reagan, the War Department ordered Van Dorn to return to Texas and assume command. He was instructed, in the event of hostilities between the United and Confederate States, to intercept and prevent the exodus of the Federal troops through Indianola. For this purpose, he was empowered to call into service whatever force he deemed necessary. "The whole of the United States force, both officers and men, must be regarded as prisoners of war," he was told. "Such of the men as may be disposed to join the Confederate States Army you are authorized to take into service; those not so inclined must be held as prisoners . . . at such place as may be judged to be most safe. The commissioned officers may be released on parole, and in special cases of which you must judge, the men may be released on oath not to serve against the Confederate States."[4]

Hawes's letter of the 9th was referred to Walker. On April 13, the day after Fort Sumter, S. Cooper, Adjutant and Inspector General, wrote to Van Dorn quoting Hawes and stating, "You are hereby instructed to give the orders heretofore received by you a liberal construction and to arrest and seize all troops and stores of the United States, in transitu or otherwise, wherever found in the State of Texas . . . "[5]

Hugh Hawes and his fellow citizens of Matagorda Bay were not the only ones alarmed over the lack of defenses on the coast. E. C.Wharton, writing from the *News* office in Galveston on the same day that Hawes had dispatched his latest letter from Indianola, addressed the War Department. "I write in a hurry by Major Bickley, a brother of General Bickley, the head of the K. G. C. [Note: Knights of the Golden Circle] . . . In case of hostilities, we are totally unprepared here. There are a number of pieces of artillery here brought from Brazos, but there is no powder, no military organization, no leader, no nothing. All our sea coast, and consequently all our ports and harbors, will be at the mercy of any small vessel of war that may choose to appear off Galveston, Indianola, &c., and dictate such terms as may please her commander. A vessel of war can come within two miles of our island, and we could be shelled without trouble . . .

"Captain Talbot of the steamship *Mexico* informed us yesterday that he learned the day before from Captain Murray of the steamship *Fashion* (chartered by the United States officers to take the . . . troops from Indianola to the transport steamships outside), that he had been told suddenly to hold off, as he would not be needed until July. He seemed to think that it was the intention to retain and concentrate the rest of the United States troops in Texas . . . at or near Indianola. We have published letters from Brownsville, Austin and Washington that show it was Houston's design, in case his late appeal to the people took effect, to call on United States troops to back him."[6] John Tyler, Jr., writing from the War Department in Montgomery on April 16, sent Wharton's message to Van Dorn with the comment, "It appears that fifteen hundred of these troops are to be concentrated at or near Indianola, and points to the complicity of General Houston in the business."[7]

Van Dorn was far ahead of his contemporaries at Montgomery in planning against the Federals. He and his companions in arms were, on April 17, prepared to execute their plans for a daring and brilliant maneuver. A nephew of the late President Andrew Jackson, Van Dorn was equal to the task. He had previously distinguished himself in the Mexican War, and had served in Texas under Colonel Albert Sidney Johnston and Lieutenant Colonel Robert E. Lee, both outstanding strategists.

The *Star of the West*, which lay at anchor in the Gulf off Indianola, was a prize too tempting to resist. Using the Confederate steamer *General Rusk*, Van Dorn and his men approached the *Star of the West* after darkness descended on April 17. Being supposed by the captain of the transport to be a Union vessel as she drew near and signaled, the *General Rusk* was permitted to tie up alongside her intended victim. Confederates with concealed arms went aboard and, in a matter of moments, outnumbered and overpowered the Federals. The gunboat *Mohawk*, which lay nearby but veiled by night, was charged with the responsibility of guarding the *Star of the West*. On the *Mohawk*, there was complete ignorance of the event occurring on the transport. Not until the capture of the *Star of the West* was a fait accompli, the vessel moved out of range of the *Mohawk*'s guns and headed to safety in Galveston harbor escorted by the *General Rusk*, did it dawn on Lieutenant Strong and the men of his command that something was amiss, but it was then too late.[8]

Thus Indianola's role in the war was launched with triumph and glory only five days after the beginning of the conflict. Upon receipt of news of the capture, a wave of exhilaration swept over the city. How easy it would be for the South to win this war!

After the capture of the *Star of the West*, vigorous efforts were made by the Federals at Green Lake and Saluria to engage the services of boats to remove them. Those efforts were almost successful. Then came the final bitterness of defeat. C. C. Sibley, Major, Third Infantry, Commanding, addressed a communication to the Adjutant General, U. S. Army at Washington. Dated at Saluria on April 25, Sibley advised that he had surrendered his command to the forces of the Confederate States under Colonel Van Dorn. He had made two attempts to escape with his command and was trying a third time when three Confederate steamers, having some 800 men and several pieces of artillery on board, came down the bay and took a position that effectively prevented Sibley's escape in two small schooners he had managed to secure. Early on the morning of the 25th, the three Confederate ships were joined by a fourth steamer carrying 400 men, one 24 and two 6 pounder pieces of artillery. Sibley had no choice but to capitulate.

The captured Federals were paroled and permitted to sail for New York, the battalion of the First Infantry being assigned by Confederates to the schooner *Horace*, that of the Eighth to the schooner *Urbana* and that of the Third Infantry to the brig *Mystic*. The *Horace* and *Urbana* were towed over Pass Cavallo bar on April 30, and proceeded to sea. The brig was unable to pass the bar until May 3, owing to low water. The two schooners arrived in New York harbor on May 31, and the brig on the following day.[9]

A Confederate force under the command of Van Dorn met the last column of the United States troops in Texas on the El Paso road at San Lucas Spring, between Castroville and San Antonio on May 9, 1861. Commanded by Lieutenant Colonel I. V. D. Reeve, the Union soldiers were from the forts of far Western Texas and were en route to Indianola for embarkation. In the face of Van Dorn's greatly superior numbers, the 347 Federals surrendered unconditionally. They were then brought to San Antonio and temporarily placed in confinement at San Pedro Springs.[10] Thus, Colonel Van Dorn completed carrying out the orders of the War Department to take as prisoners the United States troops remaining in Texas after the beginning of hostilities.

General Orders No. 4 and 5 paid tribute to the zeal and gallantry of Texan forces in the capture of Federals at Indianola and on the El Paso road. G. O. No. 4 read, "The colonel commanding the troops in Texas acknowledges with pride the valuable services of the volunteers called out by his orders to arrest the United States troops at Indianola. With short notice, they sprang to arms and joined him at Victoria with a celerity amounting to eagerness that will ever stand as proof that the State of Texas has nothing to fear from invasion from any quarter. With the fatigue of forced marches, night watches, exposure on the crowded decks of the transports in Lavaca and Matagorda Bays, and scanty provisions, there was no murmur of dissatisfaction and no unwillingness manifested to obey any order. The aged man and the youth without beard, the father and his sons, the heroes of San Jacinto and the rangers who became veterans in the Mexican War, were seen side by side in the ranks, with faces expressive of that determination to win or die that ever gives assurance of success, and which gave success.

"The companies which reported at Victoria on the 23d and 24th of April were — Captain Herbert's Company, Colorado; Captain Scarborough (Davis Guards), DeWitt; Captain McDowell, Lockhart; Captain A. C. Horton, Matagorda; Captain W. R. Friend, DeWitt Rifles; Captain G. J. Hampton, Victoria; Captain Upton, Colorado; Captain Holt, Fort Bend; Captains Jones and Harris, Colonel DeWitt's Command, Gonzales; Captain Williams, Lavaca County; Captain Fulcrod, Goliad; Captain Kyle, Hays County; Captain Stapp, Indianola; Captain Searcy, Colorado; Captain Phillips, Lavaca Town; Captain Finlay, Lavaca Town; Captain Pearson, Matagorda; Captain C. L. Owen, Texana; Captain Barkley, Fayette; Captain Gordon, Matagorda County.

"In addition to the above, there were many companies who reached Victoria too late to participate, and were turned back without reporting. Nevertheless, they are entitled to all honor for their zeal and patriotism. The command of Col. H. E. McCulloch, consisting of five companies of cavalry under Captains Pitts, Tobin, Ashby, Bogges and Nelson, and the battery of light artillery under Captain Edgar, from San Antonio made extraordinary exertions to reach Victoria on the day specified for the rendezvous, for which the greatest praise is due them and, although they were not enabled to reach Lavaca in time to participate in the maneuvers on the bay (as the movement was made before the time appointed), they proved that they could be relied upon in any emergency.

"The colonel commanding desires also to acknowledge the services of Judge Hawes of Saluria, who promptly secured two pieces of artillery unavoidably left on his wharf on the night the *Star of the West* was seized, and who tendered the hospitalities of his house during the drawing up of the agreements between the commanding officer of the United States troops and the colonel commanding.

"Captain Chubb of the *Royal Yacht* from Galveston did material service in giving facilities of communication between the vessels in the bay, and afterwards in transporting arms and ammunition of war (taken from the United States troops) to Indianola and to Galveston free of charge, for which he also deserves, and has, the thanks of the colonel commanding. . ."[11]

The matter of defense of Pass Cavallo was of urgent importance to Indianola, and to Texas. The earthworks of old Fort Washington at the site of the short-lived town of Calhoun on Matagorda Island offered possibility for protection of the pass, if suitable armament could be secured and put in position there. A disadvantage was the exposed position of the old fort. Facing directly on the Gulf, it would be susceptible to being raked by shells from Federal gunboats whose weapons might be of longer range than those of the Confederates.

Texas Governor Edward Clark, who succeeded Sam Houston after the latter refused to swear allegiance to the Confederate Government, had brought the matter of pass protection to a head by addressing a personal message to President Jefferson Davis on April 17. Clark received a reply from Secretary of War Walker advising that an officer had been sent to Indianola with instructions to determine the defenses necessary there. On the 29th, General Cooper advised Van Dorn that Governor Clark had suggested defending the harbor of Indianola by the transfer of heavy guns from Fort Clark. Van Dorn was instructed to investigate the feasibility of removing the guns to Pass Cavallo, and to keep the governor informed.

Editor Yancey printed in the *Courier-Bulletin* on May 25, a condensation of an article that had been published in the New York *Commercial Advertiser*. That news story had listed Southern port areas that would have to be included in order to make a Federal blockade of the Confederacy complete and successful. In the Western Gulf, they were given as the "Mouths of the Mississippi; Galveston, Texas; Matagorda Bay; Brazos Santiago; Mouth of the Rio Grande." Corpus Christi Bay was not named.

Writing on coast defense in the same edition, Yancey showed that Governor Clark's prodding of Montgomery had secured the desired results. The paper said, "We were pleased to meet with Capt. Dan Shea, who arrived yesterday from San Antonio where he had gone to participate in the expedition which resulted in the capture of the last body of Federal troops in our State. Capt. Shea comes with authority to enroll a company of 100 men for the term of 12 months. We learn he is authorized and directed to take position at Pass Cavallo and proceed to the erection of such fortifications as may be practicable and necessary. His company will be stationed there.

"Capt. Shea brings information that four 24-pounder guns are on the way from Fort Clark and will be put in battery at the Pass as soon as they arrive. Capt. Good of the Dallas Flying Artillery, with a full company and complete battery, has also been ordered by Col. Van Dorn to this part of the coast and may be expected within a few days. . ."

Indicating discontent with his assignment, Van Dorn wrote the War Department, "I do not know whether or not it was the intention . . . that I should be continued in command in Texas. I have executed my orders in regard to the capture of the U. S. troops and, at the same time that I do not wish to be considered as shrinking from any duty that may be imposed upon me in times like these, I must say that I would prefer being where I might have active service suitable to my age and inclinations. My duties here are now entirely in the office, where an older man would be infinitely more efficient than myself.''[12] At the time, Van Dorn was 40 years of age. His request received sympathetic attention. Promoted to major general and placed in command of the Trans-Mississippi Department, he was assassinated on May 8, 1863.[13]

J. M. Bickford, who was the school teacher at Saluria, kept a diary in brief form. His relation of events during this turbulent period gives some insight into contemporary civilian activities.

"March 15, 1861 — Had company in school today. Scholars declaimed very well.

"March 23 — Went up to Powder Horn with Burrows. All day doing it.

"March 24 — Dined at Judge Yates' & then had my picture taken for Mrs. Dubois. [Note: Bickford lived with the Dubois family on Matagorda Island]. Slept with John Van. . .

"April 17 — This evening the S. S. *General Rusk* took the S. S. *Star of the West* lying off Pass Cavallo bar.

"April 25 — U. S. troops surrendered to the C. S. forces under Col. Van Dorn.

"April 27 — Made out my report to the County.

"April 28 — Went up town [Note: Saluria] Dined at Capt. Morgan's.

"April 29 — Maj. Parr copied my report & Forrester administered the oath to self, Hill & Nichols.

"May 6 — Went up to Powder Horn on the Mail Boat. Bought saddle bags and boots, &c, &c. Spent the evening at Charlie Coen's.

"May 10 — Over to Saluria and home. Settled up my affairs generally."

In the back of the diary are the accounts for the patrons of the school, who were J. K. McCreary, Captain Wm. Hill, Captain George Morgan, R. J. Holbein, J. Wilkinson, Captain Thomas Decrow, Elijah Decrow, Captain Wm. Nichols, Louis Thibeau and L. Dubois. Each account includes "house rent" and "tuition." These were in varying amounts depending, possibly, on the number of scholars in the families. Also included were the school books, which Bickford ordered for the students. A typical bill was that of Captain Hill, which listed, "To 1 3rd Reader - $.40, 1 Speller - .15, 1 Geog & Atlas - 1.25, 2 Copy Books - .50, 1 Arithmetic - .50, House Rent - 6.70, Tuition - 86.00." Other bills included, "1 Slate - .25, 2 Rhetorics - 1.50, 1 Astronomy - 1.50, 1 Philosophy - 1.00."[14]

Published in abbreviated form, ". . . to eke out our little stock [of paper] on hand," as Editor Yancey expressed it, the *Courier-Bulletin* columns were filled with war news in late spring. One story was related to the event of April 17. "The name of the steamer *Star of the West*, lately captured near this city, has been changed to *St. Philip*. She is employed as a receiving ship at New Orleans." Another item, "New Orleans Privateers," said with obvious pride, "The steamship *Calhoun*, fitted up at New Orleans as a Confederate State privateer with several heavy guns and about 90 men armed with Mississippi rifles, went to sea a few days ago and . . . captured near Southwest Pass the bark *Ocean*

Eagle, Capt. Lace, from Rockland, Maine, with a cargo of lime. She was sent up to New Orleans in charge of a prize crew. The New Orleans privateer steamer *V. H. Ivy* . . . captured the ship *Marshall* of Providence, R. I., and the same day took another Yankee vessel, name unknown. About 20 more of these vessels [privateers] are expected at New Orleans."

Although actually organized as a result of events beginning in November 1860, the two infantry and one artillery Home Guard companies at Indianola were not incorporated until the summer of 1861. That step was taken under authorization by the Texas Legislature dated February 15, 1858, and entitled "An Act to incorporate all Military Uniformed Companies now organized, or to be organized, in the State."[15]

Section 2 of the act exempted such volunteer companies from "common Militia drills, and Battalion and Regimental reviews." Another key to the reasons for incorporation was the provision in Section 5, ". . . That drafts shall never be made from said Companies, but it shall be the privilege of their Corps to serve in body under their own officers, and only then when the number of common Militia of the Battalion is inadequate to meet the demand by draft; and in that case, these Companies will be selected by lot to supply the deficiency."

Officers were elected by the members of the individual units. Section 12 required that before any such company would be entitled to the provisions of the act, the commanding officer had to record in the office of the county clerk a certificate, under oath, showing where the company was organized, to which arm of the service it belonged, and listing the names of officers and members. A looming draft of men by the Confederacy made company incorporation very attractive. A few men were listed by the Calhoun county clerk in two companies. That may indicate over-eagerness on the part of recruiters, or a change of mind by enlistees as to the unit with which they finally wished to affiliate. It is understandable that Fletcher S. Stockdale would prefer being second lieutenant in Company B to being a private in Company A.

Company A, Indianola Guards, was incorporated June 27, 1861. Commissioned and non-commissioned officers, as shown in the county records, were D. E. Crosland - Captain, Andrew Dove - 1st Lt., Adam Murdock - 2d Lt., Charles Brandes - 2d Lt., D. C. Proctor - Orderly Sgt., Elijah Stapp - 2d Sgt., W. T. Yancey - 3d Sgt., C. C. Howerton - 4th Sgt., John Gray - 1st Corporal, G. L. Vogel - 2d Corp., S. M. Woodward - 3d Corp. and Edwin Muegge - 4th Corp.

Privates listed in Company A were James Ashworth, Sam McBride, Marx Rouff, Christopher Stapp, F. S. Stockdale, John A. Davis, Emil Reiffert, G. B. Keys, S. von Bramer, Frank Healy, A. Jani, Louis Preisig, C. M. Coen, Charles Ivy, Achilles Stapp, W. Frobese, Hugh S. Stapp, R. Rehner, W. H. Marshall, Joseph Carter, Louis Labe, Charles Kleinecke, Robert Gamble, John W. Lang, John Allen, M. Demonet, George W. Woodman, James Casey, Jacob Knopp, A. Taylor, John Ohlendorff, Joseph Hanna, C. Britz, Edw. Wood, H. J. Huck, C. Eichlitz, Joseph

Wood, B. F.Yates, Jas. S. Coates, Henry Dahme, A. Nitsche, G. L. Garey, Charles Keller, D. Stubbeman, F. Dahme, David Lewis, W. Hagerty, J. F. Madden, C. H. Bell, Joseph Coutret, I. Nolan, Robert F. Clement, C. B. Burbank, W. Bonefeldt, and W. F. Bonefeldt.[16]

Two days later, June 29, Company B, Indianola Guards was incorporated with Leon Rouff as captain. Both A and B were infantry companies, armed with rifles. In addition to Rouff, commissioned officers were W. H. Woodward - 1st Lt., F. S. Stockdale - 2d Lt. and Egmont Bulling - 2d Lt. Noncommissioned officers listed were: George W. Volk - Orderly Sgt., G. Marr - 2d Sgt., G. Baer, 3d Sgt., L. B. Schultz - 4th Sgt., Jacob Williams - 5th Sgt., J. C. Maas - 1st Corp., C. C. Mertz - 2d Corp., George W. Keehon - 3d Corp. and H. Kuester - 4th Corp.

Company B privates were shown in the records to be Fred Leibold, D. K. Woodward, F. Rohre, August Wagner, R. A. Rohner, A. Brandes, J. H. Duncan, John Freund, Henry Holzheuser, H. Cloudt, J. M. Rahm, Jno. Wilmers, Marx Rouff, M. Johannes, J. L. Allen, Jac. Garner, M. Sigmund, W. Robertson, G. Rose, F. Winkleman, Ph. Holzheuser, J. Koperz, J. Lehman, H. Bauer, B. Weinrich, S. Deutsch, F. Fuhrman, H. Walter, Chas. Metzing, Fred Holzheuser, Chas. Funk, C. V. Woodsworth, Wm. Erbs, G. Herrer, David Holzheuser, V. Steinberg, H. Courege, Fred Schraeder, F. Brandes, Charles Morrison, L. Budde, L. Sigmund, M. Haller, J. C. Weinrich, J. B. Burke, Thos. H. Mayne, Gustav Wasserman, F. Behrens, Dan Zimmerman, L. Hamm, J. G. Burke, Raymond Burke, George W. Parke, A. B. West, Peter Soper, Harry Wilson, Jac. Arto and Peyton A. Key.[17]

Company B captain, Leon Rouff, an emigrant from Europe, had become a naturalized citizen of the United States on February 19, 1861, after examination by the court, meeting in Indianola. Four months later he had become a citizen of the Confederate States and was commanding a Home Guard infantry company to stand in defense of Indianola against forces of the United States. Within a period of only weeks, he had held citizenship consecutively in Germany, the United States and the Confederate States of America.

Also on June 29, the muster roll of Indianola Artillery Company listed George Thielepape as captain. Other commissioned officers were Otto Schnaubert - 1st Lt., Otto Beyer - 2d Lt. and Joseph M. Reuss - 3d Lt. Noncommissioned officers were Charles Vollers - Orderly Sgt., J. Noll - 2d Sgt., S. Klamberg - 3d Sgt., Charles Kempel - 4th Sgt., W. Leonhardt - 1st Corp., Charles Zellney - 2d Corp. and W. Frank - 3d Corp.

Artillery company privates were J. Buss, A. Denter, H. Elbert, G. Eberhardt, G. Freund, C. French, F. Flick, J. Hamm, Charles Kaapke, J. Knopp, G. Lohrman, V. Ley, Paul Ludwig, C. Lupp, I. Miller, J. Klaus, J. Marx, H. Peschke, L. Reinecke, H. Sanders, J. Schmidt, N. Simon, H. Straube, H. Silbereisen, G. Weil, W. Witnebert, G. Goepfert, G. Wasserman, M. Funk, C. Volk, C. Lindeman, W. Sanderland and F. Westphal.

This company reported the possession of two 12-pounders, one 6-pounder and 11 balls! Captain Thielepape commented on the certificate,

"The two 12-pounders cannon in charge of this company were received from Gen'l Sherman of Galveston [Note: Sidney Sherman], supposed to be State property, and were mounted by the private subscription of the citizens of Indianola. The 6-pounder was taken from the steamship *Fashion* and was, at the expense of the citizens of Indianola, converted from a 5 to a 6-pounder, and mounted. As yet, the Company has no side arms and no ammunition for the cannons. The three cannons are of cast iron."[18]

The first emphasis after Lincoln's election the previous November had been on the organization of Home Guard companies, such as these. The possibility of war seemed real enough late in 1860 that men flocked to join local units throughout the South. It was an exciting time. Patriotism was "in" and there was a clamor on the part of hot-blooded youths to demonstrate their loyalty to their respective states. It was anticipated that when the framework of the regular army was constructed and recruitment begun, many of the men in the stop-gap Home Guards would volunteer their services to the Confederacy. When that time did arrive, some local units disbanded, but others retained their identity and became part of the reserves.

Families were divided by the conflict. Merchant and former Mayor James Ashworth, and one of his brothers, joined the Confederate military forces. Two other brothers became Union soldiers, a tragedy that rent the family, but which was commonplace in those troubled times.[19] There was a similar split in the Brackenridge family at Texana . . . two examples of many.

The first reference to the war in county records (July 13, 1861) concerned an appropriation of $1,500 for the general defense of Calhoun County, the amount to be expended solely for the purchase of munitions. Warrants were to be issued in the amount of $25 each. The total appropriation was placed at the disposition of an eight member Military Committee (or Board), two from each precinct in the county. It was the responsibility of the committee to negotiate the sale of the warrants. When sold and cash realized, munitions were to be purchased and distributed to the military companies of the county, according to the number of rank and file members of each.

Members of the committee appointed by the county court were A. H. Phillips, Jr. and R. E. Sutton from Precinct 1 (Lavaca); W. M. Blair and Ed. Beaumont, Precinct 2 (Old Town); R. W. Yates and D. E. Crosland, Precinct 3 (Indianola); James Mainland and John R. Baker, Precinct 4 (Matagorda Island). The first official meeting of the committee was at the courthouse in Indianola on Thursday, July 18. Its purpose was to plan operations and assign duties.

Concerned about the inadequate state of preparedness in counties near Matagorda Bay, D. M. Stapp, Brigadier General, 24th Brigade, Texas Militia, with headquarters at Indianola, wrote to selected citizens in the area soliciting their aid in beefing up the forces. Union blockade and the probability of movement by enemy troops into the coastal region of Texas made Stapp's action necessary.

In a letter written August 10 and addressed to John S. Menefee of Texana, Stapp said, with some facetiousness, "I have to request your assistance in organizing the Militia of Jackson County. It is too much to expect a 'Brig. Gen'l' to ride all over the country this hot weather and hence I appoint *aides de camp.* You will know who to appoint as enrolling officers and will, I believe, take pleasure in rendering me this assistance. I send you herewith enclosed partial instructions through which, with your own military genius, you can succeed in organizing the companies of your army.

"I enclose you circulars which you will please have delivered, one each to the captains of the several companies of your county. . ."[20]

Immigrant C. F. Vollers, Artillery Company sergeant and constable-elect for Precinct 3 to fill the unexpired term of Daniel Hoffman, faced the problem of inability to qualify for office due to his still being a subject of the Grand Duke of Oldenburg. Appearing before the county court, Vollers swore that in 1853 he had made, before the district court in San Antonio, declaration of his intention to become a citizen of the United States. He had failed to pursue the matter at that time.

Vollers petitioned the Calhoun county court, ". . . representing that in the dissolution of the Union, lately termed the United States, it was bona fide his intention to become a citizen of the Confederate States of America." He then "prayed this court that, on his producing such evidence, making such declaration and renunciation and taking such oaths as are required by law, he be admitted to be a citizen of the Confederate States of America, which petition was sworn to and sub-scribed by him, the said Vollers, in open court."

On fulfilling the requirements of law, Vollers was "admitted to be a citizen of the Confederate States of America . . .," whereupon he executed his official bond in the sum of $500 with Charles Kaapke and Fred Goepfert as sureties, and took the oath of office as constable for the term which would expire in October 1862.[21]

In a called meeting on September 16, 1861, the court received the report and recommendations of the Military Committee. Submission was made by D. E. Crosland, treasurer, and Wm. M. Blair, agent. The members had purchased powder "on the Rio Grande" and recom-mended that it be apportioned to the several precincts of the county, 15 kegs each to Nos. 1 and 3, and 5 kegs each to Nos. 2 and 4.

The committee further suggested that the distribution of the powder be made by its newly appointed chairman, W. P. Vaughn, only to military companies of Calhoun County and "to persons engaged in the manufacture of cartridges for the use of the County." R. W. Yates had been selected to attend to the shipping of the powder and other am-munition to the powder magazine at Lavaca, "where the whole shall be stored, subject to order of the chairman." The 16 guns and one pistol purchased by Wm. M. Blair out of the proceeds in his hands, as a committee member, were "taken into account for the use of the County and loaned to the Green Lake Cow Boys, with the understanding that the receipt of the Captain of said company be taken for the same to the Chief

Justice." The Green Lake Cow Boys Company also received 5,000 holster pistol percussion caps.

An allotment of 10,000 musket percussion caps was made to Indianola Guards Company A. The remaining 60,000 caps were held subject to the orders of captains of military companies in quantities of not more than 10,000 at one time.

J. D. Braman, the Military Committee's secretary pro tem, had been appointed to purchase 2,000 pounds of lead and to draw on the treasurer for the cost. The funds left over after payment of the approved appropriations were to be placed in the hands of the county treasurer, subject to order of the court. It was also recommended that details of the meetings of the committee be published in both the *Courier-Bulletin* and Lavaca *Gulf Key*, "so the citizens would be informed." The report was signed by Braman.[22]

The county court had ideas different from those of the Military Committee, as is so often the case when political bodies are involved. The recommendations of the committee were largely brushed aside. There was obviously an undercurrent of disagreement between the two groups. The court brusquely stated, "In view of the probability that the Military Board [committee] will be disposed (as it is understood by the Court) to close their proceedings, the Court would suggest that it would be well for the Board to turn over the ammunition purchased, and the balance of the money in their hands, to an authorized agent of the Court, taking his receipt therefor.

"It is now understood by this Court that if the Military Committee should think it proper to turn over the balance on hand to the county treasurer, as is contemplated in their report filed this day, that the said amount shall remain as a special fund in the hands of said treasurer, to be drawn for by this Court for the purpose of ammunition or arms for County uses, and further that the clerk of this Court shall be authorized to draw the same by special warrant and expend the same on such arms (fire arms, knives or swords) as he may think necessary for the use of any Home Guard . . . established for County defense."

It was astonishing to many that control of munitions in the county was to be vested in the clerk. But, the Military Committee did not die easily. On October 28, the court ordered the clerk to correspond with A. H. Phillips and endeavor to ascertain the disposition of three kegs of powder purchased by him at Lavaca as a member of the committee. The clerk reported he had received from Blair 13 guns purchased by him at Brownsville, whereupon the court instructed that inquiry be made to determine the facts connected with the distribution by him of three rifles and one revolver, which were part of the Brownsville purchase.

The court filed a receipt from Confederate Army Artillery Company Captain J. M. Reuss for 5,000 percussion caps, "the property of this Committee," and it rejected the application of Wm. Blair for 3,000 percussion caps for use in Jackson County.

Tightening its grip on military supplies, the court ordered that, "the clerk be, and he is hereby authorized and directed to take possession of the powder, lead and percussion caps now in store at Lavaca; also . . . the 16 guns and one revolver belonging to the committee, and hold the same subject to order of this court or any emergency which may take place in the County of Calhoun during the war which at present exists between the United States and the Confederate States." Noting that $314.75 remained on hand out of the original $1,500, the court instructed that amount be drawn from the committee treasurer by the clerk and loaned to Captain Reuss, "now in command of a company of Artillery of the Confederate States on Matagorda Island." The purpose of the loan was to enable Reuss, with the aid of the Ladies Sewing Society of Indianola, of which Mrs. Reuss was an active member, to clothe the company as far as the money would stretch.

Apparently the court expected the soldiers to pay their own way, even though they were on duty to protect the county and ensure the safety of its inhabitants, including the politicians. The court authorized the loan, ". . . With the further understanding that said loan is to be repaid to said clerk or said treasurer after collections are made by him [Captain Reuss] from the privates of said company for such clothing as may be distributed amongst them according to the tenor of this order."[23]

Military duty at Fort Washington was not entirely dull, nor were privations being suffered by the men there at that time. This is set out by further entries in J. M. Bickford's diary. He had been down the island and across to the Hynes Bay area, where he joined the Duke, Huff and Dubois families on a cattle drive to Louisiana. Bickford had returned to Saluria on October 28, 1861.

On October 31, the diary says, "Called over to Mr. Coen's, and after dinner went to the doctor's and the Fort.

"Nov. 2 - Went over to the Fort in the evening." He makes various references to playing euchre and whist, so it can be supposed that those evenings were occupied by card games.

"Nov. 3 — Again to the Fort and saw a dress parade.

"Nov. 8 — Went up to Powder Horn. Bought a bridle and paid Mr. Yancey for his paper.

"Nov. 10 — Went over to the doctor's and the Fort. Dined on board the *Lizzie Lake.*

"Nov. 12 — The young ladies and all hands of us visited the Fort — had a glass of champagne and then went to Captain Nichols'." There are many references to young ladies but Bickford, gentleman that he was, never named them. They figured in parties and moonlight sails.

"Nov. 15 — The officers at the Fort gave a big champagne dinner. Fine time."

R. R. Garland, Colonel, Provisional Army, C.S.A., reported from Indianola on December 6, 1861, to Major Samuel Boyer Davis, Acting Assistant Adjutant General at Galveston, on his reconnaissance of the town, the coast in the vicinity of Pass Cavallo and of Fort Washington. ". . . The point selected by Captain Shea to establish his battery is, in my opinion, the proper position to command the entrance to the bay and, if properly constructed under the supervision of an experienced engineer officer and suitably appointed, could be made to accomplish that object; but in its present condition it is totally inadequate for this purpose, and should be immediately withdrawn or put in a condition not only to command the Pass, but to be capable of defending itself from attack by sea or land."

Garland pointed to the isolated position of the fort, observing that it was totally cut off from any support from any quarter whatever and, if attacked by a superior force, either by sea or land, ". . . and it is open to attack either way or both at the same time, it must inevitably fall into the hands of the enemy, as I can conceive of no possible way of withdrawing them in the presence of an enemy, on account of several impassable bayous."

He also enclosed a report of ordnance and stores pertaining to Captain Shea's command. "The captain appears to be an energetic and industrious officer, and his command is in a fair state of discipline and instruction. . ."

Garland's enclosure was, "List of ammunition on hand at Fort Washington, Pass Cavallo, Texas (as of) December 5, 1861. Fifty-four rounds spherical case shot for 24-pounder; 24 rounds shell for 24-pounder; 156 rounds round shot for 24-pounder; 64 rounds grape shot for 24-pounder; 24 rounds canister shot for 24-pounder; 150 pounds cannon powder for 24-pounder; 10 kegs cartridges for 24-pounder (18 in each keg); 8,860 B. and B. cartridges; 2,500 rifle cartridges; 4 24-pounder siege guns; 2 12-pounder siege guns; 1 6-pounder field gun, no fixed ammunition or equipments and badly mounted; 98 rifle muskets; 33 common muskets; 36 cavalry musketoons, equipment complete. . ."[24] The inadequacy of Fort Washington's ordnance was apparent.

The Confederate force at Fort Washington had its first action on the 7th. At about 1 p.m., a sloop of war hove in sight off the pass. She sailed to the west of the bar and about five miles off, made several short tacks off the bar and steered back to the east. About 5 p.m., she came to anchor off Decrow's Channel and two miles from shore. The following day at noon, she made sail and steered westward, running close to the bar. When nearly opposite the fort and three miles distant, Shea signaled the four 24-pounder battery to open fire on her. She was struck two or three times, put about after the first round of the battery and steered seaward. She had showed no colors up to that time. Sixteen shots were fired from the fort.[25]

Five days later, Colonel Garland addressed Major Davis from "Headquarters, Camp Henry McCulloch. Sir: . . . I have just returned from Capt. Shea's camp at Pass Cavallo. The captain is making every arrangement in his power to secure a retreat, if it should become necessary. He is establishing ferries across the principal bayous for this purpose."

At the end of the week, Garland returned to Fort Washington, made a second reconnaissance and suggested to Shea the advisability of taking up a position at a point further up the pass. There he would have the same command of the channel and would be out of the range of guns from Federal vessels at sea. Garland reported to Davis that the sloop of war "was still there up to the time I left. She lies off and on, and moves up and down the coast, never getting entirely out of sight of the entrance to the bay, and it is my impression she is looking for two vessels that left that port [Indianola] for Mexico some time since with cotton, and are expected to return about this time laden with coffee. While I was at Captain Shea's camp, she fired some 8 or 10 guns. We were unable to ascertain the object of her firing, but judge she was merely practicing. At the time of firing, she was lying off the coast some 10 or 12 miles above Decrow's Point. With a good glass, from the top of the lighthouse we could distinctly see the flashes, as well as hear the report, of the guns."

Colonel Garland directed Captain Rupley's company to take position at Saluria and guard the ferry across the main bayou. Three other companies under Lieutenant Colonel Anderson took position at Indianola. In addition, Garland ordered a detachment of mounted men from Captain Beaumont's company to report to Shea for duty.[26]

Garland's suggestion for relocation of the battery was followed by Captain Shea. The Confederates moved up the island to a point nearly opposite Pelican and Bird Islands at the mouth of the pass and below Saluria. There they began construction of a fortified position where guns could control passage of vessels through the channel. A mule-powered railroad was built from the shore line to the fortification for the easy transportation of heavy materials and supplies lightered to the beach. Fieldworks lay on the Gulf side of the new location, which was given the name of Camp Esperanza. The name, Esperanza, had definite appeal to the men on duty there. A Spanish word, its meaning is "hope." As it turned out, hope was about all the Confederates at Camp Esperanza had to bolster them.

XV.

Invasion and Occupation

The winter of 1861-62 was relatively quiet around Matagorda Bay. Federal blockade had secured a stranglehold on Indianola commerce, the life-blood of the community. The same was true of Lavaca. What had been a torrent of imports and exports over the wharves of Indianola, to and from Western Texas, had diminished to a trickle. A blockade runner was occasionally able to slip past Union gunboats which patrolled the waters of the Gulf of Mexico near Pass Cavallo. The sleek, swift little ships, outbound with such valuable items of exchange as cotton and hides, and inbound with arms and ammunition, coffee, medicines, machinery and tools, were frequently caught and taken into custody by a prize crew. Some would be run aground on the Gulf beaches of the islands by Union warships in hot pursuit. Nevertheless, the enormous profits realized from a successful run through the blockade made the gamble worthwhile.

A small, but vitally important, amount of commerce was being carried on through the inland waterways from Indianola south. They were screened by the long, narrow islands separating the bays from the Gulf and, therefore, made safe from bombardment by Union boats offshore. The United States War Department, fully aware of the Matagorda Bay-Mexico trade link, determined to sever it by one means or another. Knowing this, Confederates were energetically engaged in steps designed to protect the bays from Federal attack and control.

By February 2, 1862, Major C. G. Forshey was writing to Major Davis, now at Houston, from Camp Esperanza. Forshey was major of artillery and engineer of coast defense for the Confederate Army in Texas. In his communication, Forshey referred to the earth and other works Major Shea had already prepared.[1] The name of the camp was soon given to the entire area, which eventually became officially known as Fort Esperanza.

In his report to Davis, Forshey observed that the distance to the Pelican Island side of the Pass Cavallo channel from the guns of the fort was only about 400 yards, the near side 200 yards. "With anything short of steel-clad gunboats (and nothing larger could pass the bar) the enemy could not force a passage but with a large fleet. But, on land, there is no defense. A landing could be made at any point down the island and the invaders attack this small force in the rear and cut it off. In fact, as it now stands, they furnish a strong temptation to the enemy. . ."

To thwart a Federal take-over, Forshey proposed a line of fieldworks across the land mass half a mile below the fort, manned by two or three companies of infantry, backed by the two 12-pounders and a field piece, "aided by a brass howitzer, 12-pounder, on its way hither from San Antonio." It was Forshey's theory that the fieldworks, added to the small defensive bulwarks required at the ferries of the bayous to protect retreat, would involve "something less than 10,000 cubic yards of earthwork, or, say, 1,000 days' work."

Forshey raised a policy question also. "Shall this pass and the property and inhabitants in the rear be defended at all?" If the official decision were in the affirmative, then he proposed that Fort Esperanza was unquestionably the place to do it. It was his idea that an impregnable fortification be constructed and the force increased to make it completely safe. If not, he suggested that the men and guns should be immediately removed and the public as well as private property saved. In as discreet a manner as possible, Forshey was pointing to the urgent necessity for hard decisions being made by the Confederate command, and an end to vacillation.

The maritime commerce through the bays and bayous kept a fleet of the Mexican-trade vessels in sight of the enemy during all daylight hours. "It is our main artery now, and its abandonment would be very ruinous to our people," commented Forshey. "The enemy would safely occupy the island [Matagorda] at once and cut off all communication. The large vessels outside that have recently been watching us show that the importance of the pass is understood . . . The towns around the bay . . . and all the lines of navigation to the rivers San Antonio, Guadalupe, Navidad and Colorado are the immediate dependencies of this pass. All the trade and travel toward San Antonio and the western half of Texas are the remote dependencies. Shall it be defended?" he asked again.[2] He reported that, in anticipation of an expected Federal landing in force down the coast, the inhabitants of Mustang and St. Joseph's Islands were evacuating, "leaving all their stock and their homes at the mercy of the enemy." He pointed out that Major Shea had directed that be done after the burning of several houses, "and the wanton bombardment [by the enemy] of both islands without any notice whatsoever."

Forshey continued, ". . . The intrenchments for the protection of this pass [Cavallo] are rapidly progressing. I still have a small negro force of some 30 hands, and have also a detail of 50 from the ranks in continual employment when the weather permits. I am casemating rudely the guns, and have nearly finished a bombproof cover for some 500 men near the casemates. I am making a closed work of the fort and shall soon be ready to use 1,000 men in defense of the pass."[3]

He requested permission to dismantle the valuable cast iron lighthouse tower and secrete both the plates and the lighting apparatus. The request was repeated, but he was not given the "go ahead." Instead, later in the year, an order was issued that the structure be blown up, but it proved too stout for the demolition bomb to bring it down. It was injured, several plates being broken, but it remained standing.

Neglect during the war years resulted in erosion of the land area reaching to the foundation, causing the lighthouse to tilt and assume a position somewhat like that of the leaning tower of Pisa. While the Federal forces were in control of Matagorda Island in late 1863 and early 1864, an intensive search was undertaken to locate the illuminating apparatus which had been removed and hidden by Confederates prior to setting off the charge intended to bring the structure down. A few parts of the mechanism were unearthed. By 1867, the tower was in such imminent peril of toppling, it was dismantled to forestall collapse and total loss. After considerable delay in the acquisition of a new site by the Lighthouse Board, the old tower was rebuilt two miles from its original location by July 1873. The plates that had been damaged by the blast were recast and replaced in the structure. Lighted on September 1, 1873, the revolving lantern again showed a flash every 90 seconds, this time from 91 feet above sea level.[4]

The fact that Confederate defense of the Texas coast was weak in February 1862, was made clear in Major Forshey's report of the 24th from Esperanza. The acute shortage of men and materiel was opening the path for Union capture of Galveston harbor and movement into Matagorda Bay within eight months. In late winter, the blockading bark *Arthur* had taken possession of the pass at Aransas, but had not yet planted guns on shore. The mail boat ceased to run between Indianola and Corpus Christi, and the stage on Matagorda Island bearing the mail was discontinued. Movement of maritime traffic on the inland waterway halted because of the possibility of Federal capture through Aransas Pass. In addition to Forshey's suggestions regarding dismantling the lighthouse at Pass Cavallo, he also requested authority and orders to destroy the lighthouse at Aransas. "Its possession by the enemy gives him a commanding view of all the vicinity and would render our attempt to plant our guns very precarious. It could be approached by night and blown up, as they do not occupy it."[5] Again, the requested permission was not forthcoming.

By the late spring of 1862, the general state of business at Indianola was one of stagnation. In addition, the absence of many men who were serving the Confederacy at strategic points along the Texas coast began to result in cases of hardship for their families. Indianola churches, through their Ladies Societies, undertook relief measures to aid those who had fallen into destitute circumstances. Noble as those efforts were, the need was beyond the capacity of the women involved. Help had to come through the county.

The problem was brought to a head by the appearance before the court of W. H. Woodward on behalf of "Jack Parsons, an old citizen of the county, in a very destitute condition, in bad health and wholly unable by his labor to procure the means of subsistence." Woodward requested the court to take his care into consideration and make such appropriation for his relief as might seem proper. Acknowledging the desperate nature of Parsons' situation, the court ordered that "the sum of $16 per month be allowed to Mrs. Alex Cold for the subsistence of said Jack Parsons from the first of April last to present time and as long as he ... may need assistance."[6] Thus was the precedent established in Calhoun County for a plan of welfare assistance to those who, through no fault of their own, were in want.

That action of the court was soon followed by petitions on behalf of other citizens needing aid. On May 20, 1862, the court ordered that a tax of 25¢ on each $100 of taxable property be levied and collected under the act of the Legislature of January 1 which authorized the imposition of a war tax, the proceeds of which were to be applied to the support of those in need. The act was primarily aimed at helping families of servicemen, but was loosely interpreted.

By August, the court had authorized relief payments to families of 26 soldiers. The amount was $30 per year for the wife, and the same amount for each other adult in the family. Children received $15 per year. The spreading effect of the war was to be demonstrated in the November allowance, at which time 47 families were recipients of monetary aid. A discriminatory attitude can be seen in the difference between the amount awarded Parsons and that granted to dependents of servicemen.

On the civilian front as late as April 4, the Calhoun county court was still involved in controversy with one of the members of the now-disbanded Military Committee. Wm. M. Blair was unwilling to acquiesce in the commissioners' taking away from the committee oversight of military preparedness of the county. He openly questioned the wisdom of their action and the effectiveness of their defense policy. For its part, the court groused that, "Wm. M. Blair, late of the Military Committee, has appropriated to himself a Mississippi rifle belonging to the purchase of said committee at Brownsville. The account of Mr. Blair with the county as one of said committee stands as follows — 1 revolver purchased at Brownsville, not delivered to the county, $50; 2 warrants for $25 each on ammunition account, not returned, $50; 1 Mississippi rifle purchased at Brownsville, not delivered to county, $20; 1 fine sword purchased at

Brownsville." No value was listed on the sword. Blair held his ground, to the discomfiture of the county court, whose members for some unknown reason hesitated to carry the matter further.[7]

Though Captain J. M. Reuss's artillery company was ensconced in Fort Esperanza, the unit had no banner flying over the fortification. The ladies of Indianola, being aware of that by reason of their visits across the bay to the fort, set about remedying the lack. They made a flag 12 feet by eight feet in size. It had three horizontal stripes. The bottom third of the flag was red, the center third white and top third red. In the upper left-hand corner there was a blue field with six stars in a circle. A seventh star was centered in the circle. It was almost, but not quite, the same as the first national flag of the Confederacy.

When the flag was completed, a delegation of 12 young ladies visited the fort and presented it for use by the company. Possibly they were some of those alluded to by J. M. Bickford in his diary. Miss Amelia Rouff made the presentation address, to which F. S. Stockdale responded "with eloquence." Each of Miss Rouff's 11 companions represented one of the seceding states. Holding a flag of her respective state, one by one each recited a verse appropriate to the occasion, to the rousing cheers of the soldiers. The young women were Rachel Woodward, Belle Milby, Kate Ashworth, Ida Crosland, Maggie Clement, Lissie Perrin, Zuleika Cleveland, Mollie Burke, Alice McCoppin, Eudora Moore and Emma Carter.[8]

With the guarding of Pass Cavallo in the hands of Confederate artillerymen, the commissioners appeared to feel secure enough to put up for sale "the powder, lead and caps now owned by the county." The clerk was authorized to sell these to anyone "at the highest market price." Yet, there was a contradiction in their actions because, on the same day, the court ordered that the district and county courts move the records in their offices to Victoria for safekeeping, only retaining such books and papers as were in daily use. Even those were to be kept in a state of readiness for immediate removal "on the approach of the enemy."

In connection with military surveys in the area, and the construction of Fort Esperanza, a map was prepared by Major Forshey of Pass Cavallo, the end of Matagorda Island and Decrow's Point on Matagorda Peninsula. Dated July 1, 1862, it shows the location of old Fort Washington, of the Pass Cavallo lighthouse nearby, line of redoubts below Fort Esperanza, Saluria, the old route of the bay trade from Matagorda Bay through Saluria Bayou into Espiritu Santo Bay toward Corpus Christi, also the road from Saluria to Indianola. That map labeled as "Shea's Bayou" that which separated Bayucos Island from the mainland at Alligator Head.

Felix A. Bluecher, major of artillery and assistant engineer, C.S.A., prepared a map of the same general area 14 months later, on September 6, 1863. Bluecher's map identifies the fortification as "Fort Debray," not "Esperanza." It also shows a short wharf about 500 yards above Fort Debray, a hospital on the inland side of the road from the fort to

Saluria, Captain Mainland's house in a precarious location between Fort Debray and the line of "Old Fieldworks." Wilkinson's house is also marked on Bluecher's map, as is the main lighthouse, the townsite of Saluria, Hawes's warehouse just offshore, the Saluria lighthouse across the bayou on Bayucos Island, and the road to Indianola. On Decrow's Point, the map indicates "Proposed Location of Battery."

Another, and different, map by Bluecher and Addison Denny, assistant engineer, bears the title "Map of Pass Caballo, Showing Vicinity of Fort Debray." It is undated, gives details of structures on Decrow's Point and identifies the site of Fort Washington as "Old Battery." Bluecher, in designating the island fortification as Fort Debray paid tribute to Colonel Xavier Blanchard Debray, then commanding the Sub-Military District of Houston. Debray was later advanced to brigadier general. A map by United States engineers, after the Federal takeover there, and dated December 1, 1863, shows "Fort Esperanza."

It was inevitable that Federal forces would make their way to Matagorda Bay. They had been expected for several months. When Galveston harbor fell to Union naval attack on October 4, 1862, Indianolans knew it was only a matter of time before their turn would come. The dreaded day dawned with the appearance of Union gunboats off Pass Cavallo on October 25. When the residents of the town heard the distant booming of the fort's cannons, they knew the moment of truth had arrived, though they felt confident that the artillery at Fort Esperanza would prevent the passage of enemy ships into the bay. Not so. In reply, the approaching warships peppered the fort with such withering fire that its defenders concluded that discretion was the better part of valor and retreated to Indianola before they could be cut off, a situation that Major Forshey had foreseen.

The Federal fleet, under the command of Captain William B. Renshaw, moved through Pass Cavallo and up the bay to Indianola, anchoring there in the afternoon. The following morning the *Westfield*, under flag of truce, tied up at a wharf, the commander requesting the visit of a delegation representing the citizens. H. B. Cleveland reported by letter to Major Shea, detailing the substance of the interview with Renshaw, "Indianola, Tex., October 26, 1862. Sir: At 11:30 a.m. [T. D.] Woodward, Captain [Henry] Sheppard and myself went on board the enemy's vessel, the *Westfield*, lying at the lower wharf and, in conversation with Captain Renshaw, and Captain Law of the *Clifton*, Captain Renshaw stated, in substance, that he had come into the bay to take possession of all the towns on the bay; that Indianola was already in his possession and that he should take the other towns as soon as the wind and weather favored; that he had three rifled guns and six IX-inch guns, with which he could command the bay; that he did not come to interfere with the citizens of Indianola; that he had no force to land at present, but that he would take and hold the towns by water; that the citizens could come to Indianola by land or water and go out when they pleased; that small boats bringing wood and provisions to Indianola would not be interfered with, and he hoped the citizens would unite with him in preserving the order and peace of the town. He might send a few men on shore to buy provisions, and if he did and they were interfered with, he might fire on the town. He hoped such a collision would not occur. He said he must have fresh beef, and if he could buy and pay for it, he would do so; if not, he would take it by some means and at some place . . . "[9]

Disdaining to do business with the enemy, Indianolans declined Renshaw's offer to purchase provisions and beef, whereupon he demanded the surrender of the city, advising that he would allow time for the evacuation of women, children and the ill, after which bombardment would begin.[10] In the short, but fierce, exchange of fire that ensued, the toll was one Union and two Confederates killed, with an unstated number wounded.

After the seizure of Indianola, two Federal gunboats moved toward Port Lavaca. They anchored in Lavaca Bay at 11 a.m. on October 31 and made contact with the Confederate defenders. In the official report covering the battle, details of the engagement were given. The report was prepared by George E. Conklin, Lieutenant and Adjutant, on orders of Major Daniel D. Shea, then in command of the post of Lavaca.

At 1 p.m., they sent a flag of truce on shore, which was met by Major Shea, accompanied by four of the citizens of the town. The Federals demanded the surrender of the town. Shea answered that he was able to defend it, and would do so "to the best of his ability with all the means he had at hand." Upon rejection of the demand for surrender, one hour and a half was allowed by the enemy for evacuation of women, children and the sick, Lavaca being in the grip of a yellow fever epidemic.

Upon the expiration of that period of grace, the Federal warships moved up abreast and opened fire. There were twin batteries for the protection of Lavaca. Captain John A. Vernon, assisted by Lieutenant T. D. Woodward, commanded one of them. The other was under the charge of Captain J. M. Reuss, assisted by Lieutenants Otto L. Schnaubert and G. French. "Nobly did both officers and men perform their duty," said the official report, "working their guns as coolly as though on inspection, while a perfect storm of shot and shell rained around them and this, although yellow fever had decimated their ranks." Some of the soldiers manning the batteries had not completely recovered from the disease.

Both Federal steamers were struck several times from the shore batteries, and one was partially disabled. At that juncture, they steamed out of range of the Confederate guns, where they again cast anchor and, with their longer-range guns kept up a steady fire upon the town until night. The next morning they resumed the attack. There was no return fire from land. The warships were beyond reach. "At about 11 a.m., they ceased their fire and steamed down the bay in the direction of Indianola, having in tow the schooner Lecompt, which they had captured in the bay a few days before." One of the gunboats went outside the pass and proceeded toward Galveston, "probably for a mortar boat or some additional force to assist them."

No Confederate lives were lost at Port Lavaca, "but the enemy succeeded in doing considerable damage to the town, tearing up the streets and riddling the houses . . . The enemy fired in all 252 shot and shell, 174 the first day and 78 the second, nearly all of them from 32 and 64-pounder rifled guns. Captain H. Wilke, acting ordnance officer, rendered very efficient service in keeping the batteries supplied with ammunition and freely exposing himself in the discharge of his duty. The citizens of this town acted nobly . . . and materially assisted the commanding officer . . . The ladies of the place, among them Mrs. Chesley and Mrs. Dunn, and the two . . . daughters of the former, bore a conspicuous part, acting the [role of] true Southern heroines supplying our tired soldiers with coffee, bread and meat, even during the thickest of the fight . . ."

As J. M. Bickford did, Mrs. Maurice K. (Lizzie Hatcher) Simons at Texana was keeping a diary at that time. Her entries tell of the spreading of the news about Federal gunboats entering Matagorda Bay. "Mr. Allen called, and many others. Great excitement about the yankees. Reported they've taken Powderh'n." On the 28th of October, she wrote, "Great excitement about the yanks. Milam's company gone to Carancahua Bay scouting. Militia ordered out [to] go to Lavaca. Reported that Kastenbine to be shot for disertion [sic] . . . Our theme all day & all evening as we sit round the table at work is the Yankees."

Texana, at the head of tidewater on the Navidad River, was 20 miles distant in a straight line from Lavaca. A south wind was blowing to carry the sound of battle to the frightened people of southern Jackson County. About the October 31 Federal attack on Lavaca, Mrs. Simons wrote, ". . . heard heavy firing in direction of Lavaca. Aunt Jud is with us. Milam came home to get provisions. All gloomy & sad. Aunt J & K almost sick with fear. I feel very badly but try to be cheerful to reassure the others. May God help us. I fear we are to be sorely tried this winter."

And, on November 1, "Heavy firing again this morning; all anxiety to hear the fate of Lavaca. The militia are at Kendrick's place fortifying. Call it Fort Crosland. Aunt J staid with us last night & staid til after dinner . . . I feel miserable . . ." On the following day, "2nd, Sunday. Mail in last night. No letters, no news. Northern papers insinuate there's to be an awful insurrection thro' the South, so Bro. F. tells me. I didn't go to S.S. Felt so gloomy all thro' the service at church could hardly keep tears back. The idea of an insurrection is horrible to me. Can't get it out of my mind. Lavaca has not fallen yet. A strong norther today makes against the Feds."

Soon after the capture and looting of Indianola, followed by the bombardment of Lavaca, the Federals withdrew from Matagorda Bay. The U. S. gunboat *Kittatinny*, which had been lying in the Gulf off the pass, was then ordered to move into the bay but was unable to do so because of drawing one foot more water than was over the bar. Her inability to come through Pass Cavallo made it possible for the Confederates to reoccupy Fort Esperanza and again command the channel. Additional work was done to strengthen the defensive works and make the fort less vulnerable to damage from Union attack. The military, as well as the civilian populace, had no doubt that the enemy would return.

The *Kittatinny* continued to patrol the Gulf off Pass Cavallo, her captain, C. W. Lawson, reporting on December 2 that he had seized several blockade runners, the most recent listed being the schooners *Matilda*, under English colors, and *Diana* from Campeche.

In October 1862, Confederate General John Bankhead Magruder had been transferred to Texas, a move that was believed locally to have been motivated by strategic errors on his part in the Virginia theater of war. Before the end of the year, his command was extended to include New Mexico and Arizona. Magruder's coming to Texas was to prove disastrous to the fortunes of Indianola, Lavaca and Victoria. He was convinced that Union military strategists were plotting to invade Texas from some still undetermined point on the coast. His theory had a sound basis. The Federal blockade in the Gulf of Mexico made it necessary for cotton produced west of the Mississippi to be transported to Mexico for export. There it was loaded on waiting ships from England and other industrial nations of Europe. Inasmuch as the movement on the inland waterway from Indianola had been affected by Federal presence, conveyance was largely overland by wagon. Because of the volume and importance of the traffic, it was logical to believe that Union forces would endeavor to cut the outflow by establishing a beachhead on the coast and then moving inland to San Antonio and beyond.

It was Magruder's intention to throw every possible obstacle in the path of such an invasion force by a "scorched earth" policy in the Matagorda Bay region, which he calculated would be the likely choice for a base of operation by the enemy. On December 25, he began to implement that policy. Colonel X. B. Debray, acting under orders received through Assistant Adjutant General E. P. Turner, Houston, notified Major Shea on Christmas Day, "I am instructed by Major General Magruder who is now at Virginia Point, to inform you that the enemy have landed at Galveston. Major General Magruder orders that you burn the railroad ties at Indianola, also the bridges at Indianola and Lavaca . . . You will burn or destroy the lighthouses at Saluria and Pass Cavallo, and all the houses at Pass Cavallo, if practicable . . ." The orders were not carried out in entirety.

On the same day, Debray instructed Major A. M. Hobby, commanding at Corpus Christi, "Major General Magruder . . . directs that you send a party to Aransas lighthouse to destroy it. Captain Neal or Captain Willke will know the best way of approaching it. Let them take for this purpose two kegs of powder. Major General Magruder desires me to say that he is aware of the difficulties, but he believes they can be overcome . . ."[11] The tower at Aransas was constructed of brick.

Magruder was only partially successful in his policy because of the bitter resistance of inhabitants to destruction of their property without what they considered a compelling reason. If the Federals approached, that would be time and justification enough, but not yet. However, Magruder was not easily deterred, and further ordered the destruction of the San Antonio & Mexican Gulf Railroad, as staggering a blow to Lavaca as was the burning of warehouses and wharves at Indianola to the people of that city. Such devastation would not have been unexpected from "the Yankee." For it to come through the "protecting" Confederate Army was a shocking, and unbelievable experience. A sense of frustration and futility descended upon the people of the affected region. "God protect us from our 'friends,'" commented one Victorian.[12]

The widespread yearning for peace was expressed in a wistful entry Mrs. Simons made in her diary at Texana on December 28, 1862. "Some Southern woman calls on all the women of the South to pray for peace on the 1st Jan. '63 at 12 oclk noon. Oh, is there a woman in this desolated South who will not answer to the call & plead with Almighty God for peace, honorable peace, & surely He will hear such an appeal for He has said, 'Call upon me in the day of trouble & I will deliver thee and thou shalt glorify Me.' The paper says the brute Butler is to head the army invading Texas. We have fresh incentive now to flee from our homes & seek safety anywhere . . . when the highest officer is a greater brute than any private. I wrote to M great talk about yankees coming. McGruder [Magruder] ordered all families and property within 30 miles of coast to move farther back."

The Federal fleet in Galveston Bay was routed on New Year's Day, 1863, in a naval encounter in which Renshaw's flagship, the *Westfield*, was destroyed. The *Clifton* managed to escape to the Gulf. There were losses in vessels on both sides, but total control of Galveston was recovered by the Confederacy. The off-shore blockade continued. Sagging spirits of Texans were somewhat revived by the event, but the Union defeat was not taken lightly in Washington. Although the state had been low on the list of Federal priorities, the War Department decreed that it must be taken. Public opinion in the North was critical of the loss of the foothold in Texas at Galveston.

Major Shea reported to Magruder on January 15, 1863, that the bridges and ferries affording communication between Indianola and Matagorda Island had been burned or removed. Shea said that the Federal vessels " . . . off Saluria are a three masted schooner [Note: the *Kittatinny*] with six heavy guns, and a mortar schooner with a 10 inch mortar and two 32-pounders, and between 80 and 100 men," on both ships. His comment was, "It is humiliating to us to see in our bay a small force of the enemy, and we have not the means to attack or destroy them."

In March, the *Kittatinny* was sent to Pensacola for repairs, her place at Pass Cavallo being taken by the *Owasco*. On her way to Pensacola, when off Galveston, she chased and captured a blockade runner, the *D. Sargent*, bound from Galveston to Honduras with 51 bales of cotton. The *Owasco* was, in turn, replaced at Pass Cavallo by the *Rachel Seaman*.

Although the Federals had not yet caused any difficulty with the overland traffic to and from Mexico, local elements in Texas had created

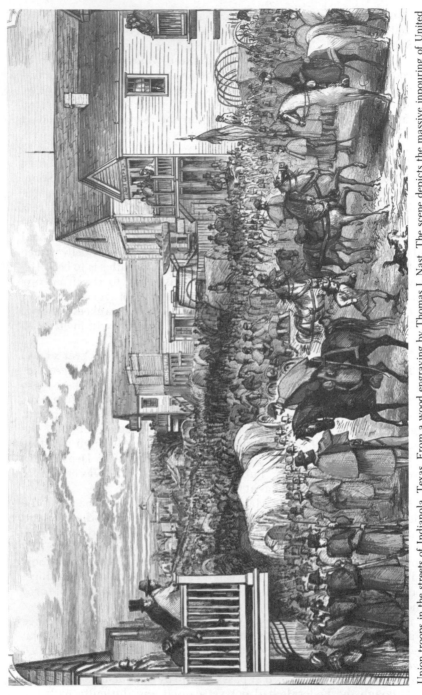

Union troops in the streets of Indianola, Texas. From a wood engraving by Thomas J. Nast. The scene depicts the massive inpouring of United States forces during the second occupation of the city, beginning in December 1863. On the right side of the street, in the distance, the roof and cupola of the Calhoun County courthouse may be seen. (*Courtesy Donald E. Cooke, President, Edraydo, Inc., Wayne, Pa.*)

problems. Writing from Alleyton on March 18, 1863, Lieutenant Colonel Henry L. Webb complained to the Assistant Adjutant General that Mexicans driving wagons and carts engaged in bringing supplies into the country had been "abused and ill-treated in the counties of DeWitt and Lavaca." Webb pointed out that it was in the interest of the Confederacy to maintain amicable relations with the Mexicans and their government, "and, as our general commanding has issued his orders to that effect, I would respectfully advise that martial law be extended over those two counties. There is evidently a disposition manifested among shirkers from the army, the conscription and the draft, to drive all Mexican transportation out of the country so that these stragglers and cowards may be assigned and employed, to screen them from service in the field.

"The Mexican trains now bringing in supplies are very large — a number of hundreds — and are owned by men of wealth and influence who reside near the frontier. All the efforts of General Magruder and General Bee will be of no avail if the most ample protection is not afforded to these Mexicans [owners of the teams] and their servants or peons . . ."

The matter of assistance to families of Confederate and State Militia servicemen became of increasing seriousness as the war progressed. In April 1863, the Calhoun county court gave the chief justice authority to have the livestock of such families marked and branded for them at a price not to exceed $1.00 per head. The court also set aside $2,500 for the purpose of supplying the families with corn, flour and other necessities of life. When the 1863 property tax rate was set at 12¢ per $100 valuation in May, a war tax of 50¢ per $100 was imposed, additional indigent families being named at most sessions of the court. A policy was also adopted that required the discontinuance of financial aid upon discharge of the family head from military service. Inflation made it necessary, in August, to increase the cash allotments for needy dependents to $50 per year for adults and $25 for children.

The time for a determined move against Texas came in September 1863, when a Union force endeavored to come in through Sabine Pass. The resounding Confederate victory at the pass under the leadership of Richard W. "Dick" Dowling on the 8th, thwarted the plans of General Nathaniel P. Banks. Indianolans derived grim satisfaction from the news that the U. S. gunboat *Clifton*, which had a part in the capture and looting of their city the previous autumn, was captured by the Confederates at Sabine Pass. But, their pleasure was soon dampened.

Banks's next move was on the lower coast with an attack on Brazos de Santiago. Brownsville was occupied on November 6 and Point Isabel two days later. Corpus Christi fell on the 16th and Aransas Pass the following day. Union troops then moved up St. Joseph's Island and were joined in a brisk fight on the 23rd at Cedar Bayou, which separates it from Matagorda Island. Flat boats were constructed, the bayou was crossed and Indianolans noted, with great alarm, the movement of the "Feds" toward Pass Cavallo.

By the 27th, Union forces under Brigadier General T. E. G. Ransom had advanced to the outer defenses of Fort Esperanza. They dug in on the night of the 28th, opening fire on the fort at daylight, November 29, continuing at intervals all day. In the meantime, the Seventh Michigan Battery advanced under cover of the sand dunes and opened fire on the fort from the right of Ransom's line. Hopelessly outnumbered and outflanked, and facing overwhelming fire power, the Confederates evacuated Fort Esperanza during the night of the 29th and retired to Indianola, after setting fire to the stores and blowing up their magazines.[13]

The Union troops immediately occupied Fort Esperanza and proceeded to make repairs. After their position was consolidated, a contingent was sent against Indianola, which was again seized and occupied after a brief but spirited fight. One of the prizes taken with the occupation was the flag that had been made by the ladies of Indianola and presented at the fort. Seventy-four years later, that flag was sent to Mrs. Howard Dudgeon of Port Lavaca by Mrs. Cora M. Hawes of Kent City, Michigan. It was presented to the Indianola Association that year by Mrs. Dudgeon and accepted by S. G. Reed, then president of the organization of former residents and descendants of Indianolans.

Flushed with victory, the Federals made plans to cross Pass Cavallo and advance up Matagorda Peninsula. After several encounters with Confederates along the way, the thrust northeastward was halted at Caney Creek. General Ransom reported that he saw 3,000 Confederate cavalry, 1,000 infantry and some artillery drawn up in the open ground just outside the fortification, which was 60 miles up the coast from Union headquarters at the pass. One Confederate, possibly posing as a deserter, came into the Union lines from Caney, stating there were 30,000 men there.

On January 27, 1864, three Confederates reached the Union lines at Indianola, having left Matagorda the night before. They reported ten regiments (about 16,000 men) and two batteries of field pieces at Caney, stating that Magruder's main force lay just behind the San Bernard in the rear of that force at Caney. They also said that the Confederate steamers *Carr*, *Cora*, *Lucy Gwin* and *Lizzie Lake*, and the schooners *Annie Dale* and *George Buckhart* were in Matagorda Bay nearby. The *Carr* and *Cora* were cotton-clads, and the former was said to have mounted the 30-pounder Parrott gun taken from the *Westfield* that had been captured in Galveston harbor. The *Cora* had a 24-pounder howitzer. Despite professed skepticism as to the reliability of the statements made by the several "deserters," being unsure as to whether the men and their information had been planted, the Union forces at length withdrew down the peninsula, and the threat to Houston was removed.

On the other side of the coin, the exact size of the Federal army was a matter of concern to Confederate military authorities. Magruder now had good reason to anticipate a move inland from the coast at Indianola, where the enemy was concentrated. Confederate Colonel James Duff gave Assistant Adjutant General W. T. Mechling at Houston his observations. A letter written at Victoria from the Headquarters of the Second Brigade, First Division, on January 24, related, "By the account given by the prisoners in my hands, the forces of the enemy at Decrow's and Indianola consist of three divisions of the Fifteenth Army Corps, one division at Indianola and two at Decrow's, say in all 15,000 men. They state that they are not as yet prepared to make an advance... My regiment is reduced so much by sickness that it is impossible to do efficient service. I have about 100 men sick in camp, exclusive of those in hospital. Spurious vaccine matter and measles are the cause of the large amount of sickness with me..."[14]

In an effort to encourage desertions from the Confederacy, Major General Napoleon J. T. Dana wrote from his Matagorda Bay headquarters to Captain Cooke, commanding the U. S. gunboat *Estrella*, lying off Pass Cavallo, about the institution of a propaganda campaign. Dated February 4, Dana said, "Two commissioned officers and 1 private, deserters from the enemy, have come in this morning. They report that so many lies are told them about the way in which they are treated here that it is very necessary some of the orders I have had printed, and Governor Hamilton's address, should be circulated among them."

Dana suggested that Cooke send an armed boat ashore at locations along Matagorda Peninsula with copies of his orders. He wanted a single copy of each order inserted in a slit in the end of a pole, and the pole stuck into the sand on the beach. "They would be sure to be picked up ... I have also some letters written by these deserters to their comrades, relating the kind of reception they meet with here, which I would like to have disposed of in the same way..."[15]

Dana addressed a communication on February 8 to Brigadier General Fitz Henry Warren, Commanding Post at Indianola, "... I wish you to preserve great vigilance and use every precaution against surprise or attack. Do not weaken your picket line or reduce its distance from the post, and scout as much as safety and your disposable means will admit. Make frequent reports in detail, and give me always your suggestions." Apparently the Union forces were as concerned about Confederate attack on Indianola as the other way around.

Further on in the letter, Dana caustically commented regarding work on fortifications at Indianola. "Hasten forward the defenses as rapidly as possible to completion... The work laid out and partly completed by Mr. J. T. Baker, engineer, on the shell mound in rear of the hospital [Note: city hospital at Indianola], is ridiculous in the extreme. It fronts the wrong way and is enfiladed from the probable approach of the enemy on the plain, the labor thus far is lost and, even worse than lost — the site is nearly spoiled.

"There was no necessity at all for a bastion work there, and the battery to be enclosed merely wanted to cover four guns and fire toward the plain and the neck, sweeping both approaches. A straight line fronting the bridge, and a flank at nearly a right angle to it facing the neck, would perfect the condition. The northern face of the battery near the wharf should be so lengthened as to cover the rear of it from a fire of a gunboat which might take up a position near the old ruined dock farthest to the westward. . . ."[16]

Although the Union soldiers stationed in Indianola stayed close to that city most of the time, occasional excursions were made into the countryside. Reconnaissance was their principal purpose, but there were instances of forays to secure fresh beef. They were at the expense of privately owned herds, from which large numbers of head were confiscated. In the course of these excursions, it was inevitable that contact would be made with outposts of the Confederates, who remained in control of the inland territory to within a few miles of Matagorda Bay at Indianola. Two such encounters on February 22, 1864, were the cause of acute embarrassment to the Union command there.

General Dana outlined, on the 23rd, one incident in an explanatory communication to Thirteenth Army Corps headquarters at New Orleans. "Brig. Gen. Warren, commanding at Indianola, reports that 25 mounted infantrymen who were scouting and driving cattle 8 miles from his post yesterday, were surrounded and charged upon by well armed and well mounted cavalry of the enemy, 55 strong. The horses of our men were poor scrubs and not trained to fire, and when the men fired a volley at the distance of 50 yards, 14 of them were unhorsed. The enemy immediately closed on them with revolvers and the 14 were captured, the other 11 escaping. General Warren reports that the affair reflects no credit on the officer in command, and I have notified him that I expect an investigation."[17]

The other incident was even more humiliating from the viewpoint of the Federal command. General Benton, reporting from Indianola on the 23rd to Assistant Adjutant General H. G. Brown, said, ". . . I send you enclosed Capt. W. Wingett's report of a scout made yesterday by the provost guard of this division under his command and which, under his bad management and disobedience of orders, resulted unfortunately in the capture by the enemy of several of his men. My instructions to the captain, given to him in person, were for him to proceed 8 or 10 miles on the Lavaca road, keeping a good lookout for the enemy and using every precaution against surprise. Instead, however, of obeying my orders, he pushed on as far as Chicolet [sic] Bayou, three miles above Port Lavaca, and 18 miles from here and this, too, notwithstanding the fact that he met the enemy's pickets within 6 miles of this place and was constantly admonished, by the presence of small scouts at different points on the prairie retreating as he advanced, that he was in the vicinity of the main rebel force, which common sense should have taught him was larger than his own.

"On arriving at Foster's house, he halted and professed, as I am informed by his men, to take dinner, although assured by Mr. Foster that the rebel camp was close at hand. While delaying here, he was notified by his picket that the enemy, apprised no doubt by their scouts of the smallness of his force, were advancing on him with near 100 cavalry.

"On receipt of this intelligence, the captain, not allowing his men to fire even a single volley, immediately ordered a hasty retreat, himself being the first to get away toward camp. No effort appears to have been made on his part to conduct his retreat in good order. The men were left to take care of themselves and were strung out according to the speed of their horses for a mile and a half on the road . . . What is still more mortifying, although the enemy diminished as they drew near this point, their fire, which had been kept up at intervals during the pursuit, was not returned, as I am informed it might have been with good effect. Captain Wingett's conduct under the circumstances is inexplicable. I have relieved him from the command of the provost guard . . . and have returned him to his regiment for the action of the major general commanding in his case . . ." The capture of the Federals was made by the Second Brigade Cavalry, C.S.A., led by Major John Thomas Brackenridge of Texana.

The instant reaction of Major General Dana to that incident, coming on top of the first, was predictable. He exploded to Warren, ". . . such scrapes are very much to be regretted and ought to be carefully avoided, as in addition to the losses and mortification they lay on us, they give great encouragement to the enemy . . . I ordered Gen. Benton to try Capt. Wingett. I wish you would report the decision and sentence in his case. Capt. Benter reports that the enemy called his name and appeared to know that he would be out there, and that the refugees and deserters report that our affairs in Indianola are known in the interior. How can this be? Is it possible that there are escapes at night, or at any time, through the picket line? The enemy will, of course, have spies in your camp if there are modes of communicating information."[18]

General Dana's dismay over rebel espionage was justified. On January 29, Colonel Duff had written to Mechling at Houston from Camp Davenport near Texana, "There is no change in matters at Indianola. The enemy is gradually increasing its cavalry force. Rifle pits have been dug, and from present indications I infer that probably the main depot for supplies will be at Indianola . . . I have now in camp two youths arrested by my pickets a few miles out of Powder Horn. These boys state that the most of the Germans have voluntarily taken the oath of allegiance to the Northern States, and that no attempt as yet has been made to compel the citizens generally to swear allegiance; that Captains Shepherd [Sheppard] and Rice [Reuss] are on parole not to leave the place and required to report on each morning to the provost marshal's office.

"My force is very weak, men and horses suffering from the effects of the salt water they are compelled to use whilst on picket duty. I have just been informed that the majority of Gregg's company of infantry, State Troops, at Victoria have deserted. I will send to their homes and endeavor to arrest them. . . ."[19]

Later the same day, Duff again reported to Mechling, "Since writing my communication to you of this date, I have received information which places the cavalry force of the enemy at Indianola stronger than I anticipated . . . It is the opinion of Captain Tevis, who reconnoitered them, that the enemy now has regular cavalry at that place. My cavalry force does not number, all told, more than 265 effective men, and many of the horses of even this number are entirely broken down from constant picket service . . . It is absolutely necessary to relieve the picket every eight or ten days to preserve the health of man and beast, as all the water near the coast is now so brackish and full of dead stock as to be absolutely loathsome . . ."[20]

On February 28, a confidential message was addressed to Brigadier General Hamilton P. Bee from Assistant Adjutant General Turner at Houston stating that General Magruder contemplated an attack on Indianola. Request was made of Bee for detailed information on available troops and supplies necessary to sustain such a venture.

By coincidence, on the same day that Turner addressed the message to Bee, and before it was received, General Bee himself had written to Brigadier General J. E. Slaughter, chief of staff, saying, "I enclose copy of communication from Colonel Duff. I respectfully request permission to attack Indianola. My scouts went [down Matagorda Peninsula] within three miles of Decrow's Point on Friday and encountered no enemy. The people living in the vicinity told them that most of the enemy had left, and the intention was to abandon the peninsula, removing what stores they had to Fort Esperanza, which is guarded with negroes. Some think that the enemy are going to Powder Horn, others to New Orleans. I shall send Captain Buchel down tomorrow with a strong scout.

"There are many reasons in favor of an attack on Indianola . . . A successful attack would inspirit and give new life to the army. I am acquainted with the country around Indianola and would submit my plans if permitted to do so by the general command. I propose to take all of the troops, except Colonel Gillespie's command. Strength of the enemy [at Indianola] from 4,000 to 6,000."[21]

By mid-March, thoughts of attacking Indianola were abandoned. The Confederates had been alerted by their scouts to a build-up of Federal forces there. Now believing that a Union plan was definitely afoot to invade Texas from Indianola, as Magruder long ago thought would happen, contingency plans were formulated. Turner advised Colonel Duff, in camp on the Navidad, on March 16, 1864, "I am instructed by the major general commanding to say that the corn at Gonzales will be placed at the disposal of Col. John S. Ford, only enough being allowed to remain for the garrison. The commissary and subsistence stores at Clinton and Victoria are placed at your disposal.

"I am further directed to say that, should you find the supply of corn and provisions at Clinton and Victoria insufficient, you will direct the officers or agents in charge of the depots at Hallettsville and Sweet Home to keep on hand corn and subsistence supplies enough to furnish your command in case it should be compelled to fall back to Columbus by way of Hallettsville This movement, however, will not take place unless you are absolutely forced to it by the enemy. Should the enemy advance from Indianola, all the stores at Victoria that you cannot take away must be burned. Notify the officer in charge of these supplies to this effect. You will withdraw all these stores from Victoria, as well as from Clinton to your present encampment . . . on the Navidad."

Demonstrating the feeling of urgency, and the detailed planning that had been done, Turner continued, "Should the enemy advance on Texana, you will fall back to Wharton, to which place you will send a part of these stores if you have time, and make a small depot (or depots) for several days' supply of corn and meal so as to be enabled to keep your scouts in presence of the advancing enemy and to ascertain his real intentions. Should the enemy pursue in numbers greatly superior, you will fall back to Richmond, but will ascertain with precision whether the enemy takes the road to Columbia or Richmond. Arriving at Richmond, you will cross the bridge and endeavor to prevent the passage of the enemy at that point, to which other troops will be sent by railroad for the same duty.

"As soon as it is ascertained that the enemy are marching on Texana, you will inform Colonel Bates, and the latter will prepare for the immediate evacuation of the mouths of Caney and Bernard. Should the enemy advance east from Texana you will, by swift courier, inform Colonel Bates, who will cause the troops at the mouths of the Caney to cross the Bernard by the pontoon bridges, breaking or burning them as soon as the troops are crossed."[22]

Preparing for the invasion from Indianola that was momentarily expected, E. R. Tarver, assistant adjutant general, moved to the Headquarters, Army in the Field, at Wharton. There, on March 17, he addressed a communication to "Colonel Bates, Commanding Army in the Field. Sir: The general commanding directs me to state that your command includes all troops from Duff's command on the west now stationed on the Lavaca River to San Luis Pass. The following regiments and companies are in your command: Duff's and Brown's regiments of cavalry, Bates' Second [Thirteenth] Texas Infantry, Waul's Legion, and three batteries, Dashiell's, Hughes' and Jones'; also the fleet in Matagorda Bay, as well as Rugeley's company at Matagorda. The latter company is dismounted all but about 20 men. The horses are in the neighborhood of that place. I would suggest that you require a field return from each regiment and battery for your information, which will give you their strength and location. . . ."[23] Rumors of an anticipated Federal invasion from Indianola alarmed civilians in the path of possible routes. Plans were made for quick evacuation to the interior of Western Texas if the war actually came to their doorstep.

Major General J. B. Magruder wrote personally to Colonel Duff saying, "You will remember that the line of retreat is on Richmond, and that Hallettsville, &c, are only mentioned as places through which you might be forced by circumstances to march on your way to Columbus . . . Recollect in all cases, if pursued by the enemy, to thoroughly destroy the bridges and boats over any stream which you have passed . . .

"Should the enemy, however, march on Victoria, you will remain near Texana to ascertain if he will take the road to Hallettsville or the road to Clinton and Gonzales. If to Hallettsville, you will fall back to Richmond as before directed. If to Clinton, you will endeavor to cut his communications and destroy his wagons, hanging on his rear and flanks, making prisoners of stragglers, &c, in all cases giving information to Colonel Bates, the commanding officer of the flotilla, and these headquarters. . . ."

A sudden, dramatic turn of events gave relief from fears of inland advance from Indianola. Developing in March was Banks's ill-starred Red River Campaign, in support of which Union troops were being secretly withdrawn in large numbers from the Texas coastal region. This directly affected the fortunes of Indianola, whose residents had been virtual prisoners since their town was occupied by the enemy. Pointing to what was then a puzzling change in Union deployment, Colonel Duff reported to General Slaughter from "Camp on Lavaca, March 18, 1864." Duff said, "The U.S. forces evacuated Indianola on the 15th instant and, as the citizens report, have gone to Saluria. My picket scouts on yesterday morning, finding no pickets this side of Powder Horn, continued to move in cautiously until they found the place abandoned [Note: by the Federals], with every indication that it is not the intention of the enemy to reoccupy it. Strange to say, none of the citizens notified us of the departure of the enemy until their absence was discovered as reported. . . ."[24]

Duff personally followed up on the report of his scouts. On his return from Indianola to headquarters on the Lavaca River near Texana on the 28th, he advised Slaughter that he had ascertained more than 5,000 Union troops were on Matagorda Island near Saluria. "General Warren's command on evacuation of Indianola consisted of 14 regiments of an average strength of about 350 each. He had eight rifled 6-pounders, four 12-pounders and two 12-pounder rifled guns. The town . . . was well fortified against an attack by land both above and below. The place is a perfect wreck, and at least one third of the houses destroyed or removed. All the money, jewels, plate &c that could be obtained were carried off. The impression left on the minds of the citizens from conversations overheard was that the main part of the command was destined for Louisiana, and that the invasion of Texas would be made from that direction." Narrowly did Texans near the coast escape the horrors of war being visited upon their communities.

Duff further stated, "On the 25th there were five steamers inside the bar and one outside; twelve sails inside and four outside. This looks as if they intended removing at least a portion of the forces now there. I trust I will be able to report in a few days whether . . . this is correct or not."[25]

The supposition of the citizens of Indianola about the destination of the Union soldiers who were being pulled out of the Matagorda Bay region was correct. The troops were sent to Northwestern Louisiana for concentration near Shreveport and an attempt to invade Texas from that quarter. On April 8, 1864, the Federals suffered a decisive defeat in the battle of Mansfield, Louisiana, which ended attempts to secure physical control of Texas.

Although nuisance movements into Matagorda Bay by the Federals occurred at intervals during the next several weeks, for all practical purposes Indianola was rid of them for the balance of the war. The last Union soldier was withdrawn from Matagorda Island on June 15, whereupon Fort Esperanza was reoccupied by the Confederates, who retained control until shortly after General Lee's surrender at Appomattox on April 9, 1865.

Indianolans quickly turned to repairing their town as best they could, erasing reminders of the unpleasant state in which they had been held during the Federal occupation. Nothing could be done about the theft of the personal property by the invaders. The loss of objects of sentimental value was much more painful than the monetary blow merchants and householders alike suffered. Able bodied men went to work to fill the rifle pits that had been dug on private and public property. The end of the war would have to come before there could be rebuilding of structures that had been burned or dismantled and their lumber used by the military, both Confederate and Union.

The Confederate-ordered burning of Saluria, coupled with Federal destruction of residences down Matagorda Island, had resulted in a general exodus of the population there. On October 7, 1864, the county court recognized the deserted condition of the island. It was acknowledged that, as long as the blockade existed and danger remained of further Union incursions in that exposed land area, it would continue in an abandoned state. The court then decreed that Precinct 4, which encompassed the island, should no longer exist as a political entity and that it be incorporated into and made a part of Precinct 3, Indianola.[26]

On the same day, A. W. Norris was called to task for the dangerous condition of the bridge across Chocolate Bayou, the site of a skirmish between Federals and Confederates on January 23. He was ordered to repair the bridge and install side rails. Inasmuch as Norris had a license from the court to charge tolls for passage over the structure, which he owned, the court made sure the repairs would be made promptly by revoking his privilege for collecting tolls until the work was done.[27]

Calhoun County Chief Justice W. H. Woodward wrote to the financial agent of the state penitentiary at Huntsville on December 19, requesting the allotment of cloth and thread which was required by the Legislature's act of November 15, 1864, to be set aside for the use of counties which had received none under the regulations existing prior to the passage of the measure. The erection of a cotton and woolen textile mill at the penitentiary had been made possible by the Legislature in 1854. The mill was an important source of denim, woolens and other heavy materials for the Confederate Army. The piece goods received by Calhoun County were made available to families of servicemen who were in dire circumstances as a result of the economic stagnation. By February 1865, there were 297 dependents of county servicemen receiving financial and other aid from the local government.[28]

The tax burden weighed heavily on the community. Income taxes paid to the county tax assessor-collector under the act of November 15,

1864, and covering the three months from December 1, 1864, to February 28, 1865, were $3,356.00. The scarcity of money made it necessary that the Legislature provide for payment of taxes in "such articles of prime necessity as the county court shall, from time to time, deem necessary for the support and maintenance of the persons provided for in this act." It called for the designation of places in each county where the items proposed to be delivered in payment of taxes, and in lieu of cash, would be received. Any taxpayer who desired to pay in produce or other articles at a fair market value set by the court, delivered them to the points of collection in Indianola and Lavaca. Provision was also made by the Legislature that "no property belonging to a soldier in the active military service, or naval or marine service of the Confederate States shall be sold for taxes."[29]

And still the need grew for relief of human suffering. On April 3, Dr. J. M. Reuss of Indianola was authorized by the court to employ "a competent person" to slaughter and distribute beeves that had been appropriated by Confederate military authorities for the support of destitute families. The pay allowance for the butcher was set at $20 per month, payable out of the county treasury. James H. Duncan was authorized to hire a drover to move appropriated beeves for the support of families in want in Old Town. The sum paid for that was $8 per month in specie.[30]

The assessment of property in Calhoun County for the year 1864 was shown on the tax rolls to be: 97,038 acres of land valued at $83,270; town lots valued at $143,930; 175 negro slaves valued at $62,400; specie $43,747; state warrants $2,091; Confederate notes $73,695; bank bills $160 and horses, cattle and miscellaneous property $223,443.[31] The listed value of some of these items was to be wiped out soon. On June 19, 1865, Union Major General Gordon Granger destroyed, in one fell swoop, $136,095. He did that by proclaiming, upon his arrival in Galveston that day, the emancipation of slaves and the end of the Confederacy in Texas. As a consequence, the Confederate notes, which had had only a paper value for a long time, were publicly acknowledged to be worthless.

The eventual outcome of the four-year-long conflict had been apparent to Indianolans for a long period of time. Its end, in defeat for the Confederacy, brought a feeling of mingled sorrow and relief. How strange it seemed that the battle of Palmito Ranch, and the resultant Federal rout, occurred on May 11, over a month after the capitulation of the South. Did the Confederates in the Rio Grande Valley actually not know of the war's end, or was it their "last fling" to inflict a humiliating defeat on the Union force that had landed at Brazos de Santiago and then moved to occupy Brownsville, expecting no opposition from a conquered foe? Whichever it was, and they suspected the latter, Indianolans were pleased by that last engagement, their thoughts going back to the occupation of their town and the looting of their valuables.

Now they began to look to the future, which they viewed with confidence. It could only be bright. Their industry and resourcefulness would lift them out of the economic collapse that was the legacy of the fratricidal war. The issue of the right of secession by states having been decided by the Union victory, as was that of the institution of slavery, now the wounds of war could be healed, they thought, and all could work together to unite and rebuild the nation. They reckoned without the steps that the vengeful Congress would take to "reconstruct" the rebellious states!

XVI.

Convalescence from War Fever

Indianolan Fletcher S. Stockdale had been elected lieutenant governor of Texas on November 5, 1863. With the collapse of the Confederacy and the flight of Governor Pendleton Murrah to Mexico in the aftermath of Appomattox, Stockdale became interim head of state. Thenceforth, he was referred to as "Governor" Stockdale. He served in that capacity until A. J. Hamilton, appointed provisional governor by President Andrew Johnson in July 1865, took over the office under the wing of the occupation army commanded by General Granger.

Union troops began to pour into the state on Granger's heels for the purpose of imposing military rule. Until they arrived on the scene, the county judge was the supreme authority. At Indianola, Judge W. H. Woodward continued to work in securing aid for the impoverished. On May 26, he wrote to Colonel O. Steele at Victoria, requesting that destitute families in Calhoun County share in the distribution of Confederate commissary supplies, which were to be parceled out there. Woodward said to Steele, "You know the helpless condition of the families of our soldiers in this county, and I feel sure you will see that they get whatever of the effects of the Government they may be entitled to."[1]

A bit more help came from D. M. Stapp. In addition to other duties he had performed during the war years, Stapp served as collector of customs for the Confederate government at Matagorda Bay. His office there was the designated depository for funds of the Confederate States. On June 1, he turned over to the county for the use of indigent families $132.00 which remained in his possession. The county acted further to relieve the hunger of the families in want. Woodward used the balance of specie in the county treasury for the purchase of 106-⅔ bushels of corn to be ground into meal. He set aside 36-⅔ bushels for use at Lavaca, the balance of 70 bushels being placed in the hands of Dr. J. M. Reuss for distribution, at his discretion, in Indianola.[2]

A great psychological boost to the county in that difficult time was receipt of a letter from the state comptroller's office in Austin giving notice that Calhoun was entitled to $5,270.80, its portion of the taxes from the county collected in 1863. It was to be used for relief. Two drafts were forwarded. One was on J. L. Allen of Indianola for $1,212.96, the other on C. .L. Thurmond of Victoria for $4,057.84.

The lifting of the Federal blockade of Matagorda Bay on June 24, 1865, by order of President Johnson reopened the gates of commerce to Indianola. Frontier forts had to be restaffed and resupplied. In some cases, partial rebuilding was necessary. Because Indianola was the Texas port at which government supplies for Western Texas, as well as for the New Mexico and Arizona Territories, were unloaded, the renewed movement of goods was a factor in the speedy recovery of the town. Silver, lead, copper and other exports of Chihuahua once more began to flow through Indianola, as did agricultural products from Western Texas. Lumber and other building material, manufactured goods, machinery, together with the passenger and freight traffic to the Southwest, long shut off by the blockade, restarted as a dribble and quickly became a flood.

Charles Morgan had been busy in New York and Washington in the waning months of the war, laying plans for the rehabilitation of his steamship empire. He had few vessels left in his possession, most having been taken over by the Union and Confederate governments. Some had been lost during the conflict, but others were seaworthy. Morgan bought back those which he needed to reestablish supremacy in the Gulf trade, and placed orders for new steamers. With availability of materials, one of the first steps taken at Indianola was rebuilding of damaged or destroyed wharves and warehouses, residences and commercial houses. Almost immediately there was employment for all who sought it, as a result of which the impoverished condition of families at the end of the war eased.

Disillusioned, angered Confederate veterans caused local difficulties in some Texas towns by giving vent to their frustrations. They did that in the seizure of merchandise still held in the name of the fallen government, and by a generally antagonistic attitude toward civil authority. Indianola was spared that problem. Hers had always been an economy based on maritime commerce. There was no dominant planter's class, as was true in the states from Louisiana eastward. Calhoun County did not have the great plantations with large slaveholdings, whose postwar

The *City of Norfolk*, which called at Indianola for many years, was typical of the steamers serving the port. An iron paddle side-wheeler, she was built at Wilmington, Del. in 1866 for Charles Morgan. (*Courtesy The Mariners Museum, Newport News, Va.*)

prostration brought down with them the economic structure of communities in the deep South. Because Western Texas was not a slaveholding region in the sense that Virginia, Louisiana and South Carolina were, emancipation had limited effect. The area's large percentage of European-born citizens, men and women steeped in the tradition of thrift and personal industriousness, was to serve it in good stead in the years following the end of the conflict. The problems to be created were inspired by reconstruction politics, and policies administered by the despised "Carpetbaggers."

Governor Hamilton's proclamation of August 19, 1865, following that which President Johnson had issued three months earlier, concerned the administration of the amnesty oath. It resulted in an order being placed by the Calhoun County court with the Victoria *Advocate* for blank forms to be used for the purpose. Included in the order were 100 amnesty blanks, 100 certificates to accompany oaths for special pardon, and 400 certificates for registering voters. However, it was not until September that the records of the district and county clerks, which had been sent to Victoria for safekeeping in May, 1862, were returned to their proper place in the courthouse at Indianola.

The city was designated as headquarters for one of the sub-assistant commissioners stationed in Texas to administer affairs for the Bureau of Refugees, Freedmen and Abandoned Lands.[3] The duties of the commissioners were concerned chiefly with former slaves, and were to ensure that their civil rights were protected in matters of employment and participation in political affairs, to provide educational opportunities and to supervise their general welfare. Because of the small number of ex-slaves in Calhoun County, the commissioner's duties there were not nearly as arduous as was the case with those assigned to plantation counties of Eastern Texas. In that section there were residing not only the locally freed slaves, but also many who had migrated from Louisiana as they sought the 40 acres and a mule they naively believed each would receive. With the approaching disenfranchisement of voters who had served the Confederacy in political or military affairs, the importance of the freed slaves to individuals plotting control of local government by use of the ballot box was obvious.

The Texas Department of State had instructed on February 1, 1866, that the county transmit to that office in Austin all the amnesty oaths taken up to January 8. Also required were the suffrage lists that had been prepared. There was, at that time, no realization that most of the names on the lists would be struck off and the right to exercise the vote denied those who supported the Confederacy. Indianola was to be no different in that respect than other Southern towns.

In the meantime, city and county matters moved forward with energy, and improvements were projected. The *Times* commented on the activity. "One unsightly object, at least, in our city is being abated. We allude to the slough, or arm, of the bayou running up to Main Street near the center of the town. This is being filled up and the foundations of buildings laid where only a few months ago was [sic] several feet of water. The reclamation of these water lots is one of the best evidences of the future expansion and prosperity of Indianola.

"There is another significant fact connected with the improvements now going on. Buildings are being erected on the back streets, near the railroad. This shows that the proprietors are looking to the completion of the road at no distant day, and the consequent attraction of business to that locality." The *Times* was referring to the railroad right of way and the embankment that had been graded prior to the beginning of the war. Plans were to revive the charter of the Indianola Railroad Company, which had lapsed because of the war and suspension of construction activity. That suspension precluded completion of the required mileage within the time set. On October 19, 1866, the Texas Legislature renewed the charter of the road, and extended the time for completion of the first 15 miles to January 1, 1871, a deadline that was met.

The county cooperated with the city in planning the construction of a bridge across Blind Bayou within the town limits. The court appropriated $200 as its part of the cost of the bridge, which was to be used as a permanent direct route for the county road that led from Powder Horn Bayou to Old Town and Lavaca. Other improvements charted included the expenditure of $800 for rebuilding the courthouse fence. Repair to and strengthening of the cupola on the courthouse was slated, as was reglazing several windows, now that glass was again available on the local market. The lightning rod on the top of the cupola was reset and firmly secured.

Reminiscent of the days before the war was the sight of caravans loaded with goods for export. The *Times* observed, "A long train of Mexican carts laden with hides were seen this morning wending their way along Main Street toward the wharf. From the large shipments of this article . . . made at this port, a stranger in Texas might be induced to inquire where all these hides come from. But, Texas is an empire in extent and can furnish pasturage for many thousand head of cattle more than are at present found on our vast prairies. Indeed, the resources of Texas in stock raising are beyond computation." On the subject of cattle movement, Editor Benton noted, "The number of beef cattle shipped from our port is a matter of astonishment to those unacquainted with the resources and exports of Texas. The *Hewes*, on her last trip, took off the largest freight of livestock, we believe, that has been shipped at any one time since the war."

A study of port statistics for the year September 1, 1865, to August 31, 1866, illustrates the recovery that Indianola was making. The data disclose that 80,389 containers of assorted merchandise came in during that period. There were also 62,306 containers of grocery items, 2,143 barrels of whiskey, 90 hogsheads sugar, 1,081 barrels sugar, 10,099 barrels flour, 2,412 kegs nails, 362 plows, 339 boxes coal oil in metal cans, 2,063 bags coffee, 452 barrels molasses, 390 bales hay, 12,003 sacks corn, 2,200 sacks oats, 145 tons coal, 1,800 palmetto logs (for wharf building), 2,210,235 feet lumber, 1,002,229 shingles, 118,000 laths, 268 doors and 648 pairs sash.

Exports in that same period were 9,342 bales cotton, 2,141 bales wool, 8,935 bags wool, 69,451 hides, 1,955 pigs lead, 2,374 containers merchandise, 44 barrels tallow, 122 boxes cotton cards, 8,962 barrels pecans, 1,028 pigs copper, 1,390 bags cotton seed, 120 barrels molasses, 25 bales sheep skins, 24,727 pounds sumac, 16 barrels nitre, 385 sacks corn, 130 tons ice, 318 head mules, 12,056 head cattle, 8,285 pounds rope, 40,028 goat skins and two barrels beeswax. Vessels entering and clearing the port of Indianola in that time were 486.[4]

Substantial as those figures were, they disclose a drastic drop in volume from the last reporting period prior to the war. Nevertheless, trade was in a state of spirited revival and would continue to increase each year until the catastrophic hurricane of 1875 selected Indianola as its target.

Ice harvested from New England ponds in mid-winter and brought to Indianola was again available on the local market through the warm months of the year. Destroyed in 1875, the Indianola icehouse was rebuilt, second only to the courthouse as the sturdiest structure in town. Its massive construction and double thick walls gave it the strength to go through the 1886 hurricane. After that storm, when Indianola was abandoned, the icehouse was floated across Matagorda Bay to Carancahua Bay, where it was hauled ashore on log rollers. There it was converted into a large two story residence that served as the home of the Ben Ward family until after World War I. In 1866, the Indianola icehouse was operated by C. L. Stadtler, whose wagons delivered the precious cargo even to customers in Victoria.

When the army of occupation reached Indianola following General Granger's arrival in Galveston, the matter of permanent quarters was of first consideration. Until housing was erected, the commissioned officers were billeted in the homes of Indianola residents. Noncommissioned officers and men were housed in tents in a large camp on the edge of town. Although the original Army Supply Depot had its facilities in Old Town, the occupation force was to be located on the block near Powder Horn Bayou bounded by Fannin, Crockett, A and B Streets. The Quartermaster and General Headquarters office was located on the half block facing Main between Milam and Travis. This was within two blocks of the bayou, 11 blocks from the courthouse and adjacent to the wharves. The post was manned by Company B, 35th United States Infantry. The Post of Indianola was maintained until the withdrawal of the military at the end of the Reconstruction period. Except for rare minor incidents related to drunkenness on the part of individual soldiers, the relations between Indianolans and the occupying forces were cordial.

Reconstruction of the San Antonio & Mexican Gulf Railroad was given priority by the Federal government. Work began in 1865 and was completed in the summer of 1866. Daily service (except Sunday) was resumed between Lavaca and Victoria on August 15. For the work of rebuilding, the government filed a claim against the SA&MG which still, in theory at least, was a privately owned corporation. The lien of

Marble soda fountain flavor-dispenser used in Reuss Drug Store, Indianola and later in the store at Cuero. Its flavors were nectar, sarsaparilla, vanilla, lemon, raspberry, chocolate, pineapple and orange. It also provided Vichy water as a mixing ingredient. Reuss's is the oldest pharmacy in continuous operation in Texas. It has been staffed by four generations of the same family. (*Courtesy Joe B. Reuss, Reuss Drug Store, Cuero, Texas.*)

$45,000 was not paid and, in 1870, the road was sold by court order, the original local owners losing their investment.

Stage lines still provided the only passenger service out of Indianola. The *Times* commented, "We observed the other day that the stages failed to make connection with the steamer. Two stages drove up to the Casimir House just in time for the passengers to witness the *Hewes* under way a few hundred yards from the wharf. We understand that there was much dissatisfaction among the passengers, who had been told somewhere above that the steamers did not leave our wharf until 6 o'clock. This is a mistake. They generally leave at about 4 o'clock p.m." Upsetting experiences such as this ceased to occur when Indianola was served by a rail line owned by Charles Morgan who was, also, owner of the principal passenger steamers. The eventual coordination of his rail and steamship schedules was a comfortable assurance for travelers through the port.

January 1867 was ushered in for Indianola with a fire that leveled the post office, the custom house, David Lewis's drug store and the merchandise houses of W. P. Milby, Dudley Schultz and John H. Dale. As a result of the disaster, the volunteer fire department received public financial support in acquiring additional fire fighting equipment. The spread of the fire was attributed to the lack of a suitable pumper which would have enabled the hard-pressed firemen to use, in large volume, the limitless supply of bay water that was only a short distance from the scene.[5]

Calhoun County was divided into four school districts by the court in January 1867 and A. T. Hensley, D. E. Crosland, Dr. J. M. Reuss, D. C. Proctor and H. J. Huck were appointed members of the Board of School Examiners. The ravages of inflation were reflected in the increase of the annual salary of the county judge from $50 to $250. The county clerk's salary was also adjusted upward to that figure. The need for a bridge across the upper reaches of Powder Horn Bayou at Caloma on the road from Indianola to Long Mott resulted in an appropriation of $200 being made for the structure. A joint board of construction supervisors for the work consisted of John Dooley, John Roemer and J. Bouquet. At the July 8 meeting of the court, R. M. Forbes presented a bill for $50 covering rental of a house occupied in Lavaca by the county clerk from September 1864 to June 30, 1865. The county office had been temporarily removed from Indianola in fear of another Federal incursion.

In 1867, Henry J. Huck reached an agreement with the trustees of the Indianola Methodist Episcopal Church for payment of the balance of the debt on the sanctuary. It dated back to June 21, 1860, when the original deed of trust was signed by the Rev. Green Orr, Joseph Carter and William J. Bloodworth. On June 7, 1867, Huck was paid $370.37 against the remaining indebtedness of $726.28, whereupon he stated to Messrs. Rooke, Benton and Rundell his decision to cancel the remainder of $355.91 due him, displaying the same attitude of kindliness and generosity that had become his hallmark in the very beginning of Indianola.

Homer S. Thrall, who had been appointed to serve the Indianola Methodist Church at the 1866 Texas Conference, wrote in his book, *Methodism in Texas*, that, "The year 1867 might, in Texas, be denominated the 'Year of Death.' The yellow fever in a malignant form appeared at Indianola in July. [Note: It happened in June, not July]. The first minister who fell its victim was Thomas F. Cook, who contracted the disease at Indianola and died July 24 at his home in Texana.

In "Year of Crucifixion: Galveston, Texas," Kathleen Davis refers to news reaching Galveston that yellow fever was present in Indianola. "Despite some confusion in civil government, day to day activity [in Galveston] apparently remained fairly calm and normal, at least until the arrival on June 28 of the steamship *Harlan* from Indianola, where 10 deaths from yellow fever were reported to have occurred. Accounts by attending physicians and contemporary newspapers trace the origin of the pestilence to Vera Cruz where 'negro vomito' was known to have been raging. A ship from that Mexican city had arrived in Indianola in May or June, depositing a family of refugees from the epidemic. The family soon afterward had been stricken and, so it seemed, had everyone who helped them or touched any of their possessions.

"A Baltimore-born young German by the name of Moller had visited Indianola in his travels through Texas. Moller arrived in Galveston on June 28, became ill the next day and died on July 3. His death, which Flake's Bulletin attributed to 'congestion of the bowels,' is generally considered the first in Galveston [Note: meaning the first that year] from yellow fever."[6]

Mayor F. E. Hughes of Indianola appeared before the county court on July 8, 1867, to discuss with the commissioners the large number of indigent persons of the county seeking admission to City Hospital for treatment of yellow fever. Mayor Hughes suggested that those individuals residing outside the city limits of Indianola were properly wards of the county. The court agreed and ordered that for all such persons treated for the disease in the hospital, the city would be reimbursed by the county at the rate of two dollars per day.

Dr. J. M. Reuss prepared a written report on the 1867 yellow fever epidemic that provided details of the disease. It also illustrated the mistaken ideas prevalent at that time, even among the most learned members of the medical profession. Dr. Reuss's writings were made part of a comprehensive history of yellow fever epidemics in Texas compiled by Greensville Dowell, M.D., and published at Philadelphia in 1876. The Reuss report is contained in Appendix A of this volume.

Commenting further on the epidemic, Thrall spoke of several ministers who died at Indianola and Lavaca. Among them were William T. Harris, Methodist, who served the churches at Lavaca and Victoria; George C. Moore, Presbyterian, and Father Alexis Renox, Catholic. Thrall was prostrated by yellow fever, but had recovered sufficiently to be present with Father Renox at the moment of his death.

The 1867 epidemic was widespread in Texas, taking a heavy toll in Galveston and Houston, and extending to parts of the state that had never before suffered greatly from it. Cases were reported from counties as far inland as Walker, Washington and Fayette. But, despite yellow fever, business boomed!

Indicative of Indianola's role in Texas trade was the amount of license taxes paid by business houses during the year ending September 30, 1867. Calhoun County ranked fourth in the state.[7] The continuing economic recovery of Western Texas from the effects of the recent war was also shown in the report of imports and exports moving through Indianola for 1867, as compared with the previous 12-month period. In cattle exports, the total had increased 50%, for cotton 70%, for general merchandise 900%. On imports, general merchandise was up by more than 600%, groceries by 59%, lumber by 300%, shingles by 130%, coffee in bags by 500% and flour in barrels by 57%.[8]

Under military rule, the court issued an order on October 2, 1867, whereby all male citizens of Calhoun County between the ages of 18 and 45 became subject to impressment for work on roads. A stipulation of the order was that this forced labor could only be required within the precinct in which each man resided. Another provision was that Henry Sheppard, overseer of the road from Indianola to Lavaca by way of Old Town, would use the men under his jurisdiction to proceed in the construction of the bridge across Blind Bayou, which had been planned as a joint project by the county and city of Indianola a year earlier, but never built.[9] There was instant furious opposition to the order. A characteristic comment was that the Union troops had come in to free the negro slaves and now sought to impose a condition of involuntary bondage on white males who had never been slave owners. The order soon proved to be unenforceable.

United States Major General Winfield Scott Hancock, commanding the Fifth Military District with headquarters at New Orleans, on December 18, 1867, had ordered that an election be held in Texas on February 10 through 14, 1868, to determine whether a constitutional convention should be called in accordance with the act of Congress of March 23, 1867. At the time, 108,799 voters were registered in the state and about 50% went to the polls. A total of 44,689 favored calling a "Texas Reconstruction Convention," 11,440 being opposed. Delegates elected from District 60, comprised of Calhoun, Victoria, Jackson and DeWitt Counties were Samuel M. Johnson from Calhoun and W. M. Varnell from DeWitt. Of the 90 delegates elected, 83 were Republicans and 7 were labeled "Conservatives." There were no Democrats.[10] Nine of the delegates were black, a surprisingly small number in view of the fact that black candidates were openly favored by the military overseeing the election. The exceedingly long constitution that resulted from the convention was unsatisfactory to Texans. Its provisions led to such abuses of power that the post-Reconstruction Constitutional Convention of 1875 strictly limited concentration of authority in a centralized state government.

Political problems had no restraining effect on plans for church expansion. Marie Melanie Goux, the Mother St. Anastasia, "Superioress of the Convent of Indianola," reached an agreement with Crittenden, Burnley, *et. al.*, on March 31, 1868, for the purchase of a full city block, number 325, on which it was intended to construct a masonry convent building. The purchase price was a token $1.00. The block was bounded by G, H, Palo Alto and Monterrey Streets. That structure was a goal of such magnitude that it would require a large investment of funds to be secured from parishioners.

Knowing that the project would require several years to fulfill, Mother St. Anastasia then bargained with Crittenden, Burnley, *et. al*, the latter-day developers of the Indianola townsite, for lots on Main Street between Hays and Burleson, where a frame building was erected to serve until the grand plan was carried to completion. She bought Lot 4, Block 52 for $350 in gold. Lot 3 in the same block was purchased for $300 in specie. The frame building housed St. Mary's Institute, the school, and was intended to be used as interim convent until funds could be raised for the masonry building on Block 325 for occupancy by the Sisters of Mercy of St. Patrick. On April 12, 1871, Mother St. Anastasia transferred ownership of Block 325 to His Excellency, C. M. Dubuis, Bishop of Galveston, with the provision that the sole use to which the property could be put was for the site of the permanent convent and school.[11] The 1875 storm put an end to the grand plan!

With the arrival of the summer of 1868, the headquarters of the Fifth Military District issued an order requiring the establishment of quarantine stations on the Gulf coast. The ravages of the yellow fever epidemic of the previous year prompted the action, which was taken in an effort to forestall a repeat of the scourge. In obedience to the military order, the Calhoun County court prepared a set of regulations governing the operation of a quarantine station in Matagorda Bay, and issued a proclamation giving notice of intention to enforce strict compliance.

A flagstaff was fastened to the wreck of the *Portland*. Attached to the staff was a yellow flag, which served as a signal of the quarantine station and gave notice to incoming ships to cast anchor and wait for a boarding party. The rules required that all vessels entering the bay would pay a fee to the Indianola quarantine surgeon covering his visit to and examination of the ships and those aboard. Rates set for the inspection were $5 for every vessel between 50 and 100 tons burthen, $10 for those between 100 and 300 tons, and $15 for all whose burthen exceeded 300 tons. Under the fee system, the quarantine surgeon was to defray all costs, including the employment of a man with suitable boat to convey him to and from arriving ships. The quarantine order went into effect on July 10 and continued until October 6, at which time it was concluded that "the health of the community is no longer endangered by the trade existing with our port," whereupon it was lifted.[12]

The Supreme Court of the United States ruled in favor of Robert S. Crittenden, Frances A. Burnley, William R. Johnson, Dr. Levi Jones and Royal A. Porter in their long legal struggle to secure control of the Juan Cano League on which Indianola was situated. Represented by their attorneys, Fletcher S. Stockdale and D. C. Proctor, the proprietors had the townsite resurveyed, platted and mapped by E. A. Hensoldt, civil engineer of Victoria, who had come to Texas from Germany in 1848. The map prepared by Hensoldt was authenticated, dated November 23, 1868, and filed for record with the Calhoun County clerk at Indianola on November 28.[13]

The proprietors kept for themselves the whole waterfront on the bay and on both sides of Powder Horn Bayou, making declaration that none was dedicated to public use. That position, which was widely shared by other property holders along the Texas coast, would later be challenged in and disallowed by the courts.

As would be expected, Crittenden, Burnley, *et. al.*, did dedicate for public use all streets, alleys and certain squares whose locations were shown on the map, and which had previously been so dedicated when the area was first laid out as Brown's Addition to Indianola. Their statement stipulated that the alleys were dedicated to the special use of the holders of property abutting upon them, but provided that the alleys could be closed by the unanimous consent of all such property holders on the block.[14] The ruling of the Supreme Court had negligible effect in the city, as those holding real property through previous purchase had already reached agreement on title with the now-recognized proprietors.

XVII.

Cattle Turned into Gold

The enormous increase in the number of cattle on the Texas range during the War Between the States, when outside markets were cut off, resulted in a total at the end of the conflict that has been variously estimated at from five to eight million head. As a consequence, the bottom dropped out of prices of cattle on the hoof. The value of the hide and tallow was greater than that of the flesh.

A ready-made opportunity was presented for men of vision and inventive genius who had been seeking means of preserving meat in a safe and palatable form. The chief method of keeping beef for long periods in those years prior to refrigeration was by packing it in salt. That process rendered it somewhat distasteful, and harmful to health if consumed in normal quantity over a period of several months.

Attempts had already been made to preserve both raw and cooked meat in tins, but results were not always ideal. The contents sometimes spoiled, caused by an imperfect seal, or by the lack of proper sanitary measures. One of the pioneer meat canneries at Indianola of which definite record can be found was that owned by the partnership of Robert Clark of that city and Charles Stillman of Brownsville. It was operated above Stevens Bayou prior to the war. Clark and Stillman jointly owned large tracts of land in Calhoun County, principally in the Green Lake area, on which they raised their own livestock for processing.

E. B. Barden, writing from Houston on May 18, 1937, said, "Mr. Clark told me that this packing house was the first to can beef [there]. They canned the meat in fresh condition and furnished it to ships. Many times they had a ship circumnavigate the globe and return to Indianola with some of the tins on hand and the meat perfectly fresh and good when the cans were opened. At other times, the whole lot would spoil on them from no apparent cause. This was the cause of considerable loss to them, so they had to discontinue packing it fresh." They then turned to canning pre-cooked beef. Shut down during the conflict because of metal shortage, the Clark and Stillman plant resumed operations after the war and continued for several years. It is likely that Robert Clark told Barden that Clark and Stillman operated the first *successful* beef canning plant at Indianola. The Cochran, Rogers and White meat cannery of 1848 preceded it, but could not be rated as successful because of its brief existence.

A different process was used by Francis Stabler, who had come to Indianola from Baltimore and opened a canning plant after the cessation of hostilities. He pioneered at Indianola in the preservation of raw meat packed in tins through the use of carbonic acid gas. The Indianola *Bulletin*, reporting on Stabler's beef packing plant, was quoted in the *Texas Almanac* of 1869, giving widespread publicity to the process. ". . . The following is a comparison of Stabler's beef, packed in 5½ and 15 pound cans, 88 and 90 pounds to the box, as shown to other beef:

"First, the meat on each beef is divided into three qualities at the following prices per pound, namely: Best cuts of beefsteak in 15 pound cans, 14¢; beefsteaks in 15 pound cans, 12¢; boiling beef in 15 pound cans, 9¢; making an average of 11⅔¢ per pound and, being free from bone, 150 pounds is equal to a 200 pound barrel of salt beef. Then 150 pounds (equal to a barrel of salt beef) costs, at 9¢, $13.50. So, in paying the above prices for Stabler's beef, it is the same as paying $17.50 and $13.50 for salt beef. . . .

"On sea voyages, it is superior to any article known to the trade and at less prices than any meat now used at sea. Sailors have been using meat put up in cans by cooking, but many of them have told us that it was so greasy and had so little of the natural beef taste that they [would] eat it as a preventive of sickness as they would take a dose of medicine. This beef of Mr. Stabler's . . . can be made into soup, broiled, boiled, fried, stewed — in fact, cooked in any way that fresh meat can be except roasted, for which the size of the pieces will not answer; while salt beef in barrels is only boiled, from the want of juiciness and the difficulty of removing the salt. It (Stabler's) can come in direct competition with fresh meat in any market, at less than salt beef prices, when the absence of bone is considered. . . ."

Because Stabler trimmed the meat to remove most fat, a by-product of his Indianola beef packery was tallow which, after rendering, was packed in barrels and shipped to New Orleans and New York. Two other by-products were hides and bones. For every legitimate hide and tallow operator, such as Stabler in his sideline, there were several which illegally and surreptitiously killed and skinned cattle. Indiscriminate slaughter of stolen cattle for their hides had been a problem in Texas for many years. The Legislature had attempted to control the situation by an act passed ȯn September 5, 1850. In the rough and tumble postwar era, the wave of rustling, killing and skinning had reached such proportions that the Union occupation army took note. The problem of thievery was especially acute in coastal and border regions, where stolen goods easily passed to dealers who asked no questions.

In an effort to stamp out the illegal traffic, General Orders No. 17 was issued on February 25, 1869, by Acting Adjutant General Louis V. Caziarc on order of Brevet Major General E. R. S. Canby, commanding the Fifth Military District with Headquarters at Austin. Referring to the 1850 law, the order required maintenance of detailed records by all persons and companies trafficking in live cattle or in hides. It also prohibited the marketing of cattle and hides without marks or brands, violation of which subjected the offending individual or business firm to fines, half of which went to the informer and the other half to the jury fund of the county. Those found guilty of not having the required lists and descriptions were liable to severe punishment. Trial was before a military tribunal, not an ordinary court of law.

In addition, the order required that "the captains of steamboats or vessels on which cattle are shipped to leave the State, or the proprietor or proprietors, or agents of the same, or of any slaughtering establishments, shall keep or cause to be kept a register book in which the marks, brands and general description of all cattle of all ages received on said boats or vessels or slaughtered at said establishments, shall be registered, together with the names of the person or persons selling them, and the county from which they were driven."

The stringency of the order had effect. Traffic in illegal hides, as well as in cattle rustled and sold live for shipment, diminished drastically. The principal deterrent appeared to be fear of judgment by the military courts, which were not noted for leniency.

Funds having become available as investors again looked south and west, work resumed on the Indianola Railroad. Thirteen miles with chair iron rails were built under the direction of an Englishman whose surname was Fry. A combined freight and passenger depot was erected at Indianola, as was a car and locomotive repair shop, in anticipation of the completion of rail laying and the acquisition of rolling stock. However, construction costs in excess of funds on hand stopped the work once more. At that juncture, Charles Morgan entered the picture. On March 15, 1869, Crittenden, Burnley, *et. al.*, sold to Morgan for $5,750 in gold coin Water Lots C1 and C2, and Wharf Lot C.[1] The land entrance of the wharf lot was at the foot of Travis Street between Blocks 3 and 4. Later events made clear that, at the time of this purchase, Morgan had set his sights on possession of the Indianola Railroad, as well as the San Antonio and Mexican Gulf.

The following year, Morgan would arrange with the city, acting through his agents, for a railroad right of way easement on Travis Street to Wharf Lot C, where a long pier would be constructed. When the wharf was completed, there was laid on it for ease in "on the spot" transfer of cargo between railroad cars and steamers a full size railroad track so trains could be backed to shipside. But, eager as Indianolans were for rail service, which they saw was tantalizingly near in 1869, travelers still used the U. S. Daily Mail Stage Line from Indianola to Victoria. There, connections were made with Risher and Hall Stage Lines running from Victoria to Austin, and to San Antonio. At the latter city, passengers, mail and light freight were transferred to the El Paso Line. L. M. Spencer was the stage line proprietor at Indianola, with the ticket office in the Magnolia Hotel.[2]

The steamship *Gov. Marvin* (Captain J. McKay, Jr.) had inaugurated a new direct competitive service between New Orleans and Indianola on February 18. She had a schedule of arrival and departure three times each month. Originally built for a route between Havana and Honduras, the *Gov. Marvin* was transferred to the more lucrative Western Gulf of Mexico trade. Her agents at Indianola were Darden, Stevens & Co.[3]

In service down the coast were three clipper-built, copper-fastened schooners, comprising the fleet of the Corpus Christi and Indianola United States Mail Line. Trim, immaculately maintained vessels with passenger accommodations, and providing connection with Morgan Line steamers from Indianola to New Orleans, they were the *Emily* (Captain William Moore), the *Agnes* (Captain N. Gardner) and the *Henrietta* (Captain John Steinhardt). Richard J. Freeman was the line's agent at Indianola. His office was at Clement and Burbank's, ship chandlers and grocers, opposite the long wharf. Clement and Burbank also supplied vessels with wood and cistern water.[4]

The gradual resettlement of Saluria and Matagorda Island made necessary a redrawing of Calhoun County precinct lines on April 5, 1869. The island was again designated as a full precinct, this time as number 5. A plan for a new county jail on the courthouse square at Indianola was presented to the court by Rooke & Wisdom, architects and contractors. Upon acceptance of the plan, payment of $20 to the firm was ordered and advertisements were scheduled calling for bids on construction. In compliance with Order No. 41, Fifth Military District, the county court imposed a special property tax of one-half of one percent of the assessed value on the tax rolls. The order stipulated that the tax must be paid in United States currency, which ruled out acceptance of produce and other goods in lieu of cash. The stated purpose of the tax was "to defray expenses necessarily incurred in arresting, guarding, subsisting and, where needed, clothing and trying prisoners, as well as repairs to the [old] jail and other places of imprisonment in the county."[5]

On May 1, 1869, a mortgage on the San Antonio and Mexican Gulf Railroad was placed on record. Mortgagees were John H. Reed of Boston and Morris K. Jessup of New York. Of the 350 bonds secured by the mortgage, 150 were cancelled on agreement, leaving outstanding 200 bonds valued at $1,000 each. Charles Morgan and Henry S. McComb were listed as holding bonds in the amount of $56,000 each. Thomas McComb held 12 bonds totaling $12,000.[6] The McCombs were business associates of Morgan, Henry being superintendent of the Morgan-controlled New Orleans, Jackson and Great Northern Railroad which ran from New Orleans to Canton, Mississippi, a distance of 206 miles. Their possession of 124 of the remaining 200 bonds gave Morgan effective control of the affairs of the SA&MG, a fact he would use to his advantage. Still to be disposed of was the claim of the United States government against the rail line.

Indicative of the esteem in which Indianolans had come to hold the men in the infantry company occupying their town was an item in the *Bulletin* of Thursday, May 6. Headed "Removed to San Antonio!" the news story also included some jabs at members of Congress held responsible for thwarting the will of the late President Lincoln, as well as that of his sorely-tried successor, Andrew Johnson, by the imposition of military rule over the people of the old Confederacy. The *Bulletin* said, "The Command of Captain Fred Bailey [Note: Frederick W. Bailey, Company B], 35th Infantry, left this city on Monday last for San Antonio. The troops of this command have been quartered in this city for over two years and their departure is regretted by all classes of our citizens. A finer set of men were never congregated together. Their uniform good manners and soldierly bearing won the respect of our people, and the time has not been when they have offended in any manner persons whom they have been compelled to arrest. Always courteous and gentlemanly in their demeanor, they had identified themselves with the prosperity of the city. Wherever they go, they will be long remembered as worthy and deserving men doing unpleasant duty over a free and sovereign people bowed down by an arbitrary and despotic will of the people's representatives in Congress assembled. We have the authority of our people in saying that they have our best wishes for their future welfare.

"May the time draw near when we may be spared the humiliation heaped upon our devoted heads by having quartered in our midst armed forces. We have full faith in the present Executive [Note: President Grant] and know that the time is not far distant when these matters will be remedied and the civil laws restored, together with all the rights and privileges belonging to a free people of a mighty Republic whose watchword shall be 'One Union, One Flag and One People!', whose rights shall be equally respected." At the time Bailey and his men left for San Antonio, the United States Revenue Cutter *Antietam*, commanded by Lieutenant Williams, arrived back in port. The *Antietam* was headquartered at Indianola.

However, with all their trials, there were pleasures to be had. Some were provided for non-tipplers by C. F. Vollers, former orderly sergeant in the Indianola Home Guard Artillery Company, at the well-patronized ginger beer garden in Old Town. There, Indianolans driving up the snow-white shell beach were wont to refresh themselves before returning to the city. At the place known as Temperance Hall, Vollers advertised that he served "Lemonade, Ginger Beer with Ice; also a good Cigar and Oysters, Sardines, or something else to keep the stomach in order." Waxing poetic, Vollers proclaimed:

"The road is good, the day is bright,
"The body strong, the mind is light,
"Let us all go to the Temperance Hall
"And give old C. F. V. a call!"

Children had their diversions, also, in the form of hay rides, swimming and fishing parties, boat excursions and picnics. Interdenominational Sunday School picnics were frequent, usually held at "the grove" below Powder Horn Bayou. Editor Ogsbury commented on one such held on Saturday, May 1. "We saw them on their return in the evening, and their smiling faces and joyous hymns indicated the happy termination of the day," he observed as they trudged past the *Bulletin* office on their way home.

Pressured by the military to proceed without delay in replacement of the old and inadequate jail, the court entered into a contract with W. H. Wisdom on May 19 for construction of the new building at a cost of $3,000. Military orders required that Wisdom be paid in United States currency. The method of payment was part of a continuing effort to force public acceptance of the distrusted paper money. The old jail was sold to G. W. Volk for $25, to be removed from the property at once so the new structure could be erected on its site.

Bulletin editor Ogsbury purred, "The 35th Infantry Company that was assigned to Indianola to replace Capt. Bailey's Company B . . . are a fine company of men and are doing their duty as becomes well behaved and courteous soldiers. They are gaining the respect of the citizens for their good and orderly conduct." If Ogsbury was using psychology to insure a genial attitude by the soldiers toward the people of Indianola, he succeeded. Army-citizen relations were as amicable as those between Bailey's command and the local residents.

Indianola witnessed two important arrivals in late May 1869. One was the installation of gas lighting to illuminate some of the business houses in the downtown section near Powder Horn Bayou. The other was the docking of the steamship *Morgan* (Captain Talbot), her distinguished passenger being Charles Morgan himself, who had journeyed from New York to inspect this Matagorda Bay port that was so rapidly increasing in commercial importance. "He was accompanied by Messrs. C. A. Whitney, Folger, Capt. Chas. Fowler and several other gentlemen from the Crescent City. They visited the depot, machine shop and the railroad and expressed some astonishment that so much progress had been made on the road and that the railroad matters were in such good condition."[7] Whitney was favorably impressed with Indianola and became its friend and benefactor until his untimely death in 1882.

Morgan was becoming concerned about the creeping of rail lines toward Texas from the Midwest. He viewed them as a potential threat to the well-being of his steamship empire by the possibility that much of the trade of Central and North Texas would be drawn toward St. Louis and Chicago, and away from the coast. His interest in the Indianola Railroad and the SA&MG was, therefore, one of self-preservation. He began to endeavor to encourage San Antonians to take a more aggressive stand toward completion of the SA&MG from their city to Matagorda Bay. He would, personally, quietly strive to promote more active area support for the extension of the road from Indianola through Victoria to Austin and beyond. Without fanfare, Morgan had been buying into the Indianola Railroad until he secured a majority interest.

The Galveston *News* of June 2, 1869, carried mention of a meeting of the Railroad Association of San Antonio. Headed "Charles Morgan's Subscription to the SA&MG Railroad," it said, "At a meeting of the Railroad Association of San Antonio on the 25th, a letter was read from Mr. Guilbeau giving an account of an interview he had, when in New Orleans, with Charles Morgan who said that if the people interested in the building of the road would come forward and take stock and the enterprise should be in the hands of honest as well as competent men who would see to it that every dollar paid in should be properly and legitimately applied, that he (Mr. Morgan) would pay in $250,000. By this, we suppose that he meant that he would take that amount of stock."

The dilatory tactics of the San Antonio business community of the period cost that city the commercial supremacy it could have had by an early rail connection to Matagorda Bay. Morgan saw the financial advantages of such an outlet to the sea for San Antonio. Had he been firmly supported in his proposal, the trade of Western Texas would not have been siphoned off eventually by Houston, leaving San Antonio something of a way station on the rail line that was completed between New Orleans and the Pacific Ocean in 1883. If San Antonians had pursued the completion of the San Antonio and Mexican Gulf when Morgan was willing to cooperate, they could have controlled a rail line to ports served by ocean-going vessels, and their city could have become the great manufacturing and trade center that the location entitled her to be.

But, Charles Morgan did not wait to see what San Antonians would do. Perhaps he foresaw their continued inaction. On August 12, he purchased for $3,250 in gold dollars Lots 3, 4, 5 and 6 in Block 3, Indianola. For $1,000 in gold dollars he bought Lot 1, Block 4. Four months later he purchased for $2,500 in gold Lots 5 and 6, Block 44. All of this property had frontage on Travis Street, down which the rail lines would later be laid to his planned new wharf.

One of the most notable events in the history of Indianola, and a world's first, was the successful shipment of a cargo of 30 beef carcasses under steamship refrigeration to New Orleans, arriving there at 10 a.m., Saturday, July 10, 1869. Messrs. Howard, Bray & Co. had directed the construction of a cold storage vault on the Morgan steamship *Agnes.* Equipped with mechanical refrigeration, the vault temperature was kept a few degrees above freezing. Upon arrival at New Orleans, the shipment was unloaded and transferred to a newly equipped refrigerating warehouse, where it was "pronounced by all who saw and tasted it to be the best beef ever brought into the market."[8] The implications of the use of this innovative chilling device were sensational. The significance of the movement of beef from Indianola was recognized on the spot by the New Orleans *Picayune*. Its edition of Tuesday morning, July 13, covered it in a front page story.

The *Picayune* exulted, "The arrival of the steamship *Agnes* on Saturday last from Texas marked a new era. It has established . . . the very important fact that beef may be brought from the prairies of Texas and laid down in the markets of the world perfectly fresh and juicy, greatly cheaper than that now offered for sale, and vastly superior in quality."

Recognizing the long-time marketing problems of the state's cattle producers, the *Picayune* commented, "Texas, heretofore, has had within her wide limits unbounded wealth which it has been impossible to make available. Millions of cattle have roamed over her vast prairies and have died without enriching anyone, because they could not be taken to market. Thousands upon thousands of cattle have been killed for their hides and tallow alone, the beef being thrown away because it could not be preserved profitably. Recently, however, a resident of New Jersey has perfected an invention that is destined to work a wonderful change. He has discovered a method whereby the cattle of Texas may be turned into gold! He has made millionaires of those who, heretofore, have been comparatively poor, since they could find no market for their almost innumerable herds."

Countering skepticism, the *Picayune* observed, ". . . Mr. Wilson Bray deserves to stand among the foremost inventors of any age . . . He has succeeded in perfecting an apparatus which defies the action of those causes which produce decay — an apparatus, the importance of which can scarcely be realized; for while it throws open to the stock raisers of the vast empire of Texas the markets of the world, it also, in effect, brings the tropics within a stone's throw of the North. It virtually annihilates space and laughs at the lapse of time, for the Boston merchant may have a fresh, juicy beefsteak from the rich pastures of Texas for dinner, and for dessert feast on the delicate, luscious but perishable fruits and vegetables of the Indies. Peaches, bananas, strawberries, figs, melons, oranges, etc. may be conveyed any distance without undergoing a perceptible change, by Bray's method; and we think it incontrovertible that a great revolution in commerce will be effected."

The process was such an extraordinary and totally new scientific development that the newspaper editor felt obliged to describe it in some detail for the edification of readers who would, otherwise, be unable to comprehend the mechanics of operation. It was a system of which they knew nothing. "Yesterday morning, in company with Mr. Bray, the patentee, Dr. Howard and a number of other gentlemen, we visited the refrigerating warehouse, Nos. 115 Fulton and 137 New Levee Streets, in which the beef brought up by the *Agnes* from Texas had been placed. This room is about 50 by 25 feet, and some 15 feet high. The walls are made double and lined with a non-conducting substance. At one end is a small fan, which is moved with great rapidity by a steam engine in an adjoining apartment, and at the other end a bulkhead is built which contains a refrigerating mixture 32 degrees colder than ice. By the rapid revolution of the fan, a current of air is created which is forced along a large tube and through the mixture in the bulkhead. By the constant repetition of this process, a temperature of 30 degrees below the freezing point may be obtained.

"For preserving purposes, however, the temperature is kept just a little above the freezing point because, at that point, there is no evaporation from meat or fruit, and because the condensation of moisture in the air is prevented and a perfect equilibrium is preserved. At this point, no decomposition can occur, nor can fermentation in liquids take place, as all chemical action is suspended. Decay, therefore, is impossible. The refrigerating mixture — the composition of which is not generally known — possesses the peculiar quality of condensing all the gaseous emanations from meat or fruit, or any impurities, such as exhalations from the lungs, etc., and consequently the air is maintained in a cold, pure and dry condition, which is essential in the preservation of meat, fruit or anything subject to decay. Poultry . . . and beef have been kept by this method 150 days without impairing the quality, flavor or appearance."

The excitement of the *Picayune* over this invention may require imagination for the twentieth century American to understand. The editor of that great newspaper correctly envisioned the commercial revolution this pioneer shipment from Indianola presaged!

"A great advantage in transporting beef by this method," the *Picayune* continued, "is that four times the quantity can be carried in the space required for livestock, the offal being dispensed with, which constitutes nearly one-half the weight. The beef being killed while in prime order, and transferred at once to the refrigerator on the vessel, is necessarily of much finer quality than that which is driven hundreds of miles overland, or that which is transported by vessel alive. In the latter case, the loss of weight amounts to nearly one-fourth, as the cattle are for several days without food and water and become heated and feverish. When driven, they lose flesh rapidly and are very much deteriorated on their arrival here.

"The apparatus on the steamship *Agnes* is precisely similar to that in the warehouse, and she is capable of bringing about 150 head of slaughtered cattle, which is equivalent to nearly, if not quite, four times that amount of live stock. The first trip, being experimental in nature, but 30 head were brought over. This beef was killed last Sunday week near Indianola, placed on the *Agnes* on Monday morning and, notwithstanding the detention of the steamer by rough weather, it was landed here in perfectly good order and looks today as though it were freshly slaughtered. . . ."

Giving the background for the experiment, the paper continued, "The present application of his [Bray's] invention to the transportation of beef from the fields of Texas happened in this way. In February last, Dr. H. P. Howard and Gen. Walter A. Bennett of San Antonio, Texas visited the North and West in the interest of a large number of stock raisers to endeavor to perfect arrangements whereby the beef of Texas should find a market. The main idea was to establish a packery in Kansas City and to drive the cattle to that point. While in Philadelphia, however, they became acquainted with Mr. Bray and, after a careful examination of his refrigerating apparatus, they were convinced of its entire feasibility and purchased one-half interest in his patent. A joint stock company was then formed and immediate steps taken to illustrate the practicability of the scheme.

"The steamship *Agnes* was fitted up expressly for the purpose, the warehouse here was constructed, and on Saturday last the first cargo of beef arrived, furnishing to the doubtful that tangible evidence of success which is so essential to conviction. This apparatus is alike applicable to railroads and steamers, and a car constructed on this principle and loaded with our most perishable fruits has been sent to Louisville, where it arrived with every article in a perfect state of preservation."

Concluding, the New Orleans *Picayune* said, "It is now proposed, we learn, to increase the capital of the company to $2,000,000 . . . We regard the inauguration of this enterprise as of great importance to Louisiana, for it will, in our opinion, lessen the price of beef and must effectually prevent any company of men from monopolizing this very necessary article of food. . . ."

The *Picayune* neglected to state that a refrigerating warehouse had been constructed in Indianola for the purpose of chilling beef after slaughtering and before placement in the vault on the *Agnes*. The complete success of this shipment meant that similarly equipped refrigerator ships were soon regularly carrying Texas beef from Indianola, not only to New Orleans but also to Baltimore, Philadelphia, New York and Boston.

The year 1869 brought the death of Indianola's co-founder, Samuel Addison White. He had purchased the Victoria *Advocate* in 1857 and was its editor at the time of his death, which occurred while he was in Indianola on a visit. White had served Texas with distinction. He was state senator in the Sixth and Tenth Legislatures and had been appointed district judge in 1865 by Provisional Governor A. J. Hamilton.[9]

A short but severe storm caused extensive damage at Indianola in August. Tornadic winds demolished the sanctuary of the Episcopal Church of the Ascension, left the rectory tottering, and unroofed several buildings in the town. Along the waterfront, there were beached and sunk boats, battered wharves and warehouses. Over the entire city there were broken windows and toppled chimneys. After the blow had passed and no loss of life was reported, Indianolans congratulated themselves upon "the obvious security of the location of our little city." Six years later, the complete fallacy of that conclusion was fully realized.

XVIII.

Hear the Whistle Blowing

Indianola City Council authorized Mayor F. E. Hughes on June 20, 1870, to enter into an agreement with the Indianola Railroad Company. Upon the payment of one dollar, and execution of a $50,000 bond, Charles Morgan's desired right of way was granted through the business district. A condition was that the grant would be forfeited by the company if the rail line "in running order" were not completed to a point 65 miles from Indianola by May 1872. Fletcher S. Stockdale was president of the company at the time.

The right of way grant began at a point on the railroad near the first bridge "to and along Canal Street, making a curve into Travis . . . along Travis Street and across Water Street to the foot of . . . Morgan's Wharf." It was stipulated by the city that the company would be obliged to maintain Travis and Canal, and all crossings, "properly graded and adjusted . . . to permit the free use of the streets by the public." To forestall monopolistic acts by Morgan and the railroad company, acting in concert, it was further provided that, whenever the needs of commerce made necessary rail connections to other wharves, such spurs would be constructed, at the request of the City Council, the expense to be borne by the city or by the person requesting the connection.[1]

In order to accommodate the new rolling stock of the narrower "standard gauge" track of four feet, eight and a half inches, rails already laid had to be reset from their original wide gauge of five feet, six inches. This necessitated alteration of axles on the equipment on hand. The final stage of track laying toward the junction with the SA&MG at Clark Station began in the second week of April 1871 and was completed before the end of the month. An incentive to get this done was the imminent arrival of Charles Morgan on a return visit from New York. He reached Indianola aboard the steamship *Harlan* on Thursday, April 20. Accompanying him were Charles A. Whitney, C. A. Weed and family, C. H. Slocumb, R. Pritchard, Page M. Baker, and several others from New Orleans. Weed was owner of the New Orleans *Times* and Baker represented the *Picayune.* Also in the party were H. S. McComb, and his son and daughter from Delaware, and Captain Charles Fowler from Galveston.

Bulletin editor C. A. Ogsbury reported on April 25 that, "Immediately on the arrival of Messrs. Morgan, McComb and party, cars were in readiness to take them out on the railroad as far as completed. By special invitation of Messrs. Morgan and Whitney, we accompanied the party, who all seemed pleased with the trip, most of the ladies and gentlemen proceeding on as far as Victoria, returning the following day. To many of the ladies, and also some of the gentlemen, the ride over the prairies was a novelty and will long be remembered as a pleasant era in life's rugged path."

The principal reason for the visit of Morgan and McComb became evident in a meeting with the directors of the Indianola Railroad Company on Saturday, April 22. In the previous year, Morgan and his associates who had financial interest in the San Antonio and Mexican Gulf, purchased that company in the foreclosure sale which had been forced by the United States government to satisfy its lien of $45,000 covering rehabilitation of the road after the war. Controlling a majority of the voting stock in the Indianola Railroad, Morgan took steps to consolidate it and the SA&MG into a single corporation to be known as the Gulf, Western Texas and Pacific Railway Company. The consolidation was ratified by the Texas Legislature on May 19.[2]

Every edition of the *Bulletin* contained railroad news — the arrival of vessels loaded with cross ties, rails and rolling stock — reports of construction activities along the line, and certainly the enthusiastic hopes of the citizens of the town for an era of unprecedented growth. On May 2, the paper said, "Great activity is displayed by those engaged in its construction. The locomotives are running constantly with cars loaded with material that gives new life and energy to this important work that will soon connect us with the great West. Cars of beautiful make, locomotives and rolling stock continue to arrive, giving confidence to our people that everything is done in earnest. The prospects are indeed encouraging, and well may we congratulate ourselves with the advent of coming prosperity, both for Western Texas and Indianola, whose destiny as a commercial mart is of no insignificant proportions."

On May 23, "New track layers have arrived from New Orleans and the work on the road will be pushed ahead with rapidity." This related to rebuilding the line from Clark Station to Victoria, and extending it from that city further into Western Texas. "We learn that a steamer is especially designated to bring new material . . . A large number of workmen passed up the road yesterday. The arrival and departure of the cars, and the sound of the whistle, indicate the advance of enterprise and capital which will, in a few years, deck our beautiful prairies with happy homes and all the great West with a fine and prosperous population." A state of euphoria existed that was to be squelched only by the Panic of 1873. In the meantime, all signals were "go."

The June 29 *Bulletin* noted, "This fine steamship [the *Matagorda*] arrived last Saturday morning with a cargo of material for the . . . railroad. The great drawback now is that the ties don't come on fast enough. The track is laid down at the rate of one mile per day, at which rate, should the material arrive fast enough, [it will be carried] to Victoria about the 4th of July next."

William Y. Conlon, who was at the throttle of the locomotive pulling the first through train from Indianola to Victoria, reminisced in an article carried in the Galveston *News* of July 31, 1910. He commented, "Colonel Upshaw from Bolivar, Tennessee was superintendent of construction and his lieutenant, Michael Grace, had charge of the track laying, and he was a man who knew his business thoroughly. Col. Upshaw was a very devout man and he held religious services in his car every Sunday morning, but I regret to say that his efforts were not always appreciated by the men. While Divine service would be going on in the colonel's car, games of chance would be in full blast under it. That certainly bothered the colonel, but with all this he never failed to have services."

Speaking of the period of construction, Conlon said, ". . . Some of these [local] people had never laid eyes upon a locomotive until they saw the 'Governor Stockdale,' the engine I was running . . . The Morgan wharf at Indianola was one of the finest I ever saw . . . Dick Finn was holding the position of master mechanic. He was an old steamship engineer and had been in the employ of the Morgan Line from his youth. During a somewhat varied experience, I must confess that I never met a more genial class of people than those of Indianola and the surrounding country during the early 1870s. Their kindness and hospitality were unbounded . . ."

Two storms sideswiped Indianola in 1871, the first in June and the second on September 30. The June blow, which was centered east of Matagorda Bay, caused only minor wind damage there. The principal problem was related to high water, which flooded the lower parts of the town. At Galveston, there was loss of life and damage to shipping. On Saturday night, September 30, a strong east wind began to blow at Indianola, which brought the tide in at an alarming rate. The lower part of town and the back portion soon became flooded. As the wind continued to increase, the water rose more rapidly until the greater part of Indianola was covered with water. There was widespread damage to merchandise in warehouses and stores near Powder Horn Bayou, where the elevation of the ground was least. At about noon Monday, October 2, the wind veered to the north, driving the water out. Again, wind damage was minor, but the fall storm brought the highest level of water that had been recorded since settlement began in the area in 1844.

Torrential rains that accompanied the storm wreaked havoc at Lavaca, where the high tides flooded the warehouses under the bluff. The Lavaca town jail was washed away and serious damage was done to the railroad property in the vicinity of Chocolate Bayou. The bridge remained standing, but the embankments were washed out and the railroad pile driver was swept down across the tracks. In the suburbs of Indianola, and for several miles inland, the flood water undermined the track in numerous places, which prevented the passage of trains. This event was a curtain-raiser to the great hurricane that would come in only four years.

The Legislature had approved on April 3, 1871, an act authorizing the incorporation of the Indianola, San Antonio and El Paso Railroad Company. Planned to be built from Indianola via Goliad to San Antonio, the route called for crossing the Guadalupe at Kemper's Bluff below Victoria and following the San Antonio River valley from Goliad to San Antonio. Incorporators were W. N. Fant, M. Kreisle, Wm. Kohler, R. W. Davis and E. Seeligson of Goliad, Henry Seeligson, William Westhoff and Samuel Johnson of Indianola, F. E. Grothaus of DeWitt County, H. H. McLean and L. S. Lawhon of Karnes County, Joseph Deutz, Charles Elmendorf, A. Siemering, Gen. Walter A. Bennett, W. J. Locke and David Bell of San Antonio, John M. Mathis of Rockport, Richard King of Corpus Christi and Albert J. Fountain of El Paso. The organizers were endeavoring to promote a rail line from San Antonio to Indianola that would by-pass Charles Morgan's GWT&P. The San Antonians and their associates feared Morgan. Fant was elected president, Siemering-vice president, Bell-secretary, J. P. Newcomb was named treasurer and S. G. Newton-attorney. Locke, E. Seeligson and McLean, together with Fant, made up the Executive Committee.

Indianolans pledged $75,000 toward the railroad, and efforts were made to raise sufficient capital to permit the beginning of construction by December 1871. The route had been surveyed. It was anticipated that improved farm lands along the line would increase sharply from their current value averaging three to five dollars per acre, and that unimproved acreage would rise in worth from an average price of one to two dollars per acre. However, it was the sparsely settled country through which the railroad would pass that made it impossible to secure adequate financing. There was not the likelihood of generation of sufficient local freight and passenger traffic along the line for several years. That made investors wary of joining in the enterprise. The ISA&EP would have opened up a vast region to settlement and would have given San Antonio an even more direct route to the Gulf than that offered by the old SA&MG.

The Gulf, Western Texas and Pacific, through its agent General H. E. McCulloch, presented the people of Travis County with a proposal in

November 1871 that would ensure the completion of the line to Austin. The company proposed that the county subscribe $500,000 of capital stock in coupon bonds payable in 30 years and bearing 8% interest. The bonds were to be delivered to the company upon completion of the railroad to its depot in the capital city. The company, in turn, upon payment of the bonds would issue to the county $500,000 worth of stock. It was contemplated that the road would be in operation within two years. The Austin *Democratic Statesman* suggested that the proposition presented advantages which the citizens of Travis County could not fail to appreciate, believing that the reduced freight rates would pay for the investment in three or four years. This proposition was doomed to failure of acceptance by reason of the fact that the extension of the Houston & Texas Central Railroad from Brenham was nearing Austin and would connect it with Houston the following month.

On January 1, 1872, public notice was given by President Richard Evans and Secretary Thos. J. Poole of the GWT&P of the issuance of 3,680 bonds, each valued at $1,000 or £200, principal and interest payable in United States gold coin or English sterling. The work of extension of the line from Victoria began in April of that year, but progress was slow. A point in central DeWitt County was selected as the terminus of the railroad and a townsite surveyed early in 1873 by Gustav Schleicher and J. C. French. Schleicher had come to Texas as one of the commune which established Bettina in 1847. The post office of Cuero, which had been opened at D. B. Friar's store in 1846, was moved four miles to the newly projected town, which became known as Cuero. Almost immediately, efforts were begun aimed at removing the county seat from nearby Clinton to the railroad terminus. Indianolans had expected the GWT&P to reach the embryo town by October 1, 1872, with completion of the line to San Antonio by April 1, 1873.

New disappointment was to be experienced, this one caused by the Panic of 1873, which began in Vienna in May. It struck the United States in full force with the collapse of Jay Cooke and Company in New York. Widespread failure of banks and other business institutions dried up the money markets, resulting in Cuero remaining the terminus of the GWT&P. As business conditions began to improve within the next two years, prospects brightened for renewed construction, again to be dashed by the hurricane of 1875 that devastated the region and caused a state of economic paralysis.

The city's volunteer firemen had received Legislative approval on April 12, 1871, to incorporate as Indianola Hook and Ladder Company, No. 1. John Eglington was foreman and Andrew Dove secretary at the time. On May 16 of that year, the Fire Department's huge new bell arrived at Indianola on the *W. G. Hewes*. Mounted on a tower at the Truck House, it was struck in code to give notice of the location of a fire.[3] The bell continued to sound the alarm for fires at Indianola until the abandonment of the city after the hurricane of 1886. It was then taken to Port Lavaca and used for the same purpose for many years before replacement.

In response to petitions submitted by residents, and the expressed concern of firemen, the Indianola City Council took steps in 1871 to control the storage of gunpowder within the corporate limits. Alarm was widespread over the danger of fire and explosion which could result in calamitous damage to property, as well as injury or death in the populace. A sturdy structure erected by J. Coutret at a cost of $150 and designated the Powder House was located at a safe distance from the occupied portion of the city. All privately owned large quantities of powder were required to be stored there. A maximum of 12½ pounds of gunpowder was permitted by ordinance to be kept on hand by merchants and gunsmiths in each place of business.[4]

The condition of the streets was a recurrent subject of complaint at Indianola. Editor Ogsbury took it up as a cause to be pursued until satisfaction was obtained by the citizens. In May, commenting on A Street, on which his newspaper office was situated, Ogsbury said, "This beautiful street running parallel with Main is becoming much traveled by pedestrians, carts and vehicles of every description, and efforts are now on foot to fill up the space covered by the small ponds that are filled by the ebb and flow of the tide. There are but two feet of water, and the cost of filling up, making the street useful, increasing the value of property, and other matters relating to the health of the city, make it an imperative duty of the city authorities to aid in its filling. . ." The perilous sea level elevation of the business section of the Indianola townsite was illustrated by the reference to the "ebb and flow of the tide" in spots along A Street. The complete disregard by Indianolans of the danger from high water set the stage for the coming destruction.

Hammering away at the condition of streets, Ogsbury editorialized on June 13 about the need to improve "gutters alongside of the curb of the sidewalks." Two weeks later, he observed that the streets would soon be dusty and disagreeable, ". . . . especially Main Street. We hope some enterprising man will take a contract to water them. We feel confident that the merchants on that thoroughfare will subscribe liberally towards it. The crowded state of this street during business hours renders it intolerable on windy days, which requires something being done to remedy [it]." A street water-wagon did finally solve the problem of the white dust from the powdered shell being stirred by the hooves of draft animals and blown into shops and residences. Bay water was used in the wagon tank and spread by means of perforated pipes set across the rear of the vehicle.[5]

Ogsbury's campaign eventually paid off, as is shown by his change in tone the following year and the comments voicing approval of work being done to properly maintain the streets of the city. He was gratified to see the improvements on Ward Street, which led to the depot of the GWT&P between C and D. Rail passengers alighting from the cars were given a good impression of Indianola as they traversed Ward between the depot and the hotels or steamer landings.

As the town grew, the need for a system of public transportation was recognized. In response to their application, a charter was granted by

Issued by Gulf, Western Texas & Pacific Railway.

FIRST CLASS.

New Orleans,

Via U. S. M. F. L. Stages; G., W. T. & P. R'y;
Morgan Line Strs.; and M's. La. & T. R.R.

Form C

3 0 3

ISSUED BY GULF, WESTERN TEXAS & PACIFIC RAILWAY.

On Presentation herewith of the Checks hereto
attached, this Ticket will be good for

ONE FIRST CLASS PASSAGE

FROM

San Antonio, Tex.,

TO

NEW ORLEANS

Via U. S. M. F. L. Stages; G., W. T. & P. R'y;
Morgan Line Strs.; and M's. La. & T. R.R.

In the event of any detention, it is expressly stipulated
that the Steamers nor railroads shall not be held liable
by the holder of this ticket for any expenses incurred
by such detention.

One hundred pounds Baggage, wearing apparel only
allowed, on Steamers and Railroads, and sixty pounds on
Stages. All above charged extra. Each Company will be
responsible only for loss or damage on its own Line.

Agent.

NEW ORLEANS.

Issued by Gulf, Western Texas & Pacific Railway.

Worthless if detached from the Contract Ticket
by any other than Clerk of Steamship.

Morgan's La. & Texas Railroad

AND

Steamship ____

Trip ____ *Room* ____ *Berth* ____

First Class Passage.

GALVESTON.

Form C

3 0 3

NEW ORLEANS.

GALVESTON.

Issued by Gulf, Western Texas & Pacific Railway.

Worthless if detached from the Contract Ticket
by any other than Clerk of Steamship.

Steamship ____

Trip ____ *Room* ____ *Berth* ____

First Class Passage.

INDIANOLA.

Form C

3 0 3

NEW ORLEANS.

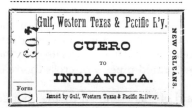

Gulf, Western Texas & Pacific R'y.

CUERO

TO

INDIANOLA.

Issued by Gulf, Western Texas & Pacific Railway.

Form C

3 0 3

NEW ORLEANS.

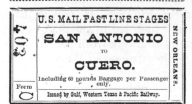

U. S. MAIL FAST LINE STAGES

SAN ANTONIO

TO

CUERO.

Including 60 pounds Baggage per Passenger
only.

Issued by Gulf, Western Texas & Pacific Railway.

Form C

3 0 3

NEW ORLEANS.

An 1873 first class ticket covering
passage from San Antonio to New Orleans. Travel was via U. S. Mail Fast Line
Stages to Cuero, GWT&P Railway to Indianola and Morgan Line steamship to
destination. (*From the author's personal
collection.*)

the state in 1871 to H. Seeligson, Casimir Villeneuve, B. F. Hunt, D. H. Regan, J. E. Mitchell and V. Weldon, as commissioners, to build and operate a street car system in the town under the name of the Indianola City Railroad Company. They were given authority to issue and sell capital stock for the purpose in an amount not less than $50,000 nor more than $250,000. The street railway company was granted the power to negotiate with the City Council for routing of the rail lines and agreement on the type of motive power to be used.[6] Inasmuch as electricity had not yet come into general use, small street cars of this type were drawn by mules treading an all-weather surfaced path between the rails.

For several years, Indianolans had, along with their fellow Texans, endured with fortitude occupation by military force, onerous taxes, disenfranchisement at the polls and the humiliation of being governed by men they did not put in office. A ground swell of reform sentiment began to be a formidable force in 1871. On September 18, Indianola Democrats filled Villeneuve Hall, the crowd overflowing onto the galleries. It was the evening before a special registration of voters was to begin. By proclamation of Governor E. J. Davis, an election was ordered to begin on Tuesday, October 3. Voter registration was set for a period of ten days and was held in the second floor office of the William Westhoff Building. The Democratic party meeting was designed to overcome apathy and whip up sentiment for registration. Senator George P. Finlay and D. C. Proctor addressed the throng. They and the stirring music of the Indianola City Brass Band roused the emotions of the listeners to a pitch that had not been witnessed there since the secessionist mass meeting of November 21, 1860.[7]

Two days later, John Hancock of Austin, the Democratic party candidate for representative to the 41st Congress from the Fourth District, spoke to Indianolans on "the political topics of the day." He had been in Victoria on the 18th and went from Indianola to Clinton for a rally on the 23rd, to Gonzales on the 25th and to Seguin on the 27th.[8] The Republican candidate for the Congressional office, Edward Degener of San Antonio, followed Hancock to speak at Indianola. In the October election, the Democratic sweep of Texas put Hancock in office.[9]

At Indianola, the bustle of commercial activity, the booming postwar growth of the community and the harmonious relations existing between the citizens and the occupation troops made it atypical. One thing that Indianola did have in common with the balance of the state was the oppressively heavy taxation. Complaints were loud and frequent about the shockingly high state levies, to which were added those of county and city. Despite the huge sums collected, state and local governments were usually short of funds. The special taxes that were frequently resorted to consistently fell on the holders of real property.

In answer to an inquiry made by Hancock for comparative figures, State Comptroller A. A. Bledsoe said, "The [state] rate of taxation in 1860 was *twelve and a half cents* on one hundred dollars; in 1867 it was *fifteen cents* on one hundred dollars; and for 1871 it is *two dollars and twenty five cents* on one hundred dollars."[10] This severe pinching of the pocketbook nerve was a powerful factor in finally arousing the people of Texas to throw off the yoke of Governor Davis's corrupt Reconstruction administration. When it fell in January 1874 after President Grant refused to support Davis with Federal troops, the end came to carpetbag politics in Texas.

XIX.

A Downtown View

The *Bolivar* (Captain Doane) ushered in a new era by inaugurating the first direct steamship service between Indianola and New York in June 1871. For 25 years, freight and passengers had been carried between the two ports by sailing vessels. For movement on the long route by steam propelled ships, transfer had been necessary at New Orleans. Now C. H. Mallory & Company moved into the Western Gulf trade in earnest as a competitor with Charles Morgan, providing service he had not offered. Before the war, Cornelius Vanderbilt had come in as a spite competitor with Morgan, but failed. Mallory was to succeed. The Indianola banking house of H. Seeligson & Company was the Mallory agent there.[1]

Telegraph service had been provided to Indianola in 1870 with completion of the Western Union line from Houston via Columbus along the right of way of the old Buffalo Bayou, Brazos & Colorado Railway. In that same year, the BBB&C was incorporated into the newly organized Galveston, Harrisburg and San Antonio Railway Company. From Columbus, the line was built across country to Morales, the first telegraph station in Jackson County, and on to Victoria.[2] For the 40 miles from Victoria to Indianola, it followed the right of way of the SA& MG to Clark Station, and that of the then-incomplete Indianola Railroad to the port.[3] From Indianola, the telegraph line was extended in 1871 through St. Mary's in Refugio County, to Corpus Christi and on to Brownsville, which was reached in November.[4] An extension of the line provided Mexico with its first telegraphic connection with the United States.[5]

Scientific events were moving forward at a fast pace. In her brief life of a quarter of a century, Indianola had witnessed the arrival of steam propelled ships, a railroad, gas illumination, the successful packing of fresh meat in tins, mechanical refrigeration, and now the transmission of written messages with the speed of lightning. It was a marvelous age of advancement in many fields, yet the means of commerce with the great West was still relatively unchanged!

A characteristic sight in Indianola before and after the war was the concentration of wagon trains bringing raw materials for export from Northern Mexico and Western Texas. In turn, they departed loaded with finished lumber, food stuffs and manufactured goods. At times, the streets in the lower part of the city near Powder Horn Bayou were so crowded with wagons and carts awaiting their turn at the warehouses and wharves that massive traffic jams developed. The extension of railroad service from Victoria to Cuero in 1873 provided only partial relief to the situation. Cattle for export were then loaded in cars at sidings along the 65-mile rail line, those cars being moved directly to the railroad pier where the animals were herded through chutes onto waiting steamers. Wagon train loads of exports were either transferred to the bayfront warehouses of the commercial agents or pulled on the wharves for direct placement on the vessels tied up there.

Risks were encountered in draft vehicle movement onto wharves, and collisions were not unusual. Occasionally, wagons drawn by fractious mules would strike a hotel hack or knock a dray into the bay.[6]

Not all such incidents involving wharf traffic were accidents. The *Bulletin* of November 28, 1871, reported on one in "An Item from the Police Court." In a spirit of humor, it said, "On Friday morning our attention was attracted by a crowd standing in the vicinity of the court of James McCoppin, J. P., and in obedience to the call of duty we sauntered into the Court House hoping that something might occur . . . of interest to our readers.

"His Honor was engaged in trying some seamen belonging to one of the schooners lying at Runge's and Sheppard's wharf, who had been on a 'regular tear' the night before. These festive votaries of Neptune were staggering in high spirits from a tour among the saloons of the town to their vessel, when their eyes fell upon a buggy standing near the warehouse of D. Sullivan & Co.

"They immediately concluded to take a starlight ride and, suiting the action to the resolution, one metamorphosed himself into a horse while the other got in to ride. He drove down the wharf a short distance when he overtook a shipmate whom the 'horse' now somewhat jaded induced, as he expressed it in court, 'to make a mule' of himself. Strengthened by this reinforcement, the party traveled faster and soon reached their vessel. But, what to do with the buggy was the question.

One proposed to place it alongside another schooner, so as to create the impression that the guilty parties were aboard her.

"Another, however, suggested a better plan, which was to throw the buggy overboard. The scheme struck his companions as a very quiet way to allay all suspicion, and they forthwith carried it out. A sudden splash, and the buggy sank beneath the waves.

"The next morning, Mr. Sullivan was very much astonished to discover that the buggy had disappeared and, believing it was stolen, he entered a complaint before the magistrate who issued a warrant for the apprehension of the offenders, if they could be found. The vehicle was traced to the wharf by the Sheriff, who inquired of one of the Captains . . . [who] interrogated his men, all of whom, with one exception, answered that they knew nothing of the affair. That one made a complete confession, as we have above related.

"The three implicated were arrested and tried for malicious mischief. One made a confession in open court and threw himself upon the mercy of the jury but was sent, with one of his companions, to the jail where they are now resolving in penitential spirit that such an occurrence 'will never happen again.' The third was acquitted and is now on the briny deep sympathising, no doubt, with the boys he left behind him."

Situated as it was, barely above high tide mark, the sights, sounds and scents of the bay were integral parts of the daily life of Indianola. Expressing a sense of communion between town and sea was an observant report of the *Bulletin*. "A beautiful sight was presented on the bay this morning by the arrival of the steamships *St. Mary*, Captain Hawthorn, and *Harlan*, Captain Lewis, both of the Morgan Line. The bay, after the cool wind of yesterday, was calm to mirror-like smoothness and the noble ships, like Le Compt and Lexington, came booming side by side for several miles up the handsomest bay of the Gulf. The *Harlan* touched the ribbons about three-quarters of a second before the '*Saint*' but the latter made fast first . . ."[7]

Various news comments gave an insight as to commercial activity in Indianola, "We notice several new buildings in the course of erection in our city; the fine two story house of Jacob Hamm on Main Street; the concrete building on the corner of Ward and Main Streets intended for business houses; and several dwellings in the upper part of the city will soon be finished, adding to the increase of Indianola. We will, no doubt, this coming summer see a large number of new buildings erected now that our railroad facilities are rapidly being extended towards the interior." And, "From the frequent arrivals of small craft plying between the different points along the coast, the coasting trade is looking up. The bayou presents daily quite a busy scene, sloops and schooners coming and going constantly, bringing produce and carrying away cargoes of merchandise. It is an evidence that the coast country is fast being settled . . .

"A fine vessel to be schooner-rigged is under construction at the yard above the city. The builders are Messrs. Idlebrook and Cleveland. Also,

Louis de Planque's photographic studio and residence in Indianola, 1875. It was commonplace for businessmen to have their residences either next door to their establishments or above them on a second floor. *(Courtesy Mrs. L. T. Barrow, Houston, and the Houston Public Library, Texas Room.)*

On the Morgan Line long wharf at Indianola. Cattle are being loaded onto the *I. C. Harris* from a GWT&P train. The ship's starboard wheelhouse is shown arching behind the locomotive smokestack. The steamship line office gallery on the T-head is at left. *(Courtesy Texas State Archives, Austin. From Samuel N. Townshend, Our Indian Summer in the Far West, London: Charles Whittingham, 1880.)*

at the shipyards below the city we notice a new vessel building on the stocks. Capt. J. E. Wetherill . . . is superintending its construction. J. H. Remschel will soon have a new vessel in the trade. She is built expressly for his business, will carry 125,000 feet of lumber and is in every respect well adapted to the trade. The lumber business is assuming large proportions . . . We now have in the city three extensive lumber yards, yet they cannot keep up a sufficient supply to satisfy the demand."[8]

Rundell & Nolda, confectioners of Indianola, in June 1871 "fitted up a magnificent saloon for the lovers of Ice Cream." Iced "soda water" in several flavors was also dispensed.[9] Hard candies made in their own factory were displayed in glass containers on shelves behind a long case in which other confections were arranged. Manufacturers of candies that were exported from Indianola throughout Western Texas, Rundell & Nolda received notice in the Houston *Times* of June 1871 for honors won at the second Grand Fair of Texas in that city. The firm took the silver medal for the best Texas-made stick candy and machine-made candy. They also won a silver medal for the best fruit drops, cable and flag candy, as well as honorable mention for their ornamental confections. In the serving of ice cream, Louis Preisig antedated Rundell & Nolda by more than a decade, his "Ice Cream Saloon, Confectionery and Fruit Store" on Main Street offering "Ice Cream and the usual summer beverages" prior to the War Between the States.[10]

Until the completion of the telegraph line, the *Bulletin* and her short-lived rivals in the city followed a practice common among members of the profession in that day — the "pirating" of foreign, national and state news stories from metropolitan papers, though usually with full credit as to the source. Seldom was an edition printed without an expression of thanks to ships' captains or pursers for New Orleans or New York papers brought to the printing office. Such public recognition in the press ensured a continuation of the practice.

Advertisements in the paper provide clues to fashionable or utilitarian merchandise in demand by the public. Sure to be listed were inventions and innovations placed in stock. On sale in Indianola were washing machines for household use, as well as dishwashers and "self dryers." Luxury merchandise such as Steinway and Chickering pianos could be purchased locally. Advertised were barber shops having "bathrooms with hot water" for the convenience of sailors and travelers who were passing through the city without benefit of hotel accommodations. One of the barbershops offered service in "cupping and bleeding" as a side line. Dry goods, grocery, hardware and jewelry stores carried enormous stocks from which selection could be made on a wholesale as well as retail basis.

There were two photographic studios. R. Rehner gave notice that he had returned from Europe and offered " . . . a collection gathered by myself in Europe of plain and colored photographs, stereoscopic views of the most noted parts of the world, the latest style of frames, and a splendid assortment of albums . . . Photographs and Ambrotypes taken in the European style . . . " Louis DePlanque's studio was located on Main Street. Following the destruction of the studio, equipment and priceless glass plates by the hurricane of 1875, DePlanque moved to Victoria where he was in business when the 1886 storm struck. It was he who took the well-known pictures of the wreckage of Indianola in that year.

Mrs. LeGros was a seamstress specializing in dresses, sacques and overskirts. Her shop, where she offered a varied assortment of "thread, needles, buttons and trimmings," was "Next door, but one, to J. M. Reuss' Drug Store." For ladies' millinery goods, Mrs. Johanna Marshall invited "the attention of the public to her large and handsome assortment of MILLINERY consisting of every variety and pattern of goods in this line, with all the appurtenances necessary to an elegant and tasteful toilet, also dress patterns of the latest bon ton, laces, ribbons, gloves, etc."

Indianola's several dry goods stores included those of M. Rouff, E. Moses, Joseph Cahn, D. H. Regan and M. Lichtenstein. The latter was joined in his firm by L. Alexander in 1872. Morris Lichtenstein suffered reverses in the Panic of 1873. He and Alexander dissolved partnership and Lichtenstein moved to Corpus Christi where he founded what later became the leading department store in that section of Texas. Commission and forwarding merchants, some of whom were wholesalers and retailers in general merchandise and groceries as well, included John H. Dale, H. Seeligson & Co., H. Runge & Co., Hartter & Beissner, Woodward Bros., C. & A. Keller, Heyck & Helferich, Vance & Bro. (R. A. and W. C.), H. Iken & Co., August Fromme and William Westhoff & Co. L. Preuss was a partner in the Westhoff firm. Seeligson and Runge were also Indianola's bankers and exchange dealers. Seeligson had the city's largest furniture store.

Whether dry goods, meat, groceries or household items, the ladies of Indianola were not obliged to carry their purchases home with them. Stores provided free delivery service to all parts of the city. Even ice was delivered to residences, as well as to hotels, restaurants and saloons. Because of the commercial nature of the port and the large number of sailors in and out every day, there was a wide choice of places of refreshment and relaxation for men. Well-known saloons were the Lone Star, Dahme's, The Office and Casimir Hall. Casimir Villeneuve branched out to become a wholesale and retail dealer in liquors, wines, brandies and beer, supplying saloons and liquor merchants in Western Texas from his large, well-stocked warehouse. Several of the grocery stores also dealt in liquors.

Casimir Hall, the largest building in the city for public assemblies and theatrical productions prior to construction of the German Casino, was equipped with a stage complete with curtain and backdrops. George French operated the ground floor bar. Upstairs, just off the balcony, was a billiard room furnished with five Phelan tables. Casimir Hall was splendidly furnished and was illuminated by chandeliers and wall fixtures using artificial gas. The interior walls were white, highlighted by panels framed with gilt moldings. The side columns and arch over the stage were decorated in rococo style.[11]

Another billiard room connected with the bar was at The Office, which had both Phelan and Collender tables. Under ownership of Fuhrman and Kleinecke, later Ingerman and Kleinecke, The Office bar was attended by Christian French.

Eglington & Miller were Indianola's undertakers, offering "a full assortment of Metallic and other coffins, and a large variety of coffin trimmings." The trimmings were for those who made their own coffins for burial of family members. A business firm of diversified interests, Eglington & Miller were also lumber merchants and builders of doors, sash, blinds and cisterns in their own mill.

In the early 1870s, physicians and surgeons at Indianola were Drs. J. M. Reuss, William A. McCamly, F. E. Hughes and H. K. Leake, the last two having joint offices. Indianola attorneys were (F. S.) Stockdale & (D. C.) Proctor, Osceola Archer, Walter Merriman and John S. Givens. William H. Crain, who studied law while working in the office of Stockdale & Proctor, was licensed to practice in 1871. Elected district attorney for the 23rd District the following year, he served until 1876, when he was elected to the Texas Senate. Two years later, he was elected representative to Congress, where he remained for five terms.[12]

Although each hotel had its own dining room for the use of guests and residents of the city, Indianola was generously supplied with restaurants. Four of the most popular were those of John Mathuly, Nicholas Cahill, Ben Weinrich and F. Barratte, the last a newcomer who had set up shop in November 1870. Cahill's was situated on the corner of Kaufman and A Streets, where he specialized in oysters stewed, raw and roasted. Mathuly's, on Main Street next to the Metropolitan Market, was noted for seafood of all kinds, as was Weinrich's. The bounty of the sea was poured onto Indianola's doorstep by oystermen, shrimpers and commercial fishermen.

Barratte's was a "restaurant extraordinary." Using "snob appeal" Barratte advertised that "The undersigned, having a thorough Parisian and New York experience, would appeal especially to that portion of the traveling public who appreciate choice cooking and a judicious selection of such viands as tempt the delicate appetite and satisfy the most fastidious tastes; confident of his ability to meet their requirements and induce them to pronounce his Restaurant worthy to be classed with the most select and noted establishments in the largest Cities . . . "

Rendall & Deviney were blacksmiths, boilermakers and machinists specializing in steam engines and fittings, castings and copper piping for gas lines. The firm also prepared mechanical drawings for all types of metal work. James E. Polhemus was bricklayer, plasterer and contractor, builder of concrete cisterns, of furnaces and grates lined with fire brick. Charles Walker, opposite the post office, operated a fabricating shop for tin, copper and sheet iron.

Custom tailors were D. Stubbeman and V. Fox. Auctioneer was William P. Milby, and jewelers were Louis Peine, F. Klamberg and L.

Looking west on Main Street, Indianola. At extreme left is the David Lewis Drug Store. Next in order are D. H. Regan's Dry Goods Emporium, L. Limott's grocery and Ingerman & Kleinecke's "The Office" saloon. On the right, through the gallery railing, is the advertising sign of August Swartz' City (meat) Market. In the foreground, just beyond the two covered wagons, is a stagecoach ready for loading. (*Courtesy DeWitt County Historical Museum, Cuero. From Mrs. Frank Elmendorf.*)

In this view down Main to the east, dimly visible in the distance are masts of coastwise sailing vessels anchored in Powder Horn Bayou at the end of the street. At right center is a buggy hitched to the covered wagon being pulled by a team of mules. This and the accompanying photograph of Main Street were made prior to the completion of the Indianola Railroad to Clark Station. (*Courtesy DeWitt County Historical Museum, Cuero. From Mrs. Frank Elmendorf.*)

Willemin. All three provided repair service for clocks and watches. In addition, Klamberg was a gold and silversmith, "manufacturing to order tea, table and soup spoons, ladles, dippers, forks and other items of cutlery."

George Stern & Bro. operated Indianola's only store that dealt exclusively in boots and shoes - exclusive with one startling exception. Incongruously, Stern's was Indianola dealer for the Howe sewing machine. In competition with Stern's was John A. Davis, general agent in Western Texas for Grover & Baker's "Family Sewing Machines."

The city's principal lumber merchants were Henry J. Huck, J. H. Remschel, Henry Runge, William Westhoff and Eglington & Miller. Hardware merchants, both wholesale and retail, were Warn & Payne, Brown & Lang and J. E. Mitchell & Co. Grocers included Wilson & Miller, L. Limott, D. Sullivan & Co., J. Wilson, Dove & Schultz, H. Seeligson, Hartter & Beissner, Woodward Bros., H. Runge & Co., James Morrison, C. & A. Keller, Vance & Bro., William H. Marshall and Charles Eichlitz. There were five meat markets in this period. One was Captain Ed Lilly's Metropolitan Market. Fay & O'Neil had two, one uptown and the other in the lower part of the business district. August Swartz owned and operated the City Meat Market and the Bayou Market, located in the upper and lower portions of the city.

The granting of permission by the county court to John F. Smith for establishment of a ferry service between Indianola and Sand Point, brought the port's stores within easy reach of residents across the bay. Sand Point was located due north of Indianola at the junction of Cox and Matagorda Bays. Smith's ferry landing was at the long wharf at the foot of Crockett Street, the heart of the downtown business district. He was authorized to charge one dollar shore to shore. The ferry proved to be a popular and convenient service to the public.[13]

The construction of an arched, fireproof vault in the courthouse was authorized in 1871. With walls of solid brick, 16 inches in thickness, and interior height of seven feet, six inches, the new vault was expected to afford ample safe storage space for county records for several decades. As it turned out, because of the two hurricanes those files would remain in Indianola for only another 15 years. The vault did protect the papers from damage during the floods.

In a move indicating an attitude of petulance, the court declared null and void an agreement with Dr. J. M. Reuss as health officer, the stated reason being the commissioners' opinion that "the rates of such services charged seem exorbitant." Bids were then invited from the several physicians of the city for medical treatment and daily board of indigent persons. Three days later, members of the court were obliged to swallow their pride. Only two bids were submitted by members of the profession in Indianola. One was from Dr. Reuss, who offered to continue at the rate of one dollar per patient, the same he had previously charged. The other bid was from Dr. H. K. Leake, whose figure was $1.50. Agreement was again entered into with Dr. Reuss, who was promptly reappointed.[14]

The Casino Society of Indianola was incorporated in 1871. Shareholders of the old Casino Association and members of the new Society met on June 17 to adopt a charter and transfer the property. Following that, the Casino building was greatly enlarged, a gymnasium added and the new-styled gas lighting installed.

The Society's building then became the focal point for performances of theatrical companies landing at Indianola and beginning tours of Western Texas. Public concerts of the Indianola City Brass Band were held there monthly, and the hall was used by the Indianola Saengerbund for performances. Like the smaller Casimir Hall, the Casino was used for both public and private dances. When necessary, folding chairs could be brought into the hall from a large storage area beneath the raised stage. Describing the Casino, Francis E. Huck estimated that the maximum seating capacity was about 400.

Baseball was a developing recreational activity in Indianola. By 1871, there were four teams there, the Lone Star Club at Old Town and the Stonewall Base Ball Club, the Excelsior and Crescents of Indianola proper. The people of the city were as sports-minded as are Americans of today and there was enthusiastic community support of the teams. When the players visited other towns, such as Corpus Christi, Galveston, Victoria and, later, Cuero in competition play, they were always accompanied by fans. Travel to Corpus Christi and Galveston was by boat. To Victoria and Cuero, teams and fans went by excursion trains on the GWT&P.

Inspection of the handsome new schooner *Thos. P. Ball* attracted a throng of Indianolans on December 6, 1871. The *Ball*, built for the New York-Indianola run, had just arrived on her maiden voyage. Woodward Bros., agents and part-owners of the ship, and Captain Rider invited citizens to come aboard and inspect the vessel. The invitation was responded to with such enthusiasm that the ship was constantly crowded during the open hours. An orchestra provided music for the occasion and Barratte's Restaurant catered "a sumptuous buffet for the guests in the beautifully finished cabin. Wine and wit flowed copiously. Appropriate speeches were delivered by Dr. F. E. Hughes and Wm. H. Crain, Esq."

Five months later the steamship *Morgan* began operating between Indianola and Brashear (later renamed Morgan City), Louisiana, her new terminus instead of New Orleans. Charles Morgan was diverting more of his ships from New Orleans, just as he had turned away from Port Lavaca in 1849 and would soon begin to by-pass Galveston. All three ports annoyed Morgan to the point that he retaliated with his ultimate weapon - a new terminus for his line of ships. Because of Lavaca's action, Indianola prospered. Though never destined to be a great port, Brashear took from New Orleans sufficient traffic, as well as commercial expenditures by Morgan, that raising wharfage fees proved to be a costly experience for the Crescent City. Houston benefited because of Galveston's attitude toward Charles Morgan, who was a man to be reckoned with. To Morgan, more than anyone else, goes credit for the development of the port of Houston.

Early in 1872, Indianolans and Galvestonians had been watching with deep concern the proposal to construct an artificial harbor at the mouth of the Brazos River. It was intended to be the terminus of the Columbia Tap Railroad, but the line was not extended to the projected port because of inadequate financing.[15] Indianola's worry about nearby competition proved to be without foundation. It was 1929 before the Brazos was diverted and the artificial harbor created. By that time, Indianola had been dead for 42 years.

As the traffic through the port continued to increase, need arose for development of better docking facilities for small vessels in Powder Horn Bayou and Lake, to relieve the crowding at the bay wharves. The Indianola Dredging Company was incorporated by Henry Seeligson, Johnathan Payne, August Heyck, Dr. F. E. Hughes and William Westhoff. The company was authorized by the state to dredge a channel across the bar at the mouth of the bayou, up that waterway and into the lake to a minimum depth of eight feet and a maximum width of 125 feet, except in the turning basin. The company was granted the right to assess fees for use of the channel and docks, remitting to the city of Indianola one half of one per cent of the gross earnings. Half of that payment was allotted to the city, the other half going into the state school fund. Vessels drawing three feet of water or less were exempt from the payment of usage fees.[16]

The Episcopal Church of the Ascension had succeeded the old St. John's in Indianola. St. John's, always a small congregation, disappeared from the scene with the catastrophic death rate of its parishioners during the yellow fever epidemics of the middle 1850s. Ascension was organized following the close of the war and prospered from the beginning, though its sanctuary had suffered destruction in the storm of 1869. From its rebuilt steeple sounded the bell given to it by Charles Morgan, who made gifts of different types but equal value to all the churches of the city in 1871.[17]

A new organ for the Church of the Ascension arrived on the steamship *Morgan* on April 7, 1871. "We were present when it was put in place and much gratified on hearing its tones," wrote Episcopalian C. A. Ogsbury in the *Bulletin*, "It was in every respect a satisfactory instrument. Mr. Law, who superintended the purchase, and under whose direction it was put in its appropriate place in the choir, deserves the thanks of the congregation for a gratuitous service on behalf of the church."[18]

The sanctuary and rectory faced B Street, being situated on Lots 11 and 12 of Block 90, at the corner of Walker. The Right Reverend Alexander Gregg, Bishop of the Diocese of Texas, came to Indianola for the specific purpose of officiating at the marriage, on Tuesday, May 9, 1871, of the Rev. Robert Jope and Mrs. Mary S. Lee, the sister of Mrs. George Seeligson. At the time, vestrymen of the church were Wm. P. Milby, F. S. Stockdale, Charles A. Ogsbury, James McCoppin, D. K. Woodward, J. E. Polhemus, John Eglington, J. S. Givens and Henry Seeligson.

The largest congregation in Indianola was that of the Presbyterian Church which, like the Catholic, had its beginning at Indian Point and later moved to Brown's Addition. The bell for that church arrived on the schooner *Franklin* from New York in June, and the new communion service came on the *Carrie* in September. "It [the communion service] is very beautiful and worthy of the noble ladies who have contributed towards its purchase through means of their Sewing Circle. Also from the same source another elegant chandelier for the church. True to their Christian instincts inherited from the crucifixion of our Savior, women are the main instruments through which the church of Christ is supported and perpetuated. This service was purchased by Mr. R. C. Warn, of Messrs. Warn & Payne of this city, who is now on a business visit to New York, where it was obtained."[19] Beginning on October 5, 1871, the Presbytery of Western Texas again convened in the Indianola Presbyterian Church.

Editor Ogsbury waxed enthusiastic on the subject of bells. "Our churches and public buildings are loud in their voices on Sunday, and days devoted to religious services. The Catholic Church has a large new bell, the Fire Department also has a loud toned bell, [and those of] the Episcopal and Presbyterian . . . together with the one . . . in the tower of the Methodist Church . . . give *tone* to the city and proclaim to its citizens that they are marching on towards a higher civilization. Nothing is more cheerful on a bright Sunday morning than to hear the church going bell pealing out its deep-toned invitation to the house of God."[20]

In addition to the Methodist Episcopal Church, South, Indianola also had a German Methodist Episcopal Church, a Baptist, Lutheran and an African Methodist Episcopal Church. On October 18, 1871, the Indianola Colored Benevolent Society was incorporated by Stephen Williams, Peter Thaupe, Jacob Harris, Philip Jones, Banister Prior and Edward Peyton for the purpose of "taking care of the aged, infirm, indigent and sick and for providing for the orphan children of their race." The organization played a key role in the improvement of the lot of black residents of Indianola, and its members did yeoman's service to both black and white during and after the great hurricane of 1875.[21]

Gun control was receiving attention by legislators and the public alike early in the decade. Proposals to regulate the keeping and carrying of weapons had been bandied for several years. It was a subject involving much controversy because it was considered by many to threaten the "right," as some citizens expressed it, to possess and bear arms on the person. It is not beyond reason to assume that one of the motivating factors in the proposal was to endeavor to bring a halt to the murderous feuds that plagued the state in the years of unrest after the war. The controls came about eventually, though their efficacy remains a matter of conflicting opinion.

On March 11, 1874, Indianola became directly involved in the Sutton-Taylor feud, one of the bloodiest in the history of Texas. Centered in DeWitt County, the feud had already cost several lives when William

Sutton, urged by his wife Laura, decided to get away from that locale until the situation quieted. He had long been a marked man. Arriving in Indianola en route to Galveston, Sutton, accompanied by his wife and young Gabe Slaughter, boarded the steamer *Clinton* lying at the Morgan wharf. Mrs. Sutton was with child, a daughter soon to be born. Their departure from Cuero on the GWT&P was not a well-kept secret. Sutton's intention to leave DeWitt County was known. That was more than members of the opposing Taylor faction could endure. Too much blood had been shed on both sides for there to have existed any spirit of forgiveness by either Suttons or Taylors. The latter would not allow Sutton to depart unharmed, if they could prevent it. Slaughter was not important to Jim and Bill Taylor. He happened to be at the murder scene and was believed to be wearing a gun.

Mrs. Sutton, in speaking of the tragedy in later years while residing in Victoria, said, "To have been there at that moment, the Taylors must have gone down to Indianola ahead of us and waited. They were not on the train, and they weren't seen until they stepped out. When I saw them, I knew they were there to kill my husband. Why else would they have made the trip to Indianola? It was not a chance meeting, but was planned. Mr. Sutton had escaped more than one ambush at home, and he supposed there would be no danger at Indianola. There were so many people around. It all happened so fast. He and Mr. Slaughter were shot and killed before anyone could move. It was assassination by cowards."[22] Bill and Jim Taylor then fled.

Mrs. Sutton placed a statement in the Victoria *Advocate* and the Indianola *Bulletin*, both of which had wide circulation in Western Texas. She offered a reward of $1,000 in addition to the state's reward of $500, for the arrest of Jim Taylor. "On the 11th of March last, Wm. Sutton, my husband, and Gabriel Slaughter, whilst engaged in getting their tickets for Galveston, on board the steamer *Clinton* at Indianola, were murdered by James and Bill Taylor in my presence without any warning or notice, James Taylor shooting my husband in the back with two six-shooters. One of the murderers, Bill Taylor, has since been arrested by Marshal Brown of Cuero and is now in Galveston jail. James Taylor, the murderer of my husband, is still at large and I offer to anyone who will arrest and deliver him inside the jail of Calhoun County, Texas, one thousand dollars in addition to the reward of $500 offered by the governor of Texas. Marshal Brown of Cuero can say whether the Governor's has been promptly paid, as he is the man that arrested the murderer Bill Taylor. As to my ability to pay the $1,000, I refer to Brownson's Bank, Victoria, Texas.

"Description of James Taylor, age 23 years; weight 165 or 170 pounds, very heavy set; height 5 feet and 10 inches; complexion dark; hair dark; round features; usually shaves clean about once a week; wears no whiskers, beard rather heavy, talks very little, has a low, dull tone, and very quiet in his manners.

MRS. LAURA SUTTON"[23]

XX.

The First Great Hurricane

The fateful year of 1875 dawned with great promise for Indianola. Maritime commerce prospered, boosted by the continuing development of Western Texas. Indianolans watched with anxiety the only cloud that then appeared on their horizon - the construction of the GH&SA from Houston toward San Antonio. By January 1, 1875, the rail line had reached the Caldwell-Guadalupe County line west of the new town of Luling.[1] That threat of railroad competition in Indianola's hinterland brought renewed agitation for resumption of construction by the GWT&P to both San Antonio and Austin.

A weather observation and reporting station had been established at Indianola by the United States Signal Service in May 1872. San Antonio's station had opened in January 1871 and Galveston's in May of that year. In September 1875, Indianola and Galveston were the Signal Service's two coastal reporting stations in Texas. It was a matter of local pride that Indianola had that distinction. The city's Chamber of Commerce had a permanent committee to confer and cooperate with the Chief Signal Officer of the Army in matters relating to the post there. Its members in 1875 were George Seeligson, Wm. P. Milby and Dan Sullivan.[2]

Connected by telegraph with headquarters in Washington, the Indianola office dispatched daily observations covering atmospheric conditions, even temperature of the water in the bay. It received from the Chief Signal Officer notices of weather changes which could affect shipping, commerce and agriculture. The network of stations connected by telegraph, which had been developed over much of the nation in the previous ten years, provided the Service with the means of studying and interpreting weather trends. It was a new science, and much was to be learned. September 1875 was to give the Signal Service its first opportunity to observe and study the movement of a gigantic hurricane. Following the blow, information was secured from all possible sources, the path charted with accuracy, wind velocity and direction, rainfall, temperature and barometric readings noted.[3] It would require several decades, and numerous hurricane-related disasters, for the art of forecasting landfall to be more nearly perfected.

Chief Signal Officer Albert J. Myer in Washington reported to Secretary of War J. D. Cameron for the year of July 1, 1875, to June 30, 1876, detailing construction and maintenance of telegraphic lines in the interior of Texas and upon the frontier. They connected military posts, and also served for the protection of the population from Indian depredations. The lines in Arizona, New Mexico and on the Texas frontier were nearly completed at the time of Myer's report, 2,482 miles having been built. As he related, selected enlisted men at each Army telegraph station were trained to make meteorological observations. A telegraphic report to Washington was required daily from each observer. "The existence of the lines in the interior of Texas permit[s] warnings to be exhibited on the Texas coast, and a knowledge of atmospheric conditions over that State, before impossible," said Myer.

The report contained the statement, "It is one of the most difficult tasks which falls to the Office to determine in advance over what ports to be selected, to the exclusion of others, an observed storm-area will pass, and in such manner as to be accompanied at these ports with a given wind velocity. Within the same area, the winds differ in force at different points. There is the danger that warnings unnecessarily given may delay the movements of shipping. A heavy responsibility is incurred if the warnings are not given when they ought to be. Time, increasing experience and . . . facilities will permit greater accuracy." That was a roundabout way of admitting that the Service had failed Indianola by not giving warning of the immensity of the storm, and the possible threat that it posed for the city's inhabitants.

When the assembling of follow-up data on the 1875 hurricane had been completed by the Signal Service, it was revealed that the first record of its existence had been entered in the log of the *Tautallon Castle* on September 1, latitude 12 °N, longitude 27 °W, southwest of the Cape Verde Islands off the coast of Africa. The ship had encountered a "heavy gale accompanied by all the peculiarities of a hurricane, veering from N.W. through W. to S. and S.W." From that first observation, the path of the growing storm can be traced across the Atlantic to the Lesser Antilles, to Cuba, the eastern Gulf of Mexico, and on to Indianola.[4]

Log entries of the many ships affected by the hurricane, even while it was still in the Atlantic, indicate the ferocity of the wind and sea. The steamer *Caribbean*, out of Liverpool on August 20, recorded, "Sunday, September 5, 2:30 p.m., gale increasing with furious squalls; glass going down; wind and squalls increasing and terrific sea. 6:30 p.m. tremendous hurricane; shipped sea, knocking away bridge, lamp-room, boats, steering gear, skylights, &c; lot of water below. 7 p.m., cargo and coal settled leeward. 9 p.m. shipped tremendous sea, carrying away boats; engines stopped; to midnight fearful hurricane, barometer 29. 6th, a.m., sea carried away man at wheel, barometer rising at 4 a.m. and weather moderating fast; barometer 29.08. On the 8th, started with one boiler, reaching St. Thomas 9 a.m., 11th."[5]

Numerous references are made in the report to sailing vessels losing deck loads, being dismasted, leaking badly. Several ships, whose route crossed the path of the hurricane in the Atlantic, simply vanished.

The hurricane reached Barbados on the 9th, causing vast damage. St. Vincent reported, "The storm, which burst over this place this morning [9th] was only indicated yesterday at 5 p.m. by barometer falling and variable. 8th, all day weather cloudy and color bright orange with occasional shower, N.N.E. light winds and rising, sea rising, intense heat . . . On the 9th, torrential rains fell, the sea . . . breaking with great violence, vessels driven ashore and wrecked."[6] All of the islands of the Lesser Antilles were affected, the extent depending on their distance and direction from the eye.

From September 1 until its passage over St. Vincent, the storm had followed a westerly path. In the Caribbean, it veered to the west northwest, moving between Haiti and Jamaica, both of which were devastated. Navassa, a small island off Haiti's Cape Carcasse, was struck with the full force of the blow on the 12th. On Friday, the 10th, the schooner *Serene* had sailed from Navassa for Wilmington, N.C. The following day, the brig *J. W. Spencer* departed for Charleston, S.C. Neither vessel was ever heard from again.

As to the effects of the storm on the island of Navassa itself, the report said, "12th. Hurricane, N.E., accompanied by deluge of rain; houses commenced to go; trees torn up by roots and others, 3 feet in diameter, snapped off; quarters, warehouse and wharves first destroyed, up to noon; afternoon, wind suddenly to S.S.E. and terrific. 2 p.m. wind came from S.S.W; rest of buildings . . . eight lighters and one gig went; railroad torn up; cars (loaded) blown from track; one building lifted bodily and smashed; all buildings wood, thermometer 78° all day . . .sea broke over cliffs 45 to 75 feet above sea-level; anchor 3,000 pounds with heavy cable 8 feet above sea washed overboard into 60 feet deep water; another 1½ tons raised out of water and left 20 feet above original place; a flat stone weighing 25 tons, 60 feet above sea level could not be found afterwards; boiler and machinery disappeared; bushes and small trees cut down by flying boards . . . men were lying down and holding onto railroad tracks; also sought shelter in holes, and in some instances were washed out by the sea breaking over them . . . More destructive by far than any since its occupation, 1856."[7]

The report from Cuba showed that the eye came onto that island a little east of Cape Cruz in Oriente Province, passed over Manzanillo and Santa Cruz, moved along the southern coast slightly south of Santa Clara, Colon, Cardenas and Matanzas, and left it north northeast of Havana. There was great havoc in Portillo, Manzanillo and Santa Cruz, most severe on the night of the 12th and on the 13th . . . "At Havana large cirro-stratus presented themselves from E.S.E. to W.N.W.; later turning into a whitish and uniform veil of fibrous structure with circles and solar and lunar halos, and heavy, damp weather; at sunset, clouds copper-red tinge. Nimbi appeared suddenly; in the east very bad looking barrier of crowded clouds in advance, and in the west, following. . . ."[8]

Key West reported many vessels driven ashore on the keys, including the steamer *City of Waco*. The steamship *St. Mary*, from Havana to New Orleans, was sideswiped by the hurricane, which had entered the Gulf of Mexico in the vicinity of Dry Tortugas, and lost her smokestack and port wheelhouse. On Tuesday morning, September 14, telegraphic dispatches from the Chief Signal Officer in Washington relayed word that "a powerful hurricane" had raged across Cuba, had battered Key West and was believed to be moving toward Mobile, Alabama. Washington sent warnings to the Mobile station, and merchants on the river front there began raising their goods above the high water mark.[9]

With only barometric readings and wind direction to guide the Signal Service, plotting the course of a hurricane was admittedly difficult in 1875. The Florida panhandle and the Alabama coast were spared. As the day passed, it began to be suspected in Washington that the storm was possibly traveling in a northwesterly direction. During the 12th, 13th, and 14th, a high pressure area covered the United States east of the Rocky Mountains, being highest over New England and the Middle Atlantic States. It was later concluded that the high caused the hurricane to veer to the west northwest, carrying it directly toward Texas.[10] By Wednesday morning the Louisiana coast was being pounded by the edge of the monster storm, sugarcane flattened, blinding torrents of rain pouring, and ships foundering, even in protected harbors along the low shore and in the Mississippi River at New Orleans. In the southwestern Louisiana bayou country around Lake Calcasieu, the tide rose to an unprecedented height — five feet above the record mark set in 1867. Still, the Signal Service in Washington faltered in deductions as to the course of the storm and eventual landfall.

The Morgan Line steamship *Austin* left Indianola on the 14th en route to Brashear with a cargo of 388 head of cattle. Completely unaware of what was ahead, she was steered into the path of the approaching storm. Five days later, the badly battered vessel limped into Sabine with only 25 of the 388 cattle alive.

At 1:25 a.m. on September 13, the steamer *State of Texas* departed Galveston for Key West. By noon she had encountered heavy squalls of rain accompanied by lightning and thunder. The fierceness of the weather increased until, at 6 p.m. on the 14th, the log entry shows that a full hurricane was blowing. "Had to slow down engine; kept head to sea and got everything tied down in case of accident to engine; sea running very high; broke over the ship and stove down engine room sides. 8 p.m., shipped a fearful sea, &c., saloon, all staterooms, port side of engine room, fire room, cook's room, completely wrecked fore and aft on port side; also upper deck, after boat and rails; stove in pilot house windows and washed overboard everything movable; complete wreck from fore to aft; making a N.N.E. drift about 2 knots an hour. Barometer fallen from 29.90 at Galveston to 28.40. 10:30 p.m., wind suddenly from N.E. to S.E. . . . 12 m., fearful sea and wind; barometer rose from 28.20 to 28.60; all hands on deck assisting engineers with hurricane bulkheads and using every available means to keep water from going below. 15th, 1:30 a.m., making 2 knots by a N.E. drift, wind S.E. and fearful hurricane; sea mountains high and completely breaking over ship; laboring heavily; 2 men at helm and 3 and third officer at relief tackles. 2 a.m., barometer still rising and hurricane has broken a little. . ."[11]

The same theme was repeated in the logs of other ships, both steamers and sailing vessels, in the central and western Gulf of Mexico. But, there were some that did not survive, as had been true in the Atlantic and Caribbean. The schooner *Witch of the Wave* left Tuxpan, Mexico on September 8 for Galveston, and was lost. The same fate was awaiting the schooner *Mabel* when she sailed out of the mouth of the Mississippi the day before the winds reached hurricane strength there. She was never heard from again.

As the storm roared on its west northwest path, its fringe reached out to slap Galveston. There, the weather station recorded solar halos during the morning of the 14th and a brisk northeast wind by night. "Wednesday, September 15: wind N. 33 miles; 11 a.m. N.E. 41 miles; 4:20 p.m. heavy rain; 9:49 immense sea. Old captains refused to go to sea. 10 p.m., wind E.N.E. 50 miles and increasing. Several bridges washed away. Water eight feet above mean tide and higher than in 1867, extending three miles inland.

"Thursday, September 16: 2 a.m., quarantine houses on breakwater, and harbor improvement buildings carried away . . . Storm continued all day. Water fell in morning but rose again in evening. Fearful night; water from Gulf covering island, except a few spots, and highest ever known.

"Friday, September 17: 12 m. to 4 a.m., terrible state of affairs, water on first floors, wind changed toward morning; 4:20 a.m. gale S.E.; at daylight water 6 to 10 feet deep towards fairgrounds, and 30 inches above that of 1867 . . .

"Saturday, September 18: at 6:55 a.m. wind N. 42 miles. Storm lasted from 4:20 a.m. September 15 to 12 m., September 18, 1875."[12]

In the target Matagorda Bay region, the wind gradually increased in intensity through the 14th with gusts up to 40 miles per hour. During the afternoon, great agitation of the air at high levels was evident from observation of the clouds, which frequently parted, momentarily exposing the sun. On the night of the 14th, the wind at Indianola backed to north, gradually increasing to "high" by daylight of the 15th. The steadily falling barometer which accompanied the wind shift contradicted "the otherwise delusive appearance of an ordinary 'norther.'" Sergeant C. A. Smith, observing at the weather station in Indianola, reported that soon after noon on the 15th the wind increased to a gale with still falling barometer. By 2 p.m., the indications were so unusually threatening that he began making hourly observations.

A study of the War Department's "hindsight" weather map for the month of September 1875, showing "tracks of centres of low barometer," discloses that as late as the 15th the path of the hurricane was headed for the Texas coast in the vicinity of Rockport. Then, the high pressure area that had forced the storm on its west northwest course began to slide rapidly to the east. With the removal of the blocking action of that center, the hurricane swerved due north and drew a bead on hapless Indianola. In its infant state of weather-watching, the Signal Service was apparently unaware of the effect the eastward movement of the high pressure center would exert on the path of the storm. In time, cause and effect would be understood, but not in 1875.

During that week of September 1875, the busy port of Indianola was more crowded than usual. The trial of Bill Taylor, charged in the murder of William Sutton and Gabriel Slaughter was in progress in the Calhoun County courthouse there. A large number of people had congregated in Indianola from DeWitt, Victoria and other nearby counties for the sensational event, and had filled the hotels.

As the daylight hours of September 15 passed and the wind velocity slowly grew, the level of the water in Matagorda Bay began to rise. It was fed by the higher stage in the Gulf, forced through Pass Cavallo. Intermittent rain squalls, characteristic of tropical disturbances, moved in. The white-crested waves pounding the bay shore were equally fascinating to Indianola children and the visitors from inland points, who watched them from sheltered spots where they were protected against the spasmodic, driving rain. The excitement of the weather was something the visitors looked forward to relating when they returned to their homes. Tragically, many of them were fated to have only one more day of life.

Indianolans buoyed their own spirits with the conviction that the wind would soon diminish, and the water recede. It had always done so. Surely this storm would be no exception. In that confident mood, the town retired for the night. The dawn of September 16 showed their unbelieving eyes that the water level was far higher than the record mark set in 1871.

Sergeant Smith reported to Washington by telegraph that throughout the night of the 15th, the tide rose rapidly, with a high sea running, that on the morning of the 16th it had broken over the beach and was rushing in torrents through the streets at right angles to the bay. Buildings facing Water Street were beginning to be undermined as the current of the inflowing water tore at the crushed shell land surface on which foundations were placed. From that time on, the work of devastation spread rapidly. By midday, the wharves were being torn apart, "whole rods of planking and timbers . . . lifted bodily and dashed into pieces among the buildings along the shore. The streets presented the appearance of narrow, swift rivers, to cross which boats and quantities of rope were brought into requisition, and even with these the passage was attended with great danger."[13]

Now those men and women who were in Indianola on business and for the Taylor trial began to panic and seek a means of exit - but, there was none! The heavy rains and rising tide had made the roads impassable. To their dismay, they learned the passenger train sitting at the railroad station could not make its scheduled run. The locomotive boiler had been drained the previous evening and, during the night, salt water had intruded into the huge underground cistern used by the railroad as its source of boiler water, thus rendering it unfit for use. Too, the track was being undercut by the swift inflowing current. Whatever future hours held, all would face it together. Actually, not quite all!

The concrete wall courthouse was becoming jammed with refugees, who were later forced to move to the second story by the surge of the storm tide. When the water around the courthouse reached a dangerous height, Bill Taylor and two other prisoners, George Blackburn and Sam Ruschau, were released from the jail, having given their pledge that they would make no attempt to escape. The pledge was not kept. The released prisoners stole horses and somehow made their way across the flooded prairie. At Green Lake, they left word where the horses could later be found by their owners, thus evincing some sense of honor and decency.

"The prairies in the rear of the town, as far as the eye could reach through the blinding rain and spray, were deeply submerged and covered with quantities of rapidly drifting debris," Sergeant Smith said. "The high grade of the G.W.T. and P. Railroad, which bounds the town on the southwest, was also submerged to such a depth as to make its use hazardous and even impossible as a means of escape from the town." At about 2 p.m. a large schooner was torn loose from her anchorage and drifted ashore stern first. She struck, and nearly demolished, the telegraph office, thus isolating Indianola from the world. After the storm, she was found sitting high and dry five miles inland.

All through the day, men buffeted the treacherous current pulling lifeboats and skiffs filled with terrified women and children, who were carried to buildings believed to be the safest. Other groups collected the "numerous cotton bales which, at every moment, came eddying around the corners, lashing them together into the most substantial rafts." Two such rafts were secured to the large safes at the H. Seeligson & Co. and H. Runge & Co. banks on Main Street, should the buildings be swept away, as appeared likely.

With the approach of night, the storm increased in intensity and the rain roared in torrents. Objects could barely be discerned across the streets, and the noise of the wind and surf became deafening. The Signal Office was now being undermined and an attempt was made to deflect the current from the east corner of the building by means of planking and other debris. That proved to be impossible because of the rapid succession of breakers which continually swept down the street. Sergeant Smith's 5 p.m. observation gave the barometer 28.90 corrected, a fall of .27 in five hours. The temperature was 75° and the anemograph showed 82 miles per hour. Fifteen minutes later, the anemometer blew away, registering 88 miles, many hours before the hurricane reached its peak. Estimates of the later wind gusts were 145 to 150 miles per hour.

"The volume and immense velocity of water pouring through the streets was now truly terrible," said Smith. "As night drew on, the work of rescuing was generally abandoned, everyone acting on the principle of 'sauve qui peut' [a general rout or stampede]. Small buildings and dwellings were being swept away on all sides, but darkness rendered assistance to the unfortunate inmates impossible." At about 6 p.m., the large hide and wool warehouse at the rear of the Signal Office collapsed. The disintegration of that building, which had stood between the office and the bay, now exposed it to the full force of the waves, increasing the danger of its fall. Evacuation became expedient. Accordingly, the people who had congregated there decided to try to get to the more secure building which housed David Lewis's drug store. It was obliquely opposite the Signal Office and somewhat better protected.

Descending to the sidewalk, they went to work constructing a raft under the lee of D. Schultz's store, the water being about breast-deep at the time. They caught a number of cedar piles which were then lashed together and covered with a door. At that moment, an empty large skiff came bobbing around the corner. As it answered the purpose better than the raft, the skiff was appropriated. "Before leaving Schultz's building, we gave all the extra rope we could spare to a party of 30 or 40 negroes who had congregated in the long hall, but were unable to help them further," said Smith. "Most of them left the building forthwith and succeeded in reaching the banks (which were already crowded) by means of rope guides.

"After the acquisition of the skiff, our party crept along under the lee of buildings until opposite our destination and succeeded, after considerable difficulty and some hard swimming, in effecting a hold on the gallery which, in our drenched condition, we climbed. . ."

Robert Clark, whose residence was next to the convent of the Sisters of Mercy of St. Patrick, waded through waist-deep water and insisted that all go to his house, which he considered to offer greater safety. Some of the sisters expressed the desire to take refuge in the church, but Mother Camillus would not consent to the separation. With great exertion, they made their way to the Clark home, where they joined other refugees. Altogether, 32 were sheltered there. By evening they were forced to go to the second floor as the great surge of water before the hurricane's eye broke over Matagorda Peninsula and Island and quickly brought the bay level to that of the Gulf. Near 10 o'clock, they moved to the attic, "where all prayed quietly and resigned themselves to God's Holy will."[14] The Catholic church and the convent were telescoped. The Clark house stood. Those exhausted occupants were saved.

Such was not the good fortune of some 300 other men, women and children. The exact number was never known, and the bodies of many of the victims were never found. Robert Jope, rector of the Episcopal Church of the Ascension, declined with thanks all offers of help from parishioners. He resolved to go through the storm with his family in the rectory next to the church, despite the earnest pleadings of vestrymen to leave.[15] Along with his wife, two daughters Anna and Jessie, son Davenport Lee, and two orphan boys residing with the family, Jope perished. Not a trace of the rectory remained. The shattered remnants of the sanctuary were deposited on the bank of Powder Horn Bayou, eight blocks from the original site.

In the hours after midnight, the wind reached its screaming peak just in advance of the arrival of the eye of the hurricane. Then a brief period of calm descended. In later years, recounting the experience, Mrs. Clark said, "We had become so steeled to the awful roar of the wind and the great waves, and the constant shuddering of the house, that when the calm came it was horrifying, for some reason. It was so strange. There was an almost abrupt lessening. I realized the noise was moving away, and then there was silence, except for the sound of our breathing. No one spoke, and I remember wondering for a moment if we really were alive or dead. We felt so oppressed, with a smothering feeling. I promised God that if we were delivered, I would take my family away and never return to Indianola. I know it sounds like a bit of foolishness to have tried to bargain at a time like that, but God did not turn away from us. I kept my promise and never went back."[16]

When the eye arrived, a change in tide was noticed. It rose several inches for a few minutes, then began setting seaward rapidly. "This evidence of abatement was hailed with shouts of joy," said Sergeant Smith. In a matter of minutes, the wind returned with explosive force, that time from the northwest as the eye passed on. The tide now moved toward the bay with racing speed. It was then that the greatest destruction to property, and the most massive loss of life occurred. Strong buildings that had withstood the movement of the water inland were now caught in the raging seaward-bound flood, torn off their foundations, tumbled in ruins and carried into the bay to the accompaniment of the screams of victims who, just moments before, had thought their trial was ending!

The actual volume of water that had been built up many miles inland behind Indianola is almost beyond calculation. At the bay shore, the maximum level above normal high tide was 15 feet. That same height was reached over Powder Horn Lake and the marshlands to the rear of the city. A single cubic yard of salt water weighs slightly in excess of 1,700 pounds, 1,728 to be exact. With the passage of the storm's eye, the weight force of the tens of millions of tons of flood water was pulled back to the bay by gravity, its speed of movement accelerated by the overwhelming pressure of the hurricane winds veering to the northwest. The strength of that rapidly returning flood was of such enormous power that almost everything in the lowest part of the city near Powder Horn Bayou was borne out to sea.

236

"It is a noteworthy fact," commented Sergeant Smith, "that the immense volumes of water, which for 18 hours poured over the beach at Matagorda Bay until for 20 miles the back country of prairie was an open sea, occupied but the short space of six hours to completely recede, on the wind changing to the northwest."

September 17 dawned cool and cloudy. A stiff gale was blowing, but the receding water soon permitted survivors to venture outside. Only then did those who lived begin to comprehend the measure of disaster that had befallen Indianola. Three-fourths of all the buildings in the town had completely disappeared. Most of those remaining were in a state of ruin and had been washed from their foundations, some a few yards and others several blocks. Twelve bayous had been cut into the townsite where large buildings had stood the day before. Five of the bayous extended completely across the town, joining the lake with the bay. The other seven, some of considerable width and depth, had been cut part way.[17]

Despite the outlook of the evening before, the signal building came through almost intact, though leaning to the southeast. The anemometer cups were gone and the large wind vane was bent, hanging off the roof at a rakish angle. Although the stairs to the second floor office were partially torn from the wall and the doors jammed from the tilt of the structure, Smith and his assistant, Charles Howard, after considerable difficulty forced their way through the front door. They found that the office and equipment sustained relatively little damage. The morning observations of the 17th were taken, with the exception of wind velocity. That could only be estimated. By evening, the wind had diminished to "high" and veered to the north, with clearing skies.

Tales of horror and heroism were to be related on all sides following the storm. Adults and youths nobly sacrificed their lives in efforts to help others. Entire families were wiped out. In some, only one or two members managed to survive after the most heartbreaking ordeals. Some people, clinging to wreckage, came through alive, though terribly bruised from the pounding of floating debris tossed by mountainous waves. Bodies of victims were strewn for 20 miles along the bay shore, many unrecognizable because of battering by heavy timbers.

At the town of Upper Saluria on Matagorda Island at Pass Cavallo, 90% of the residents were drowned. The two lighthouses on iron pilings in the bay were destroyed at a cost of the lives of both keepers and their families. Of the five Morgan Line pilots stationed at Pass Cavallo, only Captain Sim Brown survived.[18] Brown, Judge Hawes and most other islanders who lived were residents of Lower Saluria which, despite its name, was much higher than the town of Upper Saluria. That elevation saved them.

When news of the disaster at Indianola came to Victoria late Saturday night, the *Advocate* dispatched reporters on horseback. By hard riding, they reached Indianola at 9 a.m., having been in the saddle for nine hours. The *Advocate* extra edition was a masterpiece of reporting on the horrendous state of affairs found at Indianola. It was from Victoria that news of the port's destruction was flashed to the world as soon as telegraph service was restored. The people of Victoria, Cuero, San Antonio and other Western Texas communities quickly organized relief parties to aid the stricken residents. Prayers were offered and masses said throughout the state for the repose of the souls of those who were drowned.[19]

The first news that Galvestonians received about the destruction of Indianola came when the Morgan steamer *Harlan* (Captain Lewis) returned on Tuesday morning, the 21st, from the scene of devastation. Coming into port with her colors at half mast, the *Harlan* caused great excitement in the city. Residents streamed to the wharf to learn the significance of the distress signal, and then to seek information about the fate of friends and relatives in the stricken town.

Captain Lewis brought to the editor of the Galveston *News* a poignant plea from W. H. Crain of Indianola, district attorney, 16th Judicial district:

"Indianola, Sept. 20, 1875.

"We are destitute. The town is gone. One-tenth of the population are gone. Dead bodies are strewn for twenty miles along the bay. Nine-tenths of the houses are destroyed. Send us help, for God's sake."[20]

Captain Henry Sheppard, Morgan Line agent at Indianola, detailed to C. A. Whitney at New Orleans the extent of loss of human life and the massive destruction of property. The Morgan Line was hard hit. The entire planking of the railroad wharf had been torn off, the on-shore warehouse demolished, and the on-wharf office, with all records, washed away. On the T-head, the stringers remained and a large part of the planking was piled up on it, but from the T-head to the shore, not one of the stringers was left. Few of the wharf piles were in place from the shore line out 300 feet. The lower story of the railroad office at the foot of the wharf was caved in from battering by wharf timbers, and all railroad books were lost. There was likewise great damage to the track and rolling stock from Indianola to Chocolate Bayou. When the *Harlan* arrived at Indianola from Galveston after the storm, there were neither the means to unload her freight nor a warehouse in which to store it. As a consequence, Sheppard instructed Lewis to take it back to Galveston, to be kept there until arrangements could be made to get it ashore.

In the first reporting by the *News*, a letter from H. Seeligson & Co. to their representative in Galveston was quoted. ". . . Many of our acquaintances and friends are drowned . . . Our bank building is secure and funds and books dry. The writer is thoroughly exhausted, having been out with a burying party all last night, but will have to go down the bay this evening again to bury others."

H. J. Huck lost everything but his house and William Westhoff all his lumber. Only five business houses were left standing — those of H. Seeligson & Co., H. Runge & Co., Dan Sullivan & Co., Casimir Villeneuve and D. H. Regan, though each sustained damage. The first day, 60 of the bodies that were recovered and buried could not be identified, the features having been destroyed by coming in contact with floating lumber which ripped the flesh. One was found with a money belt containing $3,000.

Thursday, the 16th, was publication day for the Indianola *Bulletin* and, despite the storm, editor Ogsbury started to the newspaper plant. However, the "water from the bay [was] pouring over the beach . . . the waves dashing and cutting through at a fearful rate. Everybody was alarmed, never having witnessed water from the bay flooding the town in that direction," he said. Ogsbury found it impossible to make his way to the office, it being located in the lowest part of town. Turning back toward his residence, he secured a dray to transport his wife, two daughters and mother-in-law to R. D. Martin's two-story house, which was on higher ground. By the time he reached home with the conveyance, the water was waist deep there.

By midday, residents in the low and most exposed sections of the city were frantically seeking places of safety, their efforts to escape being made more difficult by the force of the wind and the ever deeper water. By afternoon, water began to come into the Martin house, forcing the refugees upstairs. "Night coming on, the situation was awful," Ogsbury related. "Screams from women and children could be heard in every direction. The water was then about six feet deep in the streets, some places, according to grade, more or less. Of course, I can only describe what we experienced, everyone being in the same fix."

When the eye arrived in the early morning hours and the water started its rush back to the bay, the Martin house began to sway. Martin and Ogsbury went downstairs and found the water falling. "We still had hopes the wind would lull; but no — the gusts were fearful. Mr. Martin's family consisted of his wife and two daughters, besides a young girl staying with them, and three children, two of them . . . granddaughters, and a child of Mrs. Thos. Poole."

Discovering that the rapid current was sweeping the soil from each side of the house, cutting gullies and undermining it, they abandoned the tottering building. Outside and shouting for help, they were heard by neighbor David C. Proctor. In addition to a number of local families, George Finlay of Galveston, W. S. Glass and A. B. Peticolas of Victoria and Sam C. Lackey of Clinton (attorneys who were there for the Taylor trial) had taken refuge in the Proctor residence. "We could see them in commotion, coming down to the edge of the current. . . Ropes and clothes-lines were gathered up and stretched across to a tree near Martin's house." The men then stationed themselves at intervals along the line and the eight women and three children were passed across the gully . . . "Stout arms and firm nerves conducted them safely across . . . the work was hard, but the women were brave, cool and collected. The Proctor house was reached, but here for a time the danger was great, the water cutting each side. The two-story house of H. Iken [next door] . . . had already been carried away and his family and that of C. Canfield saved themselves by a miracle."

Toward morning as the wind was perceptibly decreasing and the water getting lower, hope rose with the refugees. Daylight began to

The Half Moon Reef lighthouse erected in 1858 was in Matagorda Bay near Indianola. Nearer Pass Cavallo was the Swash lighthouse, which was identical to Half Moon and built in the same year. The structures consisted of the traditional white dwelling on screw piles, a Fifth Order lens and lantern centered on top. (*Courtesy U. S. Department of Transportation, U. S. Coast Guard.*)

break. "Then did we behold the awful destruction around us, and thanked our God that we had been saved and that our perilous position was as nothing compared with the sufferings of our neighbors and citizens along the bay. Broad daylight revealed a scene that was terrible to behold. The town could not be recognized as the Indianola of the day previous. Ruin, total ruin, everywhere. People were seen wading and jumping over one gully and another. Neighbor met neighbor and told their troubles and tribulations [of the previous night]. Death and destruction all around us. Houses crushed to the ground, others swayed around and leaning over. The wind finally dying down and the water disappearing from places in the streets, those that could sallied out to learn the news. Bodies of men, women and children were found in all directions."

Search was begun for missing relatives and friends. People were found who had floated for miles on doors, roofs or timbers they could grip. Some were trapped in collapsed structures and carried long distances. "The escape of so many of our citizens is most miraculous," said Ogsbury. "The search for bodies is still going on and the number of human beings drowned will never be known, as there were many strangers in town. Now comes to our horrified senses the news of the destruction of Saluria and Decrow's Point . . . A list of those drowned and missing is being collected and is hourly being added to . . . We are houseless and ruined . . . Churches, dwellings, stores, with some exceptions, are gone from sight and Indianola, this Monday morning [the 20th] is a sight fearful to behold."[21]

Not to his surprise, but to his dismay, the only trace of the *Bulletin* office Ogsbury found consisted of some broken pieces of the printing presses and pied type. He and his family went back to their ruined dwelling from which the furniture had been washed by the swift current. The building was without windows or doors, ". . . but it is a shelter so far, until the norther comes or until we can collect our confused senses and determine upon what we shall do, or where we can go. Like Mordecai of old, we are not, as we have no gate to sit at. Our fate is the fate of all of us. Many are leaving for Victoria and other places where they can get shelter and food. The Victoria people and neighboring towns are doing all they can to alleviate our sufferings, dealing out food and clothing."

XXI.

Death and Desolation

Ships approaching Indianola in the days subsequent to the hurricane found the surface of the Gulf of Mexico and Matagorda Bay littered with floating bits of broken furniture, wrecks of buildings, wharf lumber, trees, animal carcasses, and an occasional human body which had not yet been recovered for burial.

Coming through Pass Cavallo, the tall lighthouse was seen standing, and apparently sound. Captain Mainland's house and Judge Hawes's residence remained in place, but at Upper Saluria all buildings were wrecked. On the opposite side of the channel where there had been a cluster of buildings on Decrow's Point, nothing was to be seen except the cisterns and a small remnant of Captain Thos. Decrow's stormhouse. Everything else was gone. Even the high sand dunes on Matagorda Peninsula and Island had been washed flat. In the bay, where the two iron-framed swash lighthouses had marked the shoals, only the pilings remained. They were twisted and broken by the violence of wind and waves. At Alligator Head, the solitary house of Captain Henry Smith, though severely damaged, had successfully resisted collapse. Dwyman's Beef Packery at old LaSalle was a tangled mass.

Passengers and crew members of the ships arriving at Indianola saw only ruin and devastation, shattered buildings, some heaped one upon another, and immense piles of wooden debris blocking the streets.

Merchandise, articles of clothing and bedding were spread for drying. When the first relief ship arrived from Galveston on September 24, it was obliged to go into Powder Horn Bayou for unloading. Although reconstruction had begun on the wharves, they were still in a skeletonized state, and without flooring. In the bayou, drays came near enough to shipside for passengers and goods to be removed. The Galveston *News* reported, "On word being sent up town that a ship with provisions from Galveston for the sufferers had arrived, a short time elapsed before D. C. Proctor in his red slippers, General W. H. Woodward in a fireman's shirt, W. H. Crain driving a dray, Mr. Barlow, Mr. Milby, Judge Huck, and others, came down and received those on the boat with their usual courtesies, but showing by their appearance that they had suffered with the others."

In the five days of repairing and refitting that weather conditions had permitted, Dan Sullivan had reroofed his store building and carried a portion of his salvaged goods back inside. H. Runge & Co. had done the same, as had some other merchants. However, there were many more who found not a trace of their business houses. In some sections of the city, the streets were filled indiscriminately with merchandise and household goods of every conceivable character deposited by the storm. Running up Burleson and Hays Streets, cutting across Water, Main, A, B, C and D Streets from the bay to the railroad bridge at Canal, was a bayou 12 feet deep and 120 feet wide, over which skiffs had to be used. Where several structures, such as Charles Hubbell's Livery Stable, the Enterprise Hotel and Dr. Reuss's residence had stood the day before, there was now the rippling current of the new bayou. The Reuss residence, severely damaged, careened on the bank of the new waterway. Beyond the courthouse was another bayou that was deeper but narrower. The numerous smaller bayous cut by the waves into the city were likewise troublesome to residents. In time, all were filled, the hindrances to traffic removed and the streets again made usable from Powder Horn to Old Town.

The greatest destruction was from Powder Horn Bayou to the courthouse, over much of which there was a clean sweep, leaving the surface with the appearance of virgin beach. Of the large Gulf, Globe and Enterprise Hotels, not a recognizable fragment was to be found. The concrete courthouse came through in better condition than any other building, only its doors, windows and roof being injured. It received no structural damage.

Not a building was left from Powder Horn Bayou to the railroad track on Travis Street, except the gutted hulk of Mitchell's large hardware store.[1] In the 13 blocks alone from the bayou to the courthouse at Houston Street, 116 buildings were completely washed away, along with their contents; 90 others were critically damaged. Thirty-six buildings in that area were found to be reparable. With only three exceptions, the latter were off their foundations and wrenched. Beyond the courthouse on up the bay shore to Old Town, the story was much the same, some structures entirely gone, some on the verge of collapse, and others in a state suitable for repair. In the entire city, only 12 buildings came through the hurricane intact, all being on higher elevations above the courthouse.

Of those knocked off their foundations, some had been moved bodily as far as half a mile. One railroad car was also carried that distance. Dozens of others were moved from 50 to 500 yards. One bar of railroad iron, still attached to the ties, was found to have been carried a fourth of a mile. The lower halves of some two-story houses were washed out and the upper halves dropped down. Others lost their upper stories.

The death list grew day by day until 270 recovered corpses were counted. Some victims were never accounted for. As time passed, most of the bodies found were beyond identification. Although he died 15 miles distant at Saluria, Dr. John Leake's body was found three miles west of Indianola, beside several who drowned in the city. Dr. Leake had gone to Saluria to attend Mrs. William Nichols who had, through a tragic mistake, taken a dose of fly plaster instead of "blue mass." He broke a leg on jumping from a second floor window, was lifted onto a raft, but was soon washed off by the waves. Mrs. Nichols was in such critical condition from the effects of the poison she could not be moved. The grief-stricken Captain Nichols took their baby in his arms, got into the bed with his wife, refused assistance, and the three were drowned together.[2]

A four-year-old Indianola girl had, by some means, gotten on a floating house top alone and caught the shingles, under which her fingers became wedged as the roof structure was twisted into a warped state. She was held firmly and could not release herself. Fifteen hours later, as the flood waters receded and the roof was deposited on land, the half-crazed child was rescued. Mrs. James Wetherill, with her one-year-old baby and the nurse, was in her home when it fell, trapping them on the upper floor. All were quickly saturated from the rain and spray. As the water rose above the floor level, the mother became fearful that the cold wind roaring through the split walls would so chill the infant as to cause its death from exposure. Securing the child's bath tub, Mrs. Wetherill filled it with the warm salt water and immersed the baby. There she kept it safely until rescued 12 hours later.

Early on the 16th, the two-story residence of J. M. Morrison, which was near Powder Horn Bayou, became a place of refuge for near neighbors who judged it to be safer than their own homes. There were 31 people in the building, 13 men, six women and 12 children of various ages. At about 2 p.m. that day, the same hour that the schooner wrecked the telegraph office, the relentless smashing force of the storm-driven waves had its effect and the house began to disintegrate. As it came apart, the horrified occupants grasped at any floating object for support as they were tumbled into the water, then ten feet deep in the yard. When the last part fell, Mr. and Mrs. Morrison became separated and she was drowned, along with an adopted daughter. Morrison managed to catch a door, on which he was finally carried to land seven miles inland from Indianola. There he found his only son, who had also escaped on drift.

Along that strip were 44 men, two women and several children who had floated there on timbers.

William Coffin, his wife and two small children were in their house when it began to collapse. Coffin grasped his wife with one arm and she held one child in each arm. They were carried by the force of the water toward a splintered door where the current pinned them down. The children drowned in Mrs. Coffin's arms as her husband struggled desperately to lift all of them above the surface. As the house split apart, Mrs. Coffin was killed instantly and he was catapulted into the open air just as the building burst open and tumbled over. He managed to get on the roof and was propelled toward the railroad track, where the impact tore the framing apart. He caught a piece of lumber for support, was carried down the bayou to the bay and finally was cast onto land below the town. A short distance from that spot, Mrs. Coffin's body came ashore.[3]

Having his family in what he thought was a secure place, D. K. Woodward went out and devoted his time, along with W. H. Crain, Stephen White, Leonard Minot, and others, in carrying families to places of refuge. They had collected a large number of people in the Masonic Lodge hall which finally gave way, all falling into the raging water. Woodward and August Dahme caught the upper floor of the lodge building and drifted on it across the bayou until it went to pieces. Then they clutched a piece of scantling, finally being deposited on an inland ridge miles from their starting place. There they found Tom Clement who, with his wife, children and several others, had gotten into a boat when their house began to fall. The waves capsized the boat, casting all into the water, Clement grasping his two children. Mrs. Clement caught the gunwale, to which she, her sister and three others clung for eight hours before they were saved. The Clement children drowned as he held them. Stephen White also landed near where Morrison and his son were cast aground.[4]

Construction methods for frame buildings at that time did not call for bolting the sills to the foundation. The accepted practice was to place the piers in position and then proceed to erect the structure, resting on them. Its weight was expected to securely hold it. That was a correct and reasonable assumption, except in the instance of high flood waters, such as those experienced at Indianola. There the tightly built houses were lifted from their foundations by the 15 foot tide, floating like boats, careening and tumbling their contents (human, furniture or merchandise) until crushed.

Some resourceful individuals were able to prevent complete wreckage by using axes to chop holes in the floor, permitting the entrance of water and partial stabilization of the buildings. The most extraordinary method of weighting a house was that used at Old Town in the case of a two-story residence to which the John Garner family, along with other neighbors, fled. It was secured by leading 20 horses into the rooms of the first floor. Although the water rose to the ceiling of that lower floor, the house was not dislodged. The horses were drowned![5]

The experience of those aboard the schooner *Pee Dee* also illustrates the intense struggles to survive along the coast. The *Pee Dee* departed Calcasieu on the morning of the 14th for Indianola, laden with lumber. At 10 p.m., she passed the steamship *Australian*, lying at anchor off Galveston harbor, the wind at the time blowing strong from the northeast, with heavy sea.

By 5 a.m. of the 15th, the *Pee Dee* was off Caney, the wind then blowing nearly a gale and the sea increasing in height so as to break over the shore in the low places. Captain Gorham reefed the sails and "carried all the sail I could possibly steer the vessel with so as to get to Pass Cavallo bar as soon as possible, seeing no other chance to save our lives," he said. "My deck load was well chained and swiftered down, which helped to float the vessel and keep her from foundering going over the bar through the breakers which, in appearance, ran 30 feet high."

At 1 p.m. of the 15th, the vessel crossed the bar, got into the channel inside Pelican Spit buoy, where the crew tried to work up to Decrow's Point. Behind the point there was some shelter from the wind. The schooner *Rescue* was lying at anchor there, but the current was running with the violence of the dead-ahead wind that was blowing down Matagorda Bay. The *Pee Dee* could make no progress against it. "I came to anchor with my largest anchor and paid out 30 fathoms chain," said Gorham. "I kept my reefed mainsail up and commenced close reefing the foresail and jib, myself and mate, John Lanagan, reefing the jib. We just got it reefed when the chain parted. I told all hands to hoist the jib and get in the chains. I ran aft and managed to cant her head towards the shore where, if I had to run her on the beach, the water was deep close to the shore. If her head had canted off shore, we should have lost our lives for there were two miles of shoal water and the sea was breaking over at a fearful height.

"My men attempted to haul in the chain, but could not, it having parted near the anchor. It had to be hove in with the windlass, and being so near shore I saw no other chance for our lives, or to save anything of the vessel and cargo, but to run her on shore, which I did, it now being 3 p.m." Morgan Line Pilot Sim Brown and several other men were on shore with horses ready to give aid. The crew managed to get a rope to them, "which we bent on to our kedge anchor, with a warp to it, and by hitching the ends of the line to the horns of their saddles, they hauled the anchor up on the bank. We hauled the warp taut and, with the aid of those from the shore, we succeeded in getting ashore all safe, saving a portion of our clothing and some groceries, which were in covered buckets."

The *Pee Dee* began to break up, the loosened lumber on deck flying in every direction, carried by the hurricane wind. When the wet, shivering crew reached the land, they found Judge Hawes sitting there with an axe, which he had brought down from his residence, thinking it might be needed. He invited Captain Gorham and the crew members to take shelter at his house. "Hawes had some whiskey, which he dealt out as long as it lasted, being that night and part of the next day." Hawes had no provisions at home, as he boarded with his daughter and son-in-law, the Hortons. Gorham said that they "kept us from starving to death. Judge Hawes was like a father to us, and Mr. Horton and his wife did all they could to keep us in bread and meat. One cask of water out of six [on the boat] was saved. It washed ashore without breaking, which was the only fresh water we had for three days and [we] shared it with Mr. Horton and family, he then having at least 12 to 15 persons, mostly from houses that were broken in and washed away." The Hortons were living in what was locally known as "the Mainland house." Simeon Brown had about 20 persons at his house to feed and take care of for a week.

On Thursday evening, the 16th, as the storm raged with greater violence, all the outbuildings, horse barn and nearby kitchen were carried away from the Hawes residence. The rising water was causing the building to show signs of shifting from its foundation. Judge Hawes and the *Pee Dee* crew chopped holes in the floor of four rooms to provide ballast for the house, after which it remained steady, though everything around it went into the Gulf. Friday morning, Gorham found the *Pee Dee*'s yawl bottom up by the side of the Hortons' home.

"Soon after daylight," Gorham related, "we discovered something on Tucker's Island, about one mile from us and, although the water between us and the island was running at a fearful rate and the wind blowing heavily, Simeon Brown the pilot, with three of my crew, succeeded in getting to the island and saving the lives of Henry Nichols and Miss Decrow, who had drifted there at dark the night before on a gutter of the house, and had held on to the twigs of the bushes, with the sea breaking over them all night."

On the night of the 15th, as the wind continued to rise, the schooner *Rescue*, lying under Decrow's Point, began dragging her anchors. The crew cut away her masts to keep the ship from capsizing as it rolled violently. Then she parted her chains and was driven ashore. The mate and one man got on land without much injury, but the captain was drowned and the cook badly bruised by flying lumber. An uncounted number of vessels went ashore in the bay and Gulf, some with the drowning of crew members. One of the mail boats from Corpus Christi, the Morgan Line pilot boat and all the lighters were left ashore and wrecked when the wind abated and the tide receded to its normal bounds.[6]

The Rt. Rev. R. W. B. Elliott, D. D., Bishop of the Missionary District of Western Texas with headquarters at San Antonio, addressed the delegates to the Second Annual Convocation of the Protestant Episcopal Church. It was held in St. Andrews Church, Seguin, on June 22 to 24, 1876. Following a memorial service for the Rev. Robert Jope, Bishop Elliott outlined activities and events during the 12-month period just ended. Referring to Ascension Church, Indianola, he said, ". . . Sunday, May 16 [1875] found me at Indianola where, in the morning, I read the service, preached and administered the Holy Communion, and in the afternoon read the service, preached and confirmed two young ladies, daughters of the Rector, the Rev. Robert Jope.

"There is always a mournfulness about farewells - a last communion is a solemn occasion; but seldom has such tragic interest gathered about an administration of the Lord's Supper. Even then, the glowing sun was preparing the mighty forces of the coming storm; in grim repose the elements waited, while once more sorrowing souls, through tears, sought comfort in the all-consoling communion of the body and blood of Christ. And, when the tempest broke in its fury, and in the midst of that elemental rage, father, mother and children were swept forever from the eyes of men, I feel that these elements of the Lord's Supper were stronger than those elements of the wind and waves, for they were the memorials of Him who, throned above, rules over all, and of whom men said, when He walked upon earth, 'even the winds and the waves obey Him.' And, so sustained, I believe they voyaged on through the dark night and over the fretting seas and found their morrow dawn upon that happy shore where neither storms may beat nor billows roll.

"The sad history of that night of calamity will always in my mind be relieved by the recollection of that last communion. I shall always remember that beautiful church as it stood lit up with the softened light of that May afternoon while, with uncontrollable emotion, the pastor presented his two daughters for confirmation. When next I stood upon that spot, the winds were soft and gentle, the sea lay tranquilly within its natural bounds, but the sands where once stood church and rectory, were as freshly laid as if . . . there had never been by man any occupation . . ."

Bishop Elliott stood upon that spot on Sunday, January 23, 1876, when he returned to Indianola, preached at a morning worship service and administered Holy Communion. At 4:30 p.m., he baptized one adult and two children. At 7 p.m., the Bishop again preached and confirmed two persons. He was assisted in the services by the Rev. Mr. Carrington.

"On Monday, January 24, accompanied by the Rev. Mr. Carrington and Mr. James McCoppin, lay reader [I] went down in a wagon to LaSalle and took from the beach, where they had been cast up by the sea, the prayer desk, reading desk, lectern and altar of what was Ascension Church, Indianola."

XXII.

And Then — The End!

As Indianolans were picking up the pieces of their lives and their devastated city, with the aid of sympathetic citizens of Western Texas, news of the calamity brought an outpouring of assistance from distant places. Cash contributions and gifts of food, clothing, bedding and all types of goods flowed in great volume for the relief of the hurricane victims on the Texas coast. Not only had help come first from Victoria, but the residents there also opened their homes to Indianolans who had lost everything. The same was true of Cuero, Gonzales, New Braunfels, San Antonio, Texana, Port Lavaca and other nearby towns.

In addition to satisfying the immediate need for help by those Galvestonians whose homes were wrecked or flooded on the fringe of the great storm, the Relief Committee there, headed by J. D. Braman, George Seeligson and M. Lasker, immediately sent to Indianola $4,000 in supplies. That was the first of many shipments from kindhearted people of Galveston to the stricken residents of their neighboring port.

Outside the state, most generous were the people of New Orleans, long closely associated with Indianola. Mayor Cobb of Boston telegraphed $5,000. Cash gifts came from such widely separated communities as Detroit, New York, Chicago, St. Louis, Cincinnati, Philadelphia, Charleston, and others far too numerous to list. Relief supplies were transported by boat from New York, New Orleans,

Galveston and Corpus Christi free of charge. Refugees were given accommodations on outbound vessels gratis. Not only in the South, but also throughout the North, compassionate Americans were aghast at the magnitude of the catastrophe and reached out to help. Momentarily, at least, the chasm created by the recent war and its aftermath of Reconstruction was bridged.

Members of the 1875 Texas Constitutional Convention, then in session at Austin, acknowledged, ". . . with profound sorrow the calamities which have befallen our fellow citizens of the coast . . ." and, tendering "heartfelt sympathy to the distressed and suffering friends and relatives of those who perished in the storm . . ." voted unanimously to contribute one day's pay for relief. Delegates Ballinger, Rugeley, Stockdale and Murphy were authorized to receive the contributions, "and disburse the same so as, in their judgment, to afford the most relief." Eventually, additional assistance came from cities and towns in Europe, which were affiliated with Indianola by commercial and family ties. It was a response that touched the hearts of the disaster victims. Charles Morgan dispatched a letter, ". . . but it contained little else than an expression of sympathy."[1]

W. D. Barbour wrote from Matagorda, Texas, on October 3 about the experience of the inhabitants of the upper end of Matagorda Peninsula, near the Colorado River. In part, he said, ". . . The settlement in which I lived embraced 12 families, as many places of residence, and numbered 66 souls . . . Of this number, 21 were drowned . . . Those of us whose houses were carried away, except two or three who saved a little money, lost their all except the few shreds of clothing that covered their shivering forms. My own, and two other families, were from 60 to 70 hours without food or drink. As yet, some of us are without a mattress of our own to lie on, or a blanket to cover us, and no means to get them.

"We are profoundly grateful to the good people of Indianola, who are so generously sharing with us the flour and potatoes so kindly sent to them"[2]

The ordeal of the Barbours and their neighbors was typical of the experiences of other inhabitants throughout the Matagorda Bay region, as well as at Quintana, Velasco, along the lower reaches of the Brazos, San Bernard and Colorado Rivers. With those fellow victims, Indianolans also shared provisions, clothing, bedding and other articles necessary to continued existence, as they arrived at the port on relief ships.

Colonel A. M. Hobby, president of the Galveston Chamber of Commerce, acting in response to a request from Governor Richard Coke, on October 30 sent a detailed report on the storm to Newell V. Squarey, chairman of the International Chamber of Commerce and Mississippi Valley Society, St. Stephens Chambers, London. The report was prepared by James Sorley, chairman of the local chamber's committee on statistics. In it, Sorley apparently could not resist either the temptation to soft-pedal the storm's effect on Galveston or the opportunity to boost that city in Squarey's mind by inflating the population. He reported that to be 40,000, and gave the population of Houston as 28,000.³ The Federal census for 1870 had listed Galveston with a population of 13,898 and Houston 11,584. The 1880 census showed Galveston to have 22,248 and Houston 18,646. Galveston was not destined to reach the 40,000 population mark until the second decade of the twentieth century. At Galveston, huge cuts into the island at 20th, 25th and 29th Streets showed the tendency of the storm tide to seek passage across the island, as it did at Indianola.

The eye of the storm moved inland across Texas from Indianola through Jackson, Colorado, Austin and Washington Counties, beginning a turn to the northeast at about Navasota on to near Huntsville, where it took a course due east that carried it past Livingston and Woodville on to West Feliciana Parish, Louisiana, giving New Orleans and the southern part of that state a second battering. Near St. Francisville, the hurricane veered to a northeastwardly course that led it off the Atlantic coast at the tip of Delaware at 7:35 a.m., September 19. As it left the mainland from Sussex County, it produced heavy gales and marine disasters on the New Jersey, Delaware, Maryland and Virginia coasts. Reports from the shipping lanes of the Atlantic, and the violent storms that prevailed north of the British Isles seven to nine days later, indicate that the storm crossed the Atlantic Ocean.⁴

Labeled by the Signal Service as the most severe hurricane that had reached the United States mainland since that office began its work of charting and reporting weather phenomena, the catastrophic event was described as, ". . . furnishing one of the most perfect types of tropical storm originating in the lower latitudes and passing into the region of the temperate zone. . ."⁵ Disastrous effects of the rain on interior Texas were nowhere more graphically illustrated than in the widespread washouts on the railroads. The eastbound GH&SA passenger train from the end of the line at Kingsbury was six days en route from that place to Houston, being "delayed station after station until the road could be repaired to permit the passage of the train."

Crops were prostrated and, in the pine forests of East Texas and Louisiana, lanes from a few hundred feet to as much as a mile in width were swept clean by tornadoes spun off as the low pressure center moved to the east. The report from Austin County succinctly tells the story there. ". . . The storm commenced here a little after dark on Wednesday night and ceased about the same time on Friday. It far surpassed anything of the kind within the memory of the oldest inhabitants. For 48 hours it raged with terrible fury. Everything reeled before it . . . the amount of damage sustained by the people along this portion of the Brazos River is beyond computation. The havoc is terrible to contemplate . . . cotton plants completely stripped . . . the ground literally covered with fallen trees . . . horses and cattle driven completely out of their range, and on the prairies men are everywhere in search of them. So far, efforts have been futile.⁶

At the first of October, the Signal Offices at Indianola and Galveston, along with others on the Gulf and Atlantic coasts, received

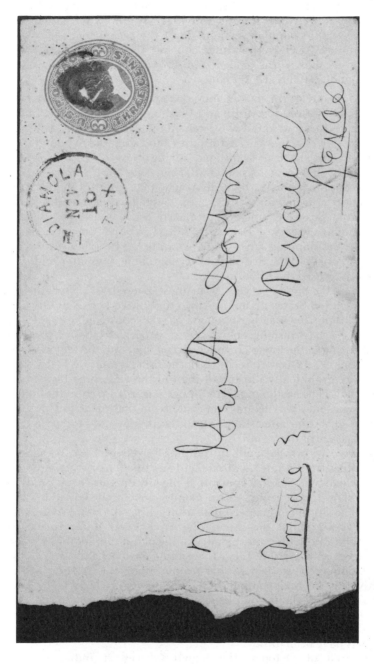

This envelope, from one ghost town to another, contained a letter dated October 4, 1875, from Sgt. C. A. Smith, U. S. Signal Service Station at Indianola. In it, he asked Texana Postmaster George Horton for information on the hurricane: wind directions, length of time, velocity, whether a period of calm was observed, and other data for use in a supplemental report he was preparing to the Chief Signal Officer in Washington. Smith sent similar letters to all other towns in or near the path of the hurricane as it moved inland across Texas. (*From the author's personal collection.*)

from Washington "cautionary signals for future use, should any occasion arise making them necessary." They were not available prior to the 1875 hurricane. The new day signal consisted of a red flag 10 by 8 feet, with a black rectangle in the center. At night, a red lantern of large size was to be displayed. The signals were to be hoisted on a tall pole at the observer's office, so they could be seen by mariners and residents alike. Their significance was, "That, from information had at the Central Office in Washington, a probability of stormy or dangerous weather has been deduced for the port, or place, at which the cautionary signal is displayed, or in that vicinity. Further, that the danger appears to be so great as to demand precaution on the part of navigators and others interested . . . It calls for frequent examinations of local barometers or other instruments by ship captains, or others interested, and the study of local signs of the weather, as clouds, etc. . . ." It can be seen that the science of charting and forecasting landfall for storms was in a rudimentary stage. So imprecise was it that 11 years later, when the second "once in a century" hurricane struck the Texas coast at Matagorda Bay and wiped Indianola off the map, no warning was issued by the Washington Signal Office until the storm was actually moving in and it was too late for residents to evacuate or take other precautionary measures.

At the end of September 1875, having learned from bitter experience that the location of Indianola was dangerous in the extreme, community leaders reached the almost unanimous conclusion that the survivors should quit the town site on the bay shore and rebuild where some protection would be afforded if and when another such hurricane should visit the area. For 30 years, they had been living under the assumption that they were safe. The storm taught them the fallacy of that belief.

A committee was appointed to correspond with C. A. Whitney and A. C. Hutchinson in New Orleans, as the representatives of the aging Charles Morgan, inviting them to visit Indianola. It was hoped that, after seeing in person the state of affairs, they might be able to induce Morgan to arrange for running his boats to points further up Powder Horn Bayou and Lake. It was a long shot, and they knew it. Without Morgan's full cooperation, they would be totally thwarted in carrying out their plan. Because of advancing years and failing health, Morgan had conferred nominal control of his Gulf steamship and rail lines on Whitney and Hutchinson, reserving for himself decisions involving change of policy.

The people of Indianola envisioned rebuilding their city on the north shore of Powder Horn Lake about three and a half miles above the mouth of the bayou. The higher elevation there would prevent a recurrence of the deep flooding experienced during the hurricane. A limited amount of dredging would provide a safe, land-locked harbor in which the large steamships and sailing vessels could tie up at short wharves. That plan would have been the salvation of their port and would have insured its permanence. It was a forlorn hope. Whitney, who had keen interest in furthering the fortunes of Indianola, was favorably disposed. Hutchinson was unyielding in his opposition to the Morgan Line expending any funds whatsoever in connection with a relocation project.[7] The Morgan Line, which had started Indianola on its boom growth, now insured its final destruction and abandonment.

In the town, there had been a "wait and see" attitude on the part of a large portion of the business community, pending receipt of word as to whether the proposal to move to a safer location would have Morgan's cooperation. When it became evident that Hutchinson's stubborn views had prevailed over those of Whitney, some of the leading merchants made their decision to leave. They were unwilling to invest in rebuilding on a location that had become recognized as being vulnerable to hurricane damage. Many families had left as soon as possible after the storm ceased. Others hesitated for weeks, some even for months.

The convent of the Sisters of Mercy having been wrecked, the members of the order were taken into the homes of two of the parishioners, D. H. Regan and Richard J. Evans. Father Mancy, temporarily assigned to the Indianola parish in the absence of Father Joseph Ferra, who was in France at the time of the hurricane, set up a temporary altar in the Evans' home and there celebrated Holy Mass. When rescue boats reached the port, three of the postulants, "Antonia, Marie and Josephine, returned to their homes in New York. The storm hastened the departure of these young ladies whose vocation was not sufficiently strong to endure either the hardships of the religious life or the unfriendly weather vagaries of the Texas coast."[8]

Those who remained had lost practically all of their possessions. Bishop Pellicer sent Mother Camillus a check for $100 to help them. He also made arrangements for her and her companions to go to the Sisters of the Incarnate Word in Victoria until convents at San Patricio and Refugio were ready to receive members of the order willing to go there. Mother Camillus was accompanied on the journey to Victoria by Sisters Mary Gertrude and Mary Catherine. Sisters Mary de Pazzi, Mary Cecilia and Mary John Berchmans remained at Indianola until late October, when Father E. A. Antoine, pastor of Our Lady of Refuge Church in Refugio, informed the Bishop that work on the new convent there was completed, whereupon they went to that town by wagon. From Indianola, this vanguard of the Sisters of Mercy paved the way for the establishment of the order in other cities of Western Texas.[9] When the Catholic Church at Indianola was rebuilt, a statue of Mary, Star of the Sea, was placed in the building as a protection from storms.

Victoria, Port Lavaca, Cuero, Texana and San Antonio received many permanent residents from Indianola. Other victims of the storm repaired or reconstructed their damaged property. They were willing to take their chances, but most of them lost heavily in that gamble in 1886. One of the merchants who built anew at Indianola was H. J. Huck. And, he honored his previous commitment to participate in the Gulf Coast Fair at Victoria, which opened on November 2. He erected on the fairgrounds an octagonal building of doors, sash, blinds and shutters manufactured in his woodworking mill at Indianola, and equipped the display

254

structure with "samples of everything in the building line." He also exhibited such varied items as church pews and garden fences.[10] In addition to his principal installation at Indianola, Huck had branch lumber yards at Victoria, Cuero, Hallettsville, Yorktown and San Antonio.

Other Indianola business houses also reached out into the trade territory with branches. William Westhoff, wholesale and retail lumber dealer, established yards at Victoria and Cuero in addition to the main yard at Indianola. Prior to the hurricane, Dr. J. M. Reuss had opened a second drug store, that one located in Cuero. H. Runge & Co. opened a branch bank in Cuero, and D. H. Regan, wholesale and retail dry goods merchant, expanded his Indianola store to branches at Texana, Victoria and Cuero.

It was not until November 29 that the Commissioners Court found time to see to storm damage repairs at the courthouse and jail. The sturdiness of the courthouse was such that relatively minor work was required — new steps and new door at one entrance, transom lights at another, restoring the blinds on the cupola and some shingle replacement on the roof. Broken window glass and split door panels had been replaced immediately after the storm.

The old fence around the jail was shattered. Another was ordered and erected. It was 15 feet high of solid planking, with a padlocked gate opening onto Main Street. An additional item on the courthouse square was the building of a new public privy with a partition "dividing it into two apartments, each . . . to have two seats . . . of good yellow pine wood . . . with two doors, one for each apartment." The court also called for the cistern to be cleaned, salt water and storm deposited debris removed, and a new top made. The damaged downspouts from the courthouse gutters were replaced "with good X X tin," and the roof of the jail was recovered with tin.

For the first time, the Indianola Signal Office displayed the new cautionary storm warning for two days beginning November 28. Sergeant Smith reported that, ". . . The display caused quite a panic among the citizens, some going so far as to make preparations to leave town. Extra warnings were carried to the shipping by agents and others interested, and general precautionary measures taken. On the winds backing to the north at 11 p.m. with indication of an ordinary norther, fears very much subsided." Smith again displayed the signals on December 26 and 27, in advance of a norther. One vessel left port during the display, and one remained in the harbor because of the warning. The Service appeared to be leaning over backward in its efforts to alert residents and mariners to possible strong winds, from any direction. A different flag was soon adopted to herald the approach of a cold front. It was a white banner with red center. That action went far toward soothing the shattered nerves of a now storm-wary populace easily frightened by the red flag with black rectangular center.[11]

The War Department's network of telegraph lines and reporting stations across Texas, and the daily bulletins being sent to Washington by inland observers, provided the means to forecast, with reasonable accuracy, the passage of strong northers which could affect shipping interests along the coast. Sergeant Smith reported, "January 9 and 10, 1876 — The display of signal on the 9th instant was followed by a series of gales which, though doing no material damage, caused heavy sea rendering it dangerous for vessels to leave port.

"February 28, 1876 — Owing to the near approach of the equinoctial season, the signal caused unusual anxiety, and numbers of seafaring men called the office in quest of information. They were most anxious to learn the character of the anticipated storm.

"March 19 to 21, 1876 — The most severe norther ever experienced; 4 or 5 bay boats blown ashore. A large warehouse was blown off its blocks. . .

"April 5 and 6, 1876 — Signals well-timed and favorably commented upon. Very many signal orders have been rendered valueless, as the orders up and down were received together or too late, caused by telegraphic interruption. . ."

Sergeant Smith was transferred to Galveston on May 18, 1876, and was succeeded by Sergeant Isaac R. Birt, who came to Indianola from Brackettville. Smith's assistant, Charles Howard, had been ordered in for promotion on November 16, 1875.[12]

C. A. Ogsbury, publisher of the Indianola *Bulletin*, was among those businessmen who, disheartened and disillusioned by Morgan's refusal to cooperate in the relocation of the city on safer ground, left the port. Ogsbury went to Cuero where, for a year, he was correspondent for the Victoria *Advocate*. When the Cuero *Star* closed shop in the summer of 1876 and "went glimmering into the west," Ogsbury was presented with the opportunity to start his own newspaper there, which he did in the fall. He was still correspondent for the *Advocate* when its plant was destroyed by fire and it was temporarily put out of business.

In that summer of 1876, the people of Western Texas witnessed an exercise of ruthless power play by Charles Morgan to enhance his own fortune regardless of the consequences to the public. In a move aimed at freezing his associates out of the Gulf, Western Texas and Pacific and assuming complete personal ownership, Morgan abruptly caused all rail traffic to cease from Indianola through Victoria to Cuero. Dispirited Indianolans saw the hand of A. C. Hutchinson behind the action. The sudden discontinuance of all rail operation caused financial distress to a large group of citizens in the three towns who were dependent on the GWT&P for a livelihood as employees. What was not known at the time was that the railroad was being deliberately maneuvered into receivership.

There arose a fast-growing feeling of antipathy on the part of newspaper editors and writers, as well as the general public, of Western Texas toward Morgan. It was in marked contrast with the friendly relationship that existed between the New Yorker and that area in the halcyon days when their interests ran parallel. His disregard of the public welfare in the 1876 shutdown was one of the factors leading to public outcry for railroad regulation by the state government. Hutchinson's influence over Morgan so inflamed the ire of Western Texans that strong antimonopoly cries began to be heard. In those early years when the public had little or no protection, such acts as suspending operation of a vital transportation agency for reasons of personal or corporate gain at the expense of others created a climate in which legislators were to be overwhelmed by an avalanche of demands for government controls. That demand, mushroomed by abuses on the part of other rail lines in Texas, culminated 14 years later in the establishment of the Texas Railroad Commission.

". . . It certainly looks singular," Ogsbury wrote, "that a whole population in Western Texas would be brought to a 'stand still' in the matter of her only railroad because of the caprice of a one-man-moneyed-power who has received all the benefits to be derived from the liberal policy bestowed by our State to those who build railroads, the donations of which, in time, more than compensate capitalists for the money expended in the construction of railways. . ."

He continued, "Austin, San Antonio and all Western and Northern Texas are deeply interested in a consolidation of their interests, both commercial and maritime, and should act together for one object, and that is to secure themselves from the blighting influence of 'railroad rings,' whose objects are to fleece them of their lands and make their trade and commerce subservient to other and extraneous sources; contributing to the wealth of strangers at the expense of their own pockets; impoverishing their children, and keeping away immigration and wealth. The proof of this is now seen in Western Texas, whose large and fertile domain is daily squandered away to enrich foreign capitalists and enable them to build railways for Eastern Texas. Should the state be divided eventually, would the land deeds thus given away to build roads in another part of the State be valid, be binding? But, we will not discuss that matter now. Our Western citizens can only hope that such a crisis may never occur."

He was not indulging in idle speculation. The matter of the giveaway of the public domain in Western Texas was the subject of frequent discussion and agitation. There was grumbling that at the current rate of granting land, Western Texas would soon be almost entirely in the hands of "railroad barons." More and more, Western Texans wondered how to halt the Legislature's profligacy.

Indianolans noted with uneasiness news that the westward extension of the Galveston, Harrisburg & San Antonio railroad had carried the line to Seguin, the first train from Houston arriving there on August 9.[13] San Antonio was only a short distance to the west. There was full realization that completion of the railroad to that city would divert from Indianola a substantial portion of the trade of Western Texas that had been hers from the beginning of the port. On February 19, 1877, the first train entered San Antonio.[14]

GWT&P Secretary-Treasurer M. D. Monserrate being unable to provide any information regarding resumption of rail service, merchants of the tri-cities were obliged to turn to the old method of transporting freight. In August, caravans of wagons and Mexican *carretas* again filled the streets of Indianola. That lasted until September 20, 1876, when operation of trains was resumed as suddenly as it had been stopped in the first place. The schedule called for departure from Indianola at 7 a.m., arrival at Victoria at 11 a.m. and at Cuero at 1:25 p.m. In the opposite direction, the train left Cuero at 6 a.m., arriving Victoria at 9 a.m. and Indianola at 1:25 p.m. Extras were operated when the accumulation of freight was more than could be handled on the regular runs.

At the end of September, in response to reports of yellow fever in New Orleans, Galveston port officials imposed another of their frequent quarantines, refusing to permit vessels from New Orleans to enter the harbor. The Indianola City Council met on Friday evening, September 29, to consider the question of a quarantine. The result of the meeting was a telegram to the Morgan Line office in New Orleans to "send along the steamships." C. A. Whitney replied that, owing to the action of the Galveston health officials, the steamers would be withdrawn until the existing interdict was removed. After a further exchange of messages with Indianola, Whitney changed his mind about suspending service. Instead, arrangements were made for vessels from the Crescent City to deposit Galveston freight on a boat at the quarantine station there, and the steamships continued to serve Indianola without interruption.[15] Galveston's quarantine was lifted within a short time when it was realized there was a substantial loss of traffic to Indianola.

On October 5, the *Advocate* reported, "We are gratified to learn that Col. C. A. Ogsbury is about perfecting arrangements for the establishment of a newspaper at Cuero. After the destruction of the Bulletin by the fearful cyclone of one year ago, this able writer did not resume the publication of his journal and subsequently removed from Indianola to Cuero. . ." Six weeks later, the *Advocate* said, "It gives us much unfeigned joy to welcome to our desk the Cuero Bulletin, under editorial management of Col. Ogsbury, formerly of the Indianola Bulletin." Ogsbury, who had come to Texas in 1836 with his twin brother and fought in the Army of the Republic, died in Cuero in 1891.

Having been repaired after damage incurred near Key West during the September storm of the previous year, the *St. Mary* had returned to the Indianola run. On the morning of December 2, 1876, her sands of time ran out as she foundered on the bar at Aransas Pass. Entering the pass in the face of a strong norther, the vessel struck hard on the outer bar and then passed to the inner. As the tide was running out, with a heavy sea, she let out both anchors to keep from drifting ashore. It was then discovered that the severe thumping blows sustained on the outer bar had caused the development of dangerous leaks. Despite the most strenuous efforts in operating the pumps they were unable to keep abreast of the inflow of water. Within 35 minutes, the *St. Mary* had settled to her upper decks. All passengers were saved, though most of the cargo was lost. The ship, valued at $125,000 was not insured in keeping with Charles Morgan's policy.[16]

Tax relief was given by the Texas Legislature in 1876 to those affected by the 1875 hurricane. Entitled "An act to exempt the persons and property of Indianola from payment of certain taxes," the measure stated, "Whereas it is known that the town of Indianola in Calhoun County in last year was devastated by a storm with very great loss of life and property . . . the persons and property of said place shall be exempted from taxation during the year 1876." A similar action for citizens of Matagorda and Brazoria Counties provided such tax relief for those living on Matagorda Peninsula and on the shore of the mainland, ". . . not more than 5 miles inland from the usual water line at ordinary tide." The waiving of taxes was given those residents likewise "on account of the great suffering and destruction of property inflicted . . . by the calamitous storm which burst upon the coast of those counties in September, 1875."

Recommendation was made in 1877 by the United States Life Saving Service that a "Life-Boat Station" be established at four points in the Eighth District on the coast of Texas. They were at Galveston, Pass Cavallo, Mustang Island and Brazos Santiago. The purpose was to place the rescue stations at passes where maritime traffic was heaviest and there was a frequency of marine disasters to vessels moving through the hazardous channels. The recent loss of the *St. Mary* was a case in point. The difficulties were caused, principally, because of the exposure of the passes to the wind force of the northers that would sweep across the bays, as well as from storms striking the coast line from the Gulf of Mexico.

The station at Pass Cavallo was erected on the northeastern tip of Matagorda Island near the location of the village of (Upper) Saluria that had been destroyed in the 1875 hurricane. It was named, and officially referred to as, "Saluria Life Saving Station."[17] After the establishment of Port O'Connor on Alligator Head in 1909, area residents frequently called it the "Port O'Connor Life Saving Station."

Sale of the GWT&P that had been the object of Charles Morgan's cutting off rail service, had been set for December 19, 1876, but was postponed until April 3 of the following year. At that time, his plan to secure total personal ownership was successful. After the 1875 storm, the badly damaged tracks from Clark Station to Port Lavaca were not again placed in operating condition. The rails were removed, leaving that town in the same isolated state in which it had existed before construction of the SA&MG to Victoria just before the war.

At the beginning of the new decade of the 1880s, events were conspiring to adversely affect Indianola's fortunes. A charter was secured from the State of Texas on November 17, 1880, for construction of the New York, Texas & Mexican Railway Company, which began at Rosenberg, not New York, and never reached Mexico. Work began in September 1881 and, on July 4, 1882, the first through train ran from Rosenberg to Victoria.[18] It carried a party of notables, including the railroad builder, Italian Count Joseph Telfener, and the Countess Telfener, the former Ada Hungerford whose sister, Marie Louise, had married John W. Mackay, one of the Silver Kings of the Comstock Lode.

Also aboard were Colonel and Mrs. D. E. Hungerford. Taking time out at Garcitas Creek for a "completion ceremony," which included the driving of a silver spike whose metal was supplied by Mackay, the party reached Victoria where a gala barbecue supper was held on the court-house square, lighted by hundreds of Japanese lanterns. A ball at the Casino finished off the evening, enhanced by the presence of "Governor" Fletcher S. Stockdale, the former Indianolan whose namesake loco-motive operated on the GWT&P between Indianola and Cuero.

Two months before the NYT&M's first train reached Victoria, the company experienced financial troubles that kept Count Telfener from realizing his original intent of building to Brownsville. A connection at the river there would have tied in with a Mexican line he had organized, the Tamaulipas Railroad, to build from Matamoros to Tuxpan on the Gulf of Mexico between Tampico and Vera Cruz. The Mexican government's promised bonus to him for the proposed line in that country was $8,000 per kilometer.

The NYT&M's problem arose from the repeal, on April 22, 1882, of the law authorizing the granting of 16 sections of land for each mile of railroad constructed in Texas. That repeal resulted from discovery that the state had already granted to railroads 8,000,000 more acres of public land than were available for such purpose.[19] The profligacy had come to a jolting halt! Although Count Telfener's building plan was aborted, the 80-mile long NYT&M was responsible for the birth of Beasley, Hungerford, El Campo, Louise, Ganado and Edna and, by 1883, for the death of Texana, which it by-passed.

Coupled with the GH&SA operating eastward from San Antonio since early 1877, the NYT&M caused a seriously large diversion of traffic from Indianola whose stub railroad, the GWT&P, did not reach far enough into Western Texas. Despite this, the port remained sur-prisingly busy, the wharves crowded with cotton and other agricultural products, as well as manufactured goods moving into and out of the state. The United States Congress had appropriated $25,000, which had been expended for dredging and other work at Pass Cavallo. Another ap-propriation of $60,000 had been approved for additional work. Im-provements were also under way on the long railroad wharf. Manufactured ice made its appearance at both Indianola and Victoria in 1882, supplementing the natural ice harvested in New England and brought by refrigerator boat.

Indianola still had her sights set on extension of the GWT&P from Cuero to San Antonio. Charles A. Whitney had become president of the ML&T (Morgan's Louisiana and Texas Railroad and Steamship Company), the Houston & Texas Central and the GWT&P, all Morgan estate properties, Commodore Charles Morgan having died on May 8, 1878. His death had caused scarcely a ripple in Western Texas. The Morgan interests were being merged with those of Collis P. Huntington, acting for the Southern Pacific Company of California.

In 1882, Whitney determined to travel to Europe to secure funding for extension of the GWT&P to San Antonio with the avowed purpose of securing for Indianola (and Morgan ships) a share of the anticipated greater volume of freight and passenger traffic that would move between the Gulf of Mexico and the Pacific coast, with the approaching completion of the southern transcontinental rail line. While in New York preparing to embark for Europe, Whitney suffered a massive stroke and died on the evening before his scheduled sailing. Again were Indianola's hopes dashed. "The news of his death cast a gloom among our public spirited citizens," said the Victoria *Advocate* on November 4, "because he was regarded as a friend to this section . . . Had his advice been followed, the GWT&P road would long since have been completed to San Antonio, thus furnishing transportation to the natural and most economical outlet for the commerce of the interior of the State. . ."

The directors of the GWT&P, meeting in Cuero on Monday, November 20, adopted a resolution which "expressed in appropriate and pointed language the regret occasioned by the recent demise of President C. A. Whitney." In commenting, the *Advocate* stated, on November 25, "The death of Mr. Whitney occurred at a most unfortunate time for our interests, as he was then on a mission which promised grand results for West Texas. He has ever been recognized as the liberal and farseeing member of the firm which controlled the Morgan interests."

Not to be missed was an opportunity to point a finger of accusation at A. C. Hutchinson. "While Mr. Hutchinson, the other member, has been persistently opposed to the extension of the railway enterprises under the Morgan control and has, with shortsightedness, illiberal and unwise opposition prevented the building of the company's line from Cuero to San Antonio, it has come to be publicly known and understood that Mr. Whitney was always an advocate of the immediate extension of the road. The recent past has demonstrated that Mr. Whitney was, of the two, the most prescient member, for no greater mistake has ever been committed than the failure of the Morgan company to extend its line westward. This error was recognized by Mr. Morgan shortly before his death and he is said to have acknowledged the mistake of the policy. With Mr. Whitney living, perhaps this policy would have been changed. Personally a good man, his death brings the regret which the loss of such must always occasion, aside from the prominent position he held . . . as the head of one of the most important of our western freight carriers." The newspaper left no doubt as to the attitude of the business communities of that portion of Western Texas toward Hutchinson.

The event to which Whitney looked forward and which he hoped to turn to Indianola's and the Morgan Line's advantage took place on January 12, 1883. The last spike was driven to complete the rail line from California across southern Arizona and New Mexico, through El Paso to San Antonio, Houston and on to New Orleans. The spike was driven at a point approximately two miles south of the station of Shumla, west of the Pecos River. The GH&SA's line first crossed the Pecos at its mouth, directly at its confluence with the Rio Grande, a point now inundated by the Amistad Dam reservoir. Upon the completion of the 321-foot high bridge across the Pecos upstream from the mouth in 1891, the original line with its two tunnels and low crossing of the Pecos was abandoned from Helmet to a point just east of Shumla. It was Whitney's plan to use Indianola as the principal Western Gulf terminus for Morgan Line ships.[20]

That plan having collapsed with Whitney's death, Indianolans were not deterred. Realizing that their economic welfare could no longer be entirely rested on freight and passenger traffic moving through their port, they turned their attention to the development of the town as a resort. Fishing, yachting, outstanding seafood restaurants, bathing in the clear waters of Matagorda Bay and the Gulf of Mexico were to be utilized as advertising attractions. There was "local color" to capitalize on, there was one of the finest and most beautiful beach drives and promenades in Texas from Indianola to Old Town and beyond, and the sea breezes were fresh and invigorating.

It was not to be. Indianola was a doomed city. The summer of 1886 was unusually hot, and a drought was widespread in Texas. Many areas of the state were suffering acute distress because of the long term deficiency in rainfall. Stephenville reported that "no seasonable rain" had fallen there in 14 months. The low level of water in the cisterns of Indianola made the appearance of cloudy, humid weather on August 18 welcome as boding the possibility of much needed rain. Instead of the expected rain, a strong easterly wind blew in with such force that, along the parched coast, clouds of dust and sand were stirred up, to the annoyance of housewives and shopkeepers alike.

The unusual wind became a subject of principal discussion. The disaster 11 years earlier was still fresh in the thoughts of Indianolans, but the situation was different in 1886. Now the Signal Service had, it was believed, adequate means to learn and warn of danger. Interest was heightened by the receipt from Washington of a telegraphic dispatch to Indianola Signal Service observer Isaac A. Reed. Dated Washington, August 18, it read, "The West India hurricane has passed south of Key West into the Gulf of Mexico, causing high winds in southern Florida and will probably cause gales on the coast of the eastern Gulf states tonight." In view of the disturbed condition of the elements, Reed was asked about the fact that no warning was displayed at the station. He had received no instructions from headquarters to hoist a signal.

When questioned after the storm had passed, "Why were you not warned of its approach?" the Signal Service Officer at Galveston replied, "I did get a signal last night [August 19] ordering 'up signals,' but the storm was well under way then, as you know. The truth of the matter is that we should have more observing stations. The Signal Service should have a station in Cuba and one at Cape Catoche or Palma Point in Yucatan. If we had stations at these points, the present storm could have been foretold and its course marked out hours and hours before we felt its first effects. Some years ago, we had stations in Yucatan and Cuba, but Congress grew economical and did away with them!"[21]

Observer Reed at Indianola received the same message, but by that time the fast moving hurricane was coming in on Indianola, the tide was rising and it was, for all practical purposes, too late for residents to take the steps that could have saved lives and property, had the official warning come in time. Before the storm reached its peak, Observer Reed died at his post.

Telegraphic communication was knocked out. The first word of the hurricane's effect came, again, from Victoria. A short dispatch from that city dated August 20 said, "One of the most terrific storms ever known here reached this section about 5 o'clock this morning. The wind gradually increased in velocity until it reached a speed never before witnessed at Victoria. On all sides may be seen the terrible evidence of its intensity. Perhaps 40 buildings yielded to the mad rush of the wind and are now simply masses of ruins. A far greater number are without roofs, while the destruction of fences, trees, shrubbery, etc. has been immense.

"Among the buildings wrecked are both of the Catholic churches, the Presbyterian church and the Methodist church, while two colored churches are totally destroyed. The standpipe collapsed for a distance of 30 feet down to the water line, while the pump house connected with the waterworks was rendered useless. Odd Fellows Hall is a complete ruin, the high school building is a wreck, while two of the engine houses belonging to the fire department were swept out of existence. . .

"The eastbound train which arrived here from Cuero, while at the depot was involved in the general wreck, two coaches and the mail car being overturned. They are now lying at the depot platform. Several passengers were on board, but fortunately no one was injured. Both depots are a mass of ruins, while the round house is a wreck. Reports from the county indicate great destruction of property . . . Considerable loss is reported from Cuero, but the extent of the damage there is not known. Several houses were destroyed at Edna. Nothing is definitely known from Indianola, but grave fears are entertained that serious damage has resulted there."

Those grave fears were well-founded. It was 1875 all over again, though on a lesser scale because of the reduced size of the community. The next dispatch from Victoria reported, "A train has just arrived from Indianola bearing the sad news of another terrible disaster there. A fire broke out this morning during the heavy storm, destroying every building except two, on both sides of the street [Main] from and including the Signal Office to the Villeneuve corner. Captain Reed, Signal Officer, was crushed and burned with Dr. Rosencranz in the Signal Office. Dr. Lewis is missing and is supposed to have been lost. The Knopp family, Mrs. Sheppard and children and a sister-in-law of Dr. Hodges of Cuero are reported among the missing.

"The water is said to have inundated the town worse than during the great storm of 1875. The railway track is washed away for two and a half miles this side of Indianola, rendering communication extremely difficult. The party from this city were compelled to wade that distance in order to reach the town. Great excitement prevails here and . . . a relief party will be organized to go to Indianola tomorrow morning. The body of a young woman, supposed to be Dr. Hodges' sister-in-law, was

263

discovered this evening alongside the railroad track by those who went down on the special train. Henry Sheppard (17 years old) was found alive, but badly bruised. The bodies of Mrs. Luther's children were also found."

Buildings in Indianola which had withstood the 1875 storm without collapse were crushed by the combination of wind and water. To the east of the railroad track toward Powder Horn Bayou nothing remained except a large safe which belonged to H. J. Huck & Co. It marked the spot where the office of the Huck lumber yard had stood. On Travis Street, the custom house was badly damaged, but remained standing. Above the railroad track, buildings were knocked from their foundations, most having collapsed. As in 1875, the streets were filled with debris. Dan Sullivan's store building was blown down, as was H. Runge & Co.'s extensive grocery establishment. A large stock of goods was buried in the ruins, most of which proved to be a total loss.

The Signal Office building stood on Main Street at one of the high points of the town. It was there that the fire originated. There were gathered in the office besides Captain Reed, Dr. H. Rosencranz, T. D. Woodward (chief clerk at the custom house), L. H. Woodworth (telegraph operator), W. J. Morrison, C. H. French and John S. Munn of Victoria, the latter visiting in Indianola. French and Munn left the office a few minutes before the crash. They had made their way to Tony Lagus's when the tower went down.

As it became evident that the swaying building was about to give way, it was suggested to Captain Reed that flight was the better part of wisdom. Reluctant to abandon his post, he at length agreed to go. Still intent upon his official duty, he delayed his departure long enough to screw down the anemograph in order that the exact velocity of the wind at the time he was forced to leave could later be determined. Unfortunately, Reed failed to extinguish the kerosene lamp in the office. The nervous Woodward, Woodworth and Morrison preceded Reed and Rosencranz down the stairs, getting clear of the building before it gave way. Rosencranz and Reed reached the sidewalk but were caught by falling timbers. The water was breast deep and they were drowned. The next day, their bodies were found, Captain Reed on the pavement, while Dr. Rosencranz lay a few feet away in the street.

Upon the disintegration of the building, the lamp exploded. Fanned by the hurricane wind, registering 102 miles per hour when the anemometer was put out of commission, the fire spread quickly. Reaching adjacent buildings, it consumed A. Frank's warehouse, Lagus's grocery store, Steinbach's market and Villeneuve's liquor store on the east side of the street. The flames leaped to the west side, destroying Dahme's corner, Lagus's hotel, Regan's dry goods store, Lewis's drug store, Anton Bauer's residence and several other structures.

John Mathuly's seafood restaurant, which withstood the 1875 storm, though in a damaged state, was destroyed in 1886. Only a portion of the rear end of the building remained standing. A few blocks from Powder Horn Bayou stood the residence of Mrs. Henry Sheppard, Sr.

During that night, of the nine persons in the house, seven were drowned, four of them small children. The Catholic church escaped serious damage in the second storm. It was in that structure that the statue of Mary, Star of the Sea, had been placed for protection following restoration after the first great storm. The Presbyterian, Union and three colored churches were wrecked. A small, unoccupied building on the east side near the courthouse was a place of refuge. When the storm abated, 39 persons were found congregated there. Miraculously, all were saved. Runge's bank, containing a heavy vault, survived the blow, but was moved several feet. On the railroad wharf, most of the pilings and stringers remained in place but the planking and rails were torn off from the shore line out about half way to the T-head which, with its office, remained virtually intact.

The wind velocity was greater in 1886 than was the case with its predecessor 11 years earlier, but its very rapid speed of forward movement, and consequent shorter duration, permitted less buildup of water on the prairie back of the town. Because of that, there was not the ruinous outflow that had wrought such havoc and cost so many lives in 1875.[22] At the Pass Cavallo lighthouse, the water stood four feet deep in the tower. "All the buildings, except the tower and the main dwelling and its kitchen, and the fences at the station, were swept away and destroyed. The tower was not badly damaged, but its rocking was so great as to shake out one of the flash panels and the first prism ring of the lens, which fell on the watch room floor and were broken. All of the keeper's rations and all oil, except 20 gallons, were lost, and all supplies, tools, etc. were destroyed. The wooden cistern was destroyed and the underground cistern burst, so that a foot of salt water came in during the night . . ."[23]

Even as far inland as San Antonio the wind was recorded at 72 miles per hour, at which moment the roof of the Signal Service building there was torn off and the anemometer wrecked. Lieutenant Sebree of the service at San Antonio calculated a maximum velocity there of at least 85 m.p.h. The 1886 hurricane's path across Texas was different from that of 1875. Cuero, Gonzales, San Antonio, Goliad, Seguin, Luling, Lockhart, New Braunfels and other towns received great damage from the force of the storm wind, and from the satellite tornadoes. At San Antonio, the greatest destruction was on Government Hill, affected by tornadic winds. The damage in the city alone was reported to be $250,000. Torrential rainfall caused serious overflow problems along the streams of Central Texas. The drought was broken at Stephenville.

All this was enough for most surviving Indianolans. There were still a few die-hards. On September 20, the Commissioners Court issued notice of a special election called for the purpose of deciding the wishes of the voters on the subject of removal of the county seat of government from "its present untenable location" in Indianola to Port Lavaca. The date set was November 2.

M. D. Monserrate arranged for an excursion train to Indianola on Sunday, October 1, "to enable those who feel so inclined to inspect the ruins of that once prosperous city." The train left Cuero at 7 a.m. and Victoria at 8:30 a.m. It arrived at the stock pens two miles from Indianola at 10 a.m. Returning, it left Indianola at 2 p.m., reaching Victoria at 3:30 p.m., and Cuero at 5 p.m. Excursionists were cautioned to take lunch and drinking water with them.[24] The special train was a sell-out.

On arrival, they saw the specter of the great port. Survivors were sadly at work dismantling broken buildings to be hauled away and rebuilt in Victoria and Cuero. Where only piles of debris remained, the owners were endeavoring to salvage those pieces which were usable. There was an atmosphere of overwhelming grief. Those who came down on the train in a carnival mood, returned to their secure homes chastened by what they had seen.[25]

As the bones of Indianola were being picked bare, there was that flicker of foolish determination on the part of a mere handful to stay. There was no hope of any further life for the town as a port. With its champion Charles A. Whitney gone and control of the Morgan properties firmly in the hands of A. C. Hutchinson, the book was closed on that aspect of its existence. The post office remained, and a few small businesses, a scattering of residents.

On November 9, the Commissioners Court met at Indianola to officially tabulate the November 2 vote. The results were already known, and were not surprising. The people's decision was for removal of the seat of government to Lavaca. On the following day, November 10, 1886, the court met in Indianola for the last time. The first meeting in the newly designated county seat was held on November 30.[26] The handsome and sturdy courthouse at Indianola was stripped of its roof, doors, windows, floors — all usable parts, leaving only the white scarred walls with their vacant openings, like eyeball sockets in a sun bleached skull.

Sorrow was the watchword of the day — sorrow for the dying town and sorrow over the tragedy of human suffering experienced there.

It was a lingering death. In April 1887, a fire destroyed the remaining fragment of the once thriving business district. The Texas Legislature approved the request of the GWT&P management to abandon the 15 miles of track from Clark Station to Indianola. On June 18, a free excursion train, the last run, was operated from Cuero and Victoria to Indianola. The rails were relaid from Clark Station to Lavaca, and the first train on that reconstructed line reached the town on November 5.

At Indianola, the post office was discontinued on October 4, 1887, and John Mahon, the postmaster, closed its door for all time. Indianola was officially declared to be dead. Now, she belonged to the ages. Only the effect of her powerful influence on the development and history of Western Texas remained!

XXIII.

Postscript. The Lesson of Indianola —

There is a natural human resistance to the learning of lessons, especially those taught in the school of experience.

During the past century, comparatively few coastal inhabitants have learned the lesson of Indianola. In Galveston, a handful of residents got the message in 1875 and tried, in vain, to open the eyes of others to the inevitable danger to their city, so remedial action could be taken in time. In 1886, the lesson was repeated for all to see and learn. And, again, some far-sighted Galvestonians shouted it from the housetops, so to speak. Their words of warning fell on deaf ears until it was too late. September 8-9, 1900, was too late. That monstrous hurricane brought the lesson home to Galveston and it could no longer be casually disregarded. As far as that city was concerned, it was finally learned, but at a ghastly, and wholly unnecessary, cost in human lives and property.

The hurricane of September 16, 1875, was the first of major category to strike a populated area since large-scale settlement of Texas. Gigantic hurricanes had occurred in 1818, and in 1837, but property damage was negligible and loss of life small because the low and exposed coastal regions of Texas were sparsely settled. Storms of lesser magnitude had been recorded all along the coast in succeeding years.

Excuses can be offered for the fact that at Indianola residents were not wise to the ways of tropical disturbances. The population was made up of German immigrants (with a scattering of other Europeans) and Americans from the northern and inland regions of the southeastern United States. They were ignorant on the subject of such storms and were simply unaware of the possibility of 15 foot tides and winds far in excess of 100 miles per hour. Those storms which had skirted their bay were minor, and damage caused was comparatively insignificant. That had been true since the community began in 1844. How could they have been expected to know of their danger?

After September 16, 1875, it was a different matter. Coastal residents did know then, but most failed to take heed. They seemed unable to grasp the fact that such an event could recur, and anywhere along the Gulf. With few exceptions, Galvestonians appeared to believe that their island was magically immune. In the 1875 report of James Sorley that was forwarded to Newell Squarey of London, it was said, "The late Lieut. Maury, U.S.N., the highest known authority on the subject of sea currents, tides, winds, etc. propounded some years ago the theory that Galveston was out of the hurricane range, that when they prevailed in this part of the Gulf of Mexico they would expend their force either east of this port on the Louisiana coast, or west on the Texas coast. So far, the experience of persons residing here for 35 years confirms this theory, nor is the recent storm an exception."

Despite the minimizing of destruction of property and loss of life in Galveston due to the combined effect of storm flooding and high wind, the Galveston *News* on September 27, 1875, stated (though in small type), ". . . It teaches us the importance of fortifying the beach against the assaults of the terrible Gulf breakers, which are dangerous at 35 miles per hour. What manner of dykes shall be built is the important question. As the city's permanent prosperity has been doubly assured by the late storm, let the work be — first, durable and, next, speedy by building one hundred feet this side of high tide two brick walls parallel to each other, twenty feet apart, five feet high, connected every ten feet by transverse walls, the entire length of the city, and then carry away the dredgings of the bay over tramways and deposit it in the spaces between the walls . . . All streets should pass over its top. The entire cost of this durable and much needed dyke would not exceed $9,000 per block, which would be $180,000 for the most needy part of the city. . ."

In another article in that same issue, the *News* pointed out that, "Within the recollection of the oldest inhabitant, the water was never so high on Galveston Island as it was between the hours of two and four o'clock, Friday morning, the 17th instant. . ." Commenting on the huge cuts into the island in three places along the Gulf beach, the paper observed that this tendency offered "strong arguments in favor of constructing a breakwater along the beach."

By October 4, the *News*'s proposal had been considered by City Council. Editorially, the *News* said in the beginning paragraph, "The Council on Friday took a step in the right direction when, in direct opposition to the policy of 'masterly inaction' recommended by the Mayor, it ordered the expenditure of five thousand dollars toward

establishing protection along the south front of the city." The paper
further suggested that representations be made to the Constitutional
Convention delegates, then in session, to include in that new document
provisions for legal authority, for financing, and for tax rebates to aid
such a project. That request was made and, with the memory of the
Indianola disaster fresh in their minds, the delegates did draft and insert
such authority, but Galveston did not get around to using it for a quarter
of a century.

The agitation for seawall protection there gradually subsided, and
was put out of mind, until August 1886 when the matter was once more
pushed onto the front page. Though again luckily on the fringe of the
storm, Galveston received a severe battering from the wind, deep
flooding and some loss of life. On the 21st, the *News* reminded its readers
that, ". . . More than ten years ago The News urged again and again that
adequate provision should be made for a system of breakwaters and
revetments that would give general security in case of a storm. . ." The
editor observed, "The fact is that Galveston should prepare for a storm
while the weather is fine . . . A couple of hundred thousand dollars,
judiciously spent, would place Galveston beyond the danger of the storm
. . . Were the whole island swept away, the people could neither retreat
to the mainland nor appeal to the mainland for assistance. . ." Prophetic
words. "There is no occasion for Galveston people being alarmed if they
and their officials will only use due precaution and practically apply the
inestimable virtue of preventive remedies."

On the following day, a lengthy letter signed "Non-Amphibian"
began, "The great overflow of yesterday [the 20th] emphasizes a
suggestion frequently made before — that Galveston must have a seawall
to protect her from Gulf overflows. The dread of the cost has prevented
even the discussion of the subject heretofore, for men who own property
dread to discuss anything that involves a possible tax. . ." The writer
then proceeded to outline a proposal for a seawall constructed of heavy
timbers and extending eight feet above ground level, concluding, "It is a
question of self preservation and should not be permitted to rest until
action is taken."

But, there were others with a different point of view. On August 27,
the *News* published a letter signed "An Old Galvestonian" filled with
patronizing comments, and the statement, ". . . It simply demonstrates
the fact that we are the safest place on the Texas coast and that we are
out of the line of these winds and waves. It further demonstrates that
Galveston cannot be overflowed. All who have observed the storms of
1867, 1875, 1877 and 1886 can but see that the gulf and bay are never
full at the same time and that a level is the entire height the water can
attain," whatever that reasoning was meant to prove.

This was too much for W. P. Ballinger who, as a member of the
Judicial Committee in the Constitutional Convention of 1875, had
worked for the provisions urged by the *News* that year regarding aid to
coastal communities in constructing protective barriers. He wrote a very
long letter to the *News* in which he expressed doubt as to the correctness

of Maury's celebrated theory that Galveston was outside the storm belt and, thus, safe, saying, ". . . It is not susceptible of demonstration." In his letter, Ballinger proposed a seawall five miles in length, at least ten feet high, wide enough for a boulevard on top, with rip rap of stone between the base of the wall and the beach. He further proposed raising the level of the city on a gradual slope up to the top of the seawall, this to be accomplished by pumping in silt from the Gulf of Mexico. Although he did not live to see it, Ballinger's proposal came nearest to being what Galveston finally adopted as its protective plan, on which construction began October 27, 1902. The value of that seawall was again proved in 1915!

At Indianola, the building of residences and business houses on the very low, exposed land had set a trap of death and destruction for the unsuspecting population in 1875. They should have known better in 1886. The examples they set and the lessons they were harshly taught are being largely ignored along the coast today in similar areas where there is no protection from the lethal combination of storm-driven high seas and destructive wind. The lesson was brought home to Corpus Christi in 1919, but many years passed before steps were taken to guard against a repeat calamity for that portion of the city below the bluff. Yet, other large areas within the corporate limits of Corpus Christi are not similarly protected.

Texas City and Freeport wisely profited from the lesson of Indianola, as well as some of their own regions. Now each is safeguarded by an extensive system of dikes designed to hold off storm tides and prevent inundation. Regretfully, there are few communities along the Texas coast between Sabine Pass and the mouth of the Rio Grande that have shown similar wisdom. On the long expanse of lowlands, hundreds of thousands of people live, work and play only a few feet above sea level. Some are in areas where land subsidence increases the hazard. Those are almost awash. The monetary value of the permanent residences, vacation homes, apartments, condominiums, hotels, motels, commercial and industrial structures within easy reach of hurricane-dashed waves must be measured in the hundreds of millions of dollars.

In time, new catastrophes comparable to those of Indianola in 1875 and 1886, of Galveston in 1900, of Corpus Christi in 1919, of hurricane Carla in 1961, to name only a few, will overwhelm parts of the Texas coast. When? Who knows? One can only say with certainty that they will come. Advance warning systems of today can keep the death toll low, although a combination of circumstances could conceivably result in a shocking loss of human life. People can get out of endangered areas when forewarned, if they will, but what of the property? It will be sacrificed on the well-used altar of folly!

APPENDIX A

Report of Dr. Joseph Martin Reuss on the Yellow Fever Epidemic of 1867 at Indianola, Texas. . . . .

Excerpt from "Yellow Fever and Malarial Diseases, Embracing a History of the Epidemics of Yellow Fever in Texas; New Views on its Diagnosis, Treatment, Propagation and Control." Greensville Dowell, M.D., Medical Publication Office, 115 South Seventh Street, Philadelphia, 1876.

Courtesy Department of Health, Education and Welfare, Public Health Service, National Library of Medicine, Bethesda, Maryland. #170626.

"Indianola, situated on the west side of Matagorda Bay, about eighteen miles from the seacoast [Note: Gulf of Mexico], a town of about twenty two hundred inhabitants, including Old-town about three miles above, is almost entirely surrounded by salt water, being on a sort of peninsula formed by Powder Horn Bayou on the southwest, a narrow outlet of the bayou running south to north, the so-called Blind Bayou northwest, and Matagorda Bay east of town. In its rear are flats which, as also parts of the town, are subject to overflow. These flats, as well as the bayous in the rear, were overflowed before the occurrence of yellow fever by fresh water in consequence of continued rains, the water running in from the surrounding prairies. This brackish water, as well as the clearing and filling up of the streets in May and early part of June, also the making of a road by the military to their camp and throwing up a bank and digging ditches on both sides of this road, by which very offensive emanations from the ground spread by the prevailing south winds over the city made, no doubt, the atmosphere a very good vehicle for the propagation of epidemic disease, and it required but the germ of yellow fever miasm to inaugurate a fearful epidemic.

"As at Galveston, this disease never appeared before its being epidemic in New Orleans and imported from there; only in 1862 when two steamers running the blockade from Havana arrived at Lavaca in August, the disease was brought here by soldiers who had visited those vessels. It then broke out about the end of September. In 1867, it appeared about the 20th of June, shortly after the arrival of a small craft from Vera Cruz, where the fever was then raging. Second-hand blankets, which were brought from there and sold here at auction, were considered the source of infection. Indeed, it was proved by sworn statements that two young men from the country who had examined these blankets, and who had only been in town a day, were attacked by yellow fever after they returned home and one died of black vomit. A

271

negro woman nursing one of them also died of well-marked symptoms of yellow fever. This occurred even before the fever broke out here. If this vessel did not bring the fever here, it must have come by a lady from New Orleans who took sick at a hotel. I did not see the lady until she was almost well; cannot, therefore, say anything more but that, from the description of her case, I suspected yellow fever. I did not know that there was yellow fever at New Orleans then, until I saw it stated in the Galveston Medical Journal of February, 1868, and of course excluded that idea at the time. In fact, I could not believe at the time that this epidemic was yellow fever, it occurring so early and being so different a type from all that I had seen before, until I had seen five or six cases of indisputable black vomit. Already, a week or two before the outbreak, I had several cases of fever of a rather continued form and more malignant type than the common climatic fevers of this region.

"The first death occurred on the 24th of June, and in less than a week the whole business part of the town was struck down, as by lightning, there being no less than 125 to 150 cases taken during that time out of a population of less than a thousand [Note: in the business section of Lower Indianola].

"In this part of the city, it had always broken out before. But, as sudden as its onset was its decline in that locality. It reached its acme in about two weeks, and after the 15th of July but very few isolated cases occurred in the central part of the city, spreading, however, in all directions to the less densely populated parts and then traveling house by house slowly until it reached the suburbs, where it lingered about for over a month.

"Persons nursing the sick for weeks, day and night, would seldom be taken until it came near their habitations or got into their own families. It would seem, then, that the infecting agent is most active at night and when persons are asleep. Several nurses, active day and night, never took sick until their patients became convalescent and they got rest and slept in infected houses.

"At Old-town, three miles distant, to which place the epidemic traveled almost house by house, some of which were separated by an interval of half a mile, it broke out on the 13th of October, weeks after the last case had occurred here, although the inhabitants of that place were in daily communication with this city during the raging of the fever, they coming here in the morning and going back in the evening. There occurred only 18 cases out of 200 inhabitants, and it lasted but two weeks owing, no doubt, to the absence of unacclimated persons. Only six adults were taken, all unacclimated.

"In this place, with about 2,000 inhabitants, no less than 550 to 600 persons must have been sick, although no certain data can be given, owing to the sudden outbreak and spread. Of six physicians then here, four were taken sick, all recovered. The number of deaths from the epidemic may be estimated at from 75 to 85.

"In my own practice, I have treated 263 cases, and about 30 in hospital; of the former with a mortality of a fraction more than nine per cent. This percentage might have been even less but for the impossibility of giving due attention to all cases, as in the height of the disease but two physicians were able to practice. In hospital practice, the result was not so favorable, from various causes incident to all such institutions. Of the 30 cases, six or seven died.

"In general, I consider the epidemic of milder type than we ever had before, compared with five previous epidemics. No acclimated persons were taken, although some old citizens died during the time, and even with some symptoms of the prevailing disease. They were in all cases broken-down constitutions and affected with chronic disease of some duration.

"In the beginning of the epidemic the temperature was unusually high, the atmosphere sultry and a marked tendency to congestion of the brain prevailed. The disease was very rapid in its course, some dying suddenly as if sunstruck, in cases that looked mild in the onset, and when such an issue was not at all expected.

"Particularly from 10 a.m. to 4 p.m. patients had to be closely watched and the fatal tendency to the brain rigidly counteracted. Delirium then was frequent, the fever at its highest, and all bad symptoms exacerbating. That the high stand of the sun exerted a dangerous influence I do not doubt. A boy of 12 years, lying sick in a room which was unceiled, having a window east, became delirious every morning at about 8 or 9 o'clock, until I moved him to an opposite room, lying west, where he remained quiet until the sun had passed its zenith, when he had to be moved back to the former room. This lasted almost a week, until he was quite well.

"After the epidemic had reached its acme, the character changed to a more slow type; a tendency to congestion of the stomach, hemorrhage, and general sepsis appeared more frequent. While in the beginning of the epidemic when black vomit occurred it was rather of less quantity, and in character of a more frothy, tenacious, bloody appearance, it now assumed the character of coffee grounds, and was thrown up in great quantity, sometimes for 48 hours. Patients now died oftener from exhaustion than hyperaemia. Symptoms of torpor were more frequent than of sthenia. Death occurred mostly on the fifth to seventh day.

"Contrary to former epidemics, there was a tendency to perspiration with a very marked peculiar offensive smell, of a musty kind, often so strong that a yellow fever patient could be detected at a distance of many yards. The same smell was perceptible on the flats in the rear of the city, and sometimes penetrated the houses at night to such an extent that fumigations had to be resorted to.

"There was, in all cases with tendency to action of the skin also a considerable vesicular rash, sometimes literally covering the patient, particularly on the neck, chest and back, resembling the eruption of miliaria or hydra, which was considered rather favorable, except where it assumed a petechial character. The average pulse was rather high, in most all cases above 100. Remissions not unfrequent, though well marked. Black vomit occurring in all stages, not always fatal, particularly in children.

"I saw one case in hospital with black vomit of an evident intermittent type (tertian), the patient throwing it up every other day for several hours. Recovered in six days after taking large doses of quinine and tincture of iron. During intermission, the patient was quite well, walking about the ward.

"Treatment in general was eliminative and expectant; in mild cases diaphoretics, as liq. ammoniae acetat., or liq. potassae citrat., with digitalis or veratrum in cases with higher vascular action, with hyoscyamus in cases with nervous excitability. In asthenic cases, no treatment would avail. The powers of nature failing from the start indicated a death blow. Ice was freely allowed by me, found grateful, and did no harm; acted to advantage in cases with gastric irritability. Ice was applied to the head in all cases with prominent cerebral symptoms, as well as cups, leeches and mustard pediluvia. Mustard wherever pain was felt, as also in local congestion, acted well.

"Creosote and chloroform seemed to be of great benefit in cases of black vomit, or where it was apprehended. Alkalies, such as lime water, with the addition of a little camphor, subdued gastric irritability, flatulency and greenish acid or bilious vomit of the second stage. The bowels were acted upon by enemata or simple aperients; mercury was only given in cases with foul tongue and offensive breath. Quinine was exhibited in occurring remissions, or after the fever had somewhat subsided. I regarded it as beneficial in preventing relapses, which were frequent and easily brought on by imprudence or excitement, often on the seventh, or even as late as the fifteenth day. I have here to state that several cases occurred where patients had a second attack after seven days, almost to the hour, after having been convalescent from a light attack, and even up and about, of which second attack they died in less than 24 hours.

"Persons after they got through the fever enjoyed, usually, good health, even more so.

"I omitted to state that much benefit was derived from cold ablutions of the skin when there was much preternatural heat and perspiration wanting. It was very grateful to the patients to sponge them with very cold water frequently, which often brought on a decline of the fever and perspiration when all other means had failed. So did the cold sheet in some very severe cases. Forcing patients to perspire by hot teas, hot bottles or bricks, and much covering, was very injurious, and cases are not rare where patients were handled by the nurses in the old accustomed way of former epidemics and put through (but forever). Such treatment always induced delirium, and patients did much better when left to nature. It was particularly dangerous to children who, with but few exceptions, got well without any interference at all. There were several cases here which were given up, and commenced improving from that time. But very few children died.

"Although many new persons came to this place after the epidemic ceased and many returned who had left at the outbreak, yet none took the fever after the 1st of August. A few strangers took sick after that time, but they invariably had contracted the disease at other places, coming from Havana or Galveston. In both places the disease was then at its height. They arrived sick or became so immediately after. This experience will contradict the frost theory. In former epidemics, cases after frost were frequent."

APPENDIX B

Hotels: Gulf, Globe, Enterprise, Baldwin, Magnolia and Cahill.

Other Business Structures: Dan Sullivan warehouse; George Seeligson
warehouse; Westhoff lumber yard; J. M. Morrison store; C. B. Burbank
store; H. J. Huck lumber yard, warehouse and sash and door factory;
English Sailor boarding house; L. Willemin jewelry store; C. W. Short
warehouse; Gradler warehouse; F. L. Beissner grocery store; Charles
Eichlitz grocery store; Casimir Villeneuve liquor warehouse; D.
Stubbeman tailor shop; Louis De Planque photographic studio; L.
Alexander dry goods store; Ice House; Custom House; David Lewis drug
store warehouse; M. Haller bakery; Eglington & Miller lumber yard,
carpenter shop and sash and door factory; Heyck & Bro. office and
warehouse; H. Iken warehouse; U. S. Bonded warehouse; Indianola
Bulletin newspaper and printing shop; Gulf, Western Texas & Pacific
Railway Company car shop, roundhouse, carpenter shop and depot;
Dudley Schultz wagon yard; Hubbell livery stable; John H. Dale
warehouse; law office of W. H. Crain; Alexander Cold store; Jesse
Parrish livery stable; J. E. Mitchell & Co. hardware store; law office of
Stockdale and Proctor; L. Peine jewelry store; H. Marx shoe store; City
Hall; R. C. Warn hardware store; B. A. Hoyt hardware store; M.
Meissner restaurant and saloon; H. Dahme's saloon; Schwartz market;
Casimir Hall; law office of Walter Merriman; Morgan Line on-shore
warehouse and office; Jos. Coutret shop.

Residences: Dan Sullivan, John McDonald, John H. Dale, Sam Marx, H.
B. Cleveland, W. H. Woodward, Mrs. Irene Poole, Andrew Dove, C.
Canfield, H. Iken, Dr. J. H. McCreary, John Burke, Mike Brennan, J. M.
Morrison, George Menefee, Henry Thiemann, G. Simon, Alex. Cold,
Wm. M. Cook, H. Dahme, J. H. Remschel, Ben Evers, Fred Hamilton, D.
K. Woodward, Mayor Burbank, Mrs. James Ashworth, Charles Huck,
Wm. Ikliff, John Mahon, Jos. Coutret, J. J. Ryan, Mrs. Leggett, Mrs.
Billups, Wm. P. Milby, Dr. H. K. Leake, George Armstrong, Louis
Bernard, Arthur Coffin, William Coffin, Wm. Thielepape, Pierson, Mrs.
Funk, Sam Kinsey, Rupert, Mrs. Lipscomb, D. E. Crosland, George
Seeligson, L. Willemin, Salvador, Louis De Planque.

Other: Thos. Colston private school, Indianola public school, Masonic
Hall, Episcopal Church of the Ascension, Episcopal rectory, German
Methodist church, Methodist Episcopal church, Casino Hall, African
Methodist church.

PARTIAL LIST OF BUILDINGS BETWEEN COURTHOUSE AND POWDER HORN BAYOU DAMAGED IN 1875 HURRICANE:

Business Structures: H. Seeligson & Co., H. Runge & Co., Dan Sullivan & Co., Casimir Villeneuve retail liquor store, D. H. Regan dry goods store, Joseph Cahn dry goods store, Tony Lagus fruit store, Tony Lagus restaurant, David Lewis drug store, Ingerman & Kleinecke saloon, Reuss drug store, L. Limott grocery store, John Mathuly restaurant, Signal Service office, Westhoff Building, Mrs. Johanna Marshall millinery store, Texas Express office, Western Union telegraph office, Jacob Hahn shoe store, U. S. post office, H. Iken store, Dr. Thurber office, The Lehman Block (four buildings).

Residences: H. A. L. Kleinecke, A. H. Keller, Henry Keller, C. W. Hartup, Casimir Villeneuve, D. C. Proctor, L. Peine, Joseph Cahn, Mrs. Wilson's boarding house, David Lewis, Henry Sheppard, George Woodman, Thos. Rooke, Anthony Platz, Mrs. Jacobs, Mrs. Frank, Capt. James Wetherill, F. L. Beissner, Walter Merriman, Robert Clark, Davis, Ben Varnell, David Schultz, Mrs. Johanna Marshall, Dr. J. M. Reuss, Emil Reiffert, Jacob Hahn, R. D. Martin, Postmaster Wagner, C. H. French, Thos. Deviney, Mrs. Karl Kaapke, Wm. Hagerty, Geo. Hyer, Mrs. Adam Murdock, J. E. Barlow, Miss McCreary, C. A. Ogsbury, L. Alexander, Mrs. Wm. Hogan, Y. O. McClanahan.

Other: Catholic church, Catholic rectory, Convent of the Sisters of Mercy of St. Patrick, Presbyterian Church.

NOTES ON THE TEXT

Abbreviation Key:
CCR — Calhoun County Records.
GET — German Element in Texas, Moritz Tiling, 1913.
GL — Gammel's Laws of Texas.
GN — Galveston News.
HBT — The Handbook of Texas.
HTR — A History of the Texas Railroads, S. G. Reed, Kingsport
    Press, 1941.
IB — Indianola Bulletin.
ICCB — Indianola Courier and Commercial Bulletin.
NA — National Archives, Washington, D. C.
TAdv — Texian Advocate.
TxAl — Texas Almanac.
VA — Victoria Advocate.
WR — War of the Rebellion.

Chapter I. The Seed is Planted: ¹HBT, II, 157. ²Topographical
Description of Texas, Geo. W. Bonnell, Austin. Clark, Wing and Brown,
1840. ³HBT, II, 60. ⁴*Ibid*, 395. ⁵GL. Act approved January 21, 1839.
⁶Map of the City of Calhoun. General Land Office, State of Texas,
Austin. ⁷GL. ⁸*Ibid.* ⁹Topographical Description of Texas, Bonnell. ¹⁰John
S. Menefee papers, University of Texas Archives, Barker Texas History
Center, Austin. ¹¹Reminiscences of George F. Simons, Edna. ¹²Texas
Under Arms, Pearce. The Encino Press, Austin, 1969. ¹³*Ibid.* ¹⁴Joutel's
Journal of LaSalle's Last Voyage. Corinth Books, New York, 1962.
¹⁵GET, 59. ¹⁶*Ibid*, 65. ¹⁷*Ibid.* ¹⁸Neu Braunfelser Zeitung, August 21,
1952. ¹⁹Texas 1844-5, Karl, Prinz zu Solms-Braunfels. ²⁰*Ibid.* ²¹CCR.
²²HBT, II, 895. ²³*Ibid*, 889. ²⁴GET. Neu Braunfelser Zeitung, August 21,
1952, gives the date of the *Johann Dethardt's* arrival as November 29.
²⁵HBT, I, 571. ²⁶Neu Braunfelser Zeitung. ²⁷GET and Answers to Interrogatories, von Meusebach. ²⁸GET, 86. ²⁹Reuss family history. ³⁰HBT,
II, 515. ³¹Huck family history, related by Francis E. Huck. ³²GET, 87.
Neu Braunfelser Zeitung. ³³NA and HBT, I, 239, 920. ³⁴NA and CCR.
³⁵Neu Braunfelser Zeitung and GET, 109.

Chapter II. A Twin-Birth — Town and County: ¹GL. (² through ⁵) CCR.
⁶Plat of Indian Point drawn by George Thielepape. University of Texas
Archives, Barker Texas History Center, Austin. ⁷TAdv, Victoria, October 10, 1850. ⁸*Ibid.* ⁹HBT, I, 540. ¹⁰CCR. ¹¹*Ibid.* ¹²TAdv, August 11,
1847, and HBT, II, 250. ¹³Incorporation of the La Vaca, Guadalupe and
San Saba Rail Road Company was approved by the Texas Legislature on
May 8, 1846. ¹⁴CCR. ¹⁵*Ibid.* ¹⁶TAdv, January 20, 1848. ¹⁷*Ibid*, October

12 and November 2, 1848. This was the post office of Cuero established in May 1846 at Friar's Store, DeWitt County, not the present city of Cuero. [18]TAdv, October 10, 1850. [19]Ibid. [20]Ibid. [21]Ibid, January 20, 1848. [22]Ibid. [23]HBT, I, 153.

Chapter III. Religion Comes to Town: [1]TAdv, April 13, 1848. [2]Ibid, June 1, 1848. [3]CCR. [4]TAdv, April 20, 1848. [5]Ibid, May 25, 1848. [6]Ibid, June 15, 1848. [7]Ibid, February 3, 1848. [8]Reminiscences of Mrs. Alexander Lowe, Victoria. [9]CCR. [10]Reminiscences of Mrs. Alexander Lowe, Victoria. [11]TAdv, August 10, 1848. [12]Life and Labours of Rev. Daniel Baker, D.D., William M. Baker, 1859.

Chapter IV. The Wave of the Future: [1]TAdv, May 18, 1848. [2]Ibid. [3]The Colorado River Raft, Southwestern Historical Quarterly, Clay, Vol. 52, No. 4, April 1949. [4]TAdv, August 3, 1848. [5]Ibid, October 6, 1848. [6]CCR. [7]TAdv, October 10, 1850.

Chapter V. Morgan Lights the Fuse: [1]The Old Morgan Line, H. M. Mayo. [2]Ibid. [3]CCR. [4]CCR. [5]CCR. [6]Plan of the City of Indianola, from Survey by E. A. Hensoldt, 1868. [7]Report of Bvt. Lt. Col. W. G. Freeman covering inspection of the Eighth Military Department in Texas, October 1, 1853. Library of Congress. [8]TAdv, February 8, 1850. [9]Ibid. February 22, 1850. [10]Ibid. [11]Ibid, April 5, 1850. [12]Ibid, March 8, 1850. [13]Ibid. [14]Report of Provisional Bishop to Second Annual Convention of the Protestant Episcopal Church in the Diocese of Texas, Trinity Church, Galveston, May 1-3, 1851. [15]TAdv, April 26, 1850. [16]Ibid. [17]Ibid, April 19, 1850. [18]Ibid, July 5, 1850. [19]Ibid, July 19, 1850. [20]GL.·

Chapter VI. The Boundary Commission Arrives: [1]TAdv, May 17, 1850. [2]Ibid, June 28, 1850. [3]Ibid, July 26, 1850. [4]Ibid. [5]HBT, I, 853. [6]Letter written by George Mason, LaSalle, August 21, 1850. [7]Personal Narrative of Explorations and Incidents Connected with the United States and Mexican Boundary Commissions. John R. Bartlett, 1854. Library of Congress. [8]Ibid. [9]HBT, I, 388. [10]TAdv, December 5, 1850. [11]Ibid, September 26, 1850. [12]Ibid, October 3, 1850. [13]Ibid, October 10, 1850. [14]Ibid. [15]Ibid. [16]Ibid, November 28, 1850. [17]Ibid, December 12, 1850.

Chapter VII. The First Newspaper: [1]Letter from John Henry Brown, Indianola, January 11, 1851. [2]TAdv, January 23, 1851. [3]Letter from John A. Rogers, Sr., Philadelphia, January 2, 1851, and Texian Advocate, February 20, 1851. [4]TAdv, March 20, 1851. [5]Ibid, February 13, 1851. [6]Ibid, February 20, 1851. [7]Ibid, May 1, 1851. [8]Ibid, June 5, 1851. [9]Letter from Charles Mason, Indianola, June 26, 1851. [10]Official notice to Victoria Postmaster James A. Moody. [11]TAdv, November 1, 1851. [12]HBT, I, 225. [13]TAdv, February 14, 1852.

Chapter VIII. A Heartrending Calamity: [1]IB, April 1, 1852. [2]Cochran had moved from Indianola to Lockhart.

Chapter IX. The County Seat is Moved: [1]TAdv, July 10, 1852. [2]CCR. [3]Records of the IOOF Grand Lodge of the State of Texas. [4]CCR. [5]Ibid. [6]Texas State Gazette, September 4, 1852. [7]TAdv, August 21, 1852. [8]Ibid,

September 4, 1852. [9]CCR. [10]Records of United States Coast Guard. [11]TAdv, August 21, 1852. [12]CCR. [13]*Ibid.* [14]GL. [15]CCR. [16]*Ibid.* [17]TAdv, September 24, 1853. [18]IB, August 31, 1853. [19]*Ibid.* [20]TAdv, September 24, 1853. [21]IB, October 19, 1853.

Chapter X. The Government Depot: [1]NA, Records of the Adjutant General's Office, 1780s-1917, Miscellaneous File #282. [2]TAdv, April 8, 1854. [3]CCR. [4]*Ibid.* [5]TAdv, September 23, 1854. [6]CCR. [7]IB, April 26, 1855. [8]*Ibid*, May 10, 1855. [9]*Ibid.* [10]CCR.

Chapter XI. The Camels are Coming: [1]Note the change in name from *Texian Advocate.* [2]Marschalk was obviously referring to John Henry Brown, former resident of Indianola, founder of the *Bulletin* and, in 1855, a co-editor of the Galveston *Civilian.* [3]The McBride Shipyard was located on Powder Horn Bayou. [4]Executive Document No. 62, 34th Congress, 3rd Session, Library of Congress, pp. 98-99. [5]*Ibid.* [6]*Ibid*, 48 and 98. [7]*Ibid*, 100. [8]*Ibid*, 198-9. [9]As told to the author by Mrs. Clark. [10]Executive Document No. 62, 34th Congress, 3rd Session, Library of Congress, pp. 154-5. [11]CCR. [12]GL. [13]CCR. [14]Letter from R. J. Clow to Mrs. Sam (Mary) Maverick, dated at Lavaca, January 9, 1857. [15]Sheppard. [16]CCR. [17]TxAl, 1859. [18]*Ibid.* [19]This was in reference to the California-bound traffic that crossed the Central American countries, the balance of the trip being made in sailing and steamships on the two oceans.

Chapter XII. Boom at Powder Horn: [1]The Indianolian, July 18, 1857. [2]TxAl, 1858. [3]Records of the Bureau of Customs. [4]CCR. [5]GL. [6]Personal communications to the author in Victoria. [7]TxAl, editions of 1859 and 1860. [8]ICCB, May 21, 1859. [9]Agreement between Charles Morgan and Buffalo Bayou Ship Channel Company ratified August 4, 1874, in possession of the author. [10]ICCB, July 30, 1859. [11]CCR. [12]*Ibid.* [13]*Ibid.* [14]ICCB, July 30, 1859. [15]*Ibid.* [16]*Ibid*, October 15, 1859. [17]*Ibid.* [18]*Ibid.* [19]*Ibid.* [20]Today the atlas lists an Indianola in Illinois, Iowa, Mississippi, Nebraska, Oklahoma and Pennsylvania, though none is shown in Kansas. [21]ICCB, October 22, 1859. [22]*Ibid*, October 29, 1859. [23]*Ibid*, October 22, 1859. [24]*Ibid.* [25]*Ibid*, October 29, 1859. [26]The bridge over Chocolate Bayou. [27]News article from San Antonio *Ledger and Texan* printed in the Indianola *Courier and Commercial Bulletin*, October 29, 1859. [28]R. E. Lee, A Biography, Douglas Southall Freeman, Charles Scribner's Sons, New York, 1934. Vol. I, p. 373. [29]*Ibid*, 405. [30]ICCB, October 29, 1859. [31]CCR.

Chapter XIII. War Clouds on the Horizon: [1]CCR. [2]HTR. ([3] through [6]) CCR. [7]*Texas State Gazette*, September 1, 1860. [8]ICCB, November 3, 1860, credited to the New Orleans *Picayune.* [9]"Outside" referred to the New Orleans-Indianola route via the Mississippi River to the Gulf of Mexico. The "inside" route was that from New Orleans to Brashear by rail, thence by steamer through Berwick and Atchafalaya Bays to the Gulf and Indianola. [10]H. M. Mayo to S. G. Reed, Houston, April 25, 1935. [11]ICCB, November 24, 1860. [12]*Ibid.* [13]*Ibid.* [14]*Ibid*, December 1, 1860. [15]*Ibid*, November 24, 1860. [16]*Ibid.* [17]The spelling of five names on this list, taken from the Indianola *Courier and Commercial Bulletin*, is suspect. The 1860 Calhoun County census script could not be deciphered in some instances to verify the spelling, so those names are shown as printed in the newspaper. [18]From report of Bishop Alexander Gregg to the 1861 Annual Convention. [19]Reminiscences of Mrs. Isaac A. Reed. [20]ICCB, January 5, 1861. [21]*Ibid.* [22]Records of the Grand Lodge of Texas, A.F. & A.M. [23]*Ibid.* [24]A History of Texas, Wortham, Vol. IV, pp. 338-9. [25]*Ibid*, 263-284. [26]HBT, II, 812. [27]Confederate Military History, Vol. XI, "Texas," Col. O. M. Roberts. [28]The Civil War Day by Day, An Almanac, 1861-65, E. B. Long, Doubleday & Co., 1971.

Chapter XIV. The Unwanted War Begins: [1]War of the Rebellion, Operations in Texas and New Mexico. Correspondence, etc. — Confederate. VII, 614-5. Government Printing Office. [2]*Ibid*, 617. [3]*Ibid*, 623-4. [4]*Ibid*, 623. [5]*Ibid*, 623-4. [6]*Ibid*, 625. [7]*Ibid*, 624-5. [8]WR — Operations in the Gulf of Mexico — Union. [9]*Ibid*, Operations in Texas and New Mexico, Reports, VII, 563-4. [10]*Ibid*, 572-4. [11]WR, Correspondence, etc. — Confederate, VII, 632-3. [12]*Ibid*, 573-4. [13]HBT, II, 831. [14]Diary in possession of Mrs. James Ardel Moore, Waco, Texas, granddaughter of J. M. Bickford. [15]GL. [16]CCR. [17]*Ibid.* [18]*Ibid.* [19]Statement by Mrs. James Ardel Moore, granddaughter of James Ashworth. [20]John S. Menefee papers, University of Texas Archives, Barker Texas History Center, Austin. [21]CCR. [22]*Ibid.* [23]*Ibid.* [24]WR, Operations in Texas, New Mexico and Arizona, Correspondence, etc. — Confederate, XI, 153-4. [25]*Ibid*, 155-6. [26]*Ibid*, 156-7.

Chapter XV. Invasion and Occupation: [1]Shea's advancement in rank indicates the value of his services to the Confederacy. [2]WR, Series I, Vol. LIII, 779-781. [3]*Ibid*, 787-8. [4]Records of United States Coast Guard. [5]WR, Series I, Vol. LIII, 778-9. [6]CCR. [7]*Ibid.* [8]Reminiscences of Mrs. Isaac A. (Alice McCoppin) Reed. [9]Official Records of the Union and Confederate Navies in the War of the Rebellion, West Gulf Blockading Squadron. [10]*Ibid.* [11]WR, Operations in W. Florida, S. Alabama, S. Mississippi, Texas, New Mexico — Correspondence, etc. Confederate, XXVII, 909-910. [12]Attributed to Captain Jesse O. Wheeler by Mrs. J. M. Brownson. [13]WR, The Rio Grande Expedition, XXXVIII, 427-8. [14]WR, Louisiana and the Trans-Mississippi, Correspondence, etc., Confederate, XLVI, 917. [15]WR, Louisiana and the Trans-Mississippi, Correspondence, etc. — Union, XVI, 238. [16]*Ibid*, 271. [17]*Ibid*, 150-1. [18]WR, Series I, XXXIV, Part 2. [19]WR, Confederate Correspondence, Louisiana and the Trans-Mississippi, XLVI, 926. [20]*Ibid*, 927. [21]*Ibid*, 1003-4. [22]*Ibid*, 1049. [23]*Ibid*, 1052-3. [24]*Ibid*, 1058. [25]*Ibid*, 1096-7. [26]CCR. [27]*Ibid.* [28]*Ibid.* [29]*Ibid.* [30]*Ibid.* [31]*Ibid.*

Chapter XVI. Convalescence from War Fever: [1]CCR. [2]*Ibid.* [3]House Executive Documents, 39th Congress, 1st Session. [4]TxAl, 1866. [5]IB, January 4, 1867. [6]Year of Crucifixion; Galveston, Texas. Kathleen Davis. Texana, Vol. VIII #2, 1970. [7]TxAl, 1869. [8]*Ibid*, 1868. [9]CCR. [10]TxAl, 1869. ([11] through [14]) CCR.

Chapter XVII. Cattle Turned into Gold: [1]CCR. [2]IB, April 1, 1869. [3]*Ibid.* [4]*Ibid.* [5]CCR. [6]*Ibid.* [7]IB, May 20, 1869. [8]TxAl, 1870. [9]HBT, II, 895.

Chapter XVIII. Hear the Whistle Blowing: [1]IB. [2]GL. [3]Reminiscences of Mrs. Robert Clark. [4]IB. [5]Reminiscences of Mrs. Robert Clark. [6]12th

Legislature, April 8, 1871, GL. [7]IB, September 19, 1871. [8]*Ibid.* [9]HBT, I, 763-4. [10]IB, September 19, 1871.

Chapter XIX. A Downtown View: [1]IB, June 13, June 29, August 15, 1871. [2]Reminiscences of George F. Simons, Edna, Texas, 1943. [3]Reminiscences of Mrs. Isaac A. Reed. [4]Galveston *Civilian*, November 12, 1871. [5]Refugio, Hobart Huson, Vol. II, 152. The Guardsman Publishing Company, Houston, 1956. [6]IB news stories. [7]IB, April 3, 1871. [8]IB, various news stories. [9]*Ibid*, June 29, 1871. [10]ICCB, November 24, 1860. [11]Reminiscences of Mrs. Isaac A. Reed. Casimir Hall was sometimes called Villeneuve Hall. [12]HBT, I, 431. [13]CCR. [14]*Ibid.* [15]IB, May 8, 1872. [16]GL. [17]The bell now hangs in the belfry of Trinity Episcopal Church, Victoria. [18]IB, April 10, 1871. [19]*Ibid*, September 19, 1871. [20]*Ibid*, June 13, 1871. [21]GL and reminiscences of Mrs. Isaac A. Reed. [22]Related to the author by Mrs. Laura Sutton. [23]The Victoria *Advocate*, June 4, 1874.

Chapter XX. The First Great Hurricane: [1]HTR. ([2] through [13]) Annual Report of the Chief Signal Officer, 1875-76. [14]History of the Sisters of Mercy of St. Patrick in Texas, by Sister Mary Aquinas O'Donohue, R.S.M. [15]Reminiscences of Mrs. Isaac A. Reed. [16]Reminiscences of Mrs. Robert Clark. [17]GN, editions of September, 1875. [18]*Ibid.* [19]VA, editions of September, 1875. [20]GN. [21]*Ibid.*

Chapter XXI. Death and Desolation: [1]GN, editions of September, 1875. [2]*Ibid.* [3]VA, editions of September, 1875. [4]GN, editions of September, 1875. [5]Related by Mrs. Bessie Garner Burleson, Port Lavaca, daughter of John and Ida Stiernberg Garner. [6]GN, editions of September, 1875.

Chapter XXII. And then — The End: [1]VA, extra edition of October 1, 1875. [2]GN, October 11, 1875. [3]*Ibid*, November 22, 1875. [4]Monthly Weather Review, September, 1875, issued by the War Department, Office of the Chief Signal Officer. [5]Annual Report of the Chief Signal Officer, 1875-76. [6]GN, October 4, 1875. [7]Related by S. G. Reed. [8]History of the Sisters of Mercy of St. Patrick in Texas, Sister Mary Aquinas O'Donohue, R.S.M. [9]*Ibid.* [10]GN, November 8, 1875. [11]Annual Report of the Chief Signal Officer, 1875-76. [12]*Ibid.* [13]VA, August 24, 1876. [14]HTR, 195. [15]VA, October 5, 1876. [16]*Ibid*, December 9, 1876, and statement by John J. A. Williams, Chief Engineer, Morgan Line, made in 1925. [17]Records of the United States Coast Guard. [18]HTR, 265. [19]GL. [20]Personal Communication, S. G. Reed. [21]GN, August 21, 1886. [22]GN and VA editions of August and September, 1886. [23]Records of the United States Coast Guard. [24]VA, September 30, 1886. [25]Reminiscences of Mrs. Isaac A. Reed. [26]CCR.

BIBLIOGRAPHY

NEWSPAPERS:

Bulletin, Cuero.
Bulletin, Indianola.
Civilian, Galveston.
Courier and Commercial Bulletin, Indianola.
Express, San Antonio.
Indianolian, Indianola.
Neu Braunfelser Zeitung, New Braunfels.
News, Galveston.
Picayune, New Orleans.
Sun, New York.
Telegraph, Houston.
Texas State Gazette, Austin.
Texian Advocate, Victoria.
Times, Indianola.
Times, New Orleans.
Tribune, New York.
Victoria Advocate, Victoria.

LETTERS:

Barden, E. B. to S. G. Reed, Houston, May 18, 1937 (in possession of author).

Eldridge, Charles W., Indianola, March 30, 1852, University of Texas Archives, Barker Texas History Center, Austin.

Eliot, George E. to L. N. Lyon, Clinton, Conn., August 23, 1935 (in possession of author).

Fellowes, Mrs. Georgina Kendall to S. G. Reed, San Antonio, June 26, 1937 (in possession of author).

Lenz, Louis, Personal Communication to S. G. Reed (in possession of author).

McCoppin, James, Secretary, to members Indianola Lodge No. 84, A.F.&A.M., December 17, 1874 (Mrs. James Ardel Moore, Waco).

Mayo, H. M. to S. G. Reed, Houston, April 25, 1935 (in possession of author).

Morgan, Charles, collection of letters to Charles A. Whitney and A. C. Hutchinson (in possession of author).

Morgan, Charles and E. M. Cave, President, Buffalo Bayou Ship Channel Co., Houston, exchange of letters February 9 and 17, 1874 (in possession of author).

Proctor, D. C. to M. D. Monserrate, Cuero, letter statement, Indianola, March 11, 1879 (in possession of author).

Sister Mary Aquinas O'Donohue, R.S.M., to S. G. Reed, Brownsville, July 31, 1945 (in possession of author).
Stadtler, C. L. to A. B. Peticolas, Indianola, July 1, 1866, University of Texas Archives, Barker Texas History Center, Austin.

MANUSCRIPTS AND PAMPHLETS:

A.F.&A.M. Grand Lodge of Texas, Waco, Records of Indianola Lodge No. 84.
Baxter, Charles, New Orleans, "Morgan Line" (in possession of author).
Calhoun County Census 1850, 1860, 1870 and 1880.
Calhoun County Deed Records.
Calhoun County Marriage Records.
Calhoun County, Minutes — Meetings of Commissioners Court.
Calhoun County Probate Records.
I00F Grand Lodge of Texas Records, Corsicana.
Jackson County Deed Records.
Kuechler, Jacob, papers, University of Texas Archives, Barker Texas History Center, Austin.
Lenz, Louis, address to Indianola Association, May 20, 1956.
Lyon, Lonnie, AGFA, SP Lines, Houston, "Morgan the Pioneer" (in possession of author).
Mayo, H. M., Houston, "The Old Morgan Line" (in possession of author).
Mayo, H. M., Houston, "Tying the Lines Together" (in possession of author).
Menefee, John S., papers, University of Texas Archives, Barker Texas History Center, Austin.
Morgan, Charles and Buffalo Bayou Ship Channel Co., Agreement Between, Houston, August 4, 1874 (in possession of author).
Morgan, Charles, various contracts with Postmaster General of the United States (in possession of author).
Sister Mary Aquinas O'Donohue, R.S.M., History of the Sisters of Mercy of St. Patrick in Texas, Laredo.
Southern Pacific Company, Report of the General Manager, Atlantic System, New Orleans, March 31, 1887.
Swanson, A. N., superintendent H&TC (c.1901), The History of the Late Commodore Charles Morgan's Contest with the City of Galveston, Texas to Hold the Coast Line Trade which he had Established Between New Orleans and Houston (in possession of author).
U. S. Department of Transportation, Records of U. S. Coast Guard, Washington and New Orleans.
Victoria County Deed Records.
Weldon, V., collection, Texas State Archives, Austin.

DIARIES, MEMOIRS (UNPUBLISHED):

Bickford, J. M., diary in possession of Mrs. James Ardel Moore, Waco.
Clark, Mrs. Robert, Victoria.
Huck Family History, related by Francis E. Huck, Victoria.
Leibold, L. P., Victoria
Lowe, Mrs. Alexander, Victoria.
Reed, Mrs. Isaac A., Victoria.

Joutel, Henri, Joutel's Journal of LaSalle's Last Voyage, Corinth Books, New York, 1962.

Long, E. B., The Civil War Day by Day, An Almanac, 1861-65, Doubleday & Co., New York, 1971.

Meinig, D. W., Imperial Texas, University of Texas Press, Austin, 1969.

Meusebach, John O., Answers to Interrogatories, Austin, 1894. Reprint by Pemberton Press, Austin, 1964.

Pearce, Gerald, Texas Under Arms, Encino Press, Austin, 1969.

Poor, Henry V., Manual of the Railroads in the United States, H. V. and H. W. Poor, annual issues 1868-1887.

Protestant Episcopal Church in the Diocese of Texas, and in the Missionary District of Western Texas, Reports to Annual Conventions, 1851-76.

Red, William Stuart, A History of the Presbyterian Church in Texas, Texas State Library, Archives Division.

Reed, S. G., A History of the Texas Railroads, Kingsport Press, Kingsport, Tennessee, 1941.

Roberts, Col. Oran Milo, Texas, Vol. XI in Evans, C. A., editor, Confederate Military History, Confederate Pub. Co., Atlanta, 1899.

Rose, Victor M., History of Victoria, Daily Times, Laredo, 1883.

Schlesinger, Arthur Meier, Political and Social History of the United States, Macmillan Co., New York, 1926.

Solms-Braunfels, Karl, Prinz zu (Carl, Prince of), Texas 1844-45, n.d. Reprint by Anson Jones Press, Houston, 1936.

Steen, Ralph W., Texas Newspapers and Lincoln, Southwestern Historical Quarterly, LI, #3, January, 1948.

Sutton, Robert C. Jr., The Sutton-Taylor Feud, Nortex Press, Quanah, Texas, 1974.

Texas Almanac, published variously by the Galveston News and newspapers in Houston and Austin, 1857-1873.

Thrall, Homer S., A History of Methodism in Texas, 1872.

Tiling, Moritz, German Element in Texas, Houston, 1913.

U. S., Department of Agriculture, Weather Bureau (National Weather Service), Records of, Climatic Survey of the United States from the Establishment of Stations to 1930, Inclusive, Sec. 33, South Eastern Texas, Government Printing Office, Washington.

U. S., Department of Commerce, National Oceanic and Atmospheric Administration, Monthly Weather Review, September, 1875, Washington.

U. S., War Department, Annual Report of the Chief Signal Officer, 1875-76, Government Printing Office, Washington, 1876.

U. S., War Department, Miscellaneous Records, National Archives, Washington.

U. S., War Department, The War of the Rebellion: A Compilation of the Official Records of the Union and Confederate Armies Published under the Direction of the Secretary of War, Government Printing Office, Washington, 1880-1901.

White, William W., The Texas Slave Insurrection in 1860, Southwestern Historical Quarterly, LII, #3, January, 1949.

Wortham, Louis J., A History of Texas, Wortham-Molyneaux Co., Fort Worth, 1924.

Young, Jo., The Battle of Sabine Pass, Southwestern Historical Quarterly, LII, #4, April, 1949.

INDEX

Point, 59; Fromme, A., 65;
Government, 43, 53, 64, 89;
LaSalle, 49, 52, 53-4, 58, 65,
83; Miller, Theodore, 23;
Morgan Line, 199, 202, 206-8,
227, 238, 260, 265; Rogers,
Capt. John A., 58; Runge &
Sheppard, 216; Verein, 23;
Western Texas, 108; White &
Co., 23, 65
Wheeler, Capt. Jesse O.: 47, 58,
107
Whig Party: 101
Whipple, Lt. A. W.: 54
White, Benjamin J.: 56
White, Samuel Addison: 7, 8, 11,
12, 15, 20, 23, 30, 32, 42, 49,
66, 77-80, 205
White, Mrs. S. A.: 13
White, Stephen: 245
White's Bayou: 83
White's Ferry: 118
Whitney, B. A.: 135
Whitney, Charles A.: 201, 207,
253-4, 258, 260-2, 266
Wilkinson, John: 153, 167
Willemin, L.: 223, 275
Williams, Jacob: 155
Williams, Stephen: 226
Willke (Wilke), Capt. H.: 169, 170
Wilmers, John: 155
Wilmington, Del.: 133
Wilmington, N. C.: 230
Wilson, Capt. David: 112
Wilson, Capt. Harry: 100, 155
Wilson & Miller: 223
Wilson's Boarding House: 276
Wingett, Capt. W.: 176-7
Winkleman, F.: 155
Winnemore, J. T.: 77
Wisdom, W. H.: 201
Witnebert, W.: 155
Wood, Edward: 108, 120, 139,
154
Wood, Joseph: 155
Woodman, George W.: 154, 276
Woods, Maj. J. C.: 110
Woodville, Tex.: 251
Woodward Bros.: 220, 223-4
Woodward, D. K.: 155, 225, 245,
275
Woodward, D. S.: 77, 135, 138
Woodward, Miss Rachel: 166
Woodward, S. M.: 154
Woodward, Thomas D.: 80, 139,
167-8, 264
Woodward, W. H.: 69, 78, 100,
114, 129, 135-6, 139, 142,
155, 165, 181, 184, 243, 275

Woodworth, L. H.: 264
Woodsworth, C. V.: 139, 155
wool industry: Saxon sheep
imported, 29; Merino sheep, 29
Worth, William Jenkins: 42
Wouffie, R.: 139
Wyoming, State of: 56

Yancey, William T.: 69, 124-6,
133, 135, 139, 140, 152-4
Yates, B. F.: 119, 120, 142, 155
Yates, R. W.: 119, 139, 156
Year of Crucifixion: 192
yellow fever: 85-7, 92-5, 115, 123,
140, 168, 192-3, 258; first
appearance, 85; Board of Health,
85, 94-5, 120; City Hospital,
85, 93-5, 120-1, 192; health
officer, 223; quarantines, 123-6,
194, 258; report of Dr. J. M.
Reuss, 192, Appendix A
Yorktown, Tex.: 27, 46, 90, 101,
255
Yucatan, Mexico: 262

Zellney, Charles: 155
Zimmerman, Dan: 155